Theatre in Balzac's
La Comédie humaine

FAUX TITRE

Etudes
de langue et littérature françaises
publiées

sous la direction de Keith Busby,
M.J. Freeman, Sjef Houppermans,
Paul Pelckmans et Co Vet

No. 181

Rodopi

Amsterdam - Atlanta, GA 2000

Theatre in Balzac's
La Comédie humaine

Linzy Erika Dickinson

♾ The paper on which this book is printed meets the requirements of "ISO
9706:1994, Information and documentation - Paper for documents -
Requirements for permanence".

♾ Le papier sur lequel le présent ouvrage est imprimé remplit les prescriptions de "ISO 9706:1994, Information et documentation - Papier pour
documents - Prescriptions pour la permanence".

ISBN: 90-420-0549-1
©Editions Rodopi B.V., Amsterdam - Atlanta, GA 2000
Printed in The Netherlands

For Harry C.

TABLE OF CONTENTS

ACKNOWLEDGEMENTS

I should like to express my thanks to colleagues from Royal Holloway, University of London, for their valuable guidance and comments, to the University of London and the Central Research Fund for financial assitance, to M. and Mme. Tagredj for their hospitality, to Dr. Matthew Schmidt for assitance with copy production, and to Dr. Emily Salines and June Garrett for their unfailing support.

LIST OF ABBREVIATIONS

Titles of works by Balzac given in the footnotes and appendices to this thesis are abbreviated as indicated below, and, unless otherwise stated, refer to these editions.

Corres	*Correspondance*, Textes réunis, classés et annotés par Roger Pierrot, 5 vols. (Paris: Garnier Frères, 1960-1969).
LMH	*Lettres à Madame Hanska*, Textes réunis, classés et annotés par Roger Pierrot, 4 vols. (Paris: Delta, 1967-1971).
LCH	*La Comédie humaine*, édition publiée sous la direction de Pierre-Georges Castex, Bibliothèque de la Pléiade, 12 vols. (Paris: Gallimard, 1976-1981).

The titles of individual works within *La Comédie humaine* are abbreviated according to the list below. The dates following each title are the dates of composition according to the new Pléiade edition, and, unless stated otherwise, are those which are used for the purpose of chronology throughout the present thesis.

Ad.	*Adieu*	(1830)
AEF	*Autre étude de femme*	(1832-39)
AP	*Avant Propos*	(1842)
AR	*l'Auberge rouge*	(1831)
AS	*Albert Savarus*	(1842)
Ath.	*La Messe de l'athée*	(1836)
B	*Béatrix*	(1838-45)
Be.	*La Cousine Bette*	(1846)
Bo.	*La Bourse*	(1832)
Boi.	*Les Héritiers Boirouge*	(1836)
Bou.	*Les Petits Bourgeois*	(1843-44)
BS	*Le Bal de Sceaux*	(1829)
CA	*Le Cabinet des antiques*	(1836-38)
Cath.	*Sur Catherine de Médicis*	(1837-41)

CB	*César Birotteau*	(1833-37)
Ch.	*Les Chouans*	(1828-29)
Ch-O	*Le Chef-d'œuvre inconnu*	(1831; 1837)
CM	*Le Contrat de mariage*	(1835)
Col.	*Le Colonel Chabert*	(1832)
Com. sal.	*La Comédienne de salon*	(1841)
Cor.	*Maître Cornélius*	(1831)
CP	*Le Cousin Pons*	(1846-47)
CSS	*Les Comédiens sans le savoir*	(1844-46)
CT	*Le Curé de Tours*	(1832)
CV	*Le Curé de village*	(1838-39)
DA	*Le Député d'Arcis*	(1839-47)
Dés.	*Une passion dans le désert*	(1830)
DF	*Une double famille*	(1830)
DL	*La Duchesse de Langeais*	(1833)
Do.	*Massimilla Doni*	(1837)
Dr.	*Un drame au bord de la mer*	(1834)
DV	*Un début dans la vie*	(1841-42)
DxA	*Les Deux Amis*	(1830-31)
E	*Les Employés*	(1837-38)
EF	*Etude de femme*	(1830)
EG	*Eugénie Grandet*	(1833)
EHC	*L'Envers de l'histoire contemporaine*	(1842-44; 1847)
ELV	*L'Elixier de longue vie*	(1830)
EM	*L'Enfant maudit*	(1831-36)
Ep.T	*Un épisode sous la Terreur*	(1829)
F	*Ferragus*	(1833)
FA	*La Femme abandonnée*	(1832)
FC	*Facino Cane*	(1836)
FE	*Une fille d'Eve*	(1838-39)
Fir.	*Madame Firmiani*	(1832)
FM	*La Fausse Maitresse*	(1841)
F30	*La Femme de trente ans*	(1829-34)
FYO	*La Fille aux yeux d'or*	(1834-35)
Gam.	*Gambara*	(1837)
Gau.	*Gaudissart II*	(1844)
Gb.	*Gobseck*	(1830)

Gr.	La Grenadière	(1832)
H	Honorine	(1842)
HA	Un homme d'affaires	(1844)
IG	L'Illustre Gaudissart	(1833)
In.	L'Interdiction	(1836)
IP	Illusions perdues	(1836-43)
Lys.	Le Lys dans la vallée	(1834-35)
Ma.	Les Marana	(1832-33)
MC	Le Médecin de campagne	(1832-33)
MCP	La Maison du chat-qui-pelote	(1829)
MD	La Muse du département	(1843)
Mes.	Le Message	(1832)
MJM	Mémoires de deux jeunes mariées	(1838-41)
MM	Modeste Mignon	(1844)
MN	La Maison Nucingen	(1837)
P	Pierrette	(1839-40)
Pay.	Les Paysans	(1838-45)
PCh.	La Peau de chagrin	(1830-31)
PG	Le Père Goriot	(1834-35)
PGr.	Pierre Grassou	(1839)
Phy.	Physiologie du mariage	(1826-29)
PM	La Paix du ménage	(1829)
PMV	Petites misères de la vie conjugale	(1830-45)
Pr.B	Un prince de la Bohème	(1840)
Pro.	Les Proscrits	(1831)
R	La Rabouilleuse	(1840-42)
RA	La Recherche de l'Absolu	(1834)
S	Sarrasine	(1830)
Sér.	Séraphîta	(1833-35)
SetM	Splendeurs et misères des courtisanes	(1838-47)
SPC	Les Secrets de la Princesse de Cadignan	(1839)
TA	Une ténébreuse affaire	(1838-40)
Th.	Le Théâtre comme il est	(1847)
UM	Ursule Mirouèt	(1840-41)

8

ZM   *Z. Marcas*   (1840)

The titles of commonly cited periodicals are abbreviated as follows:

AB   *Année balzacienne*
RLC   *Revue de littérature comparée*

INTRODUCTION

L'image que Balzac donne du théâtre et des comédiens n'a pas été étudiée.[1]

Une étude complète et minutieuse de la place qui est faite au théâtre dans *la Comédie humaine* serait extrêmement révélatrice.[2]

It may seem surprising that Balzac's representation and exploitation of the theatre in his novels have not already been examined in a systematic and comprehensive way by critics, particularly since the reader of almost any of Balzac's major novels must be struck by the abundance of references to theatres, plays, playwrights, actors, and stage characters. This is not to say that the notion of theatre in Balzac's novels has been neglected, of course. Indeed, several studies conducted during this century examine various aspects of 'theatre' in Balzac's novels. They may be divided into three distinct groups of interest.

The first group comprises source studies which reveal the extent to which Balzac's plots and characters may derive from the plays of his theatrical antecedents. P.J. Tremewan has examined in some detail the extent to which Balzac's novels may draw on the works of Shakespeare, and has focused in particular on the relationship between Shakespeare's Lear and Balzac's Goriot,[3] while Pierre Barrière,[4] and, more recently, Geneviève Delattre,[5] have examined the nature and extent of Balzac's borrowings of theme and character from the major classical dramatists, and in particular from Molière. The theatrical sources of plot and character are not the main focus of the present study.

---

[1] Roland Chollet, Introduction to *Illusions perdues*, in *LCH* ed. Pléiade, 12 vols. (Paris: Gallimard, 1977), vol. V, pp. 77-78.

[2] René Guise, Introduction to Balzac's theatre, in *Œuvres complètes illustrées*, 30 vols. (Paris: Bibliophiles de l'Original, 1965-1976), vol. XXI, p. XIII.

[3] P.-J. Tremewan, 'Balzac et Shakespeare', in *AB* (1967), pp. 259-303.

[4] Pierre Barrière, 'Les sources classiques de *la Comédie humaine*', in *Honoré de Balzac et la tradition littéraire classique* (Paris: Hachette, 1928), pp. 74-98.

[5] Geneviève Delattre, *Les Opinions littéraires de Balzac* (Paris: Presses Universitaires de France, 1961), pp. 51-83.

The second area of criticism concerned with 'theatre' in Balzac's novels comprises studies which attempt to demonstrate Balzac's adherence to a strict, 'dramatic' construction of plot. This body of criticism includes a substantial part of Barrière's work,[6] a study conducted by Ray Bowen (which appears to rely heavily on the latter),[7] and also part of a more recent study by A. Lahlou.[8] Notwithstanding Balzac's known predilection for classical theatre, the insistence in these studies on a perceived adherence to the formal construction and unities of the classical play in Balzac's novels is at best contrived, and adds little to the question of the narrative importance of theatre in *La Comédie humaine.*

The third group of works on the subject, which is most relevant to the present study, is that which is concerned with the notion of theatre, and in particular of theatrical melodrama, in *La Comédie humaine* as an expression of the central concerns of the Balzacian plot. David Bellos, for example, sees the notion of theatre as integral to the play of true and false, which characterises the action of *La Cousine Bette.*[9] In his study of this work Bellos focuses on the way in which Balzac uses allusion to the theatre, and a dramatic mode of presentation, as the means of maintaining the reader's awareness of the theatrical and tragic dimension of this novel. Bellos's treatment here is confined to a single novel, and suggests that there is much to be gained by extending the study to other novels of *La Comédie humaine.*

The play of true and false, surface and depth, illusion and disillusionment, which characterises the theatrical aspect of *La Cousine Bette,* is studied in a wider range of Balzac's novels in the works of Peter Brooks[10] and Christopher Prendergast,[11] which

---

[6] Pierre Barrière, *Honoré de Balzac et la tradition littéraire classique.* See in particular Part III, pp. 195-246.

[7] Ray Bowen, *The Dramatic Construction of Balzac's Novels* (Eugene: University of Oregon, 1940).

[8] A. Lahlou, 'Balzac auteur tragique' and 'Balzac auteur comique', in 'Balzac dramaturge dans les Scènes de la vie privée' (unpublished doctoral thesis, University of Paris-Sorbonne, 1981), pp. 26-114.

[9] David Bellos, 'True and False' and 'Novel and Drama', in *Balzac: 'La Cousine Bette'* (London: Grant & Cutler, 1980), pp. 18-32, & 46-62.

[10] Peter Brooks, *The Melodramatic Imagination* (New Haven and London: Yale University Press, 1976), pp. 110-148.

examine the function of melodrama in Balzac's plots. Peter Brooks highlights the relationship between Balzac's use of melodrama and actual stage melodrama by reference to Balzac's irresistible inclination towards the theatre. The main point of his argument is that Balzac's vision and means of expression are profoundly theatrical, the tissue of references to the theatre suggesting an awareness that he was writing for a public whose taste and responses had been formed by the melodrama. At the same time, Brooks notes that the complexities of the Balzacian vision make the literal stage too confining and that only the novel could offer Balzac the opportunity to perform the 'autopsy' of the narrative, to explain his own purposes and to examine the implications of the text.

Unlike Brooks's work, Prendergast's seminal study, *Balzac, Fiction and Melodrama* is not concerned with the influence of the stage melodrama on Balzac's novels,[12] but rather with the melodramatic dimension of *La Comédie humaine* as one of the major sources of Balzac's most compelling narrative effects. His detailed analysis of some of the major novels of *La Comédie humaine* shows how Balzac remodels the traditional conventions of melodrama in the service of his serious artistic purpose,[13] how the melodramatic devices

---

[11] Christopher Prendergast, *Balzac, Fiction and Melodrama* (New York: Holmes & Meier, 1978).

[12] *Ibid.*, pp. 5-6 'To the extent, then, that in an exact sense the term 'melodrama' is a category of dramatic criticism, the title of this book would seem to imply that it is, or in principle ought to be, a study in the influence of theatrical melodrama on the novel. Such a study, conducted in detail, remains to be done, and would doubtless prove in some degree informative and instructive. For a variety of reasons, however, it is not the theme of this book. [...] In adopting the term 'melodrama' as a focus for the analysis of some of Balzac's narrative practices, I am using the term in a fairly large and flexible sense, in a manner that is not confined to its specifically theatrical heritage. In short, 'melodrama' in the present context refers to a mode rather than to a formal genre, a mode which may be said to encompass certain dispositions of the novelistic imagination as well as the particular conventions and techniques of the stage.'

[13] *Ibid.* p. 15. 'The case I want to argue, therefore, is not that the way to rescue these texts from their damaging critical heritage is by asserting an artistic achievement located, as it were, outside Balzac's use of melodrama. On the contrary, what needs to be stressed is an idea of wholeness, a deep unity of vision and technique, entailing above all the recognition that Balzac does indeed work in and through the conventions of the melodramatic mode, but that his achievement lies in

of mystery, hyperbole, suspense and conflict serve to intensify the anxiety of a world in which nothing can be relied upon. The anagnorisis, revelation, or removal of the mask, which in the stage melodrama was designed to establish the moral order of the universe, comes in Balzac's novels to reveal further levels of falsehood, successive masks and a dark and labyrinthine social substructure. It is this 'multilayered phenomenon'[14] which is central to Prendergast's study, since it provides the basis for showing how the melodrama opens up the text, inviting the reader to see different levels of possible meaning couched in a representation of reality.

It is not just through a strictly melodramatic mode, however, that Balzac succeeds in revealing the multilayered nature of reality to his reader, but through theatre in its broadest sense – as the situation of the action; as a microcosm of the economic and moral principles governing the world at large; as the unifying metaphor which links the comedies, tragedies and dramas of the individual novels; and as the mode of presentation of many of those novels. The aim of the present study is to establish the primary importance of theatre in *La Comédie humaine*, by showing how far Balzac actually and accurately portrays the theatre of his day, how that portrayal contributes to the written history of the theatre and how it serves Balzac's wider narrative purposes. This study will also show how theatre, not just in the sense of melodrama, but in a more comprehensive sense, is the principal metaphor and mode of presentation in many of Balzac's novels, and that it is through their theatrical dimension that these novels endow the collected work of *La Comédie humaine* with a sense of unity. Finally, the present study will seek to demonstrate the close link between the novel and the theatre in Balzac's creative process, by revealing the relationship between Balzac's most 'dramatic' novel and his most successful play. In conclusion the study raises the question of whether the role of the theatre in Balzac's novels might prompt a reappraisal of Balzac's position as the father of nineteenth-century Realism and of his work as the intertext for the literature of over half a century.

---

the radical reworking of these conventions to support a serious and important artistic aim.'

[14] *Ibid.*, p. 16.

Although this is not a biographical or source study, Balzac's own experience of the theatre both as a would-be playwright and as the spectator of plays by other dramatists is not to be dismissed in an assessment of his use of theatre in his novels. An account of this experience will be given in the following sections of this introduction.

Balzac: Reader, Spectator and Critic of the Theatre

This study is concerned primarily with theatre in *La Comédie humaine*, and not with Balzac's opinions of classical and contemporary dramatists, nor with his experience as a spectator and critic of the theatre, other than in so far as these have an impact on the representation of the theatre in his novels. Only a brief summary of Balzac's activity as a reader, spectator and critic of plays will be given here in order to orientate the points which are developed in subsequent chapters. A fuller account of Balzac's critical appreciation of the theatre can be found in the work of Pierre Barrière,[15] and in the more recent and more comprehensive work of Geneviève Delattre,[16] as well as in some of the major studies of Balzac's life and work.[17]

From the statements made by Balzac in his correspondence, it has become common knowledge among critics that he wished to emulate Molière, that he had a profound admiration for Racine, and that he was at once disdainful and perhaps envious of the success of contemporary dramatists such as Hugo and Scribe. Balzac's preference for the dramatists of the preceding centuries is made clear in the earliest stages of his career in a letter to his sister in November 1819, in which he writes, 'Je dévore nos 4 auteurs tragiques: Crébillon me rassure, Voltaire m'épouvante, Corneille me transporte, Racine me fait quitter la plume'.[18]

Already a literary hierarchy is established and it is clear that Balzac holds the tradition of tragedy in high esteem. Racine reigned supreme in Balzac's estimation, both at this early stage and throughout his

---

[15] Pierre Barrière, *Honoré de Balzac et la tradition littéraire classique*, ed. cit.

[16] Geneviève Delattre, *Les Opinions littéraires de Balzac*, ed. cit.

[17] Herbert James Hunt, *Balzac's 'Comédie Humaine'* (London: Athlone Press, 1964), pp. 267-290; Pierre Barbéris, *Balzac, une mythologie réaliste* (Paris: Larousse, 1971), pp. 45-47, & pp. 71-80; André Maurois, *Prométhée ou la vie de Balzac* (Paris: Hachette, 1965), ch. IV, VII, & VIII.

[18] *Corres.*, vol. I, p. 58.

career,[19] but the first of the great classical plays that Balzac seems to have seen was Corneille's *Cinna*. 'Je n'ai pas encore vu jouer les pièces de Corneille, notre général',[20] he writes to Laure on the eve of attending that play in 1819.

Contrary to what one might expect, Léon Gozlan reports that Balzac was not a great theatre-goer in his youth, and it seems that his early opinions were largely formed from his reading of theatrical works rather than from attendance at performances: 'Il allait peu dans les théâtres; on ne l'a peut-être pas vu trois fois dans sa vie au foyer de la Comédie-française'.[21] It was through his reading that Balzac became familiar with the works of Molière,[22] and by the time his own printing firm produced an edition of Molière's work on behalf of Urbain Canel in 1825, Balzac was well equipped to write the preface, in which he limits himself to extolling Molière's virtues in general terms.[23] By 1847 Balzac immodestly declared himself a second Molière through the medium of Félix Davin in the latter's preface to *Les Comédiens sans le savoir* .[24]

Balzac's nostalgic adulation of the classical tradition in comedy and tragedy continued through the late 1820s after the production of the Molière edition, and at the same time he developed a distaste for the emerging Romantic drama on the grounds that it was not 'vrai'. This distaste became concretised in 1830 when Balzac published the *Feuilleton des journaux politiques* along with Emile Girardin, in which he devoted considerable space to active dramatic criticism. Here Balzac was vociferous in his attacks against Romantic drama

[19] *Corres.*, vol. I, pp. 35, 36, 52, 58, 60, 61, 65, 258, 356, 571.
[20] *Corres.*, vol. I, p. 52. See also Balzac's letter to Théodore Dablin p. 47, in which he requests a ticket for the performance.
[21] Léon Gozlan, *Balzac en pantoufles* (Paris: Michel Lévy & J. Hetzel,1865), p. 17.
[22] Hanotaux et Vicaire, *La Jeunesse de Balzac* (Paris: Ferroud, 1921), p. 38.
[23] *Corres.*, vol. I, pp. 256-259. This printing work was also to include editions of La Fontaine, Racine and Corneille but the latter two were never embarked upon.
[24] *LCH*, vol. VII, p. 1714, 'nous ne voyons qu'un seul nom auprès duquel nous placerions volontiers M. de Balzac... Et ce nom, c'est Molière. Qu'est-ce donc que Molière, sinon le poète qui a peint avec le plus de vérité, la société du dix-septième siècle. Si M. de Balzac avait vécu sous Louis XIV, il eût fait *Les Femmes savantes, Tartuffe, George Dandin, Le Misanthrope*; si Molière vivait de nos jours, il écrirait *La Comédie humaine*'.

and particularly against Hugo's *Hernani*.[25] The polarisation of Classicism and Romanticism in Balzac's theatrical preference endured, and in his correspondence throughout the 1830s and 1840s Balzac continued to attack Hugo, claiming, 'Victor Hugo n'est pas vrai',[26] and still upheld Racine as 'la perfection'.[27]

The works of other contemporary dramatists receive little attention in Balzac's correspondence. Scribe, for example, is often referred to as a likeable acquaintance, but whose works amount to nothing more than commercial melodramas, and is barely mentioned at all after 1840 when the melodrama fell into decline.[28] Nor does Balzac seem to subscribe, in his comments outside his novels, to the vogue for Shakespeare in the 1830s and 1840s, for although he makes a few references to the English dramatist in his correspondence, these contain no indication of admiration and seem merely to be manipulated by Balzac to demonstrate a degree of knowledge to Madame Hanska.[29]

In view of Balzac's denigration of contemporary dramatic aesthetics and the fact that he does not recommend an unaltered return to the classical tradition which he so much admired, it may seem surprising that Balzac did not express his own dramaturgy in a theoretical work. Rather this dramaturgy is to be found within *La Comédie humaine*.[30] The basis of Balzac's dramaturgy, as he expressed it in a letter to Armand Pérémé in 1838, is the need to 'faire vrai', just as he claimed to have done in the novel:

---

[25] *Le Feuilleton*, 24 March 1830 and 7 April 1830. See: *Œuvres complètes* 24 vols. (Paris: Michel Lévy, 1869-1876), vol. XXII, pp. 44-56.

[26] *LMH*, vol. II, p. 177. This judgement was made in relation to *Les Burgraves* in March 1843. *Ruy Blas* and *Lucrèce Borgia* had been similarly damned in November 1838 and May 1843 respectively. See: *LMH*, vol. I, p. 627, & *LMH*, vol. II, p. 213.

[27] In a letter to Madame Hanska on 21 December 1842 Balzac tells of a disagreement with Hugo over dinner at the Rocher de Cancale regarding the forthcoming production of *Les Burgraves*; quoting Hugo, Balzac writes: '– Je sais que je ferai mal à Balzac en disant que Racine est un homme médiocre, car il tient pour Racine... – Jusqu'à mon dernier soupir, lui ai-je répondu, car c'est la perfection'. *LMH*, vol. II, p. 139.

[28] *LMH*, vol. I, p. 45, 54, 456, 500, 512; vol. IV, p. 306.

[29] *LMH*, vol. I, pp. 533, 615, & 666; vol. II, pp. 188, 400, 438, & 500; vol. III, p. 119; vol. IV, pp. 221, 314, 347, 353, & 470.

[30] This point will be dealt with in detail in Chapter 4, section g.

> Il n'y a plus de possible que le *vrai* au théâtre, comme j'ai tenté de l'introduire dans le roman. Mais *faire vrai* n'est donné ni à Hugo, que son talent porte au lyrisme, ni à Dumas, qui l'a dépassé pour n'y jamais revenir; il ne peut être que ce qu'il a été. Scribe est à bout. Il faut chercher les nouveaux talents inconnus et changer les conditions sultanesques des directeurs. Il n'y aura jamais que la médiocrité qui subira les conditions actuelles. J'ai depuis dix ans, travaillé en vue du théâtre, et vous connaissez mes idées à cet égard. Elles sont vastes, et leur réalisation m'effraie souvent.[31]

Balzac's own attempts to write for the theatre, which span his whole career and not just the decade mentioned in this letter, are not entirely consistent with this need to 'faire vrai', however. In his finished plays Balzac experimented with tragedy, comedy and the melodrama, and desirous as he was of a commerical rather than artistic success in the theatre, he subscribed largely to what he erroneously considered to be public taste, rather than to his own vaguely articulated aesthetic ideals. Only a decade after advocating realism in the theatre did Balzac reveal to his public a realistic form of *drame bourgeois,* which he had first formulated in his novels. The success of this drama and of Balzac's other attempts to write for the stage are the subject of the next part of this introduction.

'Le plus refusé des auteurs dramatiques'[32]

Although records of Balzac's attempts with the theatre are well known, a brief account of them is relevant to the subsequent parts of the present work, for much of the experience of the theatre, which is transcribed in Balzac's novels, derived from his own attempts to write a successful play and from his dealings with theatre directors and actors. These attempts span the whole of Balzac's career from 1819, when he began to write a five-act tragedy entitled *Cromwell,* to 1848 when he wrote a *drame bourgeois* entitled *La Marâtre.* During this period of twenty-eight years Balzac repeatedly turned to the theatre in the pursuit of glory and fortune, and the more that theatrical success eluded him the more persistent he became, until in 1848 he thought of

[31] *Corres.,* vol. III, pp. 475-476.
[32] *Le Figaro,* 10 March 1839.

devoting himself entirely to the writing of plays.[33]   This life-long persistence resulted in almost fifty different dramatic projects, of which fifteen were begun and soon abandoned and only nine were finished.[34]

In the French language these projects have been traced in detail by Douchan Z. Milatchitch,[35] whose work published in 1930 remains the most comprehensive study of Balzac's theatre and substantially expands the earlier study conducted by Edmond Biré in 1897.[36] More recent accounts of Balzac's theatre have been given by René Guise[37] and Roland Chollet.[38] The latter are largely based on information already cited by Milatchitch, together with each critic's personal appraisal of the major plays.   In the English language the work of Walter Scott Hastings, published in 1917,[39] traces the genesis and production of Balzac's major plays in relation to his correspondence and to press reviews. Hastings cites, albeit in less detail, much of the same information as Milatchitch. The present account will consist in a summary of the genesis and production of only Balzac's major plays.[40] A list of all of Balzac's known dramatic projects and unfinished plays appears in an appendix at the end of this study.

Balzac's earliest attempts with the drama date from 1819 when he began work on his tragedy *Cromwell*, written in verse.   The finished

---

[33] Balzac's letters to Madame Hanska throughout 1848 attest to his obsession with the theatre.   While he makes virtually no reference to projects for novels, there are frequent references to his plays *La Marâtre* and *Le Faiseur*, and to a host of dramatic projects. See *LMH*, vol. IV, pp. 175-560.   In particular Balzac's letter of 6 August lists projects for 17 new plays. See p. 490.

[34] See Appendix V.

[35] Douchan Z. Milatchitch, *Le Théâtre de Honoré de Balzac*, 2 vols. (Paris: Hachette, 1930).

[36] Edmond Biré, 'Le Théâtre de Balzac' in *Honoré de Balzac* (Paris: Champion, 1897), pp. 165-265.

[37] René Guise, 'Un grand homme du roman à la scène, ou les illusions reparaissantes de Balzac' in *AB*, published in four parts (1966), pp. 171-216; (1967), pp. 177-214; (1968), pp. 337-368; (1969), pp. 247-280.   See also: René Guise, Introduction to Balzac's theatre, in *Œuvres complètes illustrées*, vol. XXI, pp. 1-XXXII, which is a summary of the articles published in *AB*.

[38] Roland Chollet, Introduction to Balzac's theatre in *Les Œuvres de Balzac*, 30 vols. (Lausanne: Rencontre, 1958-1962), vol. XXVII, pp. 11-31.

[39] Walter Scott Hastings, *The Drama of Honoré de Balzac* (Wisconsin: George Banta, 1917).

[40] This summary will rely on Balzac's correspondence, on press reviews and on the works cited above.

play was read to his family in April 1820 and was unanimously judged a disaster. Balzac's brother-in-law, Surville, in an act of magnanimity, sent the play to his former master at the Ecole Polytechnique, the poet, dramatist and eminent scholar François-Guillaume Andrieux. Andrieux's response was to suggest that the young Balzac should pursue any career other than literature. Undeterred, however, Balzac submitted a copy of the play to the reading committee of the Théâtre Français, who wasted no time in rejecting it.[41]

In his next finished dramatic work, *Le Nègre*, Balzac abandoned tragedy in favour of the melodrama. The change of style met with no more success, however, and the play was immediately rejected when read to the committee of the third-rate Gaîté theatre in 1822.[42]   From this point until the late 1830s Balzac's attempts with the dramatic form amounted to little more than hastily conceived ideas and outlined plans which never came to fruition,[43] and it was not until 1838 that he set about completing another full-length play. In the intervening years Balzac had found fame as a novelist, and although his thoughts repeatedly turned to the drama, the pressure to produce novels for which he had received advance payments seems to have prevented him from devoting himself to the drama in any serious way.

Nevertheless, Balzac remained convinced that the true road to literary glory, and more importantly to financial security, lay in the theatre and this belief led him to plan a play for the newly established Renaissance theatre, which had opened on 18 November 1838 with *Ruy Blas*. The directors of the theatre were seeking a second success which would match that of Hugo's play and hoped to find this by exploiting the now famous name of Balzac. The theatre accepted Balzac's offer of his play *La Première Demoiselle*, which he had first conceived and outlined in 1837, and which he now called *L'Ecole des ménages*.[44]

As Balzac tells in a letter to Zulma Carraud, the finished play was read to the committee on 25 February 1839 and was rejected in favour of *L'Alchimiste* by Alexandre Dumas.[45]   This rejection of the play

---

[41] See: Milatchitch, *Le Théâtre de Honoré de Balzac*, pp. 19-20.
[42] See: Milatchitch, *Le Théâtre de Honoré de Balzac*, p. 21.
[43] See appendix V.
[44] *LMH*, vol. I, pp. 485-486, 569, 575, 589, 593, 633, 635, & 636-638.
[45] *Corres.*, vol. III, pp. 575-576.

was announced in *La Caricature* on 3 March and in *Le Figaro* on 7 March, but Balzac went on to give two private readings of his play with great success. The first of these was in the salon of Mme Couturier de Saint-Cloud, and the second at the house of the marquis de Custine. The second reading was attended by Gautier who mentioned the occasion in laudatory terms in *La Presse* on 11 March:

> M. de Balzac a lu l'autre soir chez le marquis de C. devant le plus brillant auditoire, une comédie en cinq actes, intitulée: *L'Ecole des ménages*, où l'on retrouve la science du cœur humain, l'analyse fine et puissante, et l'exacte observation de mœurs qui ont valu à ses romans de si nombreux lecteurs [...]. Nous sommes charmés que M. de Balzac aborde enfin le théâtre.

Contemporary theatre directors failed to see the play's merit, however, and on 13 March 1839 Balzac put the play away and moved on to other projects.[46] This play was eventually produced posthumously in 1910 at the Odéon by Antoine, director and founder of the Théâtre Libre. The play was a great success with the critics but was less warmly received by the public at large and after only a short run was definitively abandoned.[47]

The accounts of Balzac's next finished play, *Vautrin*, are already well known, but are worth repeating here since this was the play which first brought Balzac fully into the milieu of the theatre. Balzac announced his new project to Madame Hanska in October 1839,[48] and by the following January the play was already in rehearsal at the Porte-Saint-Martin. Gautier recounts with great humour how Balzac woke him in the middle of the night to announce that he was to read *Vautrin* to Harel, director of the Porte-Saint-Martin, the next day. Gautier assumed that Balzac wanted him to listen to the play before the proposed meeting with Harel, but on the contrary Balzac confessed that he had not even begun to write it and insisted that together with Laurent-Jan, Ourliac and Lassailly they should work

---

[46] The readings, the subsequent rejection of the play by the Théâtre-Français, and Balzac's abandonment of it are recounted in a letter to Madame Hanska on 13 March 1839. See: *LMH*, vol. I, pp. 636-637.

[47] Milatchitch, *Le Théâtre de Honoré de Balzac*, pp. 54-55. Here Milatchitch lists the critics opinions and the journals in which reviews appeared.

[48] *LMH*, vol. I, p. 654: 'Je monte le drame de *Vautrin* à la Porte-S[ain]t-Martin'.

through the night to 'bâcler le dramorama pour toucher la monnaie'.[49]
Despite this collective effort, however, the reading was postponed and
little of this first night's work remained in the final production.

There had been many stage adaptations of Balzac's novels during
the 1830s[50] and now in 1840 the public eagerly awaited Balzac's own
inauguration in the theatre, particularly since Vautrin was one of the
most memorable characters from Balzac's novels and was to be
played by Frédérick Lemaître, then enjoying the peak of his success in
the boulevard theatres.   On the opening night of 14 March 1840,
despite the fact that Mlle Falcon[51] was giving her final performance at
the Opéra, and that the Gymnase was staging the première of Scribe's
melodrama, *La Grand' Mère*, the auditorium at the Porte-Saint-Martin
was full.[52]

Harel was counting on a success to save his theatre from
impending bankruptcy, and, according to Lemaître, when the censors
expressed concern about the criminal status of the play's hero, Harel
pleaded with Cavé, *directeur des Beaux-Arts et des Théâtres*, on the
grounds that if the play did not go ahead, the theatre's bankruptcy was
certain.   Permission to proceed was granted on the following
condition: 'si les représentations de *Vautrin* sont blâmées, elles seront
suspendues par une volonté plus forte que la mienne'.[53]   Unbeknown
to Balzac it seems, the play was condemned in advance.

The audience expected to see in the play the familiar Parisian
settings of *La Comédie humaine* and was disappointed to find the
play's tortuous plot set in the Spanish Embassy, as well as frustrated
that the main character did not appear at all in the first two acts. By
the time Lemaître eventually appeared in the third act, most members
of the audience had lost the thread of the plot entirely and had no
interest in the secondary roles played by poor actors who appeared

[49] Gautier, 'Honoré de Balzac' in *Ecrivains et Artistes Romantiques* (Paris: Plon,
1933), pp. 136-137. From articles which originally appeared in *L'Artiste* in March,
April and May 1858.
[50] See appendix IV.
[51] Mlle Falcon (Marie-Cornélie) [1812-1897], soprano at the Opéra from where
she retired early in her career in 1840.
[52] Frédérick Lemaître, *Souvenirs publiés par son fils* (Paris: Ollendorf, 1880), pp.
236-246.
[53] Henri Lecomte, *Un comédien du XIXe siècle, Frédérick Lemaître*, 2 vols. (Paris:
Hetzel, 1888), vol. II, p. 13.

like 'pommes de terre autour d'un bifteck'.[54]   In the fourth act Lemaître attempted to revive the flagging play by changing his style to burlesque comedy, in which the audience rejoiced. When he attempted to return to a serious tone in the final act, however, the audience called out for more buffoonery and the pathos of the play's closing scenes was completely lost.[55]

Vautrin was not only an abysmal failure but also a public scandal. In the fourth act Lemaître's appearance closely resembled the caricatures of Louis-Philippe which appeared at that time in the opposition press. In his correspondence Balzac blames Lemaître for this travesty and accuses him of an act of revenge against Harel.[56] In his memoirs, however, Lemaître defends his position, claiming that a slight resemblance to the king had been remarked upon at the dress-rehearsal and that the dresser and wig-maker had been instructed by Harel to exaggerate this. In any event, the appearance of Lemaître produced a furore in the audience, which contributed to the banning of the play. The duc d'Orleans, who was present at the performance, was rumoured to have stormed out of the theatre in protest, and Harel claimed that it was for this reason alone that the play was prohibited.[57] The journalists Janin and Briffault make little mention of Lemaître's burlesquing of the king, however, and no paper reports the Duc d'Orleans leaving the theatre. René Guise suggests that Harel, mindful of the fact that *Vautrin* was in any event a disaster, deliberately propagated this rumour in order to qualify for a state indemnity for the bankruptcy of the theatre.[58]

[54] *La Caricature*, 22 March 1840.

[55] See: Briffault, *Le Temps*, 16 March 1840: 'En cet instant et à dater de cette entrée gigantesque et de cette gambade incommensurable, nous avons compris que la pièce elle-même n'était qu'une énorme parade'; Janin, *Les Débats*, 16 March 1840: 'Nous l'avouons, en cet instant, voyant toute cette bouffonnerie, nous nous sommes figurés que la pièce n'était en effet qu'une parade'; Dallier, *L'Echo du théâtre*, 17 March 1840: 'Un instant nous avons cru que *Vautrin* n'était qu'une joueuse farce et nous nous en réjouissions pour M. de Balzac et sa réputation'.

[56] *LMH*, vol. I, p. 673, 'L'affaire de la ressemblance avec L[ouis]-P[hillipe] était peut-être une chose montée contre Harel, le directeur de la Porte-S[ain]t-Martin, dont il [Lemaître] voulait la chute pour avoir sa direction. Ceci est encore un mystère pour moi'.

[57] Lemaître, *Souvenirs publiés par son fils*, pp. 236-246.

[58] René Guise, 'Un grand homme du roman à la scène' in *AB* (1966), p. 209.

The play was immediately banned and Harel did in fact qualify for
an indemnity. Balzac refused the state indemnity offered to him,[59] but
made a little profit from the rapid sale of the play to a public curious
to discover 'la plus odieuse immoralité des temps modernes'.[60] The
Porte-Saint-Martin requested permission to restage *Vautrin* in 1848,
but, although the ban was lifted, the company did not proceed with
the production. Then in April 1850 the Gaîté produced the play
without Balzac's consent, and the indignant author immediately
sought an injunction which was effected on 17 May. There were two
posthumous revivals of the play, one in April 1869 at the Ambigu-
Comique, and another in September 1917 at the Sarah Bernhardt
theatre, but both were very poorly received.[61] Balzac has certainly
not succeeded in transporting the character of Vautrin from the novel
to the stage, for the hero of the play is not portrayed with any
psychological conviction and his contradictions of character remain
unexplained. In the final analysis it seems fair to agree with André le
Breton that the action is 'compliquée au point d'être par endroits
inextricable' and has a 'bizarre tissu d'inventions sans
vraisemblance'.[62]

The year after the failure of *Vautrin* Balzac's thoughts again
turned to the theatre and, more importantly, to the financial gains
which he believed could be made there. In September 1841 he
announced his latest project to Madame Hanska as a solution to his
financial crisis: 'pour pouvoir plus sûrement payer mes dettes, je
finirai une comédie pour le mois de décembre intitulée *les Rubriques
de Quinola*'.[63] The new play was intended for the Odéon and in a
letter of 5 January 1842 Balzac tells Madame Hanska that rehearsals
had already begun,[64] although, according to his friend Léon Gozlan
the play was still not finished.[65] Gozlan recalls how he heard Balzac
read his play in his lively, animated style to the committee and actors
of the Odéon and amazed them by announcing at the end of the fourth
act that the fifth was not yet written! Unshaken by the obvious

[59] See Balzac's statement to this effect in the *Revue parisienne,* 25 September1840.
[60] *La Caricature* 29 March 1840.
[61] Milatchitch, *Le Théâtre de H. de Balzac*, pp. 93-98.
[62] André Le Breton, *Balzac, l'homme et l'Œuvre* (Paris: Colin, 1905), p. 278.
[63] *LMH*, vol. II, p. 26.
[64] *LMH*, vol. II, p. 36.
[65] Léon Gozlan, *Balzac intime* (Paris: Librairie illustrée, 1886), pp. 238-239.

annoyance of all those present, Balzac went on to recount his fifth act anyway, simply making it up as he went along!

A great success was predicted for this play, but again the public was to be disappointed, for the action owes nothing to Balzac's novels and is far removed from contemporary French society. The play is set in Spain during the reign of Philip II, its main characters are expatriate Italians, and the plot hinges on the invention of a steam engine for use in shipping. Balzac, however, was blindly optimistic about his choice of theme and struck a deal with the director, securing the property right to all tickets for the first three performances. According to this agreement Balzac would sell these tickets himself at whatever price he chose and give the director fifty percent of their face value. As people came to buy advance tickets Balzac propagated the myth that the first three performances had been sold out to an illustrious audience of ministers, ambassadors, aristocrats, senior civil servants and bankers, and at the same time the press were strictly banned until the director resumed his rights at the fourth performance.[66] In this way Balzac hoped to inflate ticket prices and to generate demand, and particularly to attract the type of audience that he already claimed to be in possession of tickets. Unfortunately the scheme backfired, since the rumour was quickly exaggerated beyond all proportion, and people soon became convinced that they could not even hope to buy a ticket at any price and so did not even bother to turn up at the box-office.[67]

Consequently, on the opening night of 19 March 1842, the auditorium was half empty, and those spectators who had been duped into paying for their tickets at inflated prices were outraged to find tickets being sold outside the theatre at great reductions. Meanwhile, the journalists, who were still barred despite the poor turn-out of the public, were busy planning their revenge. According to Léon Gozlan, from the second act of the première onwards, the auditorium was a cacophony of animal noises and heckling, and at the fourth performance when the press were finally permitted entry the stalls

---

[66] See Balzac's contract with the director, d'Epagny, in *Corres.*, vol. IV, pp. 355-357.

[67] Gautier records this 'tripotage de billets', in a later account of Balzac's attempts with the drama. See: Gautier, *Histoire de l'art dramatique*, 6 vols. (Paris: Hetzel, 1858), vol. III, p. 103.

were full of police and officials, who tried in vain to maintain order.[68] Balzac tells of this disastrous outcome in his letter of 8 April 1842 to Madame Hanska:

> *Quinola* a été l'objet d'une bataille mémorable, semblable à celle d'*Hernani*. On est venu siffler toute la pièce, d'un bout jusqu'à l'autre sans vouloir l'entendre pendant 7 représentations consécutives. [...] tous mes ennemis [...] se sont mis à m'injurier et à calomnier la pièce, à qui mieux-mieux.[69]

The critics were merciless,[70] and even Gautier, who had always been supportive of Balzac's dramatic projects, makes no mention of the play in *La Presse*. After just nineteen performances *Quinola* closed,[71] and there was only one revival of the play at the Vaudeville in 1863. This time the play was treated less harshly, but was still not considered a success and closed after 43 performances.[72] The play's setting, characters and plot clearly constituted a subject which Balzac knew very little about.

The next staging of a play by Balzac was in September 1843 at the Gaîté while he was visiting Mme Hanska in St. Petersburg. Little is known about the genesis of *Paméla Giraud*, as prior to its performance there is only one mention of it in Balzac's correspondence.[73] The action of this melodrama is more contemporary than those of Balzac's previous plays. Set in the first few years of the Restoration, it tells the fairly simple story of thwarted love between the daughter of a poor tailor and the son of a wealthy bourgeois merchant. The son is condemned for a crime committed in a moment of aberration and is saved by the tailor's daughter who compromises her honour in so doing. The promised marriage between the two is forbidden, until the cunning intervention of a benevolent lawyer

---

[68] Léon Gozlan, *Balzac intime*, pp. 261-262.

[69] *LMH*, vol. II, pp. 60-61.

[70] See in particular Jules Janin in *les Débats*, 21 March 1842, who writes 'Quinola est sans excuse'. Also *La Quotidienne* , 21 March 1842 reports 'La pièce de Balzac est une des conceptions les plus bizarres, les plus incohérentes, les plus indigestes qui soient jamais sorties du cerveau d'un homme d'esprit et de talent'.

[71] *LMH*, vol. II, p. 60.

[72] Milatchitch, *Le Théâtre de Balzac*, pp. 134-137.

[73] *LMH*, vol. I, p. 683.

forces the merchants to accept the tailor's daughter as their son's wife.

Reception of the play was mixed.[74] Jules Janin condemned *Paméla Giraud* no less pitilessly than he had condemned *Vautrin* and *Quinola*,[75] while Gautier identified its 'vérité des situations', 'naturel des détails' and 'esprit du dialogue'. Gautier blames the failure of the play partly on poor acting, remarking that it was 'assez faiblement jouée'.[76] Although *Paméla Giraud* closed after only a few nights in 1843, it survived for 35 performances when it was revived in July 1859 at the Gymnase with better actors, but then a second revival at the Odéon in January 1917 met with silence from the critics and closed after just eight performances.[77]

In 1847 Balzac promised a play entitled *La Marâtre* to Hostein at the Théâtre Historique, and in 1848 devoted himself more single-mindedly to the theatre and to the writing of this play, stating in a letter to Madame Hanska: 'il faut que je fasse à *la scène* les mêmes efforts que j'ai faits en *livres,* en 1830'.[78] A few days later, on 12 March 1848, Balzac announced to Madame Hanska that he was about to begin work on this new play: '[m]on café est passé; je viens de le prendre et je commence la *Marâtre*'.[79] Balzac's subsequent letters to Madame Hanska tell how he received visits from the director Hostein, and the actress Marie Dorval, who was to play the lead.[80] The death of Marie Dorval's son caused her to take six months' leave from the theatre, however, and her role was conceded to Hostein's mistress, Mme Lacressonnière, which was clearly a disappointment for Balzac.[81]

La Marâtre is set in a bourgeois household during the Restoration period. If Balzac was ever to achieve success in the theatre then it would surely be in the portrayal of a milieu which he had already successfully depicted in his novels. The plot is finely constructed around mistaken identities, thwarted love and poisonings but is more

---

[74] See: *La Nation,* 7 October 1843; *Le Moniteur Universel,* 2 October 1843, *La Démocratie Pacifique,* 18 October 1843.

[75] *Les Débats*, 2 October, 1843.

[76] *La Presse,* 20 October, 1843.

[77] Milatchitch, *Le Théâtre de H. de Balzac,* pp. 168-169.

[78] *LMH*, vol. IV, p. 229.

[79] *LMH*, vol. IV, p. 246.

[80] *LMH*, vol. IV, p. 282.

[81] *LMH*, vol. IV, p. 350.

poignant than Balzac's previous, crude melodrama, for it ends in tragedy with the death of the hero and heroine, the resignation of their adversary and the insanity of the heroine's father.

The première of *La Marâtre* took place on 25 May 1848. There were three other premières that night in the boulevard theatres, and the public at large showed little interest in any of them, being more occupied by political events.[82]   Nevertheless, *La Marâtre* appears to have been a success with the critics and the literary world. For example, Jules Janin, previously among the harshest of Balzac's critics, now applauded Balzac for his 'œuvre charmante, ciselée, travaillée', and Balzac wrote to Madame Hanska the next day:

> Hier, nous avons eu un succès éclatant, je ne vous en parlerai pas, car l'article de J.J. vous arrivera bien certainement avant cette lettre, et il vous racontera la pièce ou en bien ou en mal. Ce que je voulais, je l'ai obtenu: une rénovation, et la littérature dramatique reconnaîtra que je vais me faire une large part. Je suis sûr de mon avenir, et d'une fortune.[83]

Despite this success with the critics, the following day Balzac wrote that the theatre was virtually empty, stating that in this time of revolution '[c]'est fini du théâtre, comme du luxe'.[84]   Financial reward for his efforts in the theatre was once more to elude him. After just five performances the noticeboards announced the temporary suspension of Balzac's play and closure of the Théâtre Historique. Alarmed by the political turbulence overtaking the capital and incapable of sustaining poor receipts, Hostein had decided to take his troupe to England.[85]   The troupe returned on 20 July and Balzac's play was immediately restaged for 36 performances with great success, although this was still a depressed period for the Parisian stage.[86]

After Balzac's death the directors of the Théâtre-Français and the Odéon approached his widow for permission to revive *La Marâtre*. Eve de Balzac objected to their suggested alterations, however, and

---

[82] *LMH*, vol. IV, p. 365.
[83] *LMH*, vol. IV, p. 365.
[84] *LMH*, vol. IV, p. 366.
[85] *LMH*, vol. IV, p. 370. See also Hostein's letter to Balzac explaining the suspension of the play in *Corres.*, vol. V, 308-310.
[86] *LMH*, vol. IV, p. 455.

prevented the directors from proceeding. Finally the play was resurrected in its original form at the Vaudeville on 1 September 1859 and enjoyed 45 performances, prompting Gautier to write: 'avec Balzac la France a perdu un auteur dramatique égal au romancier'.[87] Certainly this play demonstrates more effectively than its predecessors Balzac's powers of observation, and is something of a success in its realistic portrayal of domestic life. Nevertheless, *La Marâtre* remains inferior to the final piece of Balzac's theatre which was to be revealed to the Parisian theatre audience: *Mercadet ou Le Faiseur.*

In a letter to Madame Hanska on 6 August 1848 Balzac told of seventeen plays which he had not yet brought to fruition.[88] Of these *Mercadet* is paid particular attention in his letter the next day, in which Balzac states: 'Je vais risquer *Mercadet* aux *Français*'.[89] It is difficult to be certain of the date at which *Mercadet ou le Faiseur* was written. Already in 1839 Gautier mentions the play as forthcoming,[90] and certainly an early version of it seems to have existed in 1840 when Balzac first announced the project to Madame Hanska[91] and Gautier attended a reading of it at Les Jardies, which he was to recall in 1868:

> Nous avons entendu autrefois la lecture de *Mercadet* faite par Balzac lui-même. On ne peut se figurer quel feu, quelle animation et quelle puissance comique l'auteur donnait à sa création. Pour chaque personnage il trouvait une voix différente, il parlait, il déclamait, il mimait, et faisait vivre tout ce monde avec une turbulence fiévreuse qui vous entraînait. [...] Aucun acteur n'a jamais produit une pareille impression sur nous, non pas même Frédéric à son plus beau temps.[92]

This was not the final version of the play, however, for in 1844 Balzac's letters to Madame Hanska reveal that he had still not finished *Mercadet*.[93] There is then no mention of the play at all for

[87] *Le Moniteur Universel*, 5 September 1859.
[88] *LMH*, vol. IV, p. 490.
[89] *LMH*, vol. IV, p. 492.
[90] *La Presse*, 11 March 1839.
[91] *LMH*, vol. I, p. 675.
[92] Gautier, *Le Moniteur Universel*, 26 October 1868.
[93] *LMH*, vol. II, pp. 370, 371, 375, & 379.

the next three years, and by the time Balzac refers to it again in his correspondence, it is referred to as a finished play. On 9 August 1848 Balzac informed Madame Hanska that Frédérick Lemaître was coming to listen to the play that evening, that it would be read to the troupe at the Théâtre Français the following Monday and that rehearsals were to begin immediately.[94]

On 19 August Balzac wrote to Madame Hanska that *Mercadet* had been unanimously accepted by the actors but that some changes were required and he seemed certain of a resounding success.[95] A few weeks later on 20 September Balzac departed for Russia, leaving Laurent-Jan in charge of his literary affairs,[96] since Lockroy, then director of the Théâtre-Français, was hesitating over the production and Balzac could postpone his trip no longer. The committee of the Théâtre Français eventually changed its mind about *Mercadet* and withdrew the play from the programme. Balzac offered the play to Hostein at the Porte-Saint-Martin, but Hostein recognised that his public favoured the melodrama and asked Balzac to make substantial changes to his play.[97] Balzac's reply to Laurent-Jan from Russia on 9 February 1849 strictly forbade any such alterations.[98] Throughout 1849 Balzac was plagued by ill-health and did not return until May 1850 to Paris, where he died on 18 August with *Mercadet* still not accepted at any theatre.

In 1851 the Gymnase asked Eve de Balzac for permission to show *Mercadet*. Permission was granted but the director found the play too long and assigned to the dramatist Adolphe Dennery the task of shortening it.[99] The play was a great success when it was first performed on 23 August 1851, although the financial world was outraged by the play's exposure of financial malpractice and called for a ban, which resulted in a suspension. The furore only served to increase the public's interest in the production which, when reinstated, ran for 73 successful performances.[100]

[94] *LMH*, vol. IV, p. 495.
[95] *LMH*, vol. IV, p. 518-519.
[96] *Corres.*, vol. V, p. 365.
[97] *Corres.*, vol. v, p. 456.
[98] *Corres.*, vol. V, p. 487.
[99] The substance of this play is treated in the final chapter of the present work.
[100] *Revue et Gazette des Théâtres*, 23 August 1851; *Le Corsaire*, 26 August 1851; *Les Débats*, 25 August 1851,

Meanwhile, the Théâtre-Français retained Balzac's original version of *Mercadet ou Le Faiseur* and has staged it at various intervals from 1868 to the present day.[101] *Mercadet* is the enduring proof that, had he lived longer or applied himself more seriously at an earlier stage, Balzac might have achieved the same success with the drama as with the novel. As an isolated success, however, *Mercadet* does not establish Balzac as an *homme de théâtre*; rather it is in *La Comédie humaine* that the reader can find the most extensive evidence of Balzac's familiarity with the Parisian theatre, his knowledge of its operations and his assimilation of its aesthetics, and it is to Balzac's novels that this study now turns.

---

[101] A number of performances have been given In Paris in each of the following years:1868, 1869, 1870, 1871, 1872, 1874, 1875, 1876, 1879, 1880, 1887, 1888, 1890, 1899, 1918 and most recently in 1993. *Mercadet* has also been staged outside Paris by the Théâtre National de Strasbourg in 1964, by the Théâtre National Populaire in 1957 and by the Théâtre Populaire Romand and the Théâtre Jeune Public de Strasbourg in 1992. See: 'Le Faiseur' in *Répertoire du Théâtre Populaire Romand* (Saint-Imier: Canevas, 1992). This most recent production was played almost exactly according to Balzac's 1848 version. After the huge gains made in financial and property speculations during the 1980s, followed by enormous losses and global recession at the turn of the decade, Balzac's financial play seems to have been as relevant a comment on the finance industry in the early 1990s as it was in 1851.

PARIS THEATRES IN *LA COMEDIE HUMAINE*

Critics of Balzac have commented only superficially on his treatment of the theatre world as a background to the events of *Un grand homme de province à Paris*.[1] Most notably Donald Adamson remarks in his 1981 study of *Illusions perdues*:

> The world of the Parisian theatres is conjured up with some feeling for the character of each. Out of the ten or so Parisian theatres then (1821-1822) in existence, Balzac refers to six.[2]

Adamson goes on to cite briefly just six references to three of these theatres: the Vaudeville, the Gymnase and the Panorama-Dramatique. Roland Chollet, in his 1977 introduction to *Illusions perdues*,[3] comments more fully when claiming that Balzac's portrayal of the theatre touches only the surface of reality, because it reveals nothing of the administration, financial backing, censorship and *comités de lecture* which constituted the reality of life in the theatre. Chollet claims that Balzac's treatment of the theatre is subservient to his desire to expose the unscrupulous dealings of the press, because the theatre is shown to be 'entièrement à la merci des petites feuilles et des caprices de leurs collaborateurs'.[4] The comments of Adamson and Chollet beg a fuller examination of the historicity of Balzac's portrayal of the theatre both in *Illusions perdues* and throughout *La Comédie humaine,* and the examination here will therefore be applied to all of Balzac's novels in which there is a significant representation of the theatre.

The historicity of Balzac's portrayal of the theatre will be assessed in relation to contemporary historical sources including press publications, in particular *Le Miroir des spectacles*[5] and *Le Diable*

---

[1] Henceforth in the present study referred to as *Un grand homme.*

[2] Adamson, *Balzac, 'Illusions perdues'* (London: Grant & Cutler, 1981), p. 77.

[3] Chollet, Introduction to *Illusions perdues,* ed. Pléiade (Paris: Gallimard, 1977), vol. V, pp. 3-108.

[4] *Ibid.* p. 73.

[5] This review was edited by MM Jouy, Arnault, Emmanuel Dupaty, Cauchois-Lemaire from 15 February 1821 until 24 June 1823, after which it was relaunched as *La Pandore.* See: E. Hatin, *Bibliographie de la presse périodique française* (Paris:

boiteux,[6] the memoirs of actors, including Bouffé[7] and Lemaître,[8] and the works of critics, historians of the theatre, and social commentators, all of whom were involved in the theatre as authors and directors during the period covered by Balzac's work.[9] These contemporary sources contain detailed anecdotes of the theatre world recounted at first-hand, and it should be stressed that much of this historical material, and that used in subsequent chapters, has not previously been cited by modern historians of the theatre, nor has it been examined in relation to Balzac's work. A limited use will also be made of twentieth-century histories of the theatre in the course of this examination.[10]

The purpose of this chapter is to examine the extent to which Balzac represents the history of the theatre of his lifetime in *La Comédie humaine* and to establish how accurate that representation is and what its own contribution to the history of the theatre may be. Balzac's portrayal of the theatre will first be discussed in the context of his intentions to include a novel specifically devoted to the theatre

Anthropos, 1865), p. 348, where *Le Miroir des spectacles* is described as: 'une des feuilles les plus spirituelles et les plus populaires de la Restauration'.

    [6] A few issues of *Le Diable boiteux* first appeared in 1790 and 26 issues in 1816. From 1823-1831 it described itself as a 'journal des spectacles, des mœurs, des arts et des modes', and continued as such under the new name of *Le Frondeur* until publication ceased in 1848. See: *Grand dictionnaire universel du XIXe siècle* (Paris: Larousse, 1864-1886), vol. VI, p. 1194.

    [7] Bouffé, *Mes souvenirs, 1800-1880* (Paris: Dentu, 1880).

    [8] Lemaître, *Souvenirs publiés par son fils* (Paris: Ollendorf, 1880).

    [9] Listed below are the main contemporary sources which will be referred to in this chapter (for others used as background and orientation material see bibliography): Brazier, *Chroniques des petits théâtres de Paris depuis leur origine*, 2 vols. (Paris: Allardin, 1837); Buguet, *Foyers et Coulisses*, 15 vols. (Paris: Tresse, 1875); Duflot, *Les Secrets des coulisses* (Paris: Michel Lévy, 1865); d'Heilly, *Le scandale au théâtre* (Paris: Jules Taride, 1861); Montigny, *Le Provincial à Paris*, 3 vols. (Paris: Ladvocat, 1825); Muret, *L'Histoire par le théâtre*, 1789-1851, 3 vols. (Paris: Amyot, 1865); Royer, *Histoire universelle du théâtre* (Paris: Ollendorf, 1878).

    [10] Listed below are the main twentieth-century sources which will be referred to in this chapter (for others used as background and orientation see bibliography): Albert, *Les Théâtres des boulevards, 1789-1848* (Paris: Société française d'imprimerie, 1902); Beaulieu, *Les Théâtres du boulevard du Crime 1752-1862* (Paris: Daragon, 1905); Berthier, *Le Théâtre au XIXe siècle* (Paris: Presses universitaires de France, 1986; Carlson, *The French Stage in the Nineteenth Century* (Metuchen: Scarecrow press, 1972); Lecomte, *Histoire des théâtres de Paris* (Paris: Daragon, 1907).

in *La Comédie humaine*. This will be followed by an analysis of Balzac's portrayal of each of the theatres featured in his novels in relation to the actual histories of those theatres. Finally the portrayal of the theatre will be considered in relation to the overall narrative scheme and authorial intentions of *La Comédie humaine*.

Le Théâtre comme il est

Balzac's project for a novel which would concentrate specifically on the theatres of Paris first appears in a letter to Madame Hanska on 7 April 1844:

> Néanmoins, pour 20 000fr [...], je consentirais à leur faire *Les Misères du théâtre,* parce que c'est sans aucune[s] difficultés littéraires, vu l'abondance des figures, des types, et des événements.[11]

This was the novel which Balzac projected under different titles: by 13 April 1844 he had changed it to *Les Enfers de Paris* [12] and by 15 July of the same year to *Le Théâtre comme il est*.[13] Certainly after his own experiences at the Porte-Saint-Martin with *Vautrin* in 1840, at the Odéon with *Les Ressources de Quinola* in 1842, and at the Gaîté with *Paméla Giraud* in 1843, Balzac was well equipped to write a novel which would examine the world of the theatre from both sides of the curtain.

The intended novel was to be serialised in Dutacq's new paper, *Le Soleil,* but by 15 July 1844, according to Balzac's letter to Madame Hanska, the project had not progressed any further.   In the continuation of this letter on the next day, Balzac makes it clear that he intended to treat the world of the theatre in the same way in which he had already treated the associated world of the press in *Illusions perdues;* the novel would reveal the squalor and corruption which Balzac perceived to be the reality of life in the theatre; it would be a:

---

[11]   *LMH*, vol. II, p. 416.
[12]   *Ibid*. p. 423.
[13]   *Ibid*. p. 468.

[...] travail semblable à celui que j'ai fait sur le journalisme, et destiné à faire connaître le derrière des coulisses, le drame affreux, hideux, comique, terrible, qui précède le lever du rideau.[14]

Le Soleil was never published, but Balzac continued to refer to his projected novel in his letters,[15] until he finally began to work on it in Wierzchownia in October 1847. Here Balzac began by drafting an outline of his novel, indicating that the first part would be devoted to provincial theatre, with a fictional actor, Robert Médal, as the central character, and a familiar actress from previous novels, Florine, as the leading lady.[16] The location of this intended first part in the provinces implies that there would be a second part situated in Paris, again following the treatment of the press in *Illusions perdues* which is located in both Paris and Angoulême. In fact the few pages of the novel which were subsequently written are situated in and not in a provincial town as originally intended.

It is not clear why Balzac did not manage to make any more headway with this novel other than that he continued to be plagued by debts and increasing ill-health, and while he had claimed that the subject matter of the novel would present him with no apparent difficulties, the work was intended to be a major novel on the scale of *Illusions perdues* and circumstances demanded that he devote himself to works which could be completed more quickly. There can be no doubt that a novel devoted specifically to the theatre would have been an important addition to Balzac's work. However, its absence does not mean that the theatre is not adequately represented in *La Comédie humaine,* for, as will be seen, it is central to the portrayal of the social interaction and activity of Parisian society.

The Rise of the Boulevard du Temple

Under the Napoleonic regime the 21 theatres which existed in Paris at the beginning of the Empire were reduced to just 8; this was ratified by a decree on 29 July 1807, stating that from then on there would be

[14] *LMH,* vol. II, p. 474.

[15] *Ibid.* p. 572; vol. III, pp. 232, 233, 243; vol, IV, pp. 118, 123.

[16] This manuscript, dated October 1847 in Wierzchownia, is conserved in the Lovenjoul collection (*Lov.* A 216, fl) and is reproduced in *LCH*, vol. XII, p. 585.

four primary theatres, namely: the Théâtre-Français, the Odéon, which would now be known as the Théâtre de l'Impératrice, the Opéra, now known as the Académie impériale de musique, and the Opéra-Comique, now known as the Théâtre de l'Empereur, and including a subsidiary company specialising in Italian opera. There would also be just four minor theatres to balance the major theatres and these were: the Gaîté and the Ambigu-Comique, which were permitted to show melodramas, farces and pantomimes, and the Variétés and the Vaudeville, which were restricted to parodies, peasant plays and simple musical entertainments.   Only one exception was made and this concerned the Porte-Saint-Martin, which was authorised by an imperial decree on 11 March 1809 to show 'pièces lyriques à décorations et machines'.[17]

Dramatists and painters were encouraged by the Napoleonic court to select classical themes and to develop them in classical ways, which in the serious theatre resulted in sterile imitations of Racine and Molière. Acting styles, staging and criticism showed the same influence.[18]   The history of French theatre from the end of the Napoleonic era up to the July Revolution of 1830 is primarily that of the defeat of the neoclassical vision of Napoleon and the triumph of popular melodrama. As the harsh restrictions governing the theatre were lifted at the end of the Empire, smaller theatres began to open and flourished in the new atmosphere of relative freedom, becoming enormously prolific in the number and variety of productions which they now offered.

During the period from 1815 to 1830 the minor theatres produced 369 new comedies, 280 new melodramas, 200 new comic operas and 1300 new vaudevilles, while the declining classical tradition managed to produce only 72 tragedies.[19] In order to accommodate this huge proliferation of new work and to meet the public's demand for what was now its most popular form of entertainment, theatres would offer as many as four different productions in one evening. Rehearsals for a new production would begin on the day after its predecessor opened, even if the latter was a great success, and the programme would normally be varied each week. At most theatres the evening

---

[17] Berthier, *Le Théâtre au XIXe siècle*, p. 6.
[18] Carlson, *The French Stage in the Nineteenth Century*, pp. 12-53.
[19] *Ibid.* p. 53.

would begin between 18.00h and 19.00h or even as early as 17.00h on Sundays at the Ambigu-Comique; the latest was the Italiens which did not begin until 20.00h.

By the early 1820s, as well as the eight official theatres that had operated during the Napoleonic regime, there were four other important theatres: the Porte-Saint-Martin, which was now recognised as a theatre rather than a music-hall, the Gymnase, the Panorama-Dramatique and the Théâtre Mont-Parnasse. Along with the Vaudeville, the Variétés, the Gaîté and the Ambigu-Comique, these theatres were mostly situated on and around the boulevard du Temple, which, with its cafés, side-shows, musical entertainments and the Cirque-Olympique, had become the focal point for popular entertainment in the capital. The theatres of the boulevard du Temple, where places could be obtained for less than one franc, were worlds apart from the Théâtre-Français and the Opéra, where even a modest seat might cost in excess of 6 francs, and which consequently attracted a very different audience.

According to the historian and playwright Charles-Maurice Descombes, whose work relates mainly to the 1820s,[20] the boulevard du Temple had become the fashionable centre of entertainment for all classes of Parisian society and the impression he gives of a lively, bustling corner of the capital is also borne out by other contemporary historians of the theatre such as Montigny, d'Heilly, Brazier, Duflot, Muret, and Royer, all of whom were involved in the theatre as either playwrights or directors. Their accounts suggest that success on the boulevard du Temple lay not in the number of performances which any one play might merit, but in the number and variety of plays which any one theatre could reasonably produce. In turn this proliferation of new work in the smaller theatres provided the press with constantly changing subject matter for reviews and *feuilletons* and engendered a growth in the number of publications available in order to cover adequately the sheer volume of productions on offer.

An examination of issues of *Le Miroir des spectacles* and *Le Diable boiteux* from the early 1820s[21] reveals that increasing amounts of space were devoted to reviews of the smaller theatres and

[20] Charles-Maurice, *Histoire anecdotique du théâtre, de la littérature et de diverses impressions contemporaines*, 2 vols. (Paris: Plon, 1856).

[21] See above, pp. 30-31, n. 5 & 6, for extreme publication dates and other details.

highlights the shift in public taste which was taking place. An article in *Le Diable boiteux* of 23 July 1823 underlines how the shift in popularity from the major state theatres to the boulevard theatres was reinforced by the adherence of the state theatres to the tradition of annual closures, which in the new, dynamic climate of change they could really not afford:

> Tandis que nos grandes puissances dramatiques désertent les théâtres royaux, et courent en province rétablir leur bourse épuisée ou leur santé défaillante, les modestes acteurs du boulevard, auxquels on n'accorde pas de congés, et qui n'ont pas le loisir d'être malades, redoublent de zèle, d'activité, et le public s'habitue insensiblement à aller chercher aux théâtres du mélodrame un spectacle intéressant et varié.

A similar passage from the *Miroir des spectacles* of 18 October 1821 emphasises this shift in public taste:

> On a cru remarquer que depuis quelque temps la foule se portait de préférence aux petits théâtres, et que les bouffonneries du Gymnase et des Variétés attiraient plus de spectateurs que les grandes compositions des maîtres de la scène.

A couple of weeks earlier, on 4 October 1821, the same paper gives details of the revenues of all the theatres for the month of September, revealing that the Gymnase and the Variétés enjoyed far higher revenues than the Opéra and the Théâtre-Français.[22] Taking account of the fact that the seat prices at the latter were far higher than at the Gymnase and the Variétés the sheer volume of spectators which passed through the more popular theatres must have been enormous.

According to modern historian Maurice Albert, the social shift from the major state theatres to the boulevard du Temple in the early 1820s also reflected the more general social preoccupations of the time. The melodramatic style of antithesis and hyperbole in both the

---

[22] Académie royale de musique, 61 141F; Théâtre-Français, 47 764F; Opéra-Comique, 49 354F; L'Odéon, 22 412F; Italiens, 24 474F; Vaudeville 28 003F; Gymnase 69 362F; Variétés, 71 202F; Gaîté, 39 213F; Ambigu-Comique, 32 723F; Porte-Saint-Martin, 34 814F; Panorama-Dramatique, 26 723F.

novel and the theatre, its preoccupation with the struggle of good and
evil and with characters who are often scoundrels and criminals was,
according to Albert (although he does not cite the sources of his
information) also connected to the government's concerns with law
and order and to the public debate on the punishment of criminals,
prison conditions and the death penalty.[23]

As far as *La Comédie humaine* is concerned, although some of the
action in the Parisian novels *Un grand homme de province à Paris,
Splendeurs et misères des courtisanes* and *Le Père Goriot* takes place
at the Opéra and the Italiens, Balzac's main concern in terms of the
operations of the theatres themselves is with the boulevard theatres,
with the corruption and exploitation which existed within them and
with the economic forces by which they were driven. In *Un grand
homme* in particular, by choosing to set much of the action among the
small theatres of the boulevard du Temple, Balzac is able to reflect
their growing importance in the history of the theatre.

It should be noted, however, that although Balzac shows the
increased accessibility of the theatre to a wider and more varied
public, that public nevertheless still excluded most of the population.
Only about 10% of the inhabitants of the capital would have been
able to afford to attend even the cheapest theatres regularly, and for
the lower class, for whom the daily wage could be as little as 15 sous,
at a time when a four-pound loaf of bread would cost 17 sous, the
theatre was clearly an unaffordable luxury, although these people
would still have come to the boulevard du Temple for the side-shows
and cheaper entertainments.[24] What is presented to the reader
byBalzac as a representative truth is of course, like the total picture
offered in *La Comédie humaine,* only representative of a selected
sample of society, since Balzac does not depict the poorest classes.

The struggling fortunes of the major state theatres and in
particular of the Théâtre-Français during the 1820s are ignored by
Balzac, and this would be a serious omission in any history of the
theatre, but Balzac's concentration on the frenzied activity of the
boulevard du Temple is essential to his narrative purposes. It is
precisely the lively atmosphere, bordering on disorder and chaos,
where normal social barriers become more blurred, that permits the

[23] Albert, *Les Théâtres des boulevards*, p. 301.
[24] Berthier, *Le Théâtre au XIXe siècle*, p. 26.

type of chance encounters and changes of fortune on which the events of *Un grand homme* depend. This interpenetration of normally distinct social groups, facilitated by a change in the profile of the Parisian theatre, is vital to the narrative outcomes of the novel. For where, other than in this bustling corner of Paris, could the provincial son of a humble midwife make so many influential friends and powerful enemies in so short a time? Part of the history of this newly mobile society is revealed by Balzac through a glimpse of the history of its popular theatres.

The mood of these theatres in Balzac's novels is one of constant change, reverses of fortune, frenetic activity and fear of failure; themes which correspond to his general view of society as well as to the reality of the theatres concerned. Similarly, Balzac's actresses belong essentially to the boulevard du Temple; they are often ill-trained, fearful for their success and, as in reality, always exhausted by the proliferation of new productions, hasty rehearsals and lack of rest. The corruption, the exploitation, the rise of individualism and capitalism and the insidious spread of vice, which occupy so much of *La Comédie humaine,* were for Balzac exemplified and magnified by the boulevard du Temple.[25]

The Panorama-Dramatique

Balzac failed to write more than a few pages of his proposed novel *Le théâtre comme il est*, and it is in *Un grand homme* that he treats the theatres of the boulevard du Temple in most detail. Of these theatres, the Panorama-Dramatique has the highest profile in the novel, which is significant since this theatre existed for only a short period from April 1821 to July 1823[26] and is afforded little attention by most historians of the theatre. In historical terms the brief and ill-fated history of the Panorama-Dramatique appears relatively unimportant next to the history of, for example, the Gymnase, but for Balzac it

---

[25] The points raised here will be treated in chapters 2 and 3 of the present study.

[26] This is according to press reviews in *Le Miroir des spectacles* and *Le Diable boiteux* concerning its opening and closing performances and according to the memoirs of the actor, Bouffé, who began his career here. The definitive closure is also noted in the *Grand Dictionnaire universel du XIXe siècle*, vol. 12, p. 121: 'La salle démolie presque immédiatement, fut remplacée aussitôt par une énorme maison à six étages. Il n'en resta absolument aucune espèce de vestige'.

seems that the Panorama-Dramatique epitomises the period about which he was writing, and it does not seem to be as a result of mere accident that the events of Lucien's sojourn in the world of the theatre take place for the most part in a theatre of which the existence coincided almost exactly with the period of his stay in Paris.

Despite the relative freedom which the theatres of Paris now enjoyed, however, and in order to protect the repertoires of the major theatres, the smaller establishments continued to have restrictions placed upon them regarding the type of plays which they were allowed to produce. The Panorama-Dramatique was permitted to show dramas, comedies and vaudevilles,[27] but it also laboured under the harsh restriction of not being allowed to have more than two speaking actors on the stage at any one time and this was a considerable burden to the theatre's direction throughout its existence.

The dramatist and historian Henri Lecomte describes in 1908 how, for a sum of 64 000F, the director Alaux purchased the site where the Café du Bosquet had previously stood and had managed to accommodate almost 1,500 spectators in an auditorium which was only 31 feet wide, 23 feet deep and 39 feet high. The stage, by contrast, was 89 feet deep and facilitated some of the most impressive sets and decorations known in the French theatre at that time. During the intervals, in place of the traditional curtain, a mirrored construction measuring twenty-four feet wide by twenty high was lowered on to the stage, reflecting light throughout the auditorium and allowing the audience to participate in its favourite pastime – the observation of the social spectacle in the boxes and stalls![28]

According to Lecomte and to Bouffé's memoirs, the audience of the Panorama-Dramatique was typical of the boulevard theatres, being made up of minor nobility, ministers and their mistresses and the ladies of the faubourg St-Germain who would attend occasionally out of interest and would occupy the boxes and the *avant-scène* at prices of 3,6 and 4 francs respectively, the bougeoisie who would be in the front circle and the *baignoires* at prices of 2 and 2,4 francs, students and young bachelors who paid 1,80 and 1,25 francs for

---

[27] All references to the Vaudeville genre in this study refer to the French use of the term as a light, satiric musical play and not to its later use from the 1880s onwards in America when it was used to describe music-hall variety shows.

[28] Lecomte, *Histoires des théâtres de Paris, Le Panorama-Dramatique*.

cramped places in the orchestra stalls and rear stalls, and finally workers, apprentices and the lower classes who would pay between 0,6 and 0,9 francs to be squashed together in the balconies.

Despite two changes of director (Alaux was succeeded by Langlois in April 1822 and the latter by Chedel in January 1823), the Panorama-Dramatique never overcame its financial difficulties and the government restrictions, and on 14 July 1823 it was faced with bankruptcy. On 21 July this was notified officially on the theatre's bill-boards and then publicly announced by an article in the *Diable boiteux* on 23 July:

> Le Panorama-Dramatique, qui avait donné de si brillantes espérances a bientôt vu son dernier jour. Depuis hier ses portes sont fermées, et, faute d'avoir su s'entendre, les propriétaires et les créanciers s'exposent à perdre un privilège qui pouvait faire leur fortune.

Lecomte is the only historian to take account of the impact of this closure on the lives of those who found themselves unemployed as a result of it. He notes that the actors and actresses sought permission to continue the running of the theatre as a cooperative, but after a month of negotiations they were only granted the right to give five performances from 10 to 21 August 1823 for their own financial compensation.[29] Lecomte's work gives no sources or bibliographical references but he appears to be quoting almost directly from Bouffé's memoirs here. Lecomte states in relation to the closure that it would cause more than a hundred people to be 'sur le pavé', a phrase which echoes Bouffé's account:

> Le théâtre fut fermé le 14 Julliet 1823. Et voilà, du jour au lendemain, cent personnes sur le pavé! Nous demandâmes au ministre de l'intérieur de nous laisser jouer en société; au bout d'un mois de démarches, de prières, de supplications, nous obtînmes de donner cinq représentations! il nous fut impossible d'obtenir davantage.[30]

---

[29] Lecomte, *Le Panorama-Dramatique,* p. 80.
[30] Bouffé, *Souvenirs,* p. 57.

After the demolition of the theatre a 'maison de rapport' was erected in its place, and historian Henri Beaulieu describes this in 1905 as an example of art being forced to succumb to 'l'infâme capital'.[31] In Balzac's portrayal of this theatre, however, art is shown always to be subject to economic forces. Both in reality and in *Un grand homme,* where the Panorama-Dramatique is the most important theatre for the action of the novel, this theatre is typical of a particular and precisely defined period of history, a period characterised by the rise of individualism, capitalism, speculation and new opportunities. It is this which makes it an appropriate setting for Lucien's 'baptism of fire' in the theatrical world, for this theatre is a product of a changing society, and Lucien's social mobility is facilitated by those very same changes.

Although Balzac makes some attempt to reveal the administrative difficulties of the Panorama-Dramatique, he makes no clear reference to its greatest problem of only being allowed to have two speaking actors on the stage at the same time, and in view of the difficulties which this caused the theatre, it is a noteworthy omission on his part. The Panorama-Dramatique is introduced in the novel with a description in which the author's fictional characters Vignol and Florine, take up their places alongside real actors and actresses of the day, including the famous Potier:[32]

> Le Panorama-Dramatique, aujourd'hui remplacé par une maison était une charmante salle de spectacle située vis-à-vis la rue Charlot, sur le boulevard du Temple, et où deux administrations succombèrent sans obtenir un seul succès, quoique Vignol, l'un des acteurs qui se sont partagé la succession de Potier, y ait débuté, ainsi que Florine, actrice qui, cinq ans plus tard, devint si célèbre.[33]

The fictional name Vignol appears only in the corrected Furne edition of the novel; earlier editions refer to Bouffé who was often accused of modelling himself on Potier, and in making this change Balzac has

[31] Beaulieu, *Les théâtres du boulevard du Crime*, p. 148.

[32] Potier (Charles-Gabriel) [1774-1838], began his career at the Variétés in 1809, enjoyed the peak of his success at the Porte-Saint-Martin and retired in 1827. See: *Nouvelle Biographie générale depuis les temps les plus reculés jusqu'à nos jours*, 46 vols. (Paris: Firmin Didot Frères, 1850-1860), vol. 39, p. 898.

[33] *IP*, vol. V, p. 372.

severed a connection with historical reality. In the Pléiade edition Roland Chollet suggests that Balzac may have made this change in order to introduce the fictional character of Vignol, who would later feature in one of the novels he intended to devote to the theatre.[34] There is no evidence to support this, however, and the only fictional actor named in Balzac's projects is Robert Médal. The reference to the fictional character of Florine here and to her later fame has no connection with historical fact, for in reality no-one from the Panorama-Dramatique went on to achieve any great success other than Bouffé.

The connection with historical reality is re-established towards the end of the scene when Bouffé is indeed mentioned:

> Bouffé, qui remplissait le rôle d'un vieil alcade dans lequel il révéla pour la première fois son talent pour se grimer en vieillard, vint au milieu d'un tonnerre d'applaudissements dire: '*Messieurs, la pièce que nous avons eu l'honneur de représenter est de MM. Raoul et de Cursy.*'[35]

Not only is the name of Bouffé correctly connected with the theatre where he made his debut, but it is also connected with one of his most famous roles, for it is likely that Balzac has in mind Bouffé's later incarnation of Grandet in *La Fille de l'avare* (an adaptation of Balzac's *Eugenie Grandet*) by Bayard and Duport, first performed at the Gymnase in January 1835. This passage also supplies other historically realistic details: it was customary at the time to name the authors of a play at the end of the first performance if it was a success, and it was also usual for melodramas and vaudevilles to have more than one author.

The fortune of the Panorama-Dramatique is shown in the novel to rest on the success of a play by the fictional author de Cursy (the pseudonym of du Bruel). The situation described here by Balzac is based on what frequently happened in reality, because the competition between the theatres was fierce, and although there was no shortage of new works, the more established authors could not often be tempted away from the theatres where they already enjoyed

---

[34] *IP*, vol. V, p. 372, n. 2.
[35] *IP*, vol. V, p. 391.

success, and if they were, they would not be prepared to risk their names in any of the publicity:

> Le Panorama-Dramatique avait à rivaliser avec l'Ambigu, la Gaîté, la Porte-Saint-Martin et les théâtres de vaudeville; il ne put résister à leurs manïuvres, aux restrictions de son privilège et au manque de bonnes pièces. Les auteurs ne voulurent pas se brouiller avec les théâtres existants pour un théâtre dont la vie semblait problématique. Cependant l'administration comptait sur la pièce nouvelle, espèce de mélodrame comique d'un jeune auteur, collaborateur de quelques célébrités, nommé Du Bruel.[36]

The reference to the 'restrictions de son privilège' clearly alludes to the government regulations which stipulated that at the Panorama-Dramatique only one speaking actor could be allowed to appear on stage at any one time and which frequently necessitated the special adaptation of plays.[37]   The play in question here is *Bertram, ou le Pirate,* a three-act melodrama based on the free translation of the tragedy which was originally written by Maturin, and which in reality had been adapted for the Panorama-Dramatique by Pichot, Taylor and Nodier, who was a member of the *comité de lecture.* In reality this adaptation was first performed on 26 November 1822, but at this point in the novel the action is set almost a year earlier. The error appears to be simply an instance of Balzac's liberal treatment of chronology, however, for it seems very likely that he was familiar with the play. Although there is no record of Balzac having seen the play, the advice of the fictional character Lousteau to the real actress Florville on how best to pronounce her line: 'Arrête, malheureux!' echos actual lines of the play and thus indicates that Balzac knew the piece.[38] In the second scene of Act III one of the priests cries 'Arrête, malheureuse!' and in scene 12 of Act III one of the priests cries

---

[36] *IP*, vol. V, p. 372.
[37] See pp. 40-41.
[38] The play was particularly renowned for its spectacular scenic effects, but Balzac makes no reference to these. See: *Le Journal des théâtres* (27 Nov. 1822).

'Arrête!' Similarly, the advice of the fictional characte Nathan to
Florville echos actual lines from the play:

> Si tu veux avoir du succès, lui dit Nathan, au lieu de crier comme
> une furie: *Il est sauvé!* entre tout uniment, arrive jusqu'à la rampe et
> dis d'une voix de poitrine: *Il est sauvé*, comme la Pasta dit: *O!*
> *patria* dans *Tancrède.*[39]

In Act II, scene 13 of *Bertram ou le Pirate*, Imogène cries 'O, mon
Dieu! je te remercie, ses jours seront sauvés,' and later in the same
scene, 'Aldini! ah! du moins je sauverai tes jours,' which is not too
far removed from Balzac's quotation. Here too, the introduction of
real characters lends historical credibility to the fictional characters
and events. The reference to the real actress La Pasta evokes one of
her most famous roles and Florville herself had been performing at
the Panorama-Dramatique since its creation, after starting her career
at the Vaudeville in 1819. Contrary to the situation with Bouffé and
Vignol, where the fictional character was substituted for the real one,
here it is a real character who supplants the fictional one, for in the
original manuscript Balzac had named the actress as Coralie, not
Florville.

In the setting of the Panorama-Dramatique Balzac shows the
machinations of the press, the claque and the corrupt business world
at their worst, and his descriptions of this theatre concentrate on the
areas behind the scenes rather than the stage or the auditorium. There
is no hint of the lavish sets described by Bouffé in his memoirs, or of
the mirrored fixture which was lowered during the intervals, for
Balzac's emphasis is not on the light but on the dark side of the
theatre, and his description focuses on the obscure corridors behind
and beneath the stage, where Lucien is horrified by the squalor:

> L'étroitesse des *portants*, la hauteur du théâtre, les échelles à
> quinquets, les décorations si horribles vues de près, les acteurs
> plâtrés, leurs costumes si bizarres et faits d'étoffes si grossières, les
> garçons à vestes huileuses, les cordes qui pendent, le régisseur qui
> se promène son chapeau sur la tête, les comparses assises, les toiles
> de fond suspendues, les pompiers, cet ensemble de choses
> bouffonnes, tristes, sales, affreuses, éclatantes ressemblait si peu à

---

[39] *IP*, vol. V, p. 375.

ce que   Lucien avait vu de sa place au théâtre que son étonnement fut sans bornes.[40]

Balzac demonstrates that it is behind the scenes where intrigues are started, success is bought and sold and the sordid side of the history of the theatre is created — 'une vraie cuisine,' in the words of Lousteau.   In the novel, the Panorama-Dramatique is shown to be typical of its time in every sense, both a product of and a vehicle for a mobile and changing society, but just as those changes afforded opportunity, so too they could result in disaster, and the fortunes of the Panorama-Dramatique mirror the rapid rise and demise of the novel's central character.

Balzac places the closure of the Panorama-Dramatique in March 1822, but, as with the performance of *Bertram*, he is approximately one year out of date. The reasons for the closure are not made clear in the novel other than that the administration is in financial difficulties which are compounded by the Matifat affair.   What Balzac does make clear, like the historian Lecomte (the latter quoting Bouffé's memoirs), is the impact of the closure on private destinies. Coralie and Florine are devastated by the prospect of finding themselves without work and this fuels the rivalry between them. Through the closure of the Panorama-Dramatique Balzac is able to convey an impression of the precariousness of life within the theatre, the ephemeral nature of success and the vulnerability of those who are its victims, for the closure of the Panorama-Dramatique marks the beginning of the end for Coralie and Lucien.

Le Théâtre du Gymnase

The Gymnase was established in 1820 and, like the Panorama-Dramatique, was the product of the new growth within the theatrical world.   Its history from 1820 to 1875 has been documented by Buguet who was a member of its *comité de lecture* in the 1820s and director during the early 1830s.   Modern historians Descotes and Albert, whose histories of the theatre were first published in 1964 and 1902 respectively, do not give the sources of their information on the

---

[40] *IP*, vol. V, p. 373.

Gymnase but their phraseology is so close to that of Buguet that there can be little doubt that this is where it largely derives from.

Unlike the Panorama-Dramatique the Gymnase was favoured by the government and did not have such harsh restrictions placed upon it. From its very beginning the Gymnase had the good fortune to secure talented authors and quickly established a good reputation with the public of the faubourg Saint-Germain who considered it to be the best of the smaller theatres. This is noted by Montigny in his anecdotes of Parisian society pubished in 1825 (Montigny was himself a playwright and became director of the Gymnase in 1844):

> Décidément la mode a pris sous sa puissante protection, deux spectacles de genres bien différents: l'Opéra Italien et le Gymnase. Ces deux théâtres servent de rendez-vous à la meilleure compagnie; et par meilleure, on entend, de temps immémorial, la plus brillante.[41]

According to Montigny the popularity and success of the Gymnase were well deserved:

> Le Gymnase a d'incontestables droits à la vogue dont il jouit; aucun autre théâtre ne peut lutter avec lui d'adresse et d'activité. Aux Variétés, au Vaudeville, on s'endort quelquefois, le Gymnase veille toujours.[42]

The Gymnase had the additional advantage of being able to count Scribe among its authors and his growing personal success became inextricably linked with the success of this theatre, with the result that he could not easily be persuaded to undertake work elsewhere. On 21 November 1821 the *Journal des théâtres* states that Scribe was the co-author of every one of the 27 plays accepted at the Gymnase during the preceding months, his partners being Poirson and Mélesville. At the same time the members of the new bourgeoisie, eager to emulate their social superiors, also began to favour the Gymnase above the other boulevard theatres. In this way the audience of the Gymnase typified the new, mobile society of the

---

[41] Montigny, *Le Provincial à Paris*, vol. I, p. 44.
[42] *Ibid.* p. 47.

Restoration, for here the bourgeoisie would have been able to afford some of the best seats in the house, and thus to socialise in the same milieu as the aristocracy on what was perceived to be the same level. Consequently the Gymnase became above all else the theatre of the bourgeoisie, a middle ground between the major theatres and the rest of the boulevard theatres, just as the bourgeoisie were themselves a middle class between the aristocracy and the populace.

The demands of this largely middle-class audience are identified by Jules Janin, writing in the *Journal des Débats* on 29 July 1832:

> La société de la Restauration, qui avait adopté le Gymnase pour son théâtre, était un mélange singulier du passé, du présent et de l'avenir qui avait besoin d'une comédie faite pour lui plaire sans être chagrinée, ni dans son passé, ni dans son présent, ni dans son avenir.

For this public Scribe was the perfect author, born in the rue Saint-Denis as the son of a silk merchant and embodying the same bourgeois values as his audience. Here lay the key to his success, for according to Buguet, he was easily able to identify the tastes of the bourgeois public and to cater for them:

> M. Scribe a bien compris son temps; il a parfaitement senti qu'il se trouvait placé entre deux aristocraties, la vieille et la nouvelle; il a compris surtout que nous n'étions plus dans l'âge d'or, mais bien dans l'âge de l'or [...]. Il a, dans ses ouvrages, tout sacrifié à l'argent, l'idole du siècle.[43]

This is not to say, however, that the Gymnase came to be abandoned by the aristocracy altogether. On the contrary, such was its success that from 1824 to 1830 the duchesse de Berry was official patron and the theatre was known as Le théâtre de Madame, and an examination of the press during this period reveals that the notices of the Gymnase appeared in hierarchical order after those of the Odéon and before those of the Variétés and the Vaudeville.

In Balzac's work the only novel in which the Gymnase features is *Un grand homme,* and although the amount of exposure given to this

---

[43] Buguet, *Foyers et coulisses, Le Gymnase,* pp. 6-7.

theatre in the novel is very limited compared to the extensive treatment of the Panorama-Dramatique, the particular status of the Gymnase among the boulevard theatres is vital to the course of the narrative. As it became more successful during the early 1820s, the Gymnase expanded its troupe and procured the best acting talent of the boulevard theatres. This is confirmed by a summary of the activities of the smaller theatres in *Le Miroir des spectacles* on 7 September 1821:

> Non-seulement le Gymnase rappelle en ce moment l'élite de ses acteurs, mais il pense à s'en procurer de nouveaux. Plusieurs débuts vont avoir lieu. Celui de Mlle Fleuriet est d'un heureux présage pour ceux qui doivent suivre. La débutante a réussi complètement; elle est jeune et jolie, dit juste, et chante fort agréablement.

In the novel it is not long after this, following the demise of the Panorama-Dramatique, that thanks to the financial help of Camusot and the journalistic expertise of Lucien, Coralie gains an appointment at the Gymnase:

> Il [Lucien] trouva Coralie et Camusot ivres de joie. Le Gymnase proposait pour Pâques prochain un engagement dont les conditions, nettement formulées, surpassaient les espérances de Coralie.[44]

That Coralie's new position is at the Gymnase is significant in two respects: firstly because in simple historical terms the Gymnase was a thriving theatre which was appointing new actresses at the time and this gives credibility to the narrative, and secondly because a promotion to the Gymnase was indeed a step up for any young actress on the stages of the boulevard theatres; indeed, for many it was the pinnacle of their aspirations. This last fact is of crucial importance in the novel because Coralie's promotion to the Gymnase fuels the simmering rivalry between her and Florine, providing the enemies of Coralie and Lucien with a means of effecting their plot to bring about the downfall of the lovers. While Coralie is sincere and ingenuous,

---

[44] *IP*, vol. V, p. 428.

although not totally naïve, Florine is calculating and fiercely ambitious. Had Coralie secured an appointment at any of the less prestigious boulevard theatres, Florine's jealousy might not have been so acute, but as it is, she is enraged to the point where she gladly accepts her part in the carefully orchestrated plot, learning Coralie's lines to perfection in order to usurp her rival. While the modern reader may not be aware of the particular status of the Gymnase in the theatrical hierarchy, Balzac's contemporary reading public could be expected to appreciate the full impact of this promotion on the relationship between the two actresses.

In terms of historicity, Balzac's treatment of the Gymnase in *La Comédie humaine* is insubstantial, for while there is nothing false in its representation, little of its history is revealed other than the fact that it is shown to be subject to the same petty rivalries and intrigues as any other boulevard theatre. The history of the Gymnase is subject to the selective treatment of the novelist rather than that of the self-proclaimed historian, so that it becomes a realistic socio-historical setting and functions in *Un grand homme* not only as a background against which the plot to bring down Coralie and Lucien takes place, but also fulfils an active function in the chain of causality since it is the catalyst of the contest between Florine and Coralie.

A fleeting reference to the Gymnase is made in *Eugénie Grandet* where Florine's name was added to the Furne edition. Here she is mentioned as 'une des plus jolies actrices du théâtre de Madame',[45] which reinforces her association with this theatre. In terms of Florine's career progression through *La Comédie humaine* the Gymnase is also significant in that it is a stepping stone to her ultimate goal of appearing at the Opéra, which she is eventually seen to achieve a decade later in *Une fille d'Eve*.

The Vaudeville and the Variétés

A similar partial treatment is applied by Balzac to the Vaudeville and Variétés theatres, which are more important in terms of the narrative opportunities which they afford than in terms of any significant

---

[45] *EG,* vol. III, p. 1145.

contribution by Balzac to the recorded history of these theatres. The Vaudeville was opened in 1792 and the Variétés in 1795. Both survived the Napoleonic regime during which time they were little more than music halls, being restricted to showing simple parodies, peasant plays and popular musical entertainments. By the early 1820s, capitalising on the growth of the melodrama, the Vaudeville managed to elevate its status and now showed popular melodramas in addition to its traditional repertoire. The Variétés, however, remained largely a place of simple, popular entertainment.[46]

The Vaudeville plays a small but interesting role in *Un grand homme,* for it marks both the beginning and the end of Lucien's involvement with the world of the theatre. Although his tour of the small theatres in the company of the journalist Lousteau constitutes Lucien's 'baptism of fire' in the theatrical world, even before that, when he visits the Parisian theatre for the very first time at the invitation of du Châtelet, Lucien's illusions begin to fade:

> Le plaisir qu'éprouvait Lucien, en voyant pour la première fois le spectacle à Paris, compensa le déplaisir que lui causaient ses confusions. Cette soirée fut remarquable par la répudiation secrète d'une grande quantité de ses idées sur la vie de province.[47]

There is nothing of historical significance in the account of this evening at the Vaudeville, rather Balzac is using his readers' presumed familiarity with the social status of this theatre in order to characterise his anti-hero. Lucien is acutely aware during the visit that neither he nor Madame de Bargeton, whom he had previously idolised as a paragon of elegance, is suitably dressed, even compared to the people in the balcony. The social implications of this are clear enough to the modern reader, but to Balzac's contemporary reader this would have indicated that the provincials were very badly dressed indeed, since this a second-rate theatre, out of season (du Châtelet acquires the seats cheaply because of this), and the audience in the balcony would be made up of the lower classes of society.

The Vaudeville is also the place where Lucien is eventually snubbed by his former colleagues and where Finot and Des Lupeaulx

[46] Buguet, *Foyers et coulisses, Vaudeville, Variétés.*
[47] *IP*, vol. V, p. 265.

plan the conspiracy against him in which Coralie's promotion to the Gymnase will be a catalyst. Here in the busy foyer of the Vaudeville Lousteau makes his peace with fellow journalist and future playwright Nathan, Finot keeps abreast of events and Lucien keeps a watchful eye on his enemies. The foyer of the Vaudeville is described in the novel as the most desirable venue for meetings of journalists and critics, and, according to Buguet's account, this is historically correct. He describes it ironically as:

> [...] assez large, assez spacieux, assez aéré, orné de banquettes coquettement usées, de deux croisées soufflant la fraîcheur à la saison des frimas et d'une cheminée donnant de la chaleur pendant la canicule [...]. Au total, le foyer du Vaudeville où s'accouraient encore se reposer et s'égayer quelques autres hommes de talent était peut-être le plus décent, le plus paisible, le plus littéraire de la capitale.[48]

The Théâtre des Variétés does not feature at all in *Un grand homme* and is mentioned only briefly elsewhere in *La Comédie humaine*. There is a fleeting and incidental reference in *L'Envers de l'histoire contemporaine* where one evening Godefroid sees the first two plays at the Variétés, and there is a scene in *Un homme d'affaires* where La Palférine takes Antonia to the Variétés only to spend most of the evening engaging in business talk with Nucingen, Maxime de Trailles, Desroches and Cardot. The location is of no historical interest and merely facilitates the meeting of the protagonists.[49] It might be concluded from this scant coverage that the Vaudeville and the Variétés seem to be of less historical interest to Balzac than the Panorama-Dramatique and the Gymnase, which were not only a reflection of, but essentially the products of, the period about which he was writing.

---

[48] Buguet, *Foyers et Coulisses, Vaudeville*, pp. 61-63.
[49] *HA*, vol. VIII, p. 237.

The Ambigu-Comique, the Gaîté and the Porte-St-Martin

The Gaîté was established in 1760, and the Ambigu-Comique a few years later in 1769. These two theatres stood adjacent to each other on the boulevard du Temple, and, like the Vaudeville and the Variétés, they were permitted to continue their operations in a limited way throughout the Napoleonic regime, showing simple melodramas, farces and pantomimes. The Porte-Saint-Martin first opened in 1802 and was one of the theatres on which closure was enforced under the Empire. Although the Porte-Saint-Martin was permitted to reopen in 1808, it was really little more than a side-show and closed again in 1810. It did not achieve status as a proper theatre, with permission to show melodramas, until restrictions were lifted after the end of the Empire.

Along with the short-lived Panorama-Dramatique, these theatres were at the lower end of the theatrical hierarchy, attracting a largely unsophisticated audience occasionally enhanced by a minority from the chaussée d'Antin and the faubourg St-Germain.[50] In the early 1820s these three theatres enjoyed a period of increased prosperity while the melodrama was at the height of its popularity, but, by as early as 1823, according to claims made in an article in the *Diable boiteux* on 23 July, the Gaîté was already verging on a state of decline:

> La Gaîté avec sa salle enfumée, sa troupe d'une faiblesse extrême, son répertoire usé, son comité de lecture féminin, conserve toujours une sorte de supériorité sur ses laborieux voisins. On ne put attribuer cette faveur du public qu'à quelques anciens souvenirs.

The same article, however, reports that the Ambigu-Comique and the Porte-Saint-Martin were 'dans l'état le plus prospère'.

In *La Comédie humaine*, as with the Vaudeville and the Variétés, none of the histories of these theatres is treated in any detail. Rather they are places where characters who would not necessarily come in to contact with each other in other realms of society can easily be brought together. In many of the scenes which take place at the ᵗʰ⁻⁻ᵗʳᵉ, the precise location could indeed be at any of the boulevard

Juguet, *Foyers et coulisses, Ambigu-Comique, Gaîté, Porte-Saint-Martin.*

theatres. Where these theatres are specified by name, it is more often in order to indicate the social and intellectual mediocrity of particular characters who go there. For example, in *Un début dans la vie,* Oscar's limited means and lack of intellectual sophistication are indicated by the fact that he does not go anywhere better than the Ambigu-Comique:

> [I]l n'allait pas souvent au spectacle, et il ne s'élevait pas alors plus haut que le théâtre de l'Ambigu-Comique où ses yeux n'apercevaient pas beaucoup d'élégance, si toutefois l'attention qu'un enfant prête au mélodrame lui permet d'examiner la salle.[51]

Similarly, the indignity of the fate of Finot's play in *César Birotteau* is highlighted by the fact that he is unable to get it produced anywhere better than the Gaîté:

> Finot avait une superbe comédie en un acte pour Mlle Mars, la plus fameuse des fameuses [...] Eh bien, pour se voir jouer il a été forcé de la porter à la Gaîté.[52]

This was the type of indignity with which Balzac was himself familiar in the theatre, having had his melodrama *Le Nègre* refused even by the lowly Gaîté in 1822.[53] As with all the references which depend on the particular status of any individual theatre within the hierarchy of the theatrical world, it is presumed that the reader is aware of this hierarchy, for Balzac does not bother to point out that the Gaîté is a third rate boulevard theatre; it is taken for granted that the reader will realise that this is an artistic compromise for Finot and one which contributes to his decision to pursue a journalistic career.

It took the Porte-Saint-Martin some time to establish itself as a proper theatre but by the late 1820s and early 1830s it benefited from

[51] *DV*, vol. I, p. 766.
[52] *CB*, vol. VI, p. 138.
[53] See above, p. 17.

some resounding successes. Balzac makes reference to the most notable of these in *Splendeurs et misères des courtisanes*:

> Il y avait précisément cinq ans qu'Esther n'était allée à un théâtre. Tout Paris se portait alors à la Porte-Saint-Martin, pour y voir une de ces pièces auxquelles la puissance des acteurs communique une expression de réalité terrible, *Richard d'Arlington.* Comme toutes les natures ingénues, Esther aimait autant à ressentir les tressaillements de la frayeur qu'à se laisser aller aux larmes de la tendresse.[54]

Again Balzac, as both narrator and social historian, is using the theatrical reference to illustrate the emotional simplicity of his character and at the same time anchors his characterisation in historical reality. The reference to the success of Dumas's play at the Porte-Saint-Martin is slightly anachronistic as the narrative is in 1830 at this point and the play was not performed until December 1831. However, it is true that the play was an overwhelming success, which clearly Balzac was aware of, even though there is nothing in his correspondence at this time to indicate whether he saw the play performed.

More important in the history of the Porte-Saint-Martin is the fact that in 1822 it was the first theatre in Paris to introduce the performance of Shakespeare to the French public. These early attempts were an unmitigated disaster, as the complexity of the Shakespearian plot was simply unpalatable to an audience which expected the hyperbole and antithesis and the simple morality of the melodrama. The Porte-Saint-Martin persisted, however, and in the late 1820s and early 1830s found success where it had previously met with failure.[55] This is an important aspect of the history of the Parisian theatre which Balzac does not portray explicitly in *La Comédie humaine.* References to certain of Shakespeare's best known characters and plays are numerous throughout Balzac's novels and he assumes that his readers possess at least a basic knowledge of

---

[54] *SetM*, vol. VI, p. 619.

[55] The introduction of Shakespeare to the French audience and the influence of his work on Balzac's novels will be addressed in greater detail in Chapters 4 and 5 of the present study.

Shakespeare, but at no point does he show how Shakespeare was introduced to a wider public than that which, like himself, knew Shakespeare through the reading rather than the live performance of his plays.

The Cirque-Olympique

The Cirque-Olympique was first established in 1788 by Franconi, its first director, and after a turbulent beginning involving several changes of location, a fire and suspension during the Empire, finally settled in a site on the boulevard du Temple in 1827. As its title suggests, it was primarily a circus venue with a varied repertoire of horse-back stunts, acrobatics and its resident star, Baba the performing elephant. The Cirque-Olympique also occasionally offered a primitive type of 'movie-theatre' entertainment in the form of historical pageantry shown by means of a mechanical diorama, and by extension of this also came to be a testing ground for more worthy historical dramas which were subsequently developed in a more literary form for the larger theatres. It is here that Alexandre Dumas's first attempts at historical drama were tested.[56]

During the 1820s, *Le Miroir des spectacles* places the Cirque-Olympique after the Ambigu-Comique and before the Porte-Saint-Martin in its hierarchical listings and in January 1822 describes its repertoire as follows:

> Grands exercices d'équitation, danse et voltige à cheval.
> – L'Eléphant. – *La bataille de Bouvines.* – *La Muette.*
> – *Le Valet en goguette.* – Chevaux dressés.

In *La Comédie humaine* the Cirque-Olympique is the show place of Malaga, one of Balzac's most prominent courtesans. Although there had in reality been a performer with the stage name of Malaga, she was a dancer born in 1786 and was not associated with the Cirque-Olympique. Balzac may have simply recalled the name when creating his fictional character.

---

[56] Buguet, *Foyers et Coulisses, Le Cirque-Olympique.*

There is little detail of the repertoire or operations of the Cirque-Olympique in *La Comédie humaine,* and even in *La Fausse Maîtresse* where Malaga plays a central role. However, the few details which are given are historically correct. Paz recounts to the comtesse Laginski how Malaga performs her equestrian gymnastics, 'à la profonde admiration du peuple, du vrai peuple, les paysans et les soldats!'[57] which according to Montigny and Buguet, is an accurate description of the audience of the Cirque-Olympique. Later on in the novel, having shunned Paz's benevolence, Malaga is forced to approach him for financial assistance. The reason for this is that she must play poorly paid walk-on parts in other boulevard venues during the winter when the Cirque-Olympique is closed. Again, Buguet's records verify that the Cirque-Olympique closed during the worst of the winter months when the large, unheated venue would be too cold to attract much of an audience.

Malaga re-enters Paz's life by virtue of the historically realistic circumstances of her employment at the Cirque-Olympique with the result that in the topsy-turvy morality of the society observed by Balzac, the very thing which Paz was aiming to avoid by becoming associated with Malaga – the destruction of the Laginskis' marriage – comes about when Laginski, prompted by Paz's feigned interest in Malaga, begins to have a relationship with her himself. In this way a single aspect of the history of the Cirque-Olympique – the fact of its closure during the winter months – has been used to serve Balzac's purpose as novelist and is consistent with his general view of a society driven by financial need and sexual impulse.

The Opéra and the Italiens

The history of the French Opera and the Italian Opera in Paris during the first half of the nineteenth century is covered extensively by the playwright and critic Royer in his *Histoire universelle du théâtre,* first published in 1878. Royer was a friend of Balzac's and a member of the small literary group which Balzac formed when he lived in the rue Cassini,[58] and eventually became administrator at the

---

[57] *FM*, vol. II, p. 223.

[58] Royer, *Histoire universelle du théâtre*, vol. V, pp. 159-160. See also *Corres.* vol. V, p. 101.

Opéra in 1856.   During the period covered by Balzac's work the
Opéra staged performances on a seasonal basis and underwent several
changes of directorship in an attempt to improve its financial position
and so relieve the burden on the State. The Opéra was situated in the
rue de Richelieu from 1794 to 1820, intermittently at the Salle
Louvois and the Porte-Saint-Martin, and in the rue le Peletier from
1821 to 1873, when it relocated permanently to the lavish and now
famous building designed by Garnier.

The Italian opera, known colloquially as the *Italiens* was
performed by a separate, related company at locations in the rue
Favart and the boulevard des Italiens. The Imperial Decree of 1807
gave the Opéra the title of the Académie impériale de musique which
it retained throughout the Empire, during which period it was directed
by Picard. After the fall of the Empire the Opéra was renamed the
Académie royale de musique and in 1815 Picard was succeeded by
Papillon de la Ferté.[59]

During the 1820s the fortunes of the Opéra became more unstable
as the theatre-going public followed the fashionable trend towards the
boulevard theatres and the illustrious audience of the Opéra began to
favour the Gymnase. Despite this, however, the fact of having a box
at the Opéra remained an indicator of belonging to the most
privileged class of society. According to Montigny, writing in 1825,
it was for this reason rather than for reasons of artistic preference that
the upper classes continued to attend the Opéra:

> La haute société tient encore à ce spectacle si pompeux; mais c'est
> plutôt par étiquette que par goût; il y a des dames qui vont à l'Opéra
> à peu près comme leurs aïeuls allaient au sermon, pour s'y faire
> voir.[60]

The financial fragility of the Opéra during the Restoration was
compounded by changes of directorship, which now occurred every
few years. Viotti succeeded Papillon in 1819, followed by Habeneck
in 1821, Duplantys in 1824 and Lubbert in 1827. By the 1830s, as
the popularity of melodrama declined and the bourgeoisie became
increasingly affluent and a box, or at least a share of a box, at the

[59] Royer, *Histoire universelle du théâtre, L'Opéra*, vol. V.
[60] Montigny, *Le Provincial à Paris*, vol. II, p. 264.

Opéra became a matter of social necessity, the Opéra regained some ground, although this did little to alleviate its financial difficulties. The debts of the Opéra amounted to some 400,000 francs in 1849, which more than doubled to 900,000 francs by 1854 when the State was forced to clear them.[61] The size of this debt, particularly in view of the comparative cost of attending the Opéra, highlights the success of the smaller theatres which could not rely on State intervention in their affairs and goes some way to mitigating their unscrupulous and exploitative practices which are exposed by Balzac.

A letter to Madame Hanska on 1 July 1834 indicates that Balzac himself indulged in the common practice of taking a share in a box at the Opéra, and the passion which he declares for the Opéra explains the frequent references to particular performances which are scattered throughout *La Comédie humaine*:

> J'ai pris une place dans une loge à l'Opéra, et j'y vais deux heures tous les deux jours, la musique, pour moi, ce sont des souvenirs. Entendre de la musique, c'est mieux aimer ce qu'on aime.

On 22 August of the same year another letter announces that Balzac is only attending the Opéra once a week, but on 26 October he writes that he is again attending the Opéra and the Italiens on alternate evenings. By the time Balzac began writing *Un grand homme* in 1836, his first-hand knowledge of opera was extensive and his correspondence indicates that he was personally acquainted with Rossini, whom he first met at the home of Olympe Pélissier in 1830.[62]

In historical terms Balzac's treatment of the Opéra in *La Comédie humaine* is at best superficial and subject to his characteristic anachronisms. However, it would be unfair to accuse him of failing to portray something of the real administrative, financial and locational difficulties of the Opéra since his experience as critic, publisher and playwright did not extend to the Opéra. Balzac's experience of the Opéra is confined to that of the spectator and it is this which emerges in *La Comédie humaine*, for where in the boulevard theatres Balzac's treatment concentrates largely on the machinations behind the scenes, with which he was familiar through

---

[61] Royer, *Histoire de L'Opéra*, p. 218.
[62] *Corres*, vol. I, p. 642; *LMH*, vol. I, p. 106.

his own attempts to get his plays accepted and through his journalistic experience, his treatment of the Opéra concentrates largely on the social activity which takes place in the boxes and the foyer.

The long account of Lucien's first visit to the Opéra one Friday evening in *Un grand homme* is the most significant representation of the Opéra in the whole of *La Comédie humaine*. The account is slightly anachronistic from a strictly factual point of view in that the production on stage is *Les Danaïdes*, which according to scrutiny of the Parisian press of the 1820s was not currently being performed (actual productions on Fridays at the time were of *Les Bayadères* and *La Mort du Tasse*, followed by one of a variety of short ballets), but by the time of beginning *Un grand homme* in 1836 it is likely that Balzac was relying only on vague memory to recall what might have been performed at the Opéra in the early 1820s.

A further disparity concerns the chronology of the novel itself. Just prior to the account of the long scene at the Opéra we are told that in June the audience of the Opéra resembles a 'tapisserie usée' because so many members of its usually illustrious audience are away supervising the wine harvest on their country estates. The remark is confusing, not only because it contradicts the splendid scene which follows, but also, because according to the chronology of the novel, events are currently in October, several months after wine harvesting would normally take place. However, these minor chronological inaccuracies in no way detract from what is a sharply observed account of the behaviour of the audience at the Opéra.

Balzac exploits the behaviour and interaction of the audience to several effects. Firstly, his portrayal of the inattention of the audience to the action on stage and its indulgence in idle chatter and social intrigue is an accurate reflection of the social and intellectual position of the Opéra at the time for a large portion of its audience. This is substantiated by the memoirs of Charles de Boigne, in which he recalls how, during the period when he had shared Balzac's box at the Opéra in the early 1830s, the Opéra was something of a social playground:

> L'Opéra est un plaisir de vanité, et... de bien autre chose. Ce qu'on
> aime le plus à l'Opéra, ce n'est pas la musique. Les femmes vont à

l'Opéra pour être vues; les hommes pour voir, lorgner les femmes dans la salle, les femmes sur le théâtre.[63]

Despite the fact that the rest of the audience is paying no attention to the action on stage, Lucien is enchanted by it and confused by the attention paid to the box in which he is situated, mistakenly attributing the cause of the mockery to Louise de Bargeton's provincial dress rather than to his own exaggerated and tasteless attire and committing the unforgivable social crime of pointing to another box. While these minor details add to the portrayal of the audience and the fine nuances of its etiquette, they also, and more importantly, highlight Lucien's extreme social naivety.

As the scene progresses the drama taking place on stage is superseded by the drama taking place in the audience, when, after carefully setting the scene, Balzac introduces some of his most powerful protagonists. There is no reason why de Marsay, Vandenesse, Montriveau and Canalis could not have been introduced elsewhere in the auditorium, but they burst into the marquise d'Espard's box as though making a grand entrance on the stage itself and proceed to belittle Lucien with a lively display of wit which completely diverts his attention from the stage. The theatricality of this is further emphasised when du Châtelet then bursts in to greet Montriveau whom he has not seen since they were travelling together:

> - Se quitter dans le désert et se retrouver à l'Opéra! dit Lucien.
> - C'est une véritable reconnaissance de théâtre,' dit Canalis.[64]

In this respect the boxes of the Opéra fulfil the same functions as the *coulisses* of the boulevard theatres, at once promoting social interaction, providing a breeding ground for intrigue, and facilitating the narrative outcomes of the novel against a socially and historically realistic setting.

Most of the references to the Opéra in *La Comédie humaine* are to particular works and are not the subject of this chapter. However, it would be misleading here to imply that Balzac's representation of the

---

[63] De Boigne, *Petits mémoires de l'Opéra* (Paris: Librairie Nouvelle, 1857) p. 106.

[64] *IP*, vol. V, p. 279.

Opéra's audience reflects a total lack of appreciation of the art form on the part of his characters. Not all of Balzac's characters who attend the Opéra do so in order to socialise, to see and be seen, for there are occasional glimpses of Balzac's own passion for operatic composition in his characters. In the *Mémoires de deux jeunes mariées*, for example, Louise writes to Renée of her excitement at the prospect of seeing the performance rather than of taking part in the social spectacle:

> Les Italiens commencent à chanter dans quelques jours. Ma mère y a une loge. Je suis comme folle du désir d'entendre la musique italienne et de voir un opéra français.[65]

Similarly, in *La Duchesse de Langeais,* the officers who hear the duchess singing and playing the piano in the convent are described as 'vrais dilettanti', nostalgic for the opera of the Salle Favart where they genuinely appreciate the music.[66]

The Odéon and the Théâtre-Français

The construction of the Odéon began in 1773 and was finished in 1782; it housed the Comédie-Française for 12 years, was closed down and then re-opened in 1795 as the Théâtre de l'Egalité, eventually taking the name of the Odéon the following year. The theatre met with little success and in 1799 burnt down; its reconstruction was authorised in 1806 and in 1808 it re-opened again under the direction of Duval as the Théâtre de l'Impératrice. It burnt down a second time in 1818 and re-opened in September of the following year, finally being forced to close in 1828 until its financial difficulties had been resolved and it was able to re-open in 1829, from which time its fortunes became more stable.[67]

---

[65] *MJM,* vol. I, p. 209.

[66] Balzac's own passion was for the works of Rossini and his correspondence indicates that for him the Opéra was a means of escape from the demands of his lifestyle. On 31 October 1833 he writes to Madame Hanska how he had attended a performance of *La Gazza Ladra* at the personal invitation of Rossini where, plagued as he was by financial difficulties, he had 'noyé ses chagrins dans des torrents d'harmonie'. *LMH,* vol. I, p. 106.

[67] Buguet, *Foyers et coulisses, L'Odéon.*

The Odéon and the Théâtre-Français play only a small part in *La Comédie humaine* as far as their role as venues is concerned, and from a historical point of view the most noteworthy mention of the Odéon is in the context of the fire which ravaged the theatre in March 1818. Balzac uses the anecdote, which is recounted in *Un grand homme* by Daniel d'Arthez, to underline the difficulties of artistic endeavour, the value of patience and the precarious nature of life in the theatre, where success is never guaranteed and even when it may seem certain, is all too frequently razed to the ground.

The story of the fire at the Odéon is particularly pertinent, for fires were common in theatres during the first half of the nineteenth century before electric lighting was gradually implemented after its introduction at the Opéra in 1849. One of the things mentioned by Balzac when Lucien first goes behind the stage is the presence of the 'pompiers', who were always available to tackle the small fires which would frequently break out as a result of naked flames employed in lighting apparatus, the abundance of highly flammable materials, the wooden construction of the auditoriums and the draughts which served to fan the flames. Few theatres escaped this menace.[68]

The fortunes of the Théâtre-Français during the 1820s were seriously undermined by the increasing popularity of the boulevard theatres, and this decline was aggravated by the fact that the Théâtre-Français did not have quite the social prestige of the Opéra, and could not rely on its audience's dedication to social appearances. In September 1821, for example, the revenue of the Théâtre-Français, where seats could cost up to six francs, amounted to only 47,764 francs, compared with a revenue of 69,362 francs at the Gymnase and 71,202 francs at the Variétés, where seats could be obtained for as little as half a franc.[69] The domination of tragedy at the Théâtre-Français ended with the appointment of baron Taylor as the theatre's *Commissaire Royal* in 1825 (largely because Taylor was more

---

[68] Apart from frequent small fires which were controlled and extinguished, major fires necessitating reconstruction and in some cases relocation occurred at the following theatres: Odéon, 1799 & 1818; Ambigu-Comique, 1827; Gaîté, 1835; Vaudeville, 1838; Salle Favart, 1838 & 1887; Théâtre Lazzari, 1798; Cirque-Olympique, 1826; Opéra 1838.

[69] *Le Miroir des spectacles,* 4 October 1821.

receptive to the ideas of Romantic drama), and under his direction the popularity of the Théâtre-Français was gradually re-established.

In 1837, while he was working on *Un grand homme,* Balzac had personal experience of dealing with the Théâtre-Français when Taylor invited him to write a play specifically for this theatre. However, with the new appointment of Balzac's old enemy Buloz, the newspaper tycoon, as director, Balzac refused to pursue this opportunity further with the Théâtre-Français.[70]

In *La Comédie humaine* Balzac emphasises the rise of the boulevard theatres but neglects to show the full impact of this on the larger theatres. The Théâtre-Français is more often brought in to the narrative indirectly through reference to some of its best known actors of both tragedy and comedy, reinforcing the impression of Balzac's familiarity with the theatrical world. In *Un grand homme* Lucien's early experiences of attending the Théâtre-Français are revealed in precisely this way:

> Quel étudiant pouvait résister au bonheur de voir Talma dans les rôles qu'il a illustrés? [...] Aussi quand il cédait à la tentation de voir Fleury, Talma, les deux Baptiste, ou Michot, n'allait-il pas plus loin que l'obscure galerie où l'on faisait queue dès cinq heures et demie.[71]

This experience of the Théâtre-Français confronts Lucien with the 'rêve caressé' of being a dramatist, which, under the combined influence of the illusion which this theatre creates for him and the artistic discipline of the *cénacle,* he is convinced can only be achieved through 'la sainte voie du travail et de l'économie'.[72] Having already made acquaintance with his mephistophelean mentor Lousteau, however, it is not long before notions of artistic endeavour and patience are abandoned in favour of the 'vie des coulisses' in the boulevard theatres, and in particular the Panorama-Dramatique.

The focusing of the subsequent narrative on the corrupt activities of the boulevard theatres clearly fulfils the specific authorial purposes of revealing something of the *histoire secrète* of the theatres

---

[70] Milatchitch, *Le Théâtre de H. de Balzac,* pp. 33-41.

[71] *IP,* vol. V, p. 299.

[72] *IP,* vol. V, p. 299.

concerned. However, in apparently choosing largely to ignore the Théâtre-Français after the beginning of Lucien's stay in Paris, Balzac is not only consciously choosing to set subsequent events in the boulevard theatres in order to reflect their growing social and historical importance, but also, by implication, appears to be indicating that the Théâtre-Français is not guilty of the same kind of corruption of which he goes on to accuse the boulevard theatres. It is not so much Lucien's contact with the theatre world in general which causes the loss of his illusions but his contact with the Panorama-Dramatique in particular. This is underlined by the fact that Lousteau, who wields enormous journalistic power in the boulevard theatres and does not hesitate to exploit it, admits to being powerless to exert the same influence at the Théâtre-Français, where he simply does not dare to manipulate actors and actresses by means of petty threats and insults, for they are protected by those who are far more influential than his own journalistic friends.

Balzac's treatment of the theatre in *La Comédie humaine* is generally not concerned with a strictly factual historical account. Although, with the exception of certain anachronisms and inconsistencies, what is said is largely based in truth, the emphasis is on the theatre's place within a more generalised social history. It is the history not of the bricks and mortar of the institutions but of the people who give them their life and of the forces which motivate them.

The Social Functions of the Theatre in 'La Comédie humaine'

Balzac's representation of the histories of individual theatres may be partial and selective, and in some cases superficial, but notwithstanding its weaknesses, it offers an impression of the theatre as a dynamic, changing, and important social institution. It is here that the true value of Balzac's version of history lies, for it is an extensive observation of social manners and of a living and constantly evolving organism. This is the unifying link between the representations of the individual theatres concerned. It is not so much the actual history of the individual organisations, their companies and their performances which interest Balzac, as the particular aspects of these which reveal truths about Parisian society as a whole.

The primary social function of the theatre which emerges from *La Comédie humaine* is entertainment, whether that entertainment derives from the production itself or from the social interaction within the audience. The theatre depicted in Balzac's novels is entertainment which no longer seeks to be morally edifying according to the codes of the Classical tradition and hails the development of Romantic drama. It is a theatre which seeks to entertain through appeal to the emotions rather than to educate through appeal to the reason, if indeed the audience pays any attention to the events on stage at all. It is even suggested in *La Fille aux yeux d'or* that the average Parisian male is sexually aroused by the actresses on stage. The implication is that the theatre, as well as being a place of escapism and entertainment, fulfilled a social function which today is fulfilled by other more explicit forms of pornography, that of an external visual stimulus in sexual fantasy:

> A six heures [...] il se trouve à l'Opéra, prêt à y devenir soldat, Arabe, prisonnier, sauvage, paysan, ombre, patte de chameau, lion, diable, génie, esclave, eunuque noir ou blanc, toujours expert à produire de la joie, de la douleur, de la pitié, de l'étonnement, à pousser d'invariables cris, à se taire, à chasser, à se battre, à représenter Rome ou l'Egypte; mais toujours *in petto*, mercier. A minuit [...] il se glisse dans le lit conjugal, l'imagination encore tendue par les formes décevantes des nymphes de l'Opéra, et fait ainsi tourner, au profit de l'amour conjugal, les dépravations du monde et les voluptueux ronds de jambe de la Taglioni.[73]

If the primary function of the theatre according to Balzac's observation of society is entertainment, then for the majority of his characters that entertainment is more likely to be found in the act of attending the theatre. An article in the *Drapeau blanc* on 12 November 1821 supports the validity of Balzac's representation of the theatre as a kind of social showcase which acts as a barometer of fashionable dress and conduct:

> A la dernière représentation d'*Hamlet* j'eus le bonheur de me trouver placé dans une loge dont le devant était occupé par deux femmes charmantes qui, voulant sans doute mendier la trop grande

---

[73] *FYO*, vol. V, pp. 1043-1044.

sensibilité de leur genre nerveux, se gardèrent bien de prendre la moindre part au spectacle, et consacrèrent tout le temps à passer en revue les nombreuses et élégantes toilettes qu'il y avait dans la salle. La critique de ces dames s'exerça avec une séverité et une rigueur qui me glacèrent d'effroi, et me firent sentir bien vivement l'erreur qui m'avait égaré jusqu'alors, de regarder la mode comme l'objet d'un culte frivole.

In *Un grand homme* Lucien becomes an object of ridicule when he is subjected to this type of severe scrutiny by the ladies of the audience on his first visit to the theatre, and the provincial dress of Louise de Bargeton is excused by the critical stares only because she is related to the eminent and aristocratic Mme d'Espard. This is significant, not only in terms of Balzac's observation of the behaviour of the audience, but also because it prophesies the difficulty which Lucien will experience in adapting to the social environment of Paris, a difficulty which ultimately remains insurmountable for him.

Such difficulty is not experienced by Eugène de Rastignac whose first visit to the theatre in *Le Père Goriot*, in contrast to Lucien's, is a huge social success and foretells his success in society at large. Critics of Balzac do not comment on Eugène's experience at the theatre and yet it is significant because Eugène succeeds everywhere that Lucien fails, and since the theatre is the focal point of Parisian social life it is imperative to succeed here where one is exposed to its most harsh judgment. Lucien only manages to make connections in the *coulisses* and none of these is useful to him in terms of social success beyond the backstage of the theatre but in just one visit to the Italiens, Eugène makes connections with Delphine de Nucingen, d'Adjuda Pinto and the baron Nucingen, and succeeds in arousing jealousy in Madame de Restaud. Eugène's connections are made in the *loges* and these are connections which will open doors to him, ensuring that he is invited to the right parties and admitted to the right houses, so assuring his ultimate triumph over society.

In his memoirs, Charles de Boigne describes the opera in particular as a 'plaisir de vanité' and Balzac uses the same term in his *Petites Misères de la vie conjugale:*

> Voici ce qui soutient les théâtres: les femmes y sont un spectacle avant et après la pièce. La vanité seule paie du prix exorbitant de

quarante francs trois heures d'un plaisir contestable, pris en mauvais air et à grands frais, sans compter les rhumes attrapés en sortant.[74]

Even Louise de Chaulieu who is shown to have a genuine love of opera in Balzac's *Mémoires de deux jeunes mariées*, when she eventually attends the Opéra, is susceptible to the 'plaisir de vanité,' describing in her letters to Renée how she is 'lorgnée' and 'admirée' and how she, her mother, Madame d'Espard and the duchesse de Maufrigneuse, are 'quatre roses sur le devant de la loge'.[75]

According to Balzac's representation of the theatre, regular attendance is a social imperative if one is to maintain the appearances on which Parisian society is shown to depend. In *Le Cabinet des antiques*, for instance, the impression created by Diane's splendid attire at the Italiens is completely at odds with Victurnien's desperate financial situation which remains unsuspected by the rest of society:

Le joli couple alla aux Italiens. Jamais cette belle et séduisante femme ne parut plus sépharique ni plus éthérée. Personne dans la salle n'aurait pu croire aux dettes dont le chiffre avait été donné le matin même par de Marsay à d'Esgrignon.[76]

The fact of having a *loge* at the Italiens or the Opéra, which is indicative of only superficial impressions and is shown often to bear little relation to material circumstances, counts for more in this society obsessed with outward display than the reality which it can conceal.

For a young woman keen to play a major role in Parisian society, having a *loge* of her own comes second only to having a wealthy husband who can afford such a social asset. In *Le Cousin Pons*, Cécile's first thought upon learning of her uncle's fortune is that if she were to have a share of the inheritance she would have a 'loge aux Italiens,'[77] and in their *loges* Goriot's daughters delight in their social achievement despite their unhappy marriages. Indeed, the social status attributed to attendance at the theatre is shown to be so great in *Le Père Goriot* that Delphine de Nucingen is identified by

[74] *PMV,* vol. XII, p. 69.
[75] *MJM,* vol. I, p. 293.
[76] *CA,* vol. IV, p. 1025.
[77] *CP,* vol. VII, p. 550.

Madame de Beauséant not by association with her husband, the baron
Nucingen, or by her connection with the aristocratic de Restaud
family, but by the location of her box at the Opéra.[78]

For a man keen to impress his mistress, a visit to the right theatre
could afford an opportunity either to demonstrate his true wealth and
status or to create a deceptive semblance of wealth and status. Hulot
squanders money he can ill afford by taking Valérie Marneffe to the
theatre in resplendent gowns and always to a 'loge choisie',[79] and
when he can no longer afford this costly but imperative social luxury,
he is forced to concede the privilege to Crevel, who can afford it.
Similarly in *La Peau de chagrin*, Raphaël will go to any lengths to be
able to take Foedora to even a modest theatre rather than admit that
he cannot afford to do so:

> [J]'obtins l'honneur de la conduire à la première représentation de je
> ne sais quelle mauvaise farce. La loge coûtait à peine cent sous, je
> ne possédais pas un traître liard. [...] Mais revenons aux
> Funambules! Pour pouvoir y conduire la comtesse, je pensai à
> mettre en gage le cercle d'or qui entourait le portrait de ma mère.[80]

Clearly the social imperatives of the theatre apply only to certain
classes of society in Balzac's novels, to the aristocracy, the dandies,
the socially aspiring, and it is made clear in the opening pages of *La
Fille aux yeux d'or* that for the average member of the bourgeoisie a
share in a modest box at the Opéra is something to be achieved after a
lifetime of hard work, but this is also, in its own way, a measure of
material status.[81] More important, however, than the social status
which is demonstrated through attendance at the most prestigious
theatres, and notwithstanding the fact that that status may in any case
be a sham, is the theatre's function as a place of social interaction and
this applies to all types of theatre represented in *La Comédie
humaine*.

It has already been shown how the rise of the boulevard theatres
and their appeal to a wide and varied public did in reality bring

[78] *PG,* vol. III, p. 112.
[79] *Be.,* vol. VII, p. 189.
[80] *PCh.,* vol. X, p. 176.
[81] *FYO*, vol. V, p. 1046.

together normally distinct social groups, and certainly in *La Comédie humaine* it can be seen how other social activities such as the ball, the *salon*, the dinner, the excursion to a park, are restricted to more clearly defined social groups and are necessarily exclusive. The theatre is unique in *La Comédie humaine* in its function as a social melting pot where people of all political persuasions and all professions are able to interact, where a student can fall in love with a baroness and a courtesan can penetrate the world of high finance.

In a society where opportunities to meet members of the opposite sex were subject to more rigid social conventions than those of the present day, Balzac demonstrates how the theatre could afford such an opportunity in a socially acceptable environment and this is consistently reinforced in scenes which take place at the theatre. For example, in *Les Secrets de la princesse de Cadignan,* the princess describes how:

> Tous les vendredis, à l'Opéra, je voyais à l'orchestre un jeune homme d'environ trente ans, venu là pour moi. [...] Je trouvai dès lors mon inconnu mystérieux aux Italiens, à une stalle d'où il m'admirait en face, dans une extase naïve: c'en était joli. A la sortie de l'Opéra comme à celle des Bouffons, je le voyais planté dans la foule, immobile sur ses deux jambes.[82]

In this instance no relationship develops, but, for Eugène de Rastignac, who first sees Delphine at the theatre, the outcome is more successful, as it is for Raoul Nathan and Marie de Vandenesse who also first become aware of each other in the audience of the theatre:

---

[82] *SPC,* vol. VI, p. 960.

[L]a comtesse vint à l'Opéra, poussée par la certitude d'y voir Raoul. Raoul était en effet planté sur un des escaliers qui descendent aux stalles d'ampithéâtre. Il baissa les yeux quand la comtesse entra dans sa loge.[83]

For the Parisians of *La Comédie humaine*, the theatre epitomises the fact of being 'dans le monde' and to some extent all other social activities depend on connections which are made and invitations which are extended while at the theatre. It is significant that Balzac places familiarity with the theatre at the top of his list of social requirements for success in Paris, for the theatre is the epicentre of social life in his novels which are set in Paris:

> Un étudiant n'a pas trop de temps s'il veut connaître le répertoire de chaque théâtre, étudier les issues du labyrinthe parisien, savoir les usages, apprendre la langue et s'habituer aux plaisirs particuliers de la capitale.[84]

In contrast to this, Balzac's pious and moral heroines are expressly forbidden to attend the theatre, not only because, from the moral viewpoint of the characters concerned, the subject matter represented on stage is unsuitable and unedifying but also because the theatre is a corrupting influence, a place of vanity, intrigue and dissemblance. To some extent, ignorance of the theatre is a characteristic of the more general social ignorance of some of Balzac's provincial characters but is also equated with piety and purity as in the case of Ursule Mirouèt who turns down Minoret's invitation to the theatre on religious grounds: 'J'ai voulu la mener au spectacle à Paris où elle venait pour la première fois; elle n'a pas voulu, le curé de Nemours le lui avait défendu'.[85] Similarly, Madame Grandet expresses horror when Charles asks Eugénie if she has ever been to the theatre and denounces it as a 'péché mortel,'[86] and after her religious instruction at the convent the former prostitute Esther, in *Splendeurs et misères des courtisanes* expresses nothing but repugnance for the theatre. The Church's attitude to the theatre and to the acting profession in

---

[83] *FE,* vol. II, p. 328.
[84] *PG*, vol. III, p. 74.
[85] *UM*, vol. III, p. 879.
[86] *EG*, vol. III, p. 1088.

particular will be addressed in more detail in chapter III. Suffice to say here that the theatre was generally considered an immoral environment and those engaged in it were treated as belonging to a pariah profession.

According to Balzac's representation of the theatre in *La Comédie humaine,* the theatre is the hub of social activity in Paris during the period covered by his work and as such is subject to the same social and economic forces as society at large. In a society which Balzac portrays as governed primarily by money, the financial imperative is intensified in the theatre audience to the extent that the theatre becomes above all an opportunity for a display of wealth. The precise requirement of this wealth is made clear in a passage from *Petites Misères de la vie conjugale:*

> Donc, grisettes, bourgeoises et duchesses sont enchantées d'un bon petit dîner arrosé de vins exquis, pris en petite quantité, terminé par des fruits comme il n'en vient qu'à Paris, surtout quand on va digérer ce petit dîner au spectacle, dans une bonne loge, en écoutant des bêtises, celles de la scène, et celles qu'on leur dit à l'oreille pour expliquer celles de la scène. Seulement l'addition du restaurant est de cent francs, la loge en coûte trente, et les voitures, la toilette (gants frais, bouquet, etc.) autant. Cette galanterie monte à un total de cent soixante francs, quelque chose comme quatre mille francs par mois, si l'on va souvent à l'Opéra-Comique, aux Italiens et au grand Opéra. Quatre mille francs par mois valent aujourd'hui deux millions de capital.[87]

Conclusion – A Social Melting-pot

The social functions of the theatre which are represented in Balzac's work are broadly consistent with historical facts and contribute significantly to his desire to write the social history of his era, but at the same time Balzac exploits historicity to fulfil his wider narrative and authorial purposes. On a simple, historical level, the most important aspect of the social function of the theatre in Balzac's work, is that it is a place where normally distinct social groups come into contact. In terms of the narrative functions of the theatre, however, this fact assumes a new and far greater importance, for the

---

[87] *PMV*, vol. XII, p. 67.

theatre exists not simply as a historical background against which the narrated events take place but is itself part of the chain of causality of those events. The meetings which take place within the extended world of the theatre and the relationships and intrigues which result simply cannot be engendered elsewhere in the structure of Parisian society as represented in the novels, for all other social activities involve exclusive groups. In *Un grand homme* in particular, the theatre is the dynamic hub of the narrative which connects every significant event. It draws the characters together, acts upon them in some way by causing chance meetings or by provoking the ambition, material greed or sexual desire upon which all subsequent events depend.

Lucien's loss of illusions and his catastrophic demise, which are the subject of the narrative, begin at the point where he first enters the Vaudeville as a spectator. He is attracted by what he perceives to be the excitement of the theatre, and in order to achieve his principal aim of becoming a success in the world he becomes a theatre critic, and the lover of an actress. This is where his fatal mistake lies, because it is under Coralie's influence that Lucien learns to adopt different political and intellectual stances in the same way that the actress adopts her different roles. In switching his journalistic allegiance from a liberal to a royalist publication and in exploiting his journalistic wit to criticise others as readily as he had used it to praise them, Lucien creates enemies for himself. The situation is compounded by the fact that since he has no strong political convictions or intellectual opinions of his own but is merely assuming a role, he has no friends in either camp. It is because Lucien has no sense of where his true self lies and because he is unable to distinguish truth from role-play that he easily becomes the subject of a plot effected through the combined efforts of his enemies in the theatre world, a traitorous claque and his lover's rival on the stage. Lucien is too morally weak and becomes too much a part of the theatrical world to be able to resist the chain of causality for which the theatre is the catalyst. Lucien accepts his contemporaries at face value, failing to realise that they are also guilty of the theatrical role play which he has himself adopted. This point is also noted by Peter Brooks who states:

Lucien's experience of fashionability and of power is short-lived largely because he is never able adequately to distinguish representation from backstage manipulation. He comes to believe in appearances that he himself has put forth, and which to be operatively valid would have to be treated with sufficient distance and cynicism, with a sense of what is greasepaint and what is not.[88]

The interpenetration of normally distinct social groups which is shown to occur in the theatre and upon which the narrative outcomes of the novel depend, can be shown in a simple diagrammatic form which reveals a further dimension to the narrative importance of the theatre:

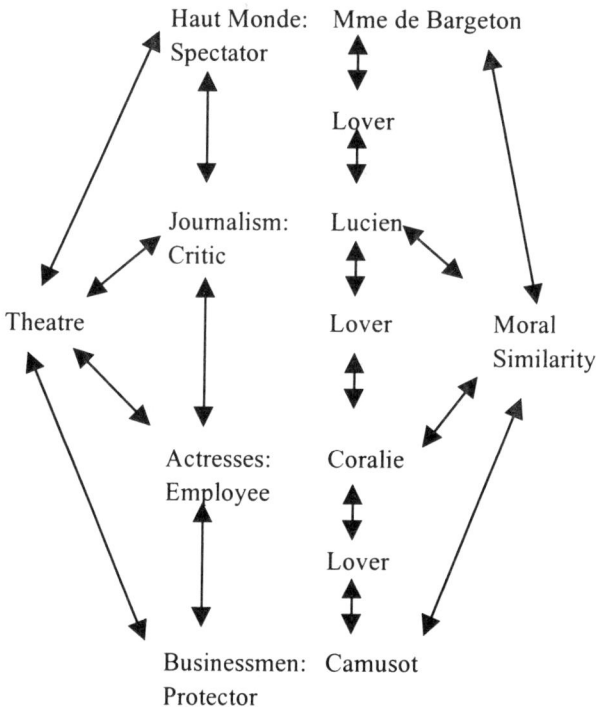

---

[88] Brooks, *The Melodramatic Imagination*, p. 123.

Normally exclusive social groups share a moral similarity and through their association with Lucien a member of the aristocracy and a third rate actress become morally similar and their fates become interconnected. The point has been made by Prendergast in his analysis of *Splendeurs et misères des courtisanes* and *La Cousine Bette* but not in relation to *Illusions perdues* and to the function of the theatre in bringing the different groups together:

> The primary task of the plot in *Splendeurs* is the bringing of different groups of characters into relationship with one another, and the primary effect of these conjunctions is the impression the novel creates of dealing with a whole social system. By creating links between characters from different social classes, by knitting together worlds as socially remote from each other as that of the banker, the prostitute, the criminal, the aristocrat, the plot, for all its cumbersome machinery, provides the formal means through which the novel projects a coherent image of a social reality grasped in its totality, seen and judged across the divisions which otherwise fragment it.[89]

In *Un grand homme* the theatre is central to this function of the plot as described by Prendergast and in this sense operates as a microcosm of the world at large. The portrayal of the theatre fulfils Balzac's wider authorial purpose by intensifying the play of ambition and greed and the twin imperatives of sexual desire and money through events told by an extradiegetic narrator. The viewpoint of this narrator is the same as that of the narrators of *Splendeurs et misères* and *La Cousine Bette,* where events depend on the same social issues dealt with in a wider and more general context than that of the theatre.

In no other novel of *La Comédie humaine* is the role of the theatre within the narrative so developed as it is in *Un grand homme.* However, it frequently functions as a convenient starting point for associations and relationships upon which subsequent events depend and contributes in some active way to the progression of the plot, as in the case of Rastignac's first meeting with Delphine in *Le Père Goriot.* This is also the case in *La Fausse Maîtresse* where a chance sighting of Malaga's name on a theatre notice provides Paz with the

---

[89] Prendergast, *Balzac, Fiction and Melodrama*, p. 81.

inspiration for his fictitious relationship with the performer which then functions in the causality of the very event which he wished at all costs to avoid: the breakdown of his friend Laginski's marriage. Again the theatrical world is not just a historically and socially realistic context in which Paz might conceivably have an expensive love affair, it plays an active role in the chain of causality, for it is a corrupting influence on those who come into contact with it. Laginski comes to meet Malaga as a result of Paz's supposed relationship with her and in this world where normal social distinctions are blurred and normally forbidden relationships are allowed, Laginski himself falls for Malaga.

A similar situation occurs when Philippe Bridau meets Malaga in *La Rabouilleuse*. Philippe is an unrepenting degenerate but the situation becomes cataclysmic when he is introduced to the world of the theatre, which encourages him to commit further thefts from his family and from his employer in order to secure an actress as his mistress. The world of the theatre intensifies the financial necessity of the world at large and gives rise to desperate measures, for it is here that the display of wealth is most apparent. In *La Peau de chagrin*, for example, while the social imperative of taking Foedora to the theatre is a small and realistic detail of Raphaèl's social circumstances, its narrative function is to contribute to the general despair at his penurious state wich causes him to accept the fantastical opportunity which is central to the novel. The social imperative and the financial imperative are indistinguishable.

It is precisely because it is partial and selective that Balzac's portrayal of the theatre in *La Comédie humaine* plays a significant role in his portrayal of the whole society which he purports to represent. It functions both as a realistic socio-historical background and as a dynamic force in the narrative. Balzac's concern in his representation of the theatre is not with artistic endeavour, or with the struggle to establish Romantic Drama, nor particularly with the mechanics or administration of the theatre. What emerges above all, and this is consistent with his treatment of every aspect of society, is an impression of the theatre's role in the economic determination of character and event, which will be treated in the next two chapters.

THE INDUSTRY OF THE THEATRE IN
LA COMEDIE HUMAINE

During the period covered by Balzac's work, from the early 1820s to the late 1840s, the theatre was a thriving industry which engaged in extensive trade with those on whom its own success depended – playwrights for their work, the press for reviews and the claque for directed applause. Twentieth-century historians of the theatre such as Albert, Beaulieu, Descotes, Dumur and Lecomte[1] focus their treatment on aspects of architecture, administration, and in particular production, and with the exception of a brief account of the operations of the claque given by Hemmings[2] in 1993, there is no comprehensive, modern study of the often corrupt trade in services which existed in the theatres. Critics and historians of the theatre, contemporary to Balzac's lifetime such as Gautier, Janin and Muret[3] concentrate almost exclusively on cataloguing particular productions and interesting anecdotes, and comments on the business activities of playwrights, the press and the claque are infrequent and fragmented. From the isolated comments of Gautier, Janin and Muret, however, taken together with the fragmented evidence which is available in press publications of the period, memoirs of those involved in the theatre including de Boigne, Bouffé, Lemaître, Dumas and Samson, and works by social commentators of the period such as Astruc,[4] Montigny[5] and Duflot,[6] a fairly full picture of the industry within the

[1] Albert, *Les Théâtres des boulevards 1789-1848*. Beaulieu, *Les Théâtres du boulevard du crime 1752-1862*. Descotes, *Le Public de théâtre et son histoire* (Paris: Presses Universitaires de France,1964). Dumur, *Histoire des spectacles* (Paris: Gallimard, 1963).

[2] Hemmings, *The Theatre Industry in Nineteenth-Century France* (Cambridge University Press, 1993), ch. 7, pp. 101-116.

[3] Gautier, *Histoire de l'art dramatique en France depuis vingt-cinq ans*, 6 vols. (Paris: Hetzel, 1858). Janin, *Histoire de la littérature dramatique,* 6 vols. (Paris: Michel Lévy, 1855-1858). Muret, *L'Histoire par le théâtre 1789-1851.*

[4] Astruc, *Le Droit privé du théâtre* (Macon: Protat frères, 1897).

[5] Montigny, *Le Provincial à Paris*: In his introduction to *Illusions perdues* (ed. Pléiade, p. 51), Raymond Chollet suggests that Balzac may have been inspired by Montigny's *Le Provincial à Paris* in the composition of *Un grand homme de province à Paris*. This is particularly apparent when the original chapter headings of Balzac's novel are taken into account: 'On ne surprend nulle part Balzac en flagrant

theatre can be pieced together. The validity and importance of Balzac's account as a reliable contribution to the history of the theatre can then be assessed in relation to this composite picture.

Modern critics of Balzac have already examined the characters of his fictional pressmen,[7] dramatists[8] and *chef de claque*,[9] and their analyses establish the extent to which these figures may be based on Balzac's contemporaries. The focus of this chapter will not be on these individual characters but on the general truths about the theatre industry which their activities and destinies reveal; its purpose is to examine Balzac's treatment of the theatre as an industry driven by capitalist economic forces and subject to the same economic determinism as he perceives to be prevalent in society at large. This will be achieved by examining Balzac's treatment of the interdependent trade between the theatres, the press, the claque and playwrights in relation to actual historical evidence. Balzac's representation of the theatre industry will then be placed in the context of his general narrative purposes in order to establish its contribution to the overall understanding of the economic code of *La Comédie humaine*.

délit d'imitation, mais il s'est très certainement inspiré de Montigny pour le choix et le découpage des tableaux. Le chapitre intitulé *Flicoteaux* a pour pendant *Les Restaurateurs à vingt-deux sous* du *Provincial*; *Le Banquier des auteurs dramatiques*, l'étude similaire sur *Mme Bolivar et ses agents*. Les deux écrivains consacrent de véritables monographies au Palais-Royal et à ses libraires. Le cas de démarquage le plus intéressant est celui du chapitre XIV de 1839; il a donné lieu, en manuscrit, à quelques hésitations révélatrices. Le premier titre rayé: *Les journalistes à l'avant-scène d'un...* correspond à *L'Avant-scène des petits théâtres*; le second également raturé: *Une première représentation* se retrouve textuellement dans *Le Provincial*; quant au titre retenu: *Les Coulisses*, Montigny l'a donné au chapitre XIII de son premier volume: *Les Coulisses d'un théâtre*. Parlera-t-on de coïncidences?'

[6] Duflot, *Les Secrets des coulisses des théâtres de Paris*.

[7] Hunt, 'Balzac's Pressmen', in *French Studies*, vol. XI (Oxford: Blackwell, 1957), pp. 230-245; Hunt, *Balzac's Comédie Humaine* (University of London: Athlone Press, 1959), pp. 209-219; Chollet, Introduction to *Illusions perdues*, pp. 61-72; Marceau, *Les Personnages de 'La Comédie humaine'* (Paris: Gallimard, 1977), pp. 209-266.

[8] Citron, 'Aux Sources d'*Une Fille d'Eve*', *AB* (1965).

[9] Felkay, 'Un banquier des auteurs dramatiques', *AB* (1972).

The Theatre and the Press - An Historical Overview

During the Restoration period the press, like the theatre, enjoyed a time of relative freedom after the restrictions which had been imposed by the Napoleonic regime. The press gained in prosperity and came to embody a certain ideal of intellectual liberty. On 3 December 1821, however, which is around the time of the earliest significant representation of relationships between the press and the theatre in *La Comédie humaine* (in *Un grand homme*, published in 1839), a bill was passed strengthening laws against the press which had already been established in 1820, and in January and February of the following year there was a lively public debate concerning the freedom of the press, culminating on 7 February in a law which imposed severe censorship on newspapers of all political persuasions.[10]

Although Charles X had proclaimed the freedom of the press in an attempt to gain favour upon his accession to the throne, Villèle and his government, acting on an idea proposed by Rochefoucauld, in 1822 began the process of *amortissement*, attempting to buy up all potentially dangerous publications one by one, even paying the sum of 300,000 francs for a paper which had only forty subscribers. A total of three million francs was spent. This inevitably gave rise to an explosion of speculative dealing in newspaper ownership, particularly among the Liberal publications which enjoyed 43,000 of the 63,000 subscriptions existing in Paris at the time.[11]

The censorship laws of 1821 and 1822 applied largely to the political papers of both Royalist and Liberal persuasion. Smaller papers and the *feuilletons*, which did not concern themselves with political issues, were considered less dangerous by the government and saw an enormous proliferation in number and circulation, which was additionally facilitated by improved technology in paper

---

[10] Collins, *Government and Newspaper Press in France 1814-1881* (Oxford University Press: 1959).

[11] *Ibid.*

production and printing. This proliferation reflects not only the relative freedom of the press at this level, but also the increased freedom and output of the theatres whose productions provided the bulk of the content of the small papers and literary supplements until around 1830.

The increase in competition among the boulevard theatres during the early 1820s which had come about as a result of the lifting of the restrictions which had been operative during the Empire, meant that poor reviews could bring about financial disaster, and so the resulting pressure for favourable criticism by the press fostered an interdependent relationship which sustained both parties. In 1821 and 1822, for example, when the productions of the small theatres were at their peak, theatre criticism constituted a higher proportion of the *feuilleton* of the *Journal des Débats* than at any other time during the Restoration – 63.9% in 1821 and 62.8% in 1822, compared with only 30.8% by 1830.[12] These statistics represent the general trend in journalism at the time, and when applied to *La Comédie humaine* they become particularly significant, for they suggest that Balzac's inclusion in *Un grand homme* of an examination of the relationship between the theatre and the press in 1821 and 1822 is far from random or arbitrary, but rather, is a calculated attempt to set events precisely in their correct historical period and thereby reflect historical truth.

Historical accounts of the relationship between the theatre and the press during the first half of the nineteenth century give differing impressions. Contemporary with Balzac's lifetime, Janin's seemingly naive account gives no indication of corruption or misuse of power by the press in relation to the theatre:

> Le petit journal [...] est un des compagnons de la liberté de la presse. Il rit en piquant, il pique en riant, [...]. Entre des mains loyales, c'est une arme charmante.[13]

---

[12] Jakoby, *Das Feuilleton des Journal des débats von 1814 bis 1830* (Tübingen: Narr, 1988), p. 68.

[13] Janin, *Histoire de la littérature dramatique*, vol. V, p. 68.

Janin's point about loyalty seems to be the pertinent issue, for in contrast to this, Berthier's modern account implies that the theatrical reviews of the small papers had little to do with the freedom of the press and were never impartial or objective:

> Il est en effet frappant de voir combien le feuilleton des petits journaux se limite, sauf exceptions, à des prises de position partisanes pour ou contre les personnes (acteurs, directeurs de théâtre).[14]

Balzac's portrayal of the press has not previously been examined in relation to the comments of either of these historians of the theatre. In his introduction to *Illusions perdues* Roland Chollet cites an anonymous extract from *Le Diable boiteux* of 16 June 1857 in order to demonstrate the corrupt and mercenary practices of the press. The extract concerned spells out how the press was then wielding its power to make and break fortunes in the theatre as a means of extorting money:

> L'opération est des plus simples: le prix d'abonnement ou de vente est dix fois plus fort que le prix de revient, et tout acteur qui ne veut pas être éreinté doit s'abonner. Chaque abonné obtient trois lignes de louanges par trimestre d'abonnement. Tout supplément louangeux doit être payé à raison de 1 ou 2 francs la ligne. Les insultes sont toutes gratuites pour les artistes non abonnés.[15]

Chollet's use of this extract is somewhat problematic since it is applied it to the activities of the press as represented in *Un grand homme* in the early 1820s although actually written in 1857. More substantial evidence of the corruption and power of the press can be found in the memoirs of Samson, actor and author at the Comédie-Française. These memoirs relate specifically to the 1820s[16] and

---

[14] Berthier, *Le Théâtre au XIXe siècle*, p. 23.

[15] Chollet, Introduction to *Illusions perdues*, p. 63.

[16] Samson began his career at the Odéon in the early 1820s and moved to the Comédie-Française in 1826 where he remained until 1830 when he accepted an offer from the Palais-Royal.

afford a valuable point of comparison with Balzac's treatment of the
press in *Un grand homme:*

> Le rédacteur en chef de cette feuille, qui composait à lui seul toute
> la rédaction, avait trouvé un moyen bien simple pour acquérir
> promptement une fortune: il fit savoir tout bonnement à tout le
> peuple des directeurs, auteurs, acteurs, compositeurs, chanteurs,
> danseurs, instrumentistes, que l'abonnement à son journal donnerait
> droit à l'éloge et l'abstention à l'injure; je dis injure, car il est
> impossible d'appeler d'un autre nom la prétendue critique de ce
> juge délicat [...]. 'Je contribue à la fortune des artistes par mes
> éloges,' disait-il hautement, 'il est donc juste qu'ils fassent   la
> mienne.' Et comme l'abonnement, vu la modicité du prix, n'était
> pas suffisant pour procurer l'opulence dont un si honnête
> homme pût se contenter, il exigea bientôt des sommes
> supplémentaires et même des cadeaux; il ne refusait rien [...]. Il
> donnait quelques dîners, et c'est là surtout qu'il se plaisait à
> étiqueter, en causant, du nom de ses donateurs, tout ce qui paraissait
> sur la table.[17]

The basis of these allegations is not revealed by Samson so it is
difficult to be certain of their reliability. However, there is no
counter-evidence offered by historians of the theatre to suggest that
they are untrue, and Samson's account, taken with the evidence
quoted by Berthier and Chollet, seems to indicate that the picture of
the theatre press in the 1820s as corrupt and mercenary has its basis
in reality and that little was to change during Balzac's lifetime.

Balzac's Experience and his Monographie de la presse parisienne

As far as is known, during his considerable activity as a pressman
Balzac was never personally guilty of the type of conduct described
in the *Diable boiteux* or in the memoirs of Samson. It is rather the
case that Balzac suffered from what other journalists wrote about his
novels and plays.[18]   Balzac contributed to *Le Diable boiteux* from
1823 to 1825, to *Le Feuilleton littéraire* from 1823 to 1824, to *La*

---

[17]   Samson de la Comédie Française, *Mémoires* (Paris: Ollendorf, 1882), p. 205.
[18]   Champfleury, *Henry Monnier* (Paris: Dentu, 1879), p. 95: 'l'abus des
personnalités particulières aux rédacteurs de petits journaux ne fut jamais le lot de
Balzac.'

Lorgnette from 1824 to 1826, and to the *Figaro* from 1826 onwards under the pseudonym of Le Poitevin de Saint Alme; in 1830, as Alfred Coudreus, he was the sole editor of *La Caricature*, and in 1835 he bought *La Chronique de Paris* from Duckett, but the paper went bankrupt soon afterwards. In 1840 Balzac made a further attempt to establish a paper of his own but *La Revue parisienne* survived for only three issues.[19] Despite the apparently effortless proliferation of small publications during the period from the early 1820s to 1840, Balzac acknowledges in 1843 the difficulty of setting up a paper successfully:

> Il ne suffit pas d'une centaine de mille francs et d'un cautionnement pour devenir directeur-rédacteur-en-chef-propriétaire-gérant d'un journal; il faut encore des circonstances, une volonté brutale et une espèce de capacité théâtrale qui manquent souvent à des gens d'un vrai talent.[20]

It is interesting that Balzac speaks of a 'capacité théâtrale' – presumably to dupe, to assume roles and to enter intrigues – here in association with the press. The parallel of the theatre and the press is constantly reinforced throughout his work, as is his vision of the theatrical quality of life outside the theatre.

Balzac had suffered as a novelist at the hands of the press upon publication of *Le Lys dans la vallée* in 1835 and it is well know that *Un grand homme* was partly written as a counter-attack against the press. Indeed, in a letter to Madame Hanska on 4 June 1839, Balzac makes this intention quite clear and also emphasises the fact that he considered himself to be in a position to reveal the truth about the world of journalism:

> C'est l'audacieuse peinture des mœurs intérieures du journalisme parisien et qui est d'une effrayante exactitude. Moi seul étais en position de dire la vérité à nos journalistes et de leur faire la guerre à outrance.[21]

---

[19] *Corres.* vol. IV, pp. 6-8.
[20] Balzac, *Monographie de la presse parisienne* (Paris: Pauvert, 1965), p. 39.
[21] *LMH*, vol. I, p. 643.

Balzac carried out his intention, and after the publication of *Un grand homme* in 1839 the journalists seized the opportunity to retaliate when *Vautrin* was first performed the following year. Gautier records how the *Vautrin* affair was treated as a scandal by the press:

> *Vautrin* compromis par la frisure de Frédérick Lemaître, d'ailleurs si admirable dans ce rôle, a été supprimé après la première représentation: les journaux trouvèrent la pièce immorale. C'est un grand mot dont on abuse maintenant et qui produit toujours beaucoup d'effet sur les simples d'esprit.[22]

The reasons for the banning of *Vautrin* were in reality more complex than Gautier suggests,[23] but it is true that the press were keen to take advantage of the opportunity to relaunch their attack on their old enemy.[24]

The republication of *Un grand homme* as part of *Illusions perdues* in 1843, coincided with the publication of Balzac's *Monographie de la presse parisienne*, the two together continuing Balzac's war with the press. The style of the *Monographie de la presse parisienne* is satirical and its content is presented as having its basis in fact. It is after all, not a work of fiction but of critical observation and commentary, and thus provides an important link between the evidence of the relationship between the theatre and the press provided by historians and literary critics and the fictional account presented in *La Comédie humaine*. The greater part of the *Monographie* concerns itself with the political functions of the press and is of no interest here. However, it is clear that Lucien, theatre critic *par excellence* of *Un grand homme,* is the embodiment of

---

[22] Gautier, *Histoire de l'art dramatique*, vol. III, p. 103.

[23] See above, pp. 20-21.

[24] Eugène Wœstyn of the *Journal du Peuple* in Orléans was alone in defending Balzac's play. Balzac acknowledges this in a letter to Wœstyn in April 1840: 'Je vous adresse mille remerciements pour votre généreux article; je n'aurais pu, pour ma défense, dire mieux, et je puis vous avouer que de si sincères témoignages spontanés adoucissent beaucoup les plaies et les coups que nous donne la calomnie. Il y a cela de particulier pour moi, que ces compensations ne me viennent jamais que de cette province tant calomniée, où l'on juge loin du cercle des inimitiés. Merci donc!' See: *Corres.*, vol. IV, p. 99.

Balzac's observation of a particular type represented in the *Monographie*:

> Le farceur aime à *faire* des acteurs, des auteurs, des danseuses, des cantatrices, des dessinateurs. Il travaille partout, il écrit sur tout; il parlera des arts sans en rien savoir. [...] il dîne et soupe, il est de toutes les parties et de tous les partis, aussi le jeune critique blond dure-t-il très peu. Vous l'avez vu jeune, élégant, passant pour avoir de l'esprit, [...] et vous le retrouvez flétri, passé, les yeux aussi éteints que son intelligence...[25]

It is precisely this misuse of his talent and switching of political allegiances which Lucien is guilty of in the novel and which leave him *flétri* and *passé*.

Similarly, the functions of the *feuilletons* which are satirically observed in the *Monographie* are precisely the functions of the press and its relationship with the theatre which are to be found, not just in *Un grand homme,* but throughout Balzac's fiction, and they reflect what have already been shown to be general historical trends in the theatre and in journalism:

> Les feuilletonistes, quoi qu'ils disent, mènent une vie joyeuse, ils règnent sur les théâtres; ils sont choyés, caressés! Mais ils se plaignent du nombre croissant des premières représentations, auxquelles ils assistent en de bonnes loges avec leurs maîtresses. Chose étrange! Les livres les plus sérieux, les œuvres d'art les plus ciselées avec patience et qui ont coûté des nuits, des mois entiers, n'obtiennent pas dans les journaux la moindre attention et y trouvent un silence complet tandis que le dernier vaudeville du dernier théâtre, les flanflons des Variétés nés de quelques déjeuners, enfin les pièces manufacturées aujourd'hui comme des bas ou du calicot, jouissent d'une analyse complète et périodique.[26]

---

[25] Balzac, *Monographie de la presse parisienne*, p. 123.
[26] *Ibid.* p. 141.

Historical Reality and The Theatre Press in La Comédie Humaine

The functions of the press feature throughout *La Comédie humaine* and most notably in four works first published over the period from 1831 to 1839. In *La Peau de chagrin,* published in 1831, the alleged corruptibility and power of the press are examined in a political context; in *Les Employés,* published in 1838, the associations of the press with commercial and ministerial departments are under scrutiny; and in *Une fille d'Eve* and *Un grand homme,* both published in 1839, the interdependent relationship of the press and the theatre is portrayed in detail.

In *Un grand homme* the correspondence of the choice of historical period with actual historical reality has already been pointed out, for the period from 1821 to 1823 saw theatre criticism at its most prolific. It should be remembered, however, that in this novel we are dealing not with serious and responsible journalism, nor with the type of publication which was of concern to the government and subjected to the most severe censorship, but rather with the *petits journaux* which were in reality often ephemeral and which, as has been illustrated, survived by means of ruses and extortion. In *Un grand homme* this type of journalism is represented mainly by *Le Courrier des théâtres,* which was in reality a thriving literary *feuilleton* throughout the 1820s and early 1830s.[27]

The single most important aspect of the relationship between the press and the theatre in this novel is economic. If the evidence of Berthier, Chollet and Samson is to be believed, then Balzac has in no way exaggerated his account in revealing the unscrupulous reality of the situation. In the novel Lucien initially uses his journalistic power for personal gain, but he soon learns from fellow journalist Lousteau that he is not at liberty to exercise his power at will and that his creative output is subject to strict economic codes:

---

[27] This daily, four-page *feuilleton* was founded in 1818 by Charles-Maurice Descombes under the title *Le Camp volant,* and thrived for fifteen years under the successive titles of *Le Journal des théâtres, Le Courrier des théâtres* and *Les Nouvelles des théâtres.* The *Grand Dictionnaire universel du XIXe siècle* records in 1869: '*le Courrier des théâtres* devint en quelque sorte, et rapidement, une feuille à la mode, qui se fit redouter de toute la gent théâtrale'. See vol. 5, p. 368.

> L'Ambigu nous prend vingt abonnements, dont neuf seulement sont servis au directeur, au chef d'orchestre, au régisseur, à leurs maîtresses et à trois copropriétaires du théâtre. Chacun des théâtres du boulevard paye ainsi huit cents francs au journal. Il y a pour tout autant d'argent en loges données à Finot, sans compter les abonnements des acteurs et des auteurs. Le drôle se fait donc huit mille francs aux boulevards. Par les petits théâtres, juge des grands! Comprends-tu? Nous sommes tenus à beaucoup d'indulgence.[28]

Lucien is shocked to discover that he cannot give his true opinion but in the novel, as in reality, the theatres are shown to be dependent on the goodwill of the press in order to ensure the success of their productions, and that goodwill is purchased at a price which in turn determines the survival of the press. It is quite simply a trade in services for mutual gain in a society which, as Balzac so often asserts, is ruled by the five franc coin. In the fictional world, as in the real world, the price of subscriptions as well as the cost of favourable reviews is extorted under pressure from those who fear the reprisals if they do not comply. Indeed the actress Coralie includes the cost of her subscriptions as part of her essential expenses which are met by the wealthy merchant Camusot, and, in the novel at least, the press is shown to be partly responsible for forcing young actresses into so-called immoral liaisons as a result of the economic imperative to which it contributes.

Success in the theatre, Balzac reveals, is a marketable commodity with a clearly identified value: a fact which is acknowledged by historians and other writers. Indeed, compared to the unscrupulous conduct described by Samson, that of Finot, the fictional editor of *Le Courrier des théâtres*, and of his team of opportunistic journalists, seems if anything to understate the reality on which it is based. Balzac also relies on real historical circumstances to provide the basis for the intrigue which is to generate wealth for Finot and increase his power as a pressman. The narrative mentions that the freedom of the press is beginning to be harnessed and that it will become increasingly difficult and expensive to establish any new publications:

[28] *IP*, vol. V, p. 466.

[I]l se prépare des lois restrictives contre la presse, les journaux existants seront seuls conservés. Dans six mois, il faudra un million pour entreprendre un nouveau journal.[29]

Both in the narrative and in reality, the restrictions introduced at this time raised the value of existing papers, and in the novel Finot plans to sell half of his third share in Dauriat's paper to Matifat for the 30,000 francs which he is paying for the whole share, thereby covering the cost of his own investment and retaining a stake in the business. Balzac then reinforces the historical credibility of the deal by pointing out that the government's action of buying up hostile newspapers and converting them in to ministerial ones will afford the opportunity to secure a highly advantageous return:

[D]ans un an le recueil vaudra deux cent mille francs à vendre à la Cour, si elle a, comme on le prétend, le bon sens d'amortir les journaux.[30]

The action of the novel is in 1822 at this stage, which coincides exactly with the actual date of the government's first plans for the *amortissement* of hostile papers.

The portrayal of the world of the press as one which affords opportunities to gain wealth, influence and status recurs in Balzac's work throughout the period from 1830 to 1839. In *La Peau de chagrin* (1830-1831), for example, it is political power which is at stake, and in *Une fille d'Eve* (1838-39) Nathan is shown to oscillate between the parallel worlds of the press and the theatre in his efforts to achieve wealth: 'Tenu de produire par son manque de fortune, il allait du théâtre à la presse, et de la presse au théâtre'.[31] Indeed, the portrayal of Nathan as both journalist and playwright underlines the close relationship of the two professions and reflects a reality in which it was commonplace for authors to exercise both professions simultaneously. If Balzac's own efforts as a pressman were not a resounding success (in economic terms at least) it was not because journalism was necessarily incompatible with other forms of artistic

---

[29] *IP*, vol. V, p. 379.
[30] *Ibid.* p. 380.
[31] *FE*, vol. II, p. 303.

production, for among his most illustrious contemporaries were those such as Hugo, Sand and Chateaubriand who regularly contributed to the   press.
Journalism, the reader is told in *Une fille d'Eve*, is at the very hub of the new, industrial and capitalist society:

> Le journalisme touche à tout dans cette époque, à l'industrie, aux intérêts publics et privés, aux entreprises nouvelles, à tous les amours-propres de la littérature et à ses produits.[32]

There can be no doubt that this was true in a wide social and political sense in a society which still required censorship of the political press and whose government viewed the increasing influence of the Liberal press with particular suspicion, but Balzac goes beyond this broad social scene in an attempt to reveal the influence of the press on private destinies, on destinies which are inextricably bound up in the relationship between the press and the theatre.

Theatre Press and Private Destinies in La Comédie humaine

The destinies under scrutiny in *La Comédie humaine* are not exclusively those of the powerful and the exploitative, but also of the vulnerable and the aspiring, whose careers in the theatre are dependent on the power of the press. Both the modern critic Sidney Braun,[33] and Balzac's contemporary Parent Duchâtelet[34] have examined the social forces which often led young girls into the theatre as a form of prostitution, and Braun takes some account of the role of the press in their exploitation. Neither of these social historians uses Balzac's work as evidence, but the role of the press in the exploitation of actresses which Balzac depicts is, at a general level, consistent with their accounts. It is in *Une fille d'Eve* (1838-39), *Un grand homme* (1836-39) and *La Rabouilleuse* (1840-42), that this role of the press is depicted in detail.

---

[32] *Ibid.* p. 338.
[33] Sidney Braun, 'The Courtesan in the French Theatre 1831-1880', in *The French Review* (Dec. 1946).
[34] Parent Duchâtelet, *De la Prostitution dans la ville de Paris*, 3rd edn. (Paris: J.B. Baillère et fils, 1857).

In all of these novels, the success of any aspiring actress's career is shown to lie in the hands of the press whose support or denigration is never a matter of objective criticism or even subjective preference, but rather of personal or collective gain. In the three novels the pressmen Nathan, Lucien and Giroudeau are able to gain the favours of a devoted mistress in Florine, Coralie and Florentine respectively in return for favourable treatment by the papers and reviews for which these pressment work. In *La Rabouilleuse* Giroudeau makes this abuse of journalistic power quite explicit to Philippe Bridau:

> A travers les vapeurs d'un certain nombre de bouteilles et de petits verres de diverses liqueurs, Giroudeau montra sur la scène à Philippe une petite, grasse et agile figurante nommée Florentine dont les bonnes grâces et l'affection lui venaient, ainsi que la loge, par la toute-puissance du journal.[35]

This is not to undermine the genuine affection which these actresses are shown to feel for their journalist lovers, for their affection as well as their talent is being exploited. Giroudeau goes on to advise Philippe that Mariette could be persuaded to be his mistress if she thinks he has some influence in the world of journalism, for this is precisely why Florentine stays with Giroudeau, who in turn is advised by Finot to ensure that she remains a hopeful *figurante* in order to retain her affections. Philippe promptly exploits Mariette in a similar fashion. The case is not quite the same with Florine and Coralie, who do in fact achieve the success which is promised to them by the journalists. This success is shown to be highly precarious, however, since it is dependent not only on the relationship between each actress and her lover, but also on the lover's relationships with his fellow journalists.

In taking an actress as a mistress, Balzac's journalists put themselves in a vulnerable position, for they provide their enemies with a means by which to attack them. After Lucien's defection from Finot's paper to a royalist publication, the plot which is hatched against him by his former colleagues is effected through the downfall of Coralie whose personal fate is of no consequence to them. The play at the Gymnase which receives disastrous reviews with Coralie

---

[35] *R*, vol. IV, p. 309.

in the lead role, is acclaimed as a huge success the next evening with Florine in her place, not because Florine is a better actress but because both women are pawns in a game of revenge which is controlled by the collective power of Lucien's enemies in the press and the theatre.

Florine's career, which is launched by the press in *Un grand homme*, is at its height in *Une fille d'Eve* where she is described as a: 'comédienne de second ordre, mais que depuis dix ans les amis de Nathan, des journaux, quelques auteurs intronisaient parmi les illustres actrices'.[36] Although Florine possesses the cunning and guile which Coralie lacks and does not fall victim to the machinations of the press in the same way as her rival, she is lulled into such a false sense of security by the continued flattery and support of the press that she is oblivious to the abyss into which Nathan's enemies are seeking to plunge him:

> Les feuilletons montraient dans Florine l'héritière de Mlle Mars. Ce triomphe étourdit assez l'actrice pour l'empêcher d'étudier le terrain sur lequel marchait Nathan, elle vécut dans un monde de fêtes et de festins.[37]

The parallel between the plots hatched against Lucien and Nathan is interesting because it reveals a damning indictment of the integrity of those who are involved in journalism. Even Nathan's close associates, who are not yet ready to declare themselves his enemies, accept that his engineered downfall will be his nemesis for harbouring ambitions beyond his status, and do nothing to alert him to the situation.

Friends can quickly become enemies in the fickle world of journalism which Balzac portrays, and yet as far as Lucien is concerned it is not just his entry into the world of journalism which marks the beginning of his loss of integrity and ultimately his downfall, but the fatal combination of simultaneous entry into two equally corrupt environments which feed from each other, propagate dissimulation and rely on the adoption of stances and roles. Coralie actively encourages Lucien to be more like her in his approach to his

---

[36] *FE*, vol. II, p. 314.
[37] *FE*, vol. II, p. 346.

work, to abandon artistic integrity and to adopt the critical stance for which he is paid just as she adopts the role for which she is paid. The longer Lucien spends with Coralie in a world where dissimulation is the norm, the more agile he becomes in his journalistic dissimulation. Balzac had already addressed this issue in *César Birotteau* (1833-37) where the opportunistic Finot is able to exploit his contacts in the theatre without becoming embroiled in its intrigues:

> Beaucoup de journalistes étaient comme les bœufs, ils ignoraient leurs forces, ils s'occupaient d'actrices, de Florine, de Tullia, de Mariette, etc. Ils régentaient tout, et ne ramassaient rien. Les prétentions d'Andoche ne concernaient ni une actrice à faire applaudir, ni une pièce à faire jouer, ni ses vaudevilles à faire recevoir.[38]

Finot is concerned only with his own success, but Lucien lacks this singlemindedness and is so caught up in the 'exercice du pouvoir de la presse' as Finot, in a demonstration of his omnipotence, divides the theatrical kingdom among his team of journalists, that he falls into the trap of wielding his power simply for its own sake and without specific goals in mind:

> Lucien, la pièce jouée, courut à la rue Saint-Fiacre y faire son article sur la pièce. Sa critique fut, par calcul, âpre et mordante; il se plut à essayer son pouvoir. Le mélodrame valait mieux que celui du Panorama-Dramatique; mais il voulait savoir s'il pouvait, comme on le lui avait dit, tuer une bonne et faire réussir une mauvaise pièce.[39]

In revealing the extent of the corruption in the relationship between the press and the theatre Balzac goes beyond an analysis of the very real economic forces which govern the interdependent relationship into a criticism of the general atmosphere of the environment which corrupts in a deterministic way. All those who are involved in the theatre and in the press we are told in *Les Employés*, are guilty of 'les mêmes vices et la même paresse',[40] and it

---

[38] *CB*, vol. VI, p. 205.
[39] *IP*, vol. V, p. 465.
[40] *E*, vol. VII, p. 924.

is this insidious and all-pervading quality of the corruption which determines the destiny of the individual. In the illusory world of the theatre, where a pauper can play a king, all men become equal but for Balzac that equality lies in a common corruptibility, a 'mauvais penchant', and it is entirely appropriate that in *La Torpille* Lucien should be forced to shake hands with his journalist enemies at the Opera Ball, where once again they become equals in the world of the theatre.

The Limitations of Balzac's Portrayal of the Petits Journaux

Since *Un grand homme* concentrates on the *feuilletons* rather than on papers of political influence, Balzac comments only superficially on the fact that censorship of the political press was tightening at the time, and there is no specific reference in the novel to the bill which was passed in December 1821 to strengthen the existing laws against the press. Nor is there any precise reference to the law which was passed in February 1822 to impose severe censorship after months of public debate in which even the smaller publications were involved.[41] It is fair to say that although Balzac's novel reflects some of the realities of the period in which it is set, he nevertheless treats the journalistic and theatrical worlds in broad, general terms which successfully recreate the atmosphere of the period without paying attention to certain historical facts.

Similarly, Balzac is partial and selective in terms of the physical setting in which he exposes the relationship between the theatre and the press, choosing to set most events in the popular establishments of the boulevard du Temple rather than the grander locations of the Opéra or the Théâtre-Français, for the less prestigious theatres were more susceptible to the power of the press and here actresses without established reputations were more easily exploited. It is also significant that throughout his work Balzac concentrates exclusively on actresses rather than actors when demonstrating the nature of the relationship between the theatre and the press.[42] In fact there is no

[41] See in particular *Le Miroir des spectacles* from November 1821 to March 1822, available as a complete series at the Bibliothèque de l'Opéra, Paris.

[42] With the exception of Robert Médal who was the proposed protagonist in Balzac's projected novel *Le Théâtre comme il est*, no male actor features in the

historical evidence that there was any distinction between male and female in terms of the economic aspects of the relationship or that both men and women in the theatre were not subjected to the same rules of extortion in subscriptions and purchased praise.

Balzac's partial and selective treatment of the relationship between the theatre and the press serves three main authorial purposes. The relationship facilitates the narrative outcomes of those novels in which it features because the relationship becomes part of the chain of causality, and because, in a deterministic way, it brings about the moral degeneration of characters who become involved in or dependent upon it. Secondly, it fulfils Balzac's self-confessed desire to take his revenge on the press. Thirdly, and most importantly, it is consistent with Balzac's overall narrative purpose to show the degeneration of society through the corrupting influence of money, with the result that almost every incident of human interaction becomes an act of trade.

La Claque – *An Historical Overview*

There is no single, comprehensive study of the history of the claque in France or of its evolution from its earliest beginnings in Roman theatre. However, it is possible to piece together a telling picture of its activities during the period covered by Balzac's work from the memoirs of actors and authors, the press and other contemporary sources. Its activities in *La Comédie humaine* are confined to the 1820s and 1830s, and since much of Hemmings's brief study of the claque in his general history of nineteenth-century French theatre refers to the middle and the second half of the century its relevance to Balzac's work is limited. It is interesting, however, that Hemmings cites Balzac's *Illusions perdues* as a source of historical evidence on

---

foreground of *La Comédie humaine*. The only references to male actors are to real actors of the time such as Lemaître, Bouffé, and Talma, whose names are often included as casual references or as points of comparison to give a sense of reality to the fiction. The point will be addressed in more detail in the following chapter.

the subject. As far as Hemmings is concerned Balzac's treatment of the claque is historically accurate, at least in relation to the 1820s.[43]

The first evidence of the use of the claque in France dates from the 1770s when, according to the memoirs of Bachaumont, it became common practice at the Comédie-Française for authors to employ paid clappers and distribute tickets among their supporters in order to resurrect a play after a disastrous first performance.[44] Interestingly, there is no evidence that anything similar was practised in the same organised way in England and it is no doubt significant that during the nineteenth century the English language adopted the French term and has never developed its own equivalent.

Just as the power of the press had increased with the increased sophistication of the technology at its disposal, so the power of the claque began to increase around the turn of the century with the changes in the design of the auditorium itself. During the eighteenth century when the *parterre* was still obliged to stand throughout the performance, and the more illustrious members of the audience would still have been seated on the stage, the services of the claque were less necessary because, for better or for worse, the audience was more actively involved in the performance. Since the abolition of seating on the stage, which had for the most part come about in 1789 with the abolition of all aristocratic privileges, and the gradual introduction of seating in the *parterre*, the audience had become increasingly distanced from the action on stage and adopted a more

---

[43] Hemmings, *The Theatre Industry in Nineteenth-Century France*, pp. 106-107: 'The hard core of the claque consisted of unskilled labourers who accepted the job – an unpaid one for the most part – because it took place after working hours and because it was their only chance of seeing the inside of a theatre and sharing in the diversions of the more fortunate members of society. Balzac's novel *Lost Illusions* includes an account of a fictional *chef de claque* to whom the hero is introduced by his friend Lousteau; at the conclusion of the interview the two young men encounter, coming up the stair case to take their orders, the smelly squad of the claqueurs and the ticket touts, [...]. Balzac has set his story in the 1820s; in the latter part of the century, in certain theatres at least, they were far from being the horny-handed automata, clapping in obedience to the word of command, that they had been under the Restoration'.

[44] Bachaumont, *Mémoires secrets*, 36 vols. (London: Adamson,1763-1789) vol. VII, p. 343.

passive stance.[45]   This is noted by de Boigne in his memoirs of the early nineteenth century:

> Le public, le vrai public n'applaudit plus, il ne prend plus la peine d'applaudir. Il craint de salir ou de déchirer ses gants, de se rougir les mains; il ne crie plus; il murmure bravo de peur de s'enrouer. Les claqueurs sont une conséquence forcée de nos habitudes de bien-être et de confortable.[46]

According to de Boigne the necessity of the claque was at least partly due to a new, bourgeois code of social behaviour, and if the noisy enthusiasm of the audience could no longer be relied upon then the members of the claque were as important to the theatre as the members of the cast:

> On a beaucoup déblatéré et l'on déblatère encore tous les jours contre les claqueurs. C'est l'habitude, c'est la mode, et l'on ne s'aperçoit pas que les claqueurs constituent avec les acteurs et les spectacles les trois éléments indispensables du théâtre.[47]

In fact de Boigne suggests that it would be better to make an honest profession of the claque and for each theatre to have its own, organised group, as was the case at the Opéra where Auguste was *chef de claque* and managed a reasonably polished team.

The practice was generally deplored and repeatedly denounced by critics during the 1820s, but this did nothing to diminish the ubiquitous presence of the claque. Montigny describes in 1825 how the *chef de claque* would always be at the front of the queue of people wanting to see an author before the first performance of a play:

> A leur tête est le chef de cabale, le directeur des applaudissments, l'entrepreneur des succès; homme indispensable et dont on peut dire: Fléau du ciel affreux, mais nécessaire![48]

---

[45] Descotes, *Le Public de théâtre et son histoire.*
[46] de Boigne, *Petits mémoires de l'Opéra*, p. 84.
[47] *Ibid.*
[48] Montigny, *Le Provincial à Paris*, vol. III, p. 46.

So necessary that in 1825, according to Bouffé's memoirs, some of the smaller theatres employed their own *chefs de claque* on a regular basis: Pompon at the Vaudeville, Sauton at the Variétés, Ely at the Cirque-Olympique and Lazare at the Folies-dramatiques.[49] Bouffé abhorred the members of the claque, claims that he never gave in to their pressure and was in the habit of ridiculing them on stage:

> Ah! que les suffrages du vrai public sont autrement flatteurs que les applaudissements convenus et payés des claqueurs, auxquels, Dieu merci, je n'ai jamais donné un seul billet, car je ne comprends pas qu'un artiste attribue quelque valeur à des applaudissements commandés par lui-même.[50]

The claque went from strength to strength and became increasingly indispensable as the audience gradually became less willing to applaud, partly because it feared reprisals from a claque which could often be drunken, volatile and violent, partly because it was often more interested in the social spectacle in the auditorium than in the spectacle on stage and partly because it would rather refrain from judgment than risk appearing foolish.

The claque might not have generated such hostility if it could at least have been relied upon to provide the service for which it was paid, but the less professional bands of claqueurs were often guilty of accepting payments from parties with conflicting interests. A satirical poem in *Le Miroir* on 8 October 1821 warns of precisely this kind of treachery and double-dealing:

La Claquomanie

Vive la claquomanie!
C'est par elle que tout va,
Depuis la ventriloquie
Jusqu'au sublime opéra.
Auteurs, acteurs, figurans,
Là chacun a ses gens;
Aussi, depuis cet abus,
On dit que l'on n'y dort plus.

[49] Bouffé, *Mes Souvenirs*, 1800-1880 (Paris: Dentu, 1880), p. 99.
[50] *Ibid.* p. 94.

A cette vile manœuvre
Les Français[51] même ont recours;
Quoiqu'ils aient plus d'un chef-d'œuvre
Qui marche bien sans secours.
Mais l'Odéon sans pitié
Réduit le corps de moitié,
Vu que l'écho du local
Répète leur bacchanal.
A Feydeau cette cohorte
Courant plus d'un mauvais sol,
Favorise de la sorte
Tantôt Pierre et tantôt Paul.
Le Théâtre Italien
Se rit d'un pareil soutien:
Là les bravos accordés
Par le goût seul sont donnés.
Suivant l'adage on sait bien
Qu'un peu d'aide fait grand bien.
Mais laissez là votre appui,
Pauvres auteurs d'aujourd'hui:
Vous que le sort persécute,
Revenez de vos erreurs;
Car bien souvent votre chute
Est l'ouvrage des claqueurs.

A.L.

This poem, whose author remains unidentifiable after cross-reference to other commentaries on the claque, it is an important testimony to the fact that the extortions of the claque applied equally to authors, actors and even those in poorly-paid walk-on parts, the *figurans*, who were particularly susceptible to the promise of success. It is particularly interesting in relation to Balzac's fiction because in the last two lines it warns of the treachery and double-dealing of which the claque is guilty in *Un grand homme*.

The status of the claque was to remain unchanged throughout the 1820s and for the rest of Balzac's lifetime and beyond. In December

---

[51] Meaning the Théâtre-Français.

1846, Gautier took the opportunity to mock the claque in his review
of Scribe's *La Protégée sans le savoir* which was an adaptation of
Balzac's *Honorine*, first performed at the Gymnase on 7 December:

> A propos d'applaudissements, témoignons à MM. les claqueurs du
> Gymnase notre admiration bien sentie! quelle exécution! comme
> c'est nourri, sonore et bien rhythmé! Quel coup de main nerveux,
> quel admirable ensemble!... Ces artistes doivent travailler quatre
> heures tous les matins pour arriver à une telle perfection! Parmi la
> section des rieurs, il y a vraiment des sujets fort distingués!
> Comme ils partent juste sur la réplique! comme aux endroits
> indiqués, ils se tordent sur les banquettes, demandant grâce, pâmés
> d'aise, se tenant les côtes, trépignant, suffoqués, étranglés, aboyant
> un bravo convulsif![52]

Similarly, an article by Emile Ségaud in 1849 sums up the general
attitude to the claque for at least three decades:

> C'est qu'avec l'institution de la claque, affreuse lèpre qui s'étend
> sur les théâtres de la capitale, on n'y obtient plus de ces succès nets,
> francs, de bon aloi, comme aussi [...] on n'y siffle plus avec cette
> vigueur dont la province a gardé seule le secret. [...] Ainsi, il est
> bien reconnu que la claque instituée dans un but de réclame
> paralyse toutes les bonnes intentions du public parisien par la
> répulsion naturelle qu'elle lui inspire.[53]

Despite the protestations of the theatrical world the claque had by
now become a firmly established part of the Parisian theatre industry
and one whose power would not diminish until the end of the century.
Its effect was to add to the industrialisation of the playwright's craft
in a way which had been predicted by an anonymous author at the
beginning of the century:

> Grâce à la claque, on fait à présent une comédie comme on faisait
> jadis une opération de commerce; et l'on se mettra bientôt auteur,
> comme on se met banquier, libraire ou marchand de draps.[54]

---

[52] Gautier, *Histoire de l'art dramatique*, vol IV, p. 379.
[53] Ségaud, *Question d'honneur littéraire et artistique. A bas la claque!* (Paris:
principaux librairies,1849), pp.8-10.
[54] Anon., *L'Art de la claque* (Paris: Pillet, 1817), p. 5. Bibliothèque de l'Opéra.

Balzac's Experience with the Claque

The only *chef de claque* with whom Balzac is known to have had contact is Porcher, who was born in 1792 and was a hairdresser until, according to the memoirs of Alexandre Dumas[55] and Frédérick Lemaître,[56] he became *chef de claque* at the Porte-Saint-Martin in 1826. Balzac's personal dealings with Porcher date from 1839 when he was in contact with him in connection with the production of *Vautrin* at the Porte-Saint-Martin. Nicole Felkay's article on Porcher[57] focuses on his role as 'un banquier des auteurs dramatiques' who would loan money to dramatists against their share of the expected box-office takings at their productions, which according to Balzac's biographer, Léon Gozlan, is what Balzac hoped to arrange with Porcher for the production of *Vautrin*.[58]

In the event, Porcher was unable to advance any money to Balzac because he had his own financial difficulties, but he did act as *chef de claque* at the fateful opening night. When Lemaître appeared on stage looking exactly like Louis-Philippe, the claque either could not or would not do anything to alter the reaction of the audience, or indeed of the censors. For Balzac this was a disastrous first experience and he blamed it at least partly on the failings of the claque.

In 1842 when *Quinola* was to be staged at the Odéon Balzac's hostility towards the claque came to the fore and according to Gozlan's account of what Balzac told him, it was largely because of the bad experience with *Vautrin* that Balzac was determined not to get involved with the claque again:

> Je ne veux pas de claqueurs. Je les exerçai à *Vautrin*, mais je les ai subis pour complaire à l'aveugle routine d'Harel, lié par mille liens d'amitié et de papiers timbrés avec Porcher. Mais je les bannis à *Quinola*, bannis à perpétuité.[59]

---

[55] Dumas, *Mes mémoires*, 5 vols. (Paris: Michel Lévy, 1865-1869; republished, Gallimard,1954-68) vol IV, p. 234.

[56] Lemaître, *Souvenirs publiés par son fils* (Paris: Ollendorf, 1880) p. 201.

[57] Felkay, 'Un Banquier des auteurs dramatiques,' *AB,* 1972.

[58] Gozlan, *Balzac en pantoufles*, p. 39.

[59] Gozlan, *Balzac chez lui*, p. 121.

Not only did Balzac not want to employ the claque for the staging of *Quinola*, he also wished to assume the *chef de claque*'s auxiliary role as *marchand de billets*. When Balzac's highly creative ticket selling scheme failed, and he was faced on the opening night with an auditorium which was more than half empty and largely hostile, he had to have recourse to the claque.[60]

The last known date of Balzac's dealings with Porcher is recorded in his correspondence in January 1849 in connection with the staging of *Le Faiseur* at the Comédie-Française. There is no mention of the claque here, however, for Balzac is writing to Laurent-Jan from Wierzchownia to entrust him with securing the correct sums for his concessionary tickets from Porcher:

> Que Porcher n'oublie pas cette fois que j'ai pour 60 francs argent c'est à dire pour 120 fr. de billets, et fais lui observer [...] que j'ai droit au double c'est-à-dire à 240 fr. de billets pendant 16 représentations[61]

Over so great a distance it is unlikely that Balzac could have been very involved in the production of his play and in this instance he expresses no opinion about the employment of the claque. In the end the production was postponed and only took place posthumously in 1851.

Balzac's personal experiences with the claque must have coloured his opinion of its activities and Felkay asserts confidently that Porcher is the main source of inspiration for Braulard, the fictional *chef de claque* in *Un grand homme*.[62] Notwithstanding the strength of Felkay's argument, it should be remembered that Balzac's main dealings with Porcher were after the first publication of *Un grand homme* in 1839, principally in connection with *Quinola* in 1842 and *Le Faiseur* in 1849. Balzac's treatment of the claque in his fiction is

---

[60] See above, pp. 23-24.
[61] *Corres.*, vol. V, 21 Janvier 1849, p. 456.
[62] Felkay, *Un Banquier des auteurs dramatiques*, p. 207.

after all not necessarily an account of his direct experiences but is an attempt to reflect the wider reality he observed around him.

The Claque and Historicity in La Comédie humaine

Balzac's concern with the claque in his fiction is concentrated in 1839 with the publication of *Un grand homme* and *Une fille d'Eve* where the action takes place in the 1820s and 1830s respectively. There is nothing in his correspondence at this time to indicate that Balzac intended his portrayal to be an attack akin to that levelled at the world of journalism. However, 1839 was the year of the staging of *Vautrin* and of Balzac's first personal involvement with the claque. The only mention of the claque in Balzac's later work is a brief reference in 1846 in *La Cousine Bette*.[63]

In *Un grand homme* the claque managed by Braulard at first appears more sordid and more corrupt than the press but in fact both industries are shown to be equally parasitic and susceptible to corruption and bribery. Goodwill has its price with the claque as it does with the *feuilletons* and the journalist Lousteau points out to Lucien the parallel between the professions engendered by the theatre – actor, author, journalist, claqueur – realising that none is superior to the others: 'Voilà les Romains! dit Lousteau en riant, voilà la gloire des actrices et des auteurs dramatiques. Vu de près, ça n'est pas plus beau que la nôtre'.[64]

In the novel Braulard operates just like Finot but at a different level and directs his squalid band just as Finot directs his journalists, extorting sums of money from actors and actressses in just the same way, by exploiting their fear of failure and their hopes of success. According to the historical evidence already cited and to Balzac's own experience, the exploitative and parasitic business operations of the claque are entirely realistic in the novel, for they constituted an accepted norm without which a production was unlikely to succeed. When Lousteau takes Lucien to meet Braulard for the first time in order to strike a deal for the profitable disposal of their concessionary tickets, Braulard automatically assumes that they have come to secure applause for Florine and Coralie who cannot hope to achieve success

---

[63] See page 113.
[64] *IP*, vol. V, p. 470.

if they do not collaborate with the claque: 'Florine et Coralie sont ses tributaires: si elles ne le subventionnaient pas, elles ne seraient point applaudies à toutes leurs entrées et leurs sorties'.[65] Braulard's subsequent dinner invitation to Lousteau and Lucien, in which he boasts of extravagance and illustrious guests from the theatre world, is reminiscent not only of Porcher's material ease, as Felkay suggests,[66] but also of Samson's account of the unnamed press editor who liked to boast at his dinner parties of his acquaintance with famous actors and the gifts he received from them:[67]

> Si vous voulez me faire l'honneur et le plaisir de venir, vous pouvez amener vos épouses, il y aura noces et festins, nous avons Adèle Dupuis, Ducange, Frédéric du Petit-Méré, Mlle Millot ma maîtresse, nous rirons bien! nous boirons mieux![68]

Finot is to be the guest of honour at this dinner where actors, the press and the claque are brought together for their mutual gain and the dining room becomes a market place where connections are made and services are exchanged. Balzac reinforces the sense of historical reality here by including in the list of guests real actors and dramatists whose names his contemporary reader might have recognised. At this point in the action, in early 1822, Adèle Dupuis had been starring at the Gaîté for five years along with Mlle Millot who was more famous for her beauty than for her talent;[69] Dupetit-Méré was a successful vaudevillist who, in the 1820s, was at the height of his career,[70] as was the melodramatist Ducange.[71] The references to these real actors and dramatists place Balzac's portrayal of the *chef de claque* and his business relationships firmly in a

---

[65] *IP*, vol. V, p. 468.
[66] Felkay, 'Un Banquier des auteurs dramatiques', p. 201 & p. 207.
[67] Samson, *Mémoires*, p. 205, see above, p. 86.
[68] *IP*, vol. V, p. 469.
[69] *IP*, vol. V, p. 469, n. 1.
[70] *Ibid.* p. 436, n. 1.
[71] Lousteau refers to the fact that Ducange has just lost his court case. This has no relevance to the narrative other than to reinforce its historicity, for in reality Ducange was sentenced to five months in prison and a fine of 500 francs on 26 June 1821 for crimes against public morality following the publication of his novel, *Valentine (IP*, p. 469, n. 2). Although Balzac places the incident at least six months later than its actual historical date, the incident has its basis in reality.

realistic context, and thus help to create a convincing portrayal of business being conducted in an informal manner during social engagements and independently of the theatre's administration.

Gautier's remarks of 7 December 1846[72] about the well-rehearsed skills of the claqueurs may have been sarcastic but in fact the presence of the *chef de claque* at rehearsals was entirely necessary and this is borne out in the novel as Coralie prepares for her debut at the Gymnase:

> Braulard promit de venir et vint à la répétition générale afin de convenir des endroits où ses romains déploieraient leurs battoirs de chair, et enlèveraient le succès.[73]

The real proof of the power of the claque in *Un grand homme* and of Braulard's claim, 'Ah! je puis faire chuter qui je veux,' comes when, as part of the wider conspiracy against them, Coralie and Lucien are betrayed by Braulard during Coralie's debut at the Gymnase. Braulard has been paid both by Coralie's protector and by the conspirators, so under his instruction the claque exaggerates its enthusiasm and is hushed into silence by the audience causing Coralie to falter and her performance to deteriorate. A performance which is not a true reflection of Coralie's talent is then treated as a disaster by the press, causing Coralie to become ill with nerves and allowing Florine to take over. That Florine is able to produce a resounding success with the same play the next day is further testimony to the ability of the press and the claque to make and break fortunes in the theatre and highlights their similarity. Coralie's career is treated by both as a piece of merchandise which can be disposed of once it has outlived its economic usefulness.

The role of the claque in this conspiracy may seem contrived and exaggerated and it is certainly more extreme than the type of generally incompetent fiasco with which Balzac was familiar and which was often the norm. However, the satirical poem from *Le Miroir* on 8 October 1821,[74] which is only a few months earlier than Coralie's disastrous debut at the Gymnase, warns of precisely the

---

[72] Gautier, *Histoire de l'art dramatique*, vol. IV, p. 379.

[73] *IP*, vol. V, p. 528.

[74] See above, p. 103.

type of treachery on the part of the claque of which Coralie and
Lucien are the victims and seems to indicate that while treachery and
double-dealing may not have been entirely typical of the claque, it
did nevertheless happen. It seems reasonable to assume from the
poem that Balzac's contemporary readers would have been familiar
with this type of conduct by the claque, and what might appear to the
modern reader to be a contrived method of bringing about the
narrative outcomes of the conspiracy, actually has some basis in
reality.[75]

In *Une fille d'Eve*, set in the 1830s, the claque is shown to be as
necessary to success in the theatre as it is in the 1820s. Balzac lists
working with the claque and paying for its services among Florine's
essential responsibilities and expenses:

> [...] travailler avec les entrepreneurs d'applaudissements pour faire
> soigner ses entrées et ses sorties, solder le compte des triomphes
> du mois passé en achetant en gros ceux du mois courant.[76]

Similarly, Florine's lover, the dramatist and journalist Nathan, is
shown to be dependent on the claque for the much needed success of
his play, a success which ultimately proves to be worthless, for no-
one of consequence in the theatrical world is fooled by the applause
of the claque. This fictional incident reflects the real irony of the
situation for although the claque was indispensable, any success
which it managed to effect was still subject to the same critical
judgments by those who were capable of making any.

In the novel it is only Marie de Vandenesse who is naive enough
to be duped by the claque:

> Elle assista naturellement, à l'avant-scène du Gymnase, à la
> première représentation de la pièce sur laquelle Nathan comptait

---

[75] A similiar incident occurs earlier in the novel when Coralie and Florine are still
performing at the Panorama-Dramatique. A conspiracy is mounted by the
neighbouring theatres who have paid the claque to ruin the play, but the director of
the Panorama-Dramatique pays them more and with the help of the actresses'
protectors ensures that there are sufficient supporters present to oust the claque and
guarantee the play's success. Since they have been paid by both parties the *claqueurs*
are happy to leave the theatre. *IP,* vol. V, p. 378.

[76] *FE*, vol. II, p. 320.

pour soutenir son entreprise, et dont le succès parut immense. Elle fut la dupe des applaudissements achetés.[77]

In reality, while the audience may have allowed itself to be persuaded by the claque, most members of the public would have remained conscious of its presence in the theatre, particularly as the main body of its members would normally sit together. Balzac's comment here is not so much on the claque itself as on the character of Marie de Vandenesse. He uses a phenomenon with which his contemporary reader would have been very familiar in order to emphasise her extreme naivety.[78]

In his treatment of the claque Balzac does not expose any aspect of its functions which was not commonly acknowledged during his lifetime. The necessity of its presence and the economic forces governing its operations which Balzac reveals are also borne out by historical reality. However, Balzac goes beyond a strictly factual account of the activities of the claque to bring it to life in his unique descriptive style. It is precisely because he is a novelist and not a historian that he is able to do this, for the act of describing the claque goes through a different, more creative series of transformations than it would if it were a purely factual account and in so doing becomes truly the author's own:

> En sortant Lucien vit défiler devant lui la puante escouade des claqueurs et des vendeurs de billets, tous gens à casquettes, à pantalons mûrs, à redingotes râpées, à figures patibulaires, bleuâtres, verdâtres, boueuses, rabougries, à barbes longues, aux yeux féroces et patelins tout à la fois, horrible population qui vit et foisonne sur les boulevards de Paris, qui, le matin, vend des chaînes de sûreté, des bijoux en or pour vingt-cinq sous, et qui claque sous les lustres le soir, qui se plie enfin à toutes les fangeuses nécessités de Paris.[79]

---

[77] *Ibid.* p. 342.

[78] This is similar to the occasions of Lucien's first visits to the Vaudeville and the Opéra in *Un grand homme* (pp. 265-266 & 272-284), where his naivety is characterised by lack of familiarity with the social code of the theatre. Worldliness and sophistication are everywhere characterised by ease and familiarity with the theatre, which is the hub of social life.

[79] *IP,* vol. V, p. 470.

Balzac's insistence here in *Un grand homme* on the repulsiveness of the claque is not simply a matter of a preoccupation with squalor, for the claque is made up of desperate individuals who are themselves caught up in the economic forces of Paris. There is plenty of historical evidence to suggest that the audience was afraid of coming to blows with the claque and if Balzac's description is accurate then it is easy to see why.[80]

Later, in 1846 in *La Cousine Bette*, Balzac insists upon the fact that the occupation of *claqueur* is that of the lowest of the low. With the exception of the *chefs de claque*, the claque is treated by historians as a collective body and this is the only instance in *La Comédie humaine* where an ordinary *claqueur* is mentioned as an individual. Instead of remaining in her liaison with Baron Hulot, Olympe Bijou deserts him in favour of a *claqueur* who in turn deserts her after squandering the money which had been given to her by Hulot. The emphasis of the narrative is upon the fact that a *claqueur* is not even worthy of a *grisette:*

> Ce *faigniant*, comme tous les jolis garçons, un *souteneur* des pièces, quoi! est la coqueluche du boulevard du Temple où il travaille aux pièces nouvelles, et *soigne les entrées* des actrices, comme il dit.[81]

As the historical documentation of the claque is fragmented and sparse, this brief portrait is valuable as a small contribution to the overall composite picture of the claque.

Within *La Comédie humaine* Balzac's portrayal of the claque rests entirely on the disorganised bands of petty criminals who operated in the boulevard theatres such as the Panorama-Dramatique, and the Gymnase and these are reduced to one generic troupe which is shown to be typical of the 'profession'. There is no mention of the semi-professional troupes which were an integrated part of the larger, more prestigious theatres such as the Opéra and the Théâtre-Français. In this sense Balzac's examination is partial, selective and, to some

---

[80] The description of the *claqueurs* given here in *Un grand homme* is strikingly similar to that given by Balzac in his article in *La Caricature* in 1830 in which he claims that the *claqueurs* spend their days 'vendant des clefs de montre et des chaînes de sûreté; des gravures prohibées; des boutons de chemise; des cure-dents, etc.' See: 'Le Claqueur' in *L'Œuvre de Balzac*, vol. 14, p. 458, and also above, p105.

[81] *Be.*, vol. VII, p. 382.

extent, simplified and has to be so in order to serve his narrative purpose. This is not to say that his account fails to reveal historical truth in any way, for the fact that he dwells exclusively on the corruption of the claque in the cheaper theatres and that his portrayal is ultimately damning, is itself a reflection of historical truth in that it is a true representation of the tide of public opinion against the claque.

Balzac's representation of the claque also takes its place in his vision of human behaviour in the wider context of his fiction and serves to reveal general truths about human nature and Parisian life as well as particular truths about the claque. As with his examination of the press, it is the economic forces governing the conduct of the claque which interest Balzac. He is at great pains to tell exactly how the trade in concessionary tickets with the claque works, just as he tells in precise detail how much money could be made from newspaper subscriptions. Lousteau describes the process to Lucien:

> Braulard a vingt mille livres de rentes, il a la griffe des auteurs dramatiques du boulevard qui tous ont un compte courant chez lui, comme chez un banquier. Les billets d'auteur et de faveur se vendent. Cette marchandise, Braulard la place [...]. A cinquante billets de faveur par soirée à chaque spectacle, tu trouveras deux cent cinquante billets par jour; si, l'un dans l'autre, ils valent quarante sous, Braulard paye cent vingt-cinq francs par jour aux auteurs et court la chance d'en gagner autant.[82]

It is not just in economic terms that the claque functions to fulfil Balzac's wider fictional aims. It also serves to demonstrate the precarious and often illusory nature of success and the fact that according to Balzac's observation of the world both within the theatre and beyond it, one could never be sure of being able to distinguish friends from enemies. The endemic moral decay and predilection towards vice which Balzac saw to be true of a society governed by self-interest and money are intensified in his representation of the theatrical world, for by its very nature the existence of that world depends upon personal ambition. Balzac's portrayal of the claque is an integral part of this representation and plays an important role in

[82] *IP*, vol. V, p. 468.

creating an atmosphere of vice and corruption which will be the downfall of those who are too good, too weak or too naive to survive.

The Career of the Dramatist – An Historical Overview

The career of the dramatist in the boulevard theatre is, both in Balzac's fiction and in reality, dependent on good relations with the press and the claque and is no less of a compromise than the career of the journalist. The contrast between the prestigious appearance and the difficult reality in the 1820s is one which is recognised by the dramatist and director Montigny:

> La profession d'écrivain dramatique, en apparence si agréable, si séduisante, et par cela si peu semblable à toutes les autres, ne laisse pas que d'avoir aussi son mauvais côté et peut occasionner des chagrins véritables.[83]

According to Montigny, one of the main difficulties that the aspiring dramatist had to face was that each theatre had a core of regular authors which it was virtually impossible to break in to. It seems reasonable to imagine that it might have been easier to get a first play acccepted at one of the smaller theatres, particularly as they changed their repertoire more frequently than the larger theatres, but evidence suggests that this was not the case:

> [...] tous les théâtres sont, plus ou moins, sous l'empire du monopole; chacun d'eux a ses fournisseurs en titre, qu'on reçoit à l'exclusion des auteurs qui n'ont que du mérite.* Il est à-peu-près inutile de se présenter, si l'on n'a pas eu le soin préalable d'entretenir des intelligences dans la place; apportassiez-vous un chef-d'œuvre, il serait refusé, si les intérêts du monopoleur en titre ou le caprice de la direction s'opposaient à son adoption définitive.
> *Ceci s'applique surtout aux petits théâtres.[84]

The question of domination by certain authors has already been raised in relation to the Gymnase where in 1821 Scribe, Poirson and

---

[83] Montigny, *Le Provincial à Paris*, vol. III, p. 45.
[84] *Ibid.* vol. II, p. 67.

Mélesville were the regular authors[85] and Montigny goes as far as to claim that unless an author writes in collaboration with 'l'heureux, le fécond, le spirituel M. Scribe,' he has little hope of having his work accepted.[86] The point is also made later in the period, in 1861, by Georges d'Heilly:

> Chaque théâtre paraît avoir adopté un auteur spécial, ou du moins quelques auteurs spéciaux qui fournissent à tour de rôle les grandes pièces de l'année.[87]

D'Heilly also claims, similarly to Montigny, that whether an author succeeds in getting his plays accepted has little to do with true talent and that the aspiring author is in need of *protection* just as the aspiring actress is:

> Règle générale, on n'arrive au théâtre que par la protection. Mais ayez du talent comme Molière, et soyez pauvre comme Job, vous êtes bien sûr de mourir de faim sur votre fumier![88]

The first step in having a work accepted for production was to submit a copy to the director of a theatre and to try to gain an audience with the *comité de lecture* who would make a supposedly democratic decision on the the merit of the play. A simple voting system was used whereby coloured balls were placed in an urn after the author had read his play to the committee. A white ball indicated unconditional acceptance, a black ball indicated rejection and a red ball indicated that the play should be accepted subject to certain alterations. An overall decision was taken strictly according to the majority colour.[89]

Although this was an attempt at democratic decision-making, it is easy to imagine that in practice the system manifested flaws. The committee at the Opéra was large and made up of connoisseurs of sound judgment and that of the Théâtre-Français was made up entirely of members of its acting company, but at the smaller theatres

[85] See chapter I, p. 48.
[86] Montigny, *Le Provincial à Paris*, vol. I, p. 70.
[87] d'Heilly, *Le Scandale au théâtre*, p. 85.
[88] d'Heilly, *Le Scandale au théâtre*, p. 92.
[89] Hemmings, *The Theatre Industry in Nineteenth-Century France*, pp. 257-275.

the impartiality and judgmental faculties of the committees were often less reliable. The Gymnase clearly favoured Scribe, and according to Montigny the small committees of the Gaîté and the Vaudeville simply acted on the instructions of the directors while the Porte-Saint-Martin employed its own rather more informal procedure:

> Les pièces nouvelles qu'on joue depuis quelques mois, c'est-à-dire les pièces des amis, ont été reçues verbalement, la réception de quelques-unes a été inscrite, *pour-mémoire*, au dos de la carte à payer dans les cabinets particuliers du restaurateur voisin.[90]

Once the committee had accepted a play it then had to be subjected to the more rigorous scrutiny of the censors. State lawyers Lacan and Paulmier explain in their catalogue of theatre legislation completed in 1853, that the origins of censorship in the theatre date back to ancient Greece and that the first records of censorship in France date from 1516 when the Court decreed that there should be no mention of princes or princesses in farce or comedy. No source is given for this information but the authors do claim that censorship is particularly necessary in the theatre because the dramatic form brings its subject matter to life in a way which is more powerful in its impact than any other art form.[91] In principle Montigny also agrees with this because people of all ages and from all walks of life attend the theatre, but he claims that in practice an author could depict the lower classes however he liked provided that he did not criticise the government or its institutions and employees.[92]

The functions of the censors were to read a draft of the play submitted in duplicate or triplicate and prohibit any offensive or dangerous passages, to attend rehearsals and ensure that the said passages had been eliminated or altered and at the same time call for the suppression of any unsuitable passages or phrases which may have slipped their attention earlier, and finally to attend the dress rehearsal in order to ensure that the costumes were not too

---

[90] Montigny, *Le Provincial à Paris*, vol. I, p. 73.

[91] Lacan & Paulmier, *Traité de la législation des théâtres*, 2 vols. (Paris: Durand, 1853), vol. I, p. 110.

[92] Montigny, *Le Provincial à Paris*, vol. III, p. 127.

provocative and that there were no subversive connotations represented by certain colour combinations. Montigny had experienced the frustrations of dealing with the censors during his own career both as an author and as a director:

> Il faut lui soumettre le manuscrit en double ou triple exécution attendre sa commodité, et bien souvent n'obtenir d'elle, après de longs délais, qu'un ouvrage tronqué, biffé, rogné, affaibli, méconnaissable à l'auteur lui-même, ou, plus souvent encore, ne le recevoir qu'avec *le refus de le représenter*.[93]

Once permission for performance had been granted, it could of course be retracted at any stage. Balzac's own experience with *Vautrin*, banned by the censors after the first performance (ostensibly because of the principal actor's resemblance to Louis-Philippe), is testimony to this.[94]

After the trials of the *comité de lecture* and the *comité de censure* came the equally taxing matter of dealing with the actors and actresses. The *collation des rôles*, which took place after the first reading of the play to the company, involved the appointment of actors and actresses to specific roles as well as making any changes to suit the whims of the individuals concerned.[95] Then finally the rehearsals would commence and the actors would start learning their lines at the pace agreed in their contracts. According to Duflot the period of time for rehearsals would be roughly two weeks for a one-act vaudeville, six weeks for a full five-act vaudeville, two months for a melodrama, three and a half months for a comic opera and anything up to nine months for a large scale opera.[96]

For the majority of dramatists a successful first production did not necessarily guarantee a future career. Apart from the pressure of having continually to produce new material, all but the most illustrious dramatists still had to compete with the other chosen

---

[93] Montigny, *Le Provincial à Paris,* vol. III, p. 122.

[94] *Corres.*, vol. IV, p. 73, letter to the editor of *La Presse*. In his letter to *La Presse* Balzac remarks that the censors had posed no objections to Lemaître's costume during the dress rehearsal and that it was only at the first performance that objections were raised. See also: *LMH*, vol. I, p. 672, 26 March 1840.

[95] Marie Colombier, *Mémoires* (Paris: Flammarion, 1898), p. 182.

[96] Duflot, *Les Secrets des coulisses*, pp. 183-184.

authors contracted to the same theatre and often apply pressure for their work to be staged, while still maintaining good relations with the director:

> Le directeur se promène gravement, distribuant à la ronde un coup d'œil protecteur, ou tâchant d'échapper à tel auteur qui demande qu'on *remonte* sa pièce; à tel autre, qui prie qu'on mette enfin la sienne à l'étude, à un troisième, qui veut connaître le répertoire de la semaine, afin de savoir si *on le joue.* [...] on se marchande, on se prend, on se quitte, on se querelle, on se raccommode, on se lutine, on se fâche.[97]

Montigny also claims that both casual acquaintances and apparently loyal friends would clamour for complimentary tickets to first performances and then deny knowing the author if the play was a failure. The author's enemies and rivals, on the other hand, would rush to console him and offer advice in these circumstances, but if the play was a success they would criticise it aloud, claiming:

> [...] ce mot m'appartient, [...] j'ai fourni l'idée de ce couplet, [...] on m'a volé cette scène toute entière, [...] et tous s'accordent à penser que la pièce ne vaut pas le diable et qu'ils feraient beaucoup mieux.

These pressures and difficulties described by Montigny will be seen to be particularly evident in Balzac's portrayal of the life of the fictional dramatist Nathan.

From the 1820s to the middle of the century it was usual for plays, and particularly for vaudevilles, to be the work of two or more authors working in collaboration and again, this is an historical circumstance which will be seen to be reflected in Balzac's novels. An examination of selected theatre reviews[98] prior to the beginning of the nineteenth century reveals few examples of plays written in collaboration. These instances increase gradually, however, after the turn of the century, through the Napoleonic years and most significantly in the 1820s and 1830s as the demand for new

---

[97] Montigny, *Le Provincial à Paris*, vol. I, pp. 117-118.

[98] *Le Diable boiteux*, 1790 & 1816; *Le Courrier des spectacles,* 1796-1807; *Le Courrier des théâtres,*1818-1833; *Le Miroir des spectacles;*1821-1823.

productions increased. This is borne out by Hemmings's statistics which show that, during the 1820s, work written in collaboration accounted for as much as 50% of the total, rising to 77% during the Restoration and only dropping back to slightly less than 50% in the 1860s.[99]

Apart from making it easier to produce plays in great volume and with great speed, co-authorship also offered new authors the opportunity to break into what was effectively a closed shop. A successful author might give his name to a new play without actually having any part in it in order that an unknown author could become established. This was, of course, not an act of altruism but a purely commercial consideration since the established author who risked his good reputation would take at least an equal share in the payment from the theatre without actually doing any work.[100]

During the period from 1820 to 1850, although dramatists were often contracted to particular theatres they were not retained on a salary but, according to Lacan and Paulmier and to Duflot were paid an average of 12% of the gross box-office takings at each performance of their play.[101] This percentage could vary according to individual negotiation and was often more at the Théâtre-Français and the Opéra. The distribution of the 12% among the co-authors of any play written in collaboration was a matter for private arrangement between the authors and was not the concern of the theatre.

In order to protect the financial interests of dramatists and to ensure that they were paid what was due to them, there were various attempts during the early nineteenth century to establish a *société des auteurs dramatiques*. Article 538 of Lacan and Paulmier's directory states that Beaumarchais had established such a society at the Comédie-Française in the previous century to ensure that payments to dramatists were administered in a proper manner. The same item goes on to say that periodically attempts were made at other theatres

---

[99] Hemmings, 'Co-authorship in French Plays', in *French Studies*, vol. 41, 1987, pp. 37-43. Hemmings has collated his statistics from the bibliography of French nineteenth-century plays *The Parisian Stage 1800-1900*, by C.B. Wicks (Alabama: University of Alabama Press, 1950-1979).

[100] Astruc, *Le Droit privé du théâtre*, p. 22.

[101] Duflot, *Les Secrets des coulisses, p. 222;* Lacan & Paulmier, *Traité de la législation des théâtres*, item 618, vol. II, p. 117.

to establish similar societies, but with little success until, in 1837, a single, large society was founded, after which time all theatres were obliged to have a contract with the society in order to engage any author. Duflot, who was himself an author of no fewer than forty-five plays, also refers to this in *Les Secrets des coulisses* in 1865:

> Chaque théâtre a un traité qui le lie avec la Société des auteurs pour la répartition des droits de chacun. Le tarif ordinaire des droits d'auteur est de 12% sur la recette brute du jour, une certaine quantité de billets d'entrée à toutes places, et son entrée à vie qu'il peut céder ou vendre au plus offrant.[102]

Duflot's comment about complimentary tickets is pertinent, for these were generally considered to make up part of the author's payment and he states that despite the attempts of theatre directors to limit or cease the issuing of authors' tickets, 'l'on en distribue chaque jour par centaines'.[103] Authors would use their free tickets to pay the claque, and would distribute them among friends and supporters. Clearly every ticket issued free of charge reduced the number of places contributing to the overall box-office takings, but it was usual for authors to trade some of their concessionary tickets with the *marchand de billets* for a good deal more than the 12% share of box-office receipts. According to d'Heilly the practice of selling authors' tickets for a proportion of the face value was widespread and such tickets were readily available:

> Les dépots de billets d'auteurs sont établis chez les marchands de vins ou autres, qui se trouvent assez près du théâtre pour faciliter la vente de ces billets au public.[104]

---

[102] Duflot, *Les Secrets des coulisses*, p. 222.
[103] *Ibid.*
[104] Georges d'Heilly, *Le Scandale au théâtre*, p. 65. See also: Felkay, 'Un Banquier des auteurs dramatiques', for an examination of Porcher's trade in tickets.

Balzac's own calculations in a letter to Madame Hanska on 4 August 1848 testify to how much money could be made through trading in *billets d'auteur:*

> Porcher, l'acquéreur des droits de billets à qui j'ai donné ma griffe pour tous mes billets de théâtre, et qui achète tous mes billets à 50pr. Car, à chaque représentation, j'ai droit de vendre pour 60fr. de billets à *la Marâtre,* et dans chaque marché nouveau ce sera ainsi. Si j'ai 4 pièces ce sera 300fr. par jour, dont j'ai 50%, c'est donc 150fr. d'assurés en dehors de mes droits.[105]

Clearly for Balzac the opportunity for making money through the sale of his *billets d'auteur* was as serious a financial consideration as his share in the box-office sales, and this preoccupation with financial success in the theatre is one of the most significant aspects of the dramatist's life which are reflected in his fiction.

The Dramatist in La Comédie humaine

The main focus of Balzac's portrayal of the dramatist is on the two fictional characters of Nathan and du Bruel, who in accordance with the overall scheme of recurring characters appear in peripheral roles throughout *La Comédie humaine.* The career of Nathan can be plotted from 1821 to 1843 and that of du Bruel from 1812 to 1845, and in *Illusions perdues, Une fille d'Eve* and *Les Employés* their roles as dramatists are examined in some detail.

In 1822 in *Un grand homme,* du Bruel, writing under the pseudonym of de Cursy, is the author of *L'Alcade dans l'embarras* in which Florine makes her debut at the Panorama-Dramatique. He is described here as: 'un jeune homme en redingote, petit, délié, tenant à la fois du bureaucrate, du propriétaire et de l'agent de change'.[106] The beginning of Nathan's role as a dramatist coincides with that of du Bruel. Having begun his career as a journalist and critic, Nathan's first attempt at writing for the stage is under his christian name of Raoul as du Bruel's co-author of *L'Alcade dans l'embarras.* A brief account of Nathan's early association with du Bruel is given

---

[105] *LMH*, vol. IV, p. 488.
[106] *IP*, vol. V, p. 376.

retrospectively in *Une fille d'Eve* where the action is set more than a decade later in 1835:

> Les revenus du théâtre l'avaient séduit; mais incapable du travail lent et soutenu que veut la mise en sène, il avait été obligé de s'associer à un vaudevilliste, à du Bruel, qui mettait en œuvre ses idées et les avait toujours réduites en petites pièces productives.[107]

Apart from Nathan and du Bruel the only other major character to achieve any success as a dramatist in *La Comédie humaine* is Félicité des Touches, who writes under the pseudonym of Camille Maupin. In 1822 in *Un grand homme* Mlle des Touches, who is then in her early thirties, is referred to as an eminent writer and in 1838 in *Béatrix* she is, according to Maxime de Trailles, an 'aubergiste de la littérature'.[108] From her first move to Paris in 1814, however, to her retirement to a convent in 1838, the story of Félicité des Touches is more that of a woman and her passions and disappointments in love than that of a dramatist and her career. The fact of her being a successful dramatist is used to highlight her creative and artistic sensibility as a woman, so that she functions in terms of her gender and emotions and not just as a representative dramatist.

Fulgence Ridal, who first appears in *La Comédie humaine* in *La Rabouilleuse* as a member of the *Cénacle* in 1819, is by 1821 a moderately successful and productive dramatist in *Un grand homme,* despite the fact that he is rather inclined to laziness. Ridal's role in *Un grand homme*, however, is very much confined to the background and contributes little to the portrayal of the dramatist's career. In *Les Comédiens sans le savoir* Ridal is, by 1845, an established *vaudevilliste* who undertakes the direction of a small theatre in association with Lousteau, but again this is a minor role.

The pressmen Finot and Lousteau also try their hand at writing for the stage but with little success. In *César Birotteau* Andoche Finot begins his career in 1818 by writing a one-act comedy but soon abandons the theatre in favour of journalism which he believes is likely to be much more profitable, and in *La Rabouilleuse* he is already, by 1820, the owner of a small theatre review. The journalist

---

[107] *FE*, vol. II, p. 302.
[108] *B*, vol. II, p. 919.

Etienne Lousteau in *Un grand homme* also makes an attempt at writing a play in collaboration with the real dramatist Ducange in 1822.[109] In the novel the play is produced the same year at the Gaîté, but like Finot, Lousteau chooses the journalistic career, preferring to exploit the work of others rather than go through the mental exertion of producing his own work. It is tempting also to classify Lucien de Rubempré in this category of failed dramatists who are lured by the press, but although Lucien's career is inextricably linked with the theatre, his early flourish of literary creativity produces an anthology of poems and a short novel but not any form of play.

The authenticity of Balzac's portrayal of the dramatist has been discussed by critics in so far as they have established that the major characters of Nathan and du Bruel may have been modelled on real dramatists with whom Balzac was acquainted,[110] but the more general historical aspects of the dramatist's career which they reveal have not been established. At the beginning of *Un grand homme*, Lucien's illusions include a naive conception of the dramatist's career, the glory of which he can only dream about: 'Etre auteur dramatique, se faire jouer, quel rêve caressé!'[111] This interior monologue expresses not Balzac's opinion but that of the central character, Lucien. The authorial voice and the character's voice become one and it is for the reader to distinguish that Balzac is ironising on the naivety of Lucien, for everywhere that Balzac makes a judgment on the theatrical world it is to criticise not to extol. If the 'rêve caressé' were ever Balzac's own then it might have been during his youth when in 1820 he read his version of *Cromwell* to his family and friends and submitted a

[109] *IP*, vol. V, p. 302. The play in question is *Agathe ou le Petit Vieillard de Calais*, which was written by Ducange in 1819.

[110] Pierre Citron proposes Gautier and Alexandre Dumas as models for Nathan. See: 'Aux Sources d'Une fille d'Eve', *AB* (1965). Citron notes in particular that Nathan's relationship witht he actress Florine, whom he eventually marries, is reminiscent of Dumas's relationship witht he actress, Mlle Ida, whom Dumas married in 1840. Citron also notes that there are elements of Balzac himself in Nathan. Certainly Nathan shares the combined interest in the novel, the theatre, journalism and politics of his creator and the failure in *Une fille d'Eve* of Nathan's attempt to establish a newspaper echos Balzac's own failure with the *Chronique de Paris* in 1836. Again, Nathan seems likely to be a composite representation of certain of Balzac's acquaintances and of his own experience.

[111] *IP*, vol. V, p. 299.

copy to the *comité de lecture* of the Théâtre-Français for it to be judged mediocre and unsuitable.[112]

In *La Comédie humaine*, however, the difficulties which the dramatist faced when submitting his work to a theatre are not revealed by Balzac. It is implied in *Un grand homme* that both Nathan and du Bruel use their journalistic influence as a lever to success, and the reader can also deduce that they benefit from the network of support in both the journalistic and commercial spheres for the launch of Florine's career since her first leading role is in their play. In *Une fille d'Eve* it is claimed that together du Bruel and Nathan have created Florine's career, but it is of course a two-way process and one in which Florine's protectors and other influential contacts have played a part; Florine's success is Nathan's and du Bruel's success and vice versa.

By the time du Bruel and Nathan are examined more closely in their role as dramatists in *Les Employés* and *Une fille d'Eve* respectively their careers are well established. Nathan's future seems assured since he has two successful plays to his name and has overcome the difficulty of making the transition from obscurity to public acclaim:

> La situation de Nathan paraissait donc extrêmement brillante. Il avait beaucoup d'amis. Deux pièces faites en collaboration et qui venaient de réussir fournissaient à son luxe et lui ôtaient tout souci pour l'avenir.[113]

It is not because of the amount of money made from these two plays that Nathan need have no worry for his future, but because now that he has had some measure of success it will be easier to have new work accepted and produced. This is not to say that he can take his future as a dramatist for granted, for he still needs to find the enormous energy to be 'à la fois sur trois théâtres: le Monde, le Journal et les Coulisses,'[114] in order to sustain the network of favour and protection which is in Balzac's view, as it was in reality, so vital to any success in the theatre.

---

[112] See above, p. 17.
[113] *FE*, vol. II, p. 347.
[114] *FE*, vol. II, p. 349.

In *Les Employés* du Bruel is sufficiently well established in both his career as a dramatist and as a bureaucrat to be able to adapt his official employment to suit the demands of the theatre, all the more so since his occasional articles in support of the Ministry afford him a certain favour with his superiors:

> Aussi, Rabourdin, très tolérant et très peu tracassier avec ses employés, le laissait-il aller à ses répétitions, venir à ses heures, et travailler à ses vaudevilles.[115]

Although the dramatists portrayed in Balzac's fiction are not seen experiencing the struggle to become established, authorial intervention in the narrative often reflects a view of the dramatist's situation which coincides with that expressed by Montigny and d'Heilly. Balzac notes the need for one of the co-authors of any play to keep in touch with the director in order to be sure that it is to be performed:

> L'*homme-mémoire* fait aussi la recette, c'est-à-dire veille à la composition de l'affiche, en ne quittant pas le directeur qu'il n'ait indiqué pour le lendemain une pièce de la société.[116]

Balzac also highlights the fickle nature of friendship where the dramatist is concerned, claiming, like Montigny, that Nathan's associates would be ready to offer advice and consolation in the face of failure, and prefer to encourage mediocrity rather than genius:

> Ainsi va le monde littéraire. On n'y aime que ses inférieurs. Chacun est l'ennemi de quiconque tend à s'élever. Cette envie générale décuple les chances des gens médiocres, qui n'excitent ni l'envie ni le soupçon, font leur chemin à la manière des taupes, et, quelque sots qu'ils soient, se trouvent casés au *Moniteur* dans trois ou quatre places au moment où les gens de talent se battent encore à la porte pour s'empêcher d'entrer.[117]

---

[115] *E*, vol. VII, p. 962.
[116] *Ibid.* p. 963.
[117] *FE*, vol. II, p. 343.

The question of mediocrity is important. Du Bruel's colleagues from the Ministry attend the performances of his plays as a group in order to support him, not because they find his plays worthy, but because he is a *bon enfant*. The implication is that they are not capable of independent critical judgment and that du Bruel is one of those who has launched his career through acceptable mediocrity rather than the gift of genius. Du Bruel's true talent lies in his ability to apply himself diligently to a proven formula: 'Du Bruel, vrai piocheur, lisait au bureau les livres nouveaux, en extrayait les mots spirituels et les enregistrait pour en émailler son dialogue'.[118] Even Ridal whose talent is not in question is said in *Un grand homme* to save his best work, that which is brightest and most original, for the private consumption of his friends because it is too sophisticated for public taste.

Balzac's concern in his portrayal of the dramatist is less with the mechanics of how a career is launched and conducted than with what that career might reveal about a character type or about Parisian life in general. The opinion expressed in *La Comédie humaine* is that in the theatre it is mediocre work which is accepted rather than the work of genius, and although Balzac had a particular, cynical interest in proposing this view, the accounts given by d'Heilly, Montigny and Duflot suggest that it is at least partly truthful.

Balzac highlights the issue of mediocrity by constant reference to the matter of co-authorship. According to Balzac's explanation of co-authorship in *Les Employés*, each of the co-authors of a play would fulfil a different function and in the case of a vaudeville there would normally need to be three authors since one would be responsible exclusively for the musical composition:

> Un auteur dramatique, comme peu de personnes le savent, se compose: d'abord d'un *homme à idées*, chargé de trouver les sujets et de construire la charpente ou *scénario* du vaudeville; puis d'un *piocheur*, chargé de rédiger la pièce; enfin d'un *homme-mémoire*, chargé de mettre en musique les couplets, d'arranger les chœurs et les morceaux d'ensemble, de les chanter, de les superposer à la situation.[119]

---

[118] *E*, vol. VII, p. 963
[119] *E*, vol. VII, p. 963.

This could of course be taken to mean that the dramatist is a multi-talented individual who must display a wide range of dramatic skills, but in the context of the discussion of Nathan and du Bruel it needs to be read literally, since each only possesses a certain part of the necessary skill. In his association with Nathan, du Bruel is the one who fulfils the function of the *piocheur* who is able to bring Nathan's ideas to fruition:

> Cursy (son nom de guerre) était estimé par ses collaborateurs, à cause de sa parfaite exactitude; avec lui, sûr d'être compris, l'homme aux sujects pouvait se croiser les bras.[120]

When his young colleague, Sébastien, asks du Bruel why he does not work alone, since he always attributes any weaknesses in a production to his co-authors, the narrator intervenes without giving the character the opportunity to reply: 'Il y avait d'excellentes raisons pour que du Bruel ne travaillât pas seul. Il était le tiers d'un auteur'.[121] On one level the remark adds to the characterisation of du Bruel, indicating both the limits of his talent and his failure to acknowledge them, but since du Bruel functions as the representative of a particular type of *employé-vaudevilliste* whom Balzac would later depict in his *Physiologie de l'employé* in 1841, the remark suggests that all authors working in this manner, like du Bruel, only possess a fraction of the necessary talent. This is the kind of authorial intervention and judgment which characterises much of Balzac's treatment of the theatrical world, for although he would pass for an impartial observer, his observation is frequently subjective.

Nathan is the *homme aux sujets*, full of ideas but lacking the tenacity and patience to carry them out, or perhaps too creative to confine himself to a prescribed formula. On the strength of the success earned in collaboration with du Bruel, a play which Nathan has written alone is staged at the Théâtre-Français, 'un grand drame tombé avec tous les honneurs de la guerre'.[122] This failure is not, however, a condemnation of Nathan's talent as a dramatist, for the play is considered a masterpiece by the 'connaisseurs' and 'vrais gens

---

[120] *Ibid.*
[121] *Ibid.*
[122] *FE*, vol. II, p. 302.

de goût'. The failure is rather a cynical observation on the theatre-going public and on the journalists who decry the play, preferring the mediocre products of Nathan's collaboration with du Bruel.

Financial necessity drives Nathan to pursue the path of co-authorship with du Bruel, for he can count on a successful and easy formula which will bring money in quickly, whereas it might take years of poverty to develop and gain recognition for his individual talent. Since Balzac is generally in the habit of describing minute calculations in the financial transactions of his characters, it is surprising that he does not give details of how much his fictional dramatists actually earn from their work; there is no mention of the financial terms agreed between authors and theatres nor of any private agreement between Nathan and du Bruel when they are working in collaboration, but this is not to say that economic issues are not important in the portrayal of the dramatist. On the contrary, where Nathan is concerned the primary issue is economic, for he is the very epitome of the dramatist driven by financial need. The prostitution of talent is a persistent concern in Balzac's examination of the artistic and literary world, and it is nowhere more apparent than in the character of Nathan who in his literary career devotes himself to churning out witty reviews and popular vaudevilles for quick financial gain rather than to developing his full potential:

> Tenu de produire par son manque de fortune, il allait du théâtre à la presse, et de la presse au théâtre, se dissipant, s'éparpillant et croyant toujours en sa veine.[123]

For modern critics of Balzac, most notably Hunt[124] and Prendergast,[125] Lousteau and Lucien are considered most guilty of prostituting their literary talent to the corrupt world of journalism. Nathan is accused of failing to fulfil his potential but is not accused of literary prostitution:

> His literary effort is dissipated and inconsistent. He is an egoist, 'paresseux au superlatif,' and thoroughly insincere. In a word,

---

[123] *FE*, vol. II, p. 303.
[124] Hunt, *Balzac's Comédie Humaine*, p. 211.
[125] Prendergast, *Balzac, Fiction and Melodrama*, p. 31.

Balzac makes of him the type of unfulfilled and ineffectual talent straining to show itself as genius.[126]

However, if Nathan chooses the easy route of collaboration with du Bruel for quick financial gain then it seems he has no more artistic integrity than his journalist colleagues. In generalised terms, sexual prostitution is considered to be a matter of necessity based on the assumption that given the opportunity to earn an equal amount of money by some other means or no need to earn money at all, one would not freely choose to engage in it. Certainly this is the case with Nathan's prostitution of talent, for the vocabulary used to describe his situation as a dramatist is the vocabulary of economic imperative, not of choice. He is 'tenu de produire',[127] the receipts from his plays are 'indispensables',[128] he is, 'sûr du succès en le voyant nécessaire',[129] and a stunning opening night is a 'nécessité'.[130] When Nathan cannot keep ahead of his creditors with the receipts from the plays he has already written, he increases the pressure to produce by borrowing against those he is yet to write: 'Florine lui conseilla d'emprunter sur des pièces de théâtre à faire, en les vendant en bloc et aliénant les revenus de son répertoire'.[131] Nathan's plays are not works of art, they are commodities to be bought and sold. As part of the industrialisation of society and the rise of bourgeois capitalism the creative urge has become an industrialised process, the success of which is measured in purely monetary terms.

Although Balzac does not specify the precise earnings of Nathan and du Bruel he does make reference to their additional payments in *billets d'auteur*. In *Un grand homme* the trade in tickets is mainly with the claque and with the journalists who in turn trade their tickets with Braulard for financial gain. In *Les Employés* there are frequent references to du Bruel's *billets d'auteur* and it is significant that Balzac, who so often intervenes as a didactic narrator to offer explanations of things with which his reader may not be familiar, does not offer any explanation or comment on this. This seems to

[126] *Ibid*, p. 221.
[127] *FE*, vol. II, p. 338.
[128] *FE*, vol. II, p. 338.
[129] *Ibid*. p. 346.
[130] *Ibid*.
[131] *Ibid*. p. 352.

suggest, as is claimed by Duflot, that the availability of such tickets to the public was so commonplace that Balzac's contemporary reader could not have failed to know about them.

Du Bruel gives his complimentary tickets to his friends and colleagues rather than trading them: one ticket each week is given to Dutocq for whom this is one of few luxuries; several are given to Sébastien; a couple each month go to Minard; and a box is offered to Mme Rabourdin at every opening night.[132] Du Bruel can afford to be generous with his tickets because he is not driven by the same financial need as Nathan. In fact, thanks to his other activities, du Bruel is in a secure financial position:

> Possédant une maison de campagne à Aulnay, rangé, plaçant son argent, du Bruel avait, outre les quatre mille cinq cents de sa place, douze cents de pension sur la Liste Civile et huit cents sur les cent mille écus d'encouragements aux Arts votés par la Chambre. Ajoutez à ces divers produits neuf mille francs gagnés par les *quarts*, les *tiers*, les *moitiés* de vaudevilles à trois théâtres différents, et vous comprendrez qu'au physique, il fût gros, gras, rond et montrât une figure de bon propriétaire.[133]

Du Bruel's position in fact reproduces something which was fairly common amongst nineteenth-century French dramatists, many of whom combined their literary career with some sort of administrative post. Balzac places this aspect of du Bruel's career firmly in reality by citing examples of these alongside his description of du Bruel:

> D'autres comme du Bruel, fabriquent des vaudevilles, des opéras-comiques, des mélodrames, ou dirigent des spectacles. En ce genre, on peut citer MM. Sewrin, Pixerécourt, Planard, etc. Dans leur temps, Pigault-Lebrun, Piis, Duvicquet avaient des places. Le premier libraire de M. Scribe fut un employé au Trésor.[134]

---

[132] *E*, vol. VII, p. 962 & p. 978.

[133] *Ibid.* p. 864.

[134] *Ibid.* Sewrin (1771-1835) was an archivist at the Hôtel des Invalides; Pixerécourt (1773-1844) was Inspecteur des Domaines; Planard (1783-1853) was employed at the Conseil d'Etat; Pigault-Lebrun (1753-1835) was Inspecteur des Salines; Piis (1755-1832) was secretary general at the Préfecture de Police and Duvicquet was secretary general at the Ministry of Police.

Eventually in *Un prince de la Bohème* du Bruel becomes a *pair de France*, the theatre having served merely as a stepping stone to his ultimate ambitions. Nathan, however, fails to amount to much after the demise of his newspaper and the thwarting of his political ambitions in a conspiracy mounted by his enemies, and ends his days 'dans une sinécure comme un homme médiocre'. Nathan's mistake, like that of Lucien, is to harbour ambitions above his station. His political aspirations arouse the jealousy of his peers in the world of journalism and the theatre and without the support of others he cannot realise his ambitions.

Somehow Balzac's representation of the dramatist is at odds with his own persistent desire to write successfully for the stage. There is no evidence of the dramatist's career as the 'rêve caressé' which constitutes part of Lucien's illusions, or of a vicarious fulfilment of Balzac's personal ambitions through his characters, nor is there a full historical account of the real difficulties which the dramatist faced with the reading committee or the censorship committee, which is surprising in view of Balzac's own experience with *Vautrin*, and there is no mention of the development of the *société des auteurs dramatiques*. Balzac's emphasis is rather on the industrialisation of the dramatist's craft, on the issue of co-authorship and the easy proliferation of mediocre work which this facilitated, and on the financial gains which were thereby afforded.

Conclusion – An Economic History

The portrayal of the claque, the theatre press and the dramatist in *La Comédie humaine* is faithful to historical reality, notwithstanding the fact that it is partial and selective. While Balzac convincingly captures the atmosphere of the period in the boulevard theatres, he also adds something of his own vision of social history. Balzac had made clear his intention to write the social history of his times in his *Avant-Propos* to *La Comédie humaine* in 1842. In the closing pages of *Illusions perdues* the following year, however, the much quoted words of Carlos Herrera clarify how Balzac viewed his interpretation of history as distinct from what he calls official history:

> Il y a deux Histoires; l'Histoire officielle, menteuse qu'on enseigne, l'Histoire ad usum delphini; puis l'Histoire secrète, où sont les véritables causes des événements, une Histoire honteuse.[135]

It is for this reason that Balzac's attention in his portrayal of the theatre industry is not focused on the administration of the theatres and on the details of their productions, which are more properly the work of such contemporaries as Gautier and Janin, but on aspects which reveal the hidden corruption and compromise beneath the surface appearance. Aspects of the theatre's history which appear to be taken for granted by the contemporary public and which are remarked upon only briefly and in a fragmented way by historians and social commentators, such as the presence of the claque, the jibes of the *feuilletons*, the issues of co-authorship and of concessionary tickets are endowed with historical importance by Balzac in accordance with his own intentions, explained in the *Avant-Propos*:

> En saisissant bien le sens de cette composition, on reconnaîtra que j'accorde aux faits constants, quotidiens, secrets ou patents, aux actes de la vie individuelle, à leurs causes et à leurs principes autant d'importance que jusqu'alors les historiens en ont attaché aux événements de la vie publique des nations.[136]

In this way Balzac is able to show the impact of those hidden or ignored aspects of the theatre's history both on society at large and on individual destinies. The impact of the theatre industry on those individuals who come into contact with it is economically determined. Money is the unifying thread between the press, the claque and the dramatist and the acquisition of it determines the behaviour and character of each individual in the chain of interaction. The press, the claque and the dramatist are shown to be interdependent within a system of trade and exchange where the individual strives for maximum financial gain. Prendergast makes the point in relation to *Le Père Goriot:*

> The model or metaphor of exchange constitutes a major focus for the 'totalizing' vision of the novel; it is, so to speak, one of the

[135] *IP*, vol. V, p. 695.
[136] *AP*, vol. I, p. 17.

lamps with which the narrator guides both reader and hero through the mysteries of the Parisian 'labyrinth' towards an understanding of its interconnected moral design.[137]

Similarly, in *Un grand homme* in particular, the system of exchange, explained at each juncture by the mephistophelean Lousteau, guides both the reader and Lucien through the 'labyrinth' of the theatre world. Each new phenomenon which Lucien meets with incredulity: the mercenariness of the claque, the trade in concessionary tickets, the obligations of the *Courrier des théâtres* to its subscribers, the moral compromises of the actress and the artistic compromises of the dramatist, is explained by Lousteau in terms of trade, exchange and mutual gain.

The effect of becoming part of an environment in which the pivotal force is a system of trade and exchange is damaging to the individual, for in Balzac's world view it is the type of opportunism which this is shown to promote which is at the root of human corruption. *l'intérêt*, we are told by Balzc, develops man's *penchants mauvais*. This is certainly the case in the theatre where all who come into contact with its backstage operations are corrupted or compromised by economic opportunism: Lousteau and Finot abandon any aspirations to be dramatists in favour of the unscrupulous spoils of theatre journalism, becoming cynical and exploitative, Braulard and the claque are shown to be treacherous parasites, and Nathan and du Bruel thrive on mediocrity while the members of the *cénacle* strive for artistic recognition.

The struggle for triumph and survival in the economic system of the theatre is one of perpetual combat. Again this is consistent with Balzac's view of Parisian society as a whole as exemplified by Rastignac's defiant assertion at the end of *Le Père Goriot* where he threatens to fight and win. The combat is intensified in the theatre not only because the selective emphasis is on its most corrupt and compromising aspects but also because there are no characters who do not enter the fight. Even Coralie battles until her dying breath to re-establish her ruined career.

All those involved in the combat against Lucien and Coralie have a different personal motive, but the effect is that the two individuals are impotent in the face of the collective power. Braulard and the claque

---

[137] Prendergast, *Balzac: Fiction and Melodrama*, p. 77.

are prepared to become the instruments of Lucien's enemies in the press because they succumb to the financial imperative. Similarly Florine enters the pact for the benefit of her own career. The motives of Florine and the claque who will execute the plan are different from those of the main group of conspirators, but all have self-interest in common.

Rastignac will be able to triumph over society partly because he adopts some its values which are most abhorrent to him and partly because he already has influential friends. In the world of the theatre, Lucien cannot succeed, for it is the adoption of its amoral value system and the subsequent switching of newspapers for personal gain without any secure allegiances on either side of the political camp which creates so many enemies for him. The fight for survival in Paris may be a combat of the individual against society but as Hemmings has pointed out, it is a fight which can only be won with support from others:

> In *La Comédie humaine* the unsupported individual almost always goes under. Only when he can form an alliance with those whose interests coincide with his is he able to flout society, its laws and institutions. However strong the individual real strength lies in numbers.[138]

Lucien falls because he steps outside the chain of interdependency on which the theatre world depends. The same fate befalls Nathan when he too steps out of the theatre world to advance his career in politics. The dramatist Nathan creates enemies in the same way as the journalist Lucien by harbouring ideas above his station, and is forced to resign himself to the mediocrity which is a part of the theatre environment.

While the social institution of the theatre performs a unique function in so far as it brings together otherwise exclusive social groups, the industry which it generates operates according to the same economic system as society at large, and in this sense it is a microcosm of that society. The portrayal of the theatre industry is consistent with Balzac's intention to write the *Histoire Secrète* because it shows the theatre developing not just as a result of political

---

[138] Hemmings, *Balzac, An Interpretation of La Comédie humaine* (New York: Random House, 1967) p. 139.

and legislative changes but as a result of underlying economic and social forces.

The outcome of the economic imperative of the theatre in *La Comédie humaine* is the industrialisation of the art form, so that plays are treated as commodities and the theatre is a market place for the corrupt enterprises of the press and the claque. In his portrayal of the theatre Balzac endows the machinations of the press and the claque with more importance than the productions themselves firstly in order to facilitate the narrative outcomes of the plot and secondly in order to emphasise the industrialisation of the creative process, which, as Lucien discovers in *Un grand homme,* applies to all literature:

> Depuis deux heures, aux oreilles de Lucien tout se résolvait par de l'argent. Au théâtre comme en Librairie, en Librairie comme au Journal, de l'art et de la gloire, il n'en était pas question.[139]

In 1840 Sainte-Beuve directly accused Balzac himself of this industrialisation of art in *Dix ans après en littérature,* claiming that his novels were more remarkable for their quantity than their quality, and indirectly his criticisms of the *feuilletonistes* and the *Société des Gens de Lettres* contained in an article published in the *Revue des deux mondes* in 1839 under the title of *De la littérature industrielle* were also levelled at Balzac.[140] It is well known that much of Balzac's work was produced at great speed and with a sense of financial opportunism,[141] for the fact is of course that Balzac was himself caught up in and conditioned by the very processes of historical and social change which he had set out to observe.

---

[139]   *IP*, vol. V, pp. 303 & 378.
[140]   Sainte-Beuve, 'De la littérature industrielle', in *Revue des deux mondes* (Aug. 1839), pp. 675-691.
[141]   See for example: *Corres*, vol. III, p. 575 à Zulma Carraud, March 1839: 'La Renaissance m'avait promis 6 000fr. de prime pour lui faire une pièce en 5 actes; [...] Comme il me fallait 6 000 francs à la fin de fevrier, je me mets à l'Œuvre.' *LMH*, vol. I, p. 663, 20 Jan. 1840: 'Je ne puis avoir de tranquillité, qu'après avoir gagné par un succès au théâtre assez d'argent pour tout apaiser [...]. Je prépare plusieurs ouvrages pour la scène, afin de payer le plus possible dans cette année-ci.' *LMH*, vol. II, p. 26, 30 Sept. 1841: 'Songez que pour pouvoir plus sûrement payer mes dettes, je finirai une comédie pour le mois de décembre.'

'L'HORRIBLE CARRIERE DU THEATRE'

'L'horrible carrière du théâtre'[1] – Balzac as author/narrator, uses this phrase in *La Rabouilleuse* when describing the launch of Mariette's career as an actress. The image of the theatrical world which Balzac presents to his reader is such that members of the acting profession are seen to be pursuing a career which is morally and artistically compromising as well as physically draining. This particular view of the theatre must surely have been coloured by Balzac's own frustrations and disappointments as his repeated attempts to break into the theatrical world as a dramatist met with failure.

The actresses of *La Comédie humaine* have been the subject of extensive critical study in relation to the role of women in nineteenth-century society and most specifically to the role of the courtesan. In *La Courtisane romantique,* W.H. Van der Gun pays particular attention to Balzac's fictional actresses as the representation of a necessary element of the social group which constitutes 'le monde littéraire, politique et galant':

> *Illusions perdues* explique pourquoi une carrière littéraire ou politique implique nécessairement la présence d'une courtisane. C'est dans son salon que s'affrontent éditeurs et écrivains ou que des politiciens pressés d'arriver flairent le bon vent. [...] Tout s'enchaîne, c'est le jeune auteur du Bruel et le journaliste Nathan qui ont lancé Coralie et Florine sur la scène du Panorama-Dramatique, mais le succès de la pièce dépend surtout de quelques articles de journaux. C'est surtout dans *Illusions perdues* que la vénalité des actrices acquiert le sens symbolique de la corruption des âmes et de la prostitution de l'esprit.[2]

No distinction is made here between the serious actress and the actress who uses her profession merely in order to ply her alternative trade and the actress/courtesan is assessed only in relation to her role in the moral degeneration of society. For Maurice Bardèche the

---

[1] *R*, vol. IV, p. 317.
[2] W.H. Van der Gun, *La Courtisane Romantique et son rôle dans 'la Comédie humaine' de Balzac* (Assen, Pays-Bas: Van Gorcum, 1963), p. 97.

prostitution in which Balzac's fictional actresses engage is central to an understanding of certain novels because it is the 'lierre monstrueux qui tapisse toute la façade de la société capitaliste.'[3]

H.J. Hunt extends his analysis of the actress/courtesan Coralie, to take account of her individual qualities, but still his emphasis is on her sexuality and function as a prostitute and not on her role as an actress:

> When Coralie meets Lucien she falls in love for the first time: violently, for Balzac was ready to allow an unlimited capacity for genuine passion and selfless devotion to the soiled dolls of the theatre and the opera house. [...] Coralie is vulgar, uneducated and unintelligent yet Balzac has made her unreflecting forthrightness a corrective to her amorality. Her passionate and humble attachment gives her something which might be called saintliness, if it were manifested in a better cause and with less sensual gusto.[4]

Donald Adamson takes some account of Coralie's experience as an actress as the catalyst of Lucien's undoing, for it is she who encourages him to adopt the skills of her profession and to assume roles:

> As an actress she is used to appearing before the widest of Parisian worlds, the theatre; but, as an actress, she also has two faces: the inner self and the theatrical mask. This ability to superimpose an artificial identity upon her true self is helpful to her, [...]. But it is also of the greatest possible detriment to Lucien that she should encourage him, not to strive to hammer out his own identity, but instead to dissolve and destroy that identity beneath an endless succession of masks.[5]

No critic, however, looks at how Balzac actually represents the mechanics, legalities and conditions of the actress's career in the theatre – conditions which were often responsible for forcing the actress into a life of prostitution. An important feature of the actresses' prostitution is the role played by the wealthy businessmen

---

[3] Maurice Bardèche, *Une lecture de Balzac* (Paris: Les Sept Couleurs,1964) p. 150.

[4] Herbert J. Hunt, *Balzac's 'Comédie humaine'*, p. 219.

[5] Donald Adamson, *Balzac, 'Illusions perdues'*, p. 32.

who support them.   These protectors are, without exception, driven
by the twin imperatives of sex and money and it is in this context that
modern critics have analysed their role in Balzac's fiction, however,
the historical basis of the role of the protector has not been
established.

       The purpose of this examination is to establish the extent to
which Balzac's portrayal of the actress's career reflects general
historical and sociological truths and how those truths or falsehoods
function in the overall narrative scheme of *La Comédie humaine*.
The historicity of Balzac's portrayal of careers in the theatre will be
assessed here in relation to the evidence found in contemporary
historical and modern critical sources.   The history of theatrical
careers is an immense subject, rich in examples from the lives of the
hundreds of actors and actresses who were employed in the Parisian
theatres during the first half of the century; the treatment here will
therefore be selective and confined to aspects of historical evidence
which are of particular relevance to *La Comédie humaine*.

The Acting Profession – An Historical Overview

Just as the boulevard theatres began to flourish in the 1820s,
engendering many new plays and legions of aspiring dramatists, so
too the number of actors and actresses engaged by the theatres
increased.   The opportunity to offer a wider variety of productions
than those strictly prescribed by the Napoleonic regime meant that
most theatres would employ several different troupes at the same
time, and particularly those boulevard theatres which offered three or
four short pieces in the course of the same evening.   Duflot explains
in *Les Secrets des coulisses* that each theatre had its 'troupe d'or'
which was composed of its best actors and only performed plays by
the most successful authors, its 'troupe d'argent,' the members of
which were generally talented but needed good plays in order to
make money for the theatre, and the 'rogunes de fer-blanc,' who
would perform the short plays at the beginning of the programme.[6]

       Additionally, short production runs and frequent changes of
programme afforded ample opportunity for the ambitious newcomer
to break into this growth industry.   Montigny claims that according to

---

[6] Duflot, *Les secrets des coulisses*, p. 226.

the *Almanach des théâtres* for 1825 the number of people employed on the stage in Paris alone was around 450 and this figure does not include musicians, extras and chorus girls:

> Le nombre des acteurs, chanteurs, danseurs, actrices, chanteuses, et danseuses qui exploitent les douze théâtres de la capitale, est de quatre cent cinquante environ; à aucune époque ce nombre n'a été dépassé.[7]

Alhoy's *Grande biographie dramatique*, published the previous year, gives details of many of these artists,[8] but it seems fair to assume that there would have been many more who made only a brief appearance and disappeared into obscurity without ever attracting the attention of the press or the biographers.

It was not uncommon during the first half of the nineteenth century for an actress's career to begin at a very early age, particularly since the minimum age requirement for entrance to the Conservatoire, where actors and actresses were trained for the major state theatres, was only eleven. Indeed, the actress, Léontine Fay, born in 1810, first appeared on stage at only five years of age and caused a sensation when she first appeared at the Gymnase at the age of eleven.[9] However, there were few actresses who could enjoy such acclaim so soon in their career. The majority, particularly in the boulevard theatres where there was little or no formal training, would be struggling for recognition among the extras and chorus girls for many years, possibly without ever achieving any measure of success.

Gautier, in his ironic style, remarks how in this struggle for recognition actresses would employ all the skills of their craft both on and off stage, demonstrating a natural propensity to intrigue and subterfuge:

> Quelque compliquée que soit l'intrigue du drame qu'on vient de jouer, elle est d'une simplicité extrême en comparaison des imbroglios dédaliens qui s'ourdissent au foyer, derrière la toile de fond, ou d'un portant à un autre. [...] Il est difficile d'imaginer ce

---

[7] Montigny, *Le Provincial à Paris*, vol. II, p. 336.

[8] Alhoy, *Grande biographie dramatique* (Paris: chez les marchands de nouveautés, 1824).

[9] *LCH*, vol. XII, Index, p. 1678.

> qu'une actrice dépense de finesse, de talent, de patience, de ruses, de machinations, pour se faire accorder un rôle, et surtout pour l'ôter à une rivale.[10]

It is precisely this type of backstage drama described by Gautier which will be seen to be central to Balzac's portrayal of the actress's career.

During the period covered by Balzac's work, the theatre was the only area of employment where the opportunities available to women were equal in both number and remuneration to those available to men. As could be expected, however, salaries and conditions in the boulevard theatres which were run on purely commercial lines, were generally poorer than in the major state theatres. Since the portrayal of the acting profession in *La Comédie humaine* is confined almost exclusively to the boulevard theatres it is sufficient here to say that at the state theatres it was usual for established members of the troupe to be *sociétaires*, giving them the right to an agreed salary and/or a share of the box office takings, to take part in decisions relating to production, casting and administration, and to remain employed until their death or voluntary retirement.[11]

This security was far from the norm in the boulevard theatres, however, where average salaries during the period from 1820 to the mid 1840s ranged between approximately 300 and 3,000 francs per annum. Bouffé began his career at the Panorama-Dramatique in 1820 on just 25 francs per month, gradually working his way up to 3,000 francs per annum before the closure of this theatre in 1823.[12] Lecomte's history of the Panorama-Dramatique gives details from the theatre's accounts in April 1822 which show that the actress, Florville, was earning 1,100 francs per annum at that time.[13] It was usual at most theatres for part of any salary to be made up of what were known as *feux*, an agreed allowance for each performance. According to Duflot's glossary (1865) the term dates from the previous century when actors were responsible for heating their own

---

[10]   Gautier, *Souvenirs de théâtre, d'art et de critique* (Paris: Charpentier, 1882), p. 184

[11]   Hemmings, *The Theatre Industry in Nineteenth-Century France*, pp.183-198.

[12]   Bouffé, *Mes Souvenirs*, p. 41.

[13]   Lecomte, *Le Panorama-Dramatique*, p. 32.

dressing rooms and were granted a special allowance in order to do so.[14]

Most actresses would spend the greater part of their salary on costumes and accessories, since in all theatres costumes were provided only for period dramas. For male actors the expense of providing contemporary costumes was not too much of a burden, but for women with many costume changes and rapidly changing fashions it was a different matter entirely.[15] As well as costumes the actress also had to have an extensive range of make-up and wigs at her disposal, all of which had to be paid for out of her own purse.[16]

Hemmings quotes Antoine's *Le Théâtre Libre* published in 1892 as the main source of information on the subject of costume provision. However, evidence not previously cited by historians of the theatre can be found which relates specifically to the first half of the century. While Lacan and Paulmier's directory of laws governing the theatre makes no mention of any formal obligation on the part of either actors or theatres regarding the provision of costumes, it does mention costumes in article 210 as follows:

> L'acteur qui fait des achats de costumes pour ses rôles ne fait pas un acte de commerce, car il n'achète ni pour revendre, ni pour louer, ni pour l'exploitation d'une industrie commerciale. La seule chose qu'il loue c'est son travail. Les costumes ne sont que des moyens accessoires à l'aide desquels le travail doit se produire.[17]

The fact that written clarification of this was necessary at all implies that, contrary to what has now become the norm, it was indeed common practice for actors to purchase their own costumes during the period leading to the publication of this work in 1853. Lacan and Paulmier also note that it was not uncommon for a theatre to pay an

---

[14] Duflot, *Les Secrets des coulisses*, p. 104.

[15] Gautier claims in an article on Parisian actresses (*La Presse* 11 August1845), that actresses could have to change costume as many as ten or twelve times in one evening.

[16] Duflot, *Les Secrets des coulisses*, p. 132; the make-up items listed by Duflot are: *Rouge végétal, Rouge liquide, Blanc de baleine, Poudre de riz, Poudre d'iris, Pomade de concombre, Cire vierge fondue et parfumée* and *Eau de la Floride* for hair styling.

[17] Lacan & Paulmier, *Traité de la législation des théâtres*, p. 244.

actress an advance on her salary in order to help her meet her
expenses for the production but in the event of her debut being
unsuccessful, the theatre had the legal right to cancel the appointment
without notice and the actress was legally obliged to pay back any
sum advancd by the theatre.[18] It seems reasonable to assume that any
such expenses incurred by an actress would be for costumes and
accessories.

Further evidence regarding the provision of costumes can be
found in d'Heilly's work published in 1861:

> Je sais d'avance que Mlle X..., du théâtre de ..., gagne 2 000 francs
> par an, et je la vois, dans une pièce nouvelle, afficher pour 10 000
> fr. de dentelles et de diamants. Comment voulez-vous que j'aille
> supposer autre chose que cette naturelle et simple vérité: Mlle X...
> a un amant![19]

D'Heilly's point highlights the role of the protector in the theatre
which will be addressed later in this chapter, however, it is significant
here that the extravagance of the actress's costume is compared not to
what the theatre company itself might have otherwise provided, but
with what the actress actually earns. Although it is not explicitly
stated, the implication is that the actress would otherwise have had to
fund her costume from her own meagre salary.

There was no legal obligation for theatres to make any payments
to actors during periods of illness[20] and until baron Taylor set up the
Association de secours mutuels entre les artistes in 1840 there was no
official system of financial aid for actors and actresses who became
ill or unemployed. A letter from the actor Samson to the director of
the *Revue et gazette des théâtres* on 2 June 1855 outlines the
purposes of the society:

> Il y a quatorze ans, M. le baron Taylor réunissait chez lui des
> acteurs de différens théâtres; il les entretenait de leurs camarades
> pauvres, et (chose plus cruelle) languissant dans une pauvreté sans
> espoir; il leur montrait l'incertitude de leur avenir, la nécessité de

---

[18] Lacan & Paulmier, *Traité de la législation des théâtres,* art. 315-317, p. 327.
[19] Georges d'Heilly, *Le Scandale au théâtre*, p. 99.
[20] Lacan & Paulmier, *Traité de la législation des théâtres*, art. 330, p. 347.

s'unir entre eux pour conjurer des chances propre fatales, pour
secourir des misères nombreuses

Additionally, an examination of the press reveals that it was common
for acting companies to conduct benefit performances in aid of
colleagues who were either ill, without work or facing retirement and
prior to the establishment of Taylor's society this would have been
the only source of aid for the actor or actress in distress.[21]
Many actresses still found themselves in desperate financial
circumstances even after an illustrious career. Léontine Fay who had
made such a promising start at the Gymnase in 1821, which Balzac
refers to in *Un grand homme* saying that in 1822 she was 'la grande
merveille du moment,'[22] was, according to Balzac's letter to Madame
Hanska on 11 May 1843, burnt out by her early thirties and could no
longer make 'cent écus de recette'.[23]   Similarly, according to
Lemonnier, even the famous actress Déjazet whose career had
extended from 1828 to 1844, ended her days in penury, relying on
colleagues and friends to give on her account one of the benefit
performances so often advertised in the press:

> J'eus l'honneur d'être un des amis de Déjazet, qui fut la comédienne
> la plus fêtée de Paris. Elle mourut pauvre, et encore, trois ans avant
> sa fin, dut-on lui organiser une représentation de retraite.[24]

If such could be the fate of the famous it seems hardly surprising that
the ephemeral actresses of the boulevard theatres should have been
inclined to exploit their physical attributes for as long as they were
able to.

Balzac's Acquaintance with the Actress/Courtesan

According to Balzac's biographers, the only actress/courtesan with
whom he was personally aquainted was Olympe Descuilliers, known

---

[21] The *Miroir des spectacles* in particular details benefit performances almost
weekly.
[22] *IP*, vol. V, p. 536.
[23] *LMH*, vol. II, p. 213.
[24] Lemonnier, *Les Abus du théâtre* (Paris: Tresse & Stock, 1895), p. 16.

as Olympe Pélissier. Born in 1799, Olympe began her career as a *petit rat*, one of the groups of hopeful young girls as young as ten or eleven employed in the theatres, and in particular at the opera, on pitiful wages to make up the dance troupes, choirs, extras and so on. Olympe had been sold by her mother to a young duke, but by 1830 when Balzac met her for the first time, she had grown into a beautiful and intelligent woman who was the mistress of Eugène Sue and the hostess of a *salon* frequented by Rossini whom she was eventually to marry in 1847.[25]

During the course of 1831 Balzac had a brief relationship with Olympe and their correspondence indicates that even after this ended he continued to be invited to her *salon*: This is confirmed by a letter of 2 January 1832 from Olympe to Balzac:

> Puis-je compter sur vous pour lundi prochain 9 courant. Rossini dîne chez moi ce sera bien pour commencer l'année; vous devez être en amabilité plus que jamais. Ce temps de repos n'a dû que vous rendre plus brillant.[26]

Olympe's life seems to have provided Balzac with some of the biographical details of many of his fictional actress/courtesans. Esther, the reader is told in *La Torpille*, had begun her career as a *petit rat*;[27] Coralie is said in *Un grand homme* to have been sold by her mother to de Marsay in 1819 at the age of fifteen;[28] and Tullia is said in *Un prince de la Bohème* to have been supported through the early years of her career at least partly by the young duc du Rhétoré.[29] However, it is Olympe's *salon* which seems to have been the greatest inspiration to Balzac, for his courtesans are not just mistresses, but more importantly are hostesses whose lavish homes become the stages for the interplay of the bohemian world of the artist and the corrupt world of business.

---

[25] Arrigon, *Les Années romantiques de Balzac* (Paris: Perrin, 1927), pp. 82-85; and Wurmser, *La Comédie inhumaine* (Paris: Gallimard, 1964), p. 311.

[26] *Corres.*, vol. I, p. 642.

[27] *SetM*, vol. VI, pp.440-442.

[28] *IP*, vol. V, p. 387.

[29] *Pr.B*, vol. VII, p. 826.

The Actresses of La Comédie humaine

The first thing to recognise in Balzac's portrayal of stage careers is that he confines his treatment exclusively to female performers. While this fact highlights the importance of the theatre as an area of female employment, this is rather incidental to the narrative since it is not primarily their talents and achievements as actresses which are portrayed in Balzac's actresses, but rather their talents as seductresses, for they are, without exception, also courtesans. The exclusion of male actors from the foreground of *La Comédie humaine* appears to be a deliberate move to maintain a particular balance of power and trade in relationships which Balzac was keen to expose, and will be addressed in more detail in the final part of this chapter. In contrast to other fields of female employment, which are portrayed as menial and domestic or somehow not serious and gainful, the theatre is shown as an area where a woman could have some semblance of competing with men on equal terms, where she could talk in terms of a career and of personal ambition. The only female character of *La Comédie humaine* who has any kind of notable career other than that of a stage performer is Mlle des Touches who is a dramatist under the name of Camille Maupin, for it is only in the world of the theatre where normal social conventions no longer apply, that her sex achieves any degree of liberation.

The theatrical careers of Balzac's fictional actresses are often brief and serve only as a lever to their more prominent roles as courtesans. The reference to Esther having been a *rat* at the Opéra is fleeting and incidental and is her only contact with the theatre, for after this, through the course of *Splendeurs et misères des courtisanes,* she becomes one of Paris's most prominent courtesans.[30] Malaga, born in 1817, is a horse-back performer at the Cirque-Olympique in 1837 where she makes acquaintance with Paz and Laginski who become her protectors.[31] Later, in 1845 she is being supported by Cardot and nothing is known of her after this date.[32] Jenny Cadine is referred to as one of the best actresses of the boulevard theatres, from where she

---

[30] *SetM*, vol. VI, pp. 440-442.
[31] *FM*, vol. II, p. 222.
[32] *CP*, vol. VII, p. 701.

progresses to the Italiens,[33] but she is never actually seen at work in the theatre. Rather, her importance in *La Comédie humaine* is as Hulot's *protégée* at the age of thirteen.[34] The same is true of Josépha Mirah who begins her career under the protection of Crevel in 1829,[35] secures a position at the Italiens in 1834 thanks to Hulot's financial support[36] and finally ends as *prima donna* at the Opéra in 1843.[37] The reader is told of Josépha's professional achievements but Josépha is never actually seen at work in the theatre.

Other actresses, Florentine, Mariette, Olympe Cardinal, Héloïse Brisetout, are but background characters in the general scene of the 'monde littéraire et galant' whose reappearance throughout *La Comédie humaine*, often included alongside references to real actors and actresses of the day, serves as part of the general scheme of recurring characters, giving a sense of cohesion, continuity and reality to the events in which they otherwise play only a minor part. Florentine is born in 1804, makes her debut at the Gaîté as a dancer in 1820[38] and disappears into obscurity after 1840. Mariette, born in 1804, is a friend of Florentine and also a dancer but considerably more successful, making her debut at the Opéra in 1821[39] where she is still a celebrated *premier sujet* in 1845.[40] Olympe Cardinal, born in 1824, leaves home at the age of fourteen after refusing the advances of Cérizet and is discovered by her mother in 1841 at the Théâtre Bobino,[41] a third-rate boulevard theatre notorious for its poor productions and its riotous audiences. Héloïse Brisetout is protected by Crevel in the 1830s[42] and in 1845 is the mistress of Gaudissart at whose theatre she is *première danseuse*.[43]

In terms of the historicity of Balzac's representation of the theatre in *La Comédie humaine*, the actresses who are most important are

[33] *Be.*, vol. VII, p. 1173.
[34] *Ibid.*, p. 64.
[35] *Ibid.*, p. 63.
[36] *Ibid.*, p . 65.
[37] *Ibid.*, p. 376.
[38] *MD*, vol. IV, p. 738.
[39] *R*, vol. IV, p. 316.
[40] *CP*, vol. VII, p. 699.
[41] *Bou.*, vol. VIII, p. 172.
[42] *Be.*, vol. VII, p. 158.
[43] *CP*, vol. VII, p. 531.

Tullia, Coralie and Florine. Tullia, born in 1799 is *premier suject de danse* at the Opéra from 1817 to 1827.[44]   In 1830 she marries the dramatist du Bruel after a relationship lasting seven years[45] and finally achieves her ambition to become a *comtesse* in 1839 when du Bruel becomes a pair de France.[46] Coralie, born in 1804, is sold by her mother to de Marsay at the age of fifteen and enters the theatre 'par désespoir' when he is bored with her.[47] Her first acting success is at the Panorama-Dramatique in 1822 where she demonstrates real talent.[48]   Coralie dies later that year, exhausted by excessive work, repeated illnesses and the emotional strain of the conspiracy against Lucien.[49] Florine is less gifted than her rival, Coralie, but among the actresses of *La Comédie humaine* her career is the most prominent. Born in 1805, she makes her debut at an unnamed boulevard theatre at the age of fifteen although she has played minor walk-on parts since the age of thirteen.[50]   Florine works her way up from the Panorama-Dramatique, via the Gymnase to the Opéra, until in 1845 she eventually marries Nathan, after which no more is known of her.[51]

Clearly it is dangerous to make too great a distinction in an analysis of Balzac's work between the function of the courtesan and the function of the actress since the two are inextricably linked in his characters. The amalgamation of the two roles is highlighted by the fact that the skills of simulation, role-playing, feigned emotions and capacity to handle intrigue convincingly, all of which are required of

---

[44] *PrB*, vol. VII, pp. 825-826.
[45] *Ibid.*
[46] *Ibid.*, p. 836.
[47] *IP*, vol. V, p. 388.
[48] *Ibid.*, p. 372.
[49] *Ibid.*, p. 546.
[50] *FE*, vol. II, p. 316.
[51] *CSS*, vol. VII, p. 1211.

the boulevard actress, are precisely the qualities which equip those same characters for their roles as accomplished courtesans. Nevertheless, the acting experiences of Tullia, Coralie and Florine reveal general observations on the social and historical position of their profession from the early 1820s to the mid 1840s.

The promotion of Balzac's fictional actresses from *rats* or *comparses* to leading ladies is shown to depend not only on their protectors, on the claque and on the press but also on their own capacity to survive in a treacherous and competitive environment. It is the sense of rivalry and capacity for intrigue described by Gautier in his *Souvenirs de théâtre*[52] which are the key to Florine's success, and it is because Coralie does not possess these that she cannot survive. Coralie has genuine talent but she does not have the wiles necessary to exploit it:

> Le talent, déjà si rare dans l'art extraordinaire du comédien, n'est qu'une condition du succès, le talent est même longtemps nuisible s'il n'est accompagné d'un certain génie d'intrigue qui manquait absolument à Coralie.[53]

Coralie and Florine are supposed to be friends but Balzac shows that where personal ambition is concerned the actress can no more rely on supposed friendship than can her journalist lover and in the battle of rivalry which follows Coralie is no match for Florine:

> Coralie était incapable de se défendre contre les rivalités et les manœuvres des coulisses auxquelles s'adonnait Florine, fille aussi dangereuse, aussi dépravée déjà que son amie était simple et généreuse.[54]

The intrigue to which Coralie falls victim is essentially a male conspiracy against Lucien but it is one in which Florine's complicity is advantageous to her own career. In the face of failure Coralie is offered the same hollow consolations as are offered to the dramatist in the same circumstances; her *loge* is filled with people proffering

---

[52] See above, p. 134.
[53] *IP*, vol. V, p. 527.
[54] *IP*, vol. V, p. 527.

advice but these are the very people who have engineered the failure of the play.

Coralie earns 500 francs per month,[55] but although this is considerably more than the 25 francs per month which the real actor Bouffé earned as a debutant and the 1,100 francs per annum which Florville earned at the Panorama-Dramatique,[56] it is still not enough for her to avoid accumulating debts and her failure is a blow to both her pride and her purse. Lucien attempts to console Coralie by telling her that if the director of the Gymnase wants to he can buy back her appointment and dashes out to Frascati's gaming house in a desperate bid to win some money. It is a small detail in the narrative but one which reveals the very real pressure which an actress was under when making her debut. It can be assumed that Coralie has already received and spent at least some of her salary in advance and, as has been shown by reference to Lacan and Paulmier, she would have been legally obliged to repay this even if it had been spent on costumes for the production.

Coralie's subsequent illness can only aggravate her financial difficulties, since in reality there would have been no sick-pay or other financial help available as Taylor's poor fund was not founded until 1840 and the action here is in 1822. Coralie is devastated to have lost her role to Florine, but it is not just *amour-propre* which is at the centre of the rivalry between them. It is also, according to actual employment conditions prevailing in the theatre at the time, a financial imperative. A benefit performance might have been a possible source of help but since Coralie and Lucien are by this stage without friends in the theatre and since it is Balzac's specific intention to depict 'l'horrible carrière du théâtre' in its most negative

---

[55] *IP*, vol. V, p. 430. In a note in the Pléiade edition (p. 1310), Roland Chollet claims by reference to Lecomte's history of the Panorama-Dramatique, that 'ces appointements correspondent à ce que pouvait gagner un débutant au Panorama-Dramatique. En avril 1822, l'actrice Florville y recevait 1 100 francs et Bouffé 300.' (p. 1310). However, I have to disagree with this since the accounts which are reproduced by Lecomte, although computed in April 1822, are for a whole year, and Coralie's salary seems very high by comparison. This can be established by close scrutiny of other entries in the accounts which are shown as multiples of 12 months, and by cross-calculation to the final balance sheet. See Lecomte, *Histoire des théâtres, Le Panorama-Dramatique*, pp. 97-105.

[56] Bouffé, *Mes Souvenirs*, p. 41.

light, no such benefit performance is offered to Coralie and so, continually unwell and exhausted by her efforts to re-establish her acting career, she is finally forced to seek the help of her protector, Camusot, and to promise to return to him.   It is this moral compromise which deals the final blow to Coralie and leaves Lucien with the indignity of composing vulgar songs in order to pay for her funeral.

In his long, didactic commentary on Parisian life at the beginning of *La Fille aux yeux d'or* (1834-1835), Balzac emphasises that he sees life on the stage as morally, physically and emotionally draining:

> Le comédien joue jusqu'à minuit, étudie le matin, répète à midi [...]
> La concurrence, les rivalités, les calomnies assassinent ces talents.
> Les uns désespérés, roulent dans les abîmes du vice, les autres
> meurent jeunes et ignorés pour s'être escompté trop tôt leur avenir.
> Peu de ces figures, primitivement sublimes, restent belles.[57]

The point is reiterated in *Une fille d'Eve* (1838-39), where Balzac again insists that the glamorous appearance of the actress's life hides cruel realites:

> Beaucoup de gens, séduits par le magnifique piédestal que le
> Théâtre fait à une femme, la supposent menant la joie d'un
> perpétuel carnaval. Au fond de bien des loges de portiers, sous la
> tuile de plus d'une mansarde, de pauvres créatures rêvent, au retour
> du spectacle, perles et diamants, robes lamées d'or et cordelières
> somptueuses, se voient les chevelures illuminées, se supposent
> applaudies, achetées, adorées, enlevées; mais toutes ignorent les
> réalités de cette vie de cheval de manège où l'actrice est soumise à
> des répétitions sous peine d'amende, à des lectures de pièces, à des
> études constantes de rôles nouveaux, par un temps où l'on joue
> deux ou trois cents pièces par an à Paris.[58]

It is precisely the demands of this type which exhaust the sensitive nature of Coralie and contribute to her premature death.

---

[57] *FYO*, vol. V, p. 1049.
[58] *FE*, vol. II, p. 320.

The Role of the Protector

The final blow is dealt to Coralie when she is faced with the prospect of having to return to Camusot, the wealthy businessman who is her protector. This is one of the most interesting aspects of Balzac's portrayal of the acting profession, as all of his actresses in addition to having their *amant de cœur,* also have a wealthy lover who finances their lifestyle. There has been no comprehensive historical study of the role of the protector in the theatre but it is possible to piece together fragmented evidence from contemporary sources in order to establish the historical basis of Balzac's portrayal.

The insufficiency of actress's salaries, particularly in view of their costume and lifestyle expenses has already been discussed, and the natural conclusion of d'Heilly on seeing a poorly paid actress in an extravagant costume is that she has a lover.[59]   This was the consequence of financial necessity and appears to have been common practice. The actress Marie Colombier explains in her memoirs of the end of the Empire and the early 1820s how the young girls at the Conservatoire would all have protectors who assumed a semi-paternal role for the sake of propriety.[60] A review of the Variétés in *Le Miroir* on 22 September 1821 tells of just such a young girl whose training has been financed by an English Lord: 'On parle déjà d'une jolie danseuse, Mlle Maria, qui doit débuter incessament: c'est un lord qui a fait les frais de l'éducation de cette jeune espagnole'.

Whatever the outward appearance, it was usually not simply a question of benevolence on the part of the protector. Samson relates an incident in his memoirs of the first half of the century in which a young actress is discussing in veiled terms with Madame Crosnier, the *portière*, the prospect of having sex with her protector:

> - Ah! Je comprends! rien pour rien, n'est-ce pas? un ami qui ne
>   donne pas sa protection, qui...
> - N'en dites pas de mal, il est si bon, il m'aime tant!
> - Et toi?
> - Moi... moi... je voudrais être premier sujet.[61]

[59] See above, p. 136.
[60] Colombier, *Mémoires, Fin d'Empire*, p. 20. This evidence has already been quoted by Hemmings, *The Theatre Industry in Nineteenth-Century France*, p. 200.
[61] Samson, *Mémoires*, pp. 60-61.

It is not a question of feelings as far as the girl is concerned but of the fulfilment of her ambition, particularly since there would not only be costumes to pay for, but, as has been shown in the previous chapter, also press subscriptions and the claque.

According to Duflot's definition of the protector in his theatrical glossary of 1865, the protector would generally be a respected member of society, wealthy and too old to be desired as a lover without the attraction of his money:

> Bienfaiteur – Quelquefois protecteur ou le monsieur sérieux.
> – C'est ordinairement un agent de change, un général, un riche
> négociant ou un coulissier. Quand ils n'ont pas passé trente ans
> les bienfaiteurs prennent le nom d'amants. Les bienfaits se passent
> régulièrement de mois en mois, sans préjudice du terme et des
> cadeaux. Le cumul n'est pas permis, mais il est assez généralement
> pratiqué.[62]

The last line of Duflot's explanation calls to mind Zola's depiction of the fictional actress Nana, in 1880, who is expert at managing the complications of her plural relationships and is perhaps the greatest fictional representation of the actress/courtesan.

Montigny does not explicitly attest to the existence of the protector in the theatre but he suggests in his description of the actress's dressing-room that the wealthy, elderly gentleman who is present may be there out of carnal rather than artistic interests:

> Mais quelle est cette tête poudrée qui cherche à s'approcher du feu
> pour réchauffer ses pieds et n'a fait de bruit jusqu'à présent qu'en
> se mouchant, en crachant et en prenant du tabac? serait-ce un
> homme riche qui vient chercher des plaisirs cotés ici comme les
> eaux-de-vie et les sucres le sont à la Bourse?[63]

As far as Montigny is concerned, the presence of the the rich, elderly gentleman is by no means unusual since he chooses to feature this figure in a representative scene of the actress's dressing-room.

Montigny's description of the dressing-room conjures up a scene which is comparable to the paintings of Gavarni who is famed for the

---

[62] Duflot, *Les Secrets des coulisses*, p. 36.
[63] Montigny, *Le Provincial à Paris*, vol. III, p. 278.

accuracy of his depiction of backstage scenes during the 1840s and 1850s. In particular his painting of 1851 entitled *La Loge* shows in the background a bearded gentleman in rich evening dress. Within the literal frame of the painting is a frame of light which surrounds the actress and the most prominent feature to emerge from the obscurity outside this frame of light is the eyes of the gentleman. These eyes are wide, bright and glaring as they stare from the outer frame of darkness into the inner frame of light, directed downwards at the actress's naked shoulders. The representation of sexual excitement and attraction is clear.[64]

In an article on Parisian actresses in *La Presse* on 11 August 1845, Gautier asserts that Gavarni's depiction of actresses behind the scenes is both detailed and accurate, which goes some way to substantiating the usefulness of Gavarni's painting in relation to Balzac's fiction. In the same article Gautier also lists the protector among those with whom the actress must maintain good relations in order to assure her success:

> Quel art! être bien avec le directeur, avec le régisseur, avec le costumier, avec le souffleur, avec l'avertisseur, et, en dernier ressort, sans compter le protecteur, avec l'amant favorisé, celui qui l'était, celui qui va l'être, les hommes de lettres, les chorégraphes, les compositeurs, les journalistes et les claqueurs!

With the exception of Hemmings, modern historians of the theatre devote little attention to the role of the protector in the theatre from the early 1820s to the mid 1840s. Hemmings's treatment covers the whole of the century and it is interesting that in relation to the first half of the century he uses *Illusions perdues* as a source of historical evidence:

> Balzac was as ever faithfully describing in *Illusions perdues* a commonplace situation when he showed the actress Coralie impatient for the embraces of the hot-blooded young journalist Lucien de Rubempré while giving her spare moments to the middle-

[64] Guillaume Sulpice Chevallier, dit Gavarni. Bibliothèque de l'Opéra, Paris, MUS. 1731.

aged silk merchant Camusot who pays the rent of her flat and buys her dresses and jewels: Camusot, her protector.[65]

Hemmings assertion that this was a commonplace situation at the time of *Illusions perdues* in the 1820s is based on the evidence in Marie Colombier's memoirs, and on Alhoy's *Grande biographie dramatique* of 1824. The rest of Hemmings' sources relate more specifically to later decades.

Maurice Descotes, in his study of the theatre-going public published in 1964, does not explore the role of the protector in any detail but in his examination of the changing status of the bourgeoisie in the theatre he refers to certain of Balzac's bourgeois characters by way of example and notes the fact that they are shown to penetrate the theatrical world and contribute to the careers of actresses:

> Ceux qui tiennent le haut du pavé, ce sont les bourgeois de Balzac, les Birotteau, les Matifat, les Rogron, les Poiret; ils envahissent les coulisses comme les salles de spectacle, contribuent à faire et à défaire les réputations.[66]

Descotes does not give any sources for his claim that bourgeois businessmen were instrumental in actress's careers and relies entirely on Balzac's characters as evidence. Although Balzac's portrayal of the bourgeois protector will be shown to be accurate, Descotes' reliance on these particular characters is somewhat misguided as Poiret and Rogron are never seen to attend the theatre or to have any involvement with it and although Birotteau attends as a spectator he certainly never becomes part of the backstage world. Matifat, however, is very much part of the theatrical world, and along with Cardot, Camusot, Crevel and Hulot, who would have served as better examples for Descotes, he features in *La Comédie humaine* as part of Balzac's incarnation of the protector.

In the narrative chronology of *La Comédie humaine* the first example of a bourgeois businessman assuming the role of an actress's protector is in 1817 in *Un début dans la vie,* which was written in 1841 and 1842. The main narrative is set in the late 1820s, but

[65] Hemmings, *The Theatre Industry in Nineteenth Century France*, p. 200.
[66] Descotes, *Le Public de théâtre et son histoire*, p. 289.

Balzac digresses from this to explain the development of Cardot's relationship with the actress, Florentine, which had begun in 1817 when she was only thirteen years old. Within two weeks of meeting her Cardot has established Florentine and her mother in smart lodgings, purchased furniture and provided an allowance of 250 francs per month, the equivalent of an entire year's salary for a young, unknown actress:

> Le père Cardot, orné de ses ailes de pigeon, parut alors être un ange, et fut traité comme devait l'être un bienfaiteur. Pour la passion du bonhomme, ce fut l'*âge d'or*.[67]

If the sexual arrangements of the relationship are not made as explicitly clear as the financial arrangements, there is nevertheless no evidence to suggest that Cardot has any reason to be dissatisfied with the deal. The fact that Cardot is married, has a family and is at great pains to keep the two sides of his life strictly separated by conducting his liaison in secret is reason enough to suppose that his support of Florentine is not merely an act of charitable benevolence. Although Balzac presents the relationship as a normal and accepted way for an actress to further her career and seems to dissociate himself from any moral judgment, he nevertheless accuses Cardot of hypocrisy in his double standards: 'L'oncle Cardot, grave et poli, passait pour être presque froid, tant il affichait de decorum, et une dévote l'eût appelé hypocrite'.[68] Balzac's main concern in his portrayal of the protector, however, is not so much with moral criticism as with presenting a view of sex and money as the driving forces of human behaviour. In his portrayal of the relationship between actress and protector there is always a trade in these twin imperatives, a trade which constituted part of the historical reality of the actress's life.

In addition to paying for her accommodation and expenses, Cardot pays for Florentine to take dancing lessons, which according to the memoirs of Marie Colombier, was how all the young girls at the Conservatoire afforded their classes.[69] Historical authenticity is added to the portrayal here in that Florentine's lessons are with

---

[67] *DV*, vol. I, p. 856.
[68] *DV*, vol. I, p. 836.
[69] Marie Colombier, *Mémoires, Fin d'Empire*, p. 133.

Vestris, who is not a fictional character but was a dancer at the Opéra from 1772 to 1816 and subsequently ballet master at the Conservatoire.[70]   This authenticity is further strengthened when in 1820 Florentine makes her debut at the Gaîté in *Les Ruines de Babylone*, the melodrama by Pixerécourt, which was first performed there in 1810.

By 1822 Florentine is well established, and although she continues her relationship with Cardot she has begun also to take younger lovers, a common situation according to the claims of Duflot and to Zola's portrayal of Nana.[71]   Marie Colombier had described the role of the protector as *semi-paternel* and it is this vocabulary which Balzac uses to describe the status of Florentine's relationship with Cardot from 1822 onwards, implying that while he is partly a father figure he is also partly something else:

> Comme le petit père Cardot avait acquis de son côté cinq ans de plus, il était tombé dans l'indulgence de cette demi-paternité que conçoivent les vieillards pour les jeunes talents qu'ils ont élevés et dont les succès sont devenus les leurs.[72]

Balzac's concern in this relationship is with Florentine's financial dependence on Cardot and with the implications of this for Cardot's heirs.   During the course of their relationship Cardot amasses a fortune of 90,000 francs, not for the future security of his family, but because he knows that with his support Florentine will eventually work her way up from the boulevard to the Opéra and that when she does she will expect 'le luxe d'un Premier Sujet'.[73]   When this day arrives in 1825, when Florentine is twenty-one and Cardot is seventy, he spends exactly half of his life's savings on her, and includes in this expenditure the purchase of the luxurious apartment where Coralie had lived in 1821 when she was supported by Camusot.[74]   Family wealth is dissipated by individual desire and the male sexual ego, in

[70] *DV*, vol. I, p. 857 & n. 1.
[71] See above, p. 146.
[72] *DV*, vol. I, p. 857.
[73] *Ibid.*
[74] *Ibid.*, p. 858. The impression of reality is strengthened here and elsewhere by establishing the familiarity of a background in which actresses inherit each other's apartments, lovers, and *salons*.

Balzac's view destabilising an already weakened social structure by diluting wealth and power downwards through the established social hierarchy. Nowhere is this more acute than in the Cardot household where, unbeknown to their daughter and wife, both father and son-in-law, Camusot, squander their wealth on actresses.

Cardot simply accepts that his son-in-law should behave in exactly the same way as he does. The characters do not question their own or others' involvement in these extra-marital relationships because they are shown to be an inevitable and established element of the social system. This is partly because Balzac shows the trafficking in sex and money to be a two-way process in which both parties of any contract are equally guilty of exploitation and neither is presented as a victim. In a world where values and morals are subordinate to financial considerations and individual desires and ambitions an exchange is shown to be easily effected when the satisfaction of each party's desires is compatible .

At the same time as we see Florentine supported by Cardot in *Un début dans la vie*, we also see her in *La Rabouilleuse* simultaneously conducting a relationship with Giroudeau. In the narrative it is late 1819 and early 1820, and Florentine has made her debut at the Gaîté but is not yet fully established as a leading lady. Giroudeau also acts as Florentine's protector but in a different way, for he is the uncle of Finot, chief editor and owner of the *Courrier des théâtres* where, as the paper's book-keeper, he has a certain influence which Florentine intends should be exercised to the benefit of her career. Neither narrator nor character questions the circumstances of this triangular relationship, but rather Balzac presents the situation precisely as it appears to his characters – as a matter of financial necessity and therefore as normal and acceptable. This is underlined by Giroudeau when he explains the relationship to Philippe Bridau:

> Je te ferai voir ce soir le ménage de Florentine. Quoique ma Dulcinée n'ait que cinquante francs par mois au théâtre, grâce à un ancien marchand de soieries nommé Cardot, qui lui offre cinq cents francs par mois, elle est encore assez bien ficelée![75]

---

[75] *R*, vol. IV, p. 310.

The effect of the recurring character of Cardot here serves to intensify the incestuous atmosphere within the theatrical world and the insidious nature of the trade in relationships, for all participants in the theatrical world – the press, the claque, actresses and the bourgeois businessmen who support them – operate according to the same system of trade and exchange and through their participation in that system become morally identical.

When Giroudeau and Philippe arrive at Florentine's that evening, sixteen year-old Mariette is there and she too is looking for a protector:

> Mlle Godeschal, qui voulait alors débuter au Panorama-Dramatique sous le nom de Mariette, comptait sur la protection d'un premier gentilhomme de la Chambre, à qui Vestris devait la présenter depuis longtemps.[76]

The underlying implication here is that Vestris is procuring young ladies for wealthy gentlemen. It is not clear who is paying for Mariette's lessons with Vestris at this time, but what is clear is that, like Florentine, Mariette has to have a protector before she can hope to make her debut on the stage. For as long as he is able to afford to, Philippe Bridau fills this role. In the case of Bridau it is the combined effect of lust, boredom after the dissolution of the Napoleonic army, and wanting to belong to the social group of the 'monde littéraire et galant' which urges him to become Mariette's protector. Balzac uses Bridau's relationship with Mariette to show the destructive effect of the individual desire on the family unit in so far as Bridau meets the actress's expenses by stealing from his family and from Finot's paper where he has secured a job. Mariette's expenses are unwittingly met by Madame Bridau, an elderly widow and Philippe's brother, Joseph, a struggling artist. In this way Balzac is able to demonstrate the destructive impact of Philippe's relationship with the actress on the family unit. The exploitation which takes place between Mariette and Philippe is for mutual gain and those who suffer through it are the ignorant and the innocent who do not enter into the trading contract. Mariette is certainly not a victim, she may only be sixteen but she is shrewd enough to have

[76] *R*, vol. IV, p. 310.

contingency plans for when Philippe runs out of money and confesses
to only ever having seen him as a stepping stone in her career path:

> [E]lle n'avait jamais vu dans ce garçon qu'un militaire brutal et sans
> esprit, un premier échelon sur lequel elle ne voulait pas longtemps
> rester. Aussi, prévoyant le moment où Philippe n'aurait plus˙
> d'argent, la danseuse avait-elle su conquérir des appuis dans le
> journalisme qui la dispensaient de conserver Philippe; néanmoins,
> elle eut la reconnaissance particulière à ces sortes de femmes pour
> celui qui, le premier, leur a pour ainsi dire aplani les difficultés de
> l'horrible carrière du théâtre.[77]

While the reader might judge this to be a moral compromise, no such
judgment is made by the actress herself. Neither Mariette nor
Florentine questions their relationship with their protector in terms of
their personal integrity, for each simply sees it as a necessary fact of
theatrical life.

If Cardot is financially exploited by Florentine then his son-in-
law, Camusot, is all the more so by Coralie in *Un grand homme,*
where his money is used to support not only the actress but also her
lover, Lucien. Here the morality of the functions of the protector in
the theatre is called into question, at least temporarily, by Lucien who
is uninitiated in the corrupt, topsy-turvy world of the Parisian theatre.
Lucien is shocked by the fact that Coralie overtly desires him as a
lover while making no pretence about her relationship with Camusot.
This is not so much a comment on the morals of Parisian society,
however, as a reinforcement of Lucien's extreme naivety in a way
which the contemporary Parisian reader would recognise.

Just as Coralie is maintained by the silk-merchant, Camusot, so
Florine, in the same novel, is maintained by the pharmacist, Matifat,
but she is abandoned by her protector when he learns of the plot
hatched by Florine and her lover, Lousteau,[78] together with Finot, to
extort money from him through an over-inflated sale of a share in
Finot's paper. The financial implications of this desertion for Florine
are not discussed; what is important to Balzac is that his bourgeois

---

[77] *R,* vol. IV, p. 317.

[78] Florine's relationship with Nathan begins shortly after this episode. The actress
abandons Lousteau in favour of Nathan because Nathan is able to help her to be
appointed at the Gymnase.

protectors, although driven by the sexual imperative, are not always the fools they might first appear to be. Sexuality and money are inextricably bound up together so that each is valued in relation to the other. Matifat is one of the new bourgeoisie who have worked hard for their money and learned to value economic power; in this case he judges Florine's sexual favours not to be worth the expense.

The novel in which the figure of the protector features most prominently is *La Fausse maîtresse* (1841), where it is central to the plot and its narrative outcomes. The action of this novel begins in 1835 by which time the actress Florine, who had been supported through the early stages of her career by Matifat some fifteen years previously, is now well established partly thanks to the support of the father of the novel's heroine, Clémentine Laginski:

> Par un effet du hasard, malgré les dissipations insensées du marquis du Rouvre pour Florine, une des plus charmantes actrices de Paris, Clémentine devint donc une héritière.[79]

The marquis du Rouvre does not have the economic shrewdness of the bourgeoisie and it is chance which saves him from squandering the entire family fortune on the actress. It is not his role as Florine's protector which is central to the plot, however, but that of Paz, the friend of Clémentine's husband, as protector to Malaga. Paz fabricates a story about a relationship with Malaga in order to conceal the fact that he is in love with Clémentine. The charade is entirely credible to Clémentine because it is based on a normal and commonly acknowledged phenomenon. Balzac uses a situation which has its basis in the social reality of his time around which to weave an otherwise highly improbable intrigue which is the product of his creativity.

When Paz and Laginski pass off the latter's considerable gambling debts as Paz's expenses in supporting Malaga, Clémentine, however displeased, has no reason to suspect the truth and understands that such sums are necessary to the function of a protector. Paz turns the charade partly into reality in his attempt to drive a wedge between himself and Clémentine by actually offering paternal support to Malaga. He pays her 320 francs a month and here Balzac is quite

[79] *FM*, vol. II, p. 195-196.

specific about the sexual arrangements – Paz requires nothing from Malaga. This is met with such astonishment and profound suspicion by Malaga and her servants and treated as so extraordinary that the reader can be left in no doubt about the sexual deals made by the other protectors in *La Comédie humaine*. It is an ironic observation by Balzac of the moral climate of his time that sexual trade is presented as the norm and an act of altruism is treated as highly suspicious.

While Florine, Florentine, Coralie and Malaga are presented as actresses who take their careers seriously and use protectors specifically for their career advancement, this is not true of the actresses portrayed in *La Cousine Bette*. Although Jenny Cadine and Josépha Mirah have achieved considerable success in the theatre, they are first and foremost courtesans, having begun their teenage years as such, turning to the stage later on as a secondary occupation and it is in relation exclusively to their talents as courtesans that they are portrayed in the novel. Josépha's only comment on the theatre is to justify her relationships to Adeline Hulot by explaining the dilemma of the actress in pursuing her career:

> Dans la carrière du théâtre une protection nous est nécessaire à toutes au moment où nous y débutons. Nos appointements ne soldent pas la moitié de nos dépenses; nous nous donnons donc des maris temporaires.[80]

Josépha was discovered by Crevel at the age of fifteen and despite Josépha's justifications to Adeline the theatre did not figure in their early relationship; the same is true of Hulot and Jenny Cadine. Balzac's portrayal of these relationships demonstrates that in some cases the theatrical world merely exploited a trade in relationships which went on anyway, regardless of any specific financial need generated by a career in the theatre.

Crevel, who began his career working for César Birotteau in 1818 is socially inept and morally corrupt, but like Matifat, he is no fool where money is concerned and when baron Hulot begins to compete

---

[80] *Be.*, vol. VII, p. 380.

for Josépha's attentions in the late 1830s he concedes defeat to his competitor. As in the case of Matifat, the sexual imperative succumbs to the financial imperative. Hulot, without the financial acumen of Crevel and Matifat, nor the bourgeois instinct to control his money, and without the fortune to permit such excess, spends over 100,000 francs as Josépha's protector in just two years.

The focus of the relationship between actress and protector in *La Cousine Bette* is not so much a matter of trade for mutual benefit as of monomanic sexual excess and the devastating effect which this has on the Hulot family. The issue which had previously been presented as at worst a matter of financial necessity and at best an unavoidable aspect of life in the theatre in works written in the late 1830s and early 1840s, has by the time of publishing *La Cousine Bette* in 1846 been subjected to Balzac's narrative transformations so that it has been exaggerated to excessive proportions and becomes a further incarnation of the monomanic, destructive passion with which Goriot had loved his daughters in *Le Père Goriot* (1834-35). It is not the theatre itself or the fact of Josépha being an actress which are put on trial by Balzac, but rather Hulot's monomania and his wife's inadequacy in the face of it. Within the moral and social context of the novel Hulot could just as easily have spent his 100, 000 francs on any other expensive courtesan, such as Valérie Marneffe, who is not an actress.

Balzac was himself of the opinion that his representation of the relationships of actresses with their protectors should be viewed as historically reliable, for in the early 1840s, in the second part of *Béatrix,* when discussing the dangerous influence of actresses and courtesans on the fabric of society, Balzac clearly presents himself as a historian rather than a novelist:

> Ce monde si dangereux a déjà fait irruption dans cette histoire des mœurs par les figures typiques de Florine et de l'illustre Malaga d'*Une fille d'Eve* et de *La Fausse maîtresse*; mais pour le peindre avec fidélité, l'historien doit proportionner le nombre de ces personnages à la diversité des dénouements de leurs singulières existences.

As is borne out by *La Cousine Bette*, however, Balzac's treatment of history is always subject to the creative process of his writing.

The Actress in Society

It is common knowledge that prior to the nineteenth century members of the acting profession had been excommunicated by the Catholic Church and ostracised by polite society, so only a brief summary of the historical position will be given here. Prior to the nineteenth century actors and actresses could not give evidence as witnesses in any civil court case, were prohibited from taking up any public function or office, and could not receive a christian burial or get married unless they renounced their profession. Even as early as the seventeenth century La Bruyère had commented on the hypocrisy of a Christian audience which sought to be entertained by excommunicates,[81] and it was not until the Revolution of 1789 that attempts were made to establish equal civil and religious rights for actors and actresses.

On 21 December 1789 a motion was put to the National Assembly to cancel the existing law which prevented non-Catholics, namely Protestants, Jews and actors, from holding positions of public employment.[82]   Equal civil rights for actors were won but the deep-rooted prejudice which had built up during the preceding centuries would take almost an entire century to alter significantly.   The Napoleonic regime strengthened the newly established equality of actors as it was successfully able to stamp out any resistance from the Catholic Church.   However, as soon as Napoleon fell from power the Church tried to re-establish the excommunication of members of the acting profession.   Louis XVIII had a moderating influence on the Church and there were no major conflicts during his reign, but from 1824, under Charles X, the Church resumed its campaign against the acting profession and this continued until the revolution of 1830 which finally reinforced the equality which had initially been won in 1789.[83]

Hemmings cites many instances during the period from 1789 to 1830 of Christian burials being refused to actors and of funeral processions arriving at churches to find the doors firmly locked. Among the most famous of these is the tragedian Talma, who in

---

[81]   La Bruyère, *De quelques usages*, in *Les Caractères*, para. 21.
[82]   Hemmings, *The Theatre Industry in Nineteenth-Century France*, p. 138.
[83]   Hemmings, *The Theatre Industry in Nineteenth-Century France,* p. 141.

1826 was refused the last rites and in turn refused to renounce the profession which he loved, requesting instead that his body be taken directly to Père-Lachaise cemetery upon his death.

In Balzac's fiction there is only one example of an actress's death but in this case the representation is true to reality. When Coralie is on the point of death in 1822 she specifically requests to be reconciled with the Church:

> Par un retour étrange,[84] Coralie exigea que Lucien lui amenât un prêtre. L'actrice voulut se réconcilier avec l'Eglise, et mourir en paix. Elle fit une fin chrétienne, son repentir fut sincère.[85]

Strictly speaking Coralie would have been entitled to a Christian burial without making a formal request in 1822 but since in practice this was difficult to obtain, a repentance and reconciliation of this kind would still have been necessary. Historical circumstances reinforce the characterisation of Coralie here for the sincerity of her repentance is a reflection of the sanctifying quality of her love for Lucien; once purified by true love, despite the fact that this is outside the bond of a Christian marriage, she cannot return to her former life of moral compromise and the only way forward is to a Christian death.

In *La Comédie humaine*, however, it is not so much the legal and religious marginalisation of the acting profession which is in evidence as the social prejudice which resulted from this. Balzac points out that in the minds of the public actors and actresses are considered to lead extraordinary lives which are far removed from reality:

> Potier, Talma, Mlle Mars, étaient dix fois millionnaires et ne vivaient pas comme les autres humains: le grand tragédien mangeait de la chair crue, Mlle Mars faisait parfois fricasser des perles, pour imiter une célèbre actrice égyptienne.[86]

[84] The use of the word 'étrange' here seems at odds with the fact that elsewhere Balzac is at pains to stress the sanctifying quality of Coralie's love for Lucien. It does not seem at all strange in fact that this sensitive creature should wish to be reconciled with the Church.

[85] *IP*, vol. V, p. 546.

[86] *CB*, vol. VI, p. 69.

At the same time, however, there is no distinction in the minds of the women of polite society between actresses, courtesans and common prostitutes. Louise expresses this to Renée in *Mémoires de deux jeunes mariées:*

> Je roulais dans la fange sociale au-dessous de la grisette, de la fille mal élevée, côte à côte avec les courtisanes, les actrices, les créatures sans éducation.[87]

When a term is required by the women of polite society to describe some moral undoing it often takes the form of abhorrent reference to the *fille d'Opéra*.[88] Interestingly, it is always the women of polite society who express their prejudice in these terms, for their husbands and fathers are often the very men who have actresses and *filles d'Opéra* as mistresses.

It is this type of prejudice which the actress Tullia, has to face in her relationship with the playwright du Bruel, for in Balzac's fiction, as in reality, it is the interpreter of a play who is considered immoral by society and not the author. In *Un prince de la Bohème* (1840), when Tullia retires from the stage in 1829 at the age of thirty, it is partly because she feels she has become a little too fat 'pour se montrer quasi nue au parterre,' but more importantly it is, 'pour devenir une bonne et charmante femme,' to du Bruel. The playwright who has pursued his career in precisely the same industry is under no apparent social pressure to renounce it, while Tullia must adopt all the outward signs of religious devotion in order to prove herself a worthy wife: 'Tullia sut se faire adopter par les femmes les plus jansénistes de la famille du Bruel. [...] La danseuse se confessa, reçut l'absolution, communial'.[89]

Legally speaking Tullia would now, in 1829, have the same civil rights as any other citizen but it is not her legal status which is a bar to her integration and advancement in society; it is the social prejudice against her former profession. Not only must Tullia retire

---

[87] *MJM*, vol. I, p. 392.

[88] For example, see: *DF*, vol. II, p. 75: 'L'amour des filles de l'Opéra, dit la comtesse avec horreur'; *MJM*, vol. I, p. 344: 'Oh! chère, je suis pire qu'une fille d'Opéra'.

[89] *Pr.B*, vol. VII, 827.

from the theatre but also, in order to reinforce her renunciation, she must sever her connections with all of her friends and associates in the theatre so that her new life is not compromised in any way.

By 1836 Tullia has made herself acceptable to polite society and Balzac's comment on her integration acknowledges the extent to which it is due to the changes in the political and social structure of the country after 1830:

> Claudine fit comprendre à du Bruel que le système élastique du gouvernement bourgeois, de la royauté bourgeoise, de la cour bourgeoise était le seul qui pût permettre à une Tullia, devenue Mme du Bruel, de faire partie du monde où elle eut le bon sens de ne pas vouloir pénétrer.[90]

In this sense Balzac reflects the actual social history of his time. He shows through Tullia that the change in the legal status of actors and actresses which came about in 1789 and remained valid despite opposition from the Church, did not have any real, practical impact until well after 1830 when the social mobility of the actress began to be an element of the mobility of society as a whole.

The ultimate proof of this shift in social values comes in 1839 when du Bruel becomes a *pair de France* and Tullia a *comtesse*. While this particular social promotion does not appear to have any basis in fact, the important issue is that in Balzac's view of post-1830 society any social advancement is possible. Certainly an actress in Tullia's position could never have become *Mme la comtesse* prior to 1830, but by 1839 this would at least seem a credible possibility to Balzac's reader.

When Tullia renounces the theatre she also ceases to hold her *salon*, as does Florine when she marries Nathan. Married respectability is clearly not compatible with the type of *salon* frequented by people of the theatrical world, and the courtesan, Carabine, takes over:

> Carabine, rivale de la non moins célèbre Malaga, s'était enfin portée héritière du salon de Florine, devenue Mme Nathan; de celui de

[90] *Ibid.*

Tullia, devenue Mme du Bruel; de celui de Mme Schontz devenue Mme la présidente du Ronceret.[91]

Interestingly, du Bruel is seen attending Carabine's *salon* as late as 1845. Social prejudice prohibits his wife from holding such a *salon* but does not prohibit the *pair de France* from attending it. In this way Balzac highlights a social distinction which is not emphasised by historians of the theatre. Since male actors do not feature in *La Comédie humaine* they do not fall within the scope of this investigation, but given the social conventions governing the position of women generally in the early nineteenth century, it seems fair to assume that the prejudice which the actress had to combat must have been far greater than that faced by her male counterpart. As far as *La Comédie humaine* is concerned, the social prejudice attached to the acting profession is directed at women by women.

To some extent the actresses of *La Comédie humaine* are defined by their differences from the women of polite society. On the whole, if the women of polite society appear to be more morally upstanding then the actresses appear to be more exciting. Blondet makes this point in *Une fille d'Eve*:

> Quand on a Florine, qui tour à tour est duchesse de vaudeville, bourgeoise de drame, négresse, marquise, colonel, paysanne en Suisse, vierge du Soleil au Pérou, sa seule manière d'être vierge, je ne sais pas comment on s'aventure avec les femmes du monde.[92]

However, they are also defined in terms of their similarity, for just as it is their natural adaptability and experience of assuming roles which befits Balzac's reformed actresses to take up positions as respectable members of society, so it is a natural propensity for role playing and dissimulation which characterises the society women who are rarely quite what they seem.

---

[91] *Pr.B*, vol. VII, p. 1211.
[92] *FE*, vol. II, p. 382.

Conclusion – A Twin Imperative

As the theatre is the hub of social activity in *La Comédie humaine* the role of the actress constitutes an important element of the social history which Balzac presents to his reader. In order to fulfil their role in the portrayal of a total social history Balzac's fictional actresses form part of the overall scheme of recurring characters. This fictional device has been criticised by Percy Lubbock as an obstacle to the reader's understanding and experience of each individual novel because, in his opinion, recollections of previous characters obscure the relationship with the character now in question.[93]   While Lubbock's view may be valid, the recurring characters are nevertheless essential to the creation of a total social scheme in which events and destinies become interconnected. For the reader of the whole *Comédie* the scheme reinforces the sense of reality in which certain characters become increasingly familiar and for the reader of the individual novel it has the effect of situating the present narrative in relation to a past and future reality.

The reduction of the hundreds of real actresses employed in Paris from the 1820s to the 1840s to a representative handful of fictional characters may seem oversimplified, but at the same time it is powerfully convincing since most readers' experience of social reality is likely to be confined to small groups of individuals who are connected by common interests. In *La Muse du département* the reader is told that Mariette, Coralie, Florine, Florentine and Tullia are 'comme les cinq doigts de la main',[94]   a small exclusive group belonging to a bohemian underworld of performers, journalists and pleasure-seekers. Mariette is mentioned in eleven novels, Coralie in eight including two after her death, Florine in fourteen, Florentine in six, and Tullia in twelve, and their frequent reappearance and the emergence of fragmented aspects of their destinies create both a sense of intimacy with the reader and an impression of belonging to a larger social group as they move in and out of the narrative foreground.

---

[93] Lubbock, *The Craft of Fiction* (London: Cape, 1921), pp. 207-210.
[94] *MD*, VI, p. 739.

When they are in the foreground of the narrative the actresses are shown to move in intimate social groups where only selected *invités* are admitted, and their *salons* and *soupers* involve the same regular visitors. As the actresses inherit each other's lovers, protectors, appointments and apartments, an atmosphere of exclusivity and incestuousness is established which encourages the reader to accept the narrowness of the representation. Then as they are alluded to in other novels their circles of activity are widened and an impression of belonging to a larger social reality is established as they touch the lives of new characters beyond their intimate group. In this way, for example, Florine in *Un grand homme* and in *Une fille d'Eve* moves in a small group of actresses and journalists but when she is mentioned by characters in other novels this works to establish the credibility of the new fiction, since the characters in question obviously form part of a social scene which is already familiar.

The link with a wider social context is reinforced by admitting the wealthy businessman to the actress's immediate social group in the role of protector. In this way the actress's *salon* becomes an extension of the theatre itself where normally distinct social groups are able to interact and where Balzac is able to show the chaos and corruption existing beneath the apparently calm surface of society. In his preface to *Une fille d'Eve* in 1839 Balzac writes: 'Il n'y a rien qui soit d'un seul bloc dans ce monde; tout y est mosaïque'. Consistent with this interpretation of the world, aspects of the lives of the wealthy businessmen who support actresses are revealed which would not ordinarily be revealed in their normal spheres of activity but which make up part of their total 'mosaic' picture. Thus, when Lucien visits Camusot at home to plead for help on the part of Coralie, he finds the family man very different from the drunken libertine he had known from the supper parties and the backstage of the theatre, for the protector does not belong exclusively to one world or the other. The actress and her protector belong rather to a total, interconnected social scheme which is characteristic of Balzac's view of a mosaic reality.

Balzac's treatment of the actress and her protector is, of course, not just a question of portraying the possibly hidden connections in social reality through the use of representative types. It embodies a particular ideological drive and deliberately pursues a particular vision of reality in which all relationships are based on a system of trade and exchange. It seems to have escaped the attention of critics that Balzac has a particular interest in always showing the *amant de clur* of the actress to be a journalist or a playwright and never a fellow actor. In reality, there were many instances of actresses and actors enjoying long and happy relationships with each other, but to introduce these to *La Comédie humaine* would be to undermine Balzac's comment on the theatrical world and on society at large. It would establish the kind of economic and social equality between male and female characters which would upset the entire interplay of sex and money in the narrative scheme. Notwithstanding the true affection which the actress may feel for her journalist lover, she is nevertheless almost always motivated by self-interest, engaging in relationships with journalists or playwrights to ensure favourable reviews and good roles, and with wealthy businessmen to meet her expenses.

Money and sex are the twin imperatives which drive the theatrical world of *La Comédie humaine*. These twin imperatives are fused in the figure of the actress who is both the object of sexual desire and of commercial arrangements, and they are inextricable since the actress's sexual relationships are determined by her economic circumstances. Although the role of the protector has its basis in the historical reality of the period, it also serves Balzac's wider fictional aims for it is consistent with his vision of a society in which choices are determined by financial considerations. The financial imperative in Balzac's fiction is widely acknowledged; in Hunt's interpretation it is:

> [...] the 'Open sesame' to passionate adventure, the avenue to success, luxury, power and all the many forms of self-fulfilment which the many kinds of men and women desire.[95]

---

[95] Hunt, *Balzac's 'Comédie Humaine'*, p. 446.

In the theatre world depicted by Balzac it is only through money that the actress can achieve her ambitions and the protector can fulfil his desires.

The corruption and decay which are prevalent in the theatre and which are epitomised by the actress's life have effects beyond the closely confined world of the theatre. The unquestioned acceptance of the sexual prostitution of the actress to her protector is symptomatic of the general moral decay which Balzac saw to be prevalent in society at large. It is, in the words of Christopher Prendergast, characteristic of: 'The disruptive pressure on the social order of a developing nineteenth-century individualism'.[96] In so far as they are driven by their individual desires and ambitions, the middle-class business men who act as protectors become morally identical to the corrupt journalists who operate their relationships with actresses according to the same code of exchange and mutual exploitation. This impression of moral similarity corresponds with Balzac's view of the interpenetration of vice through all levels of society, as each becomes connected with the other by sexual interaction with the actress. In his *Avant-Propos* in 1842, Balzac had stressed the importance of passion in human motivation, and in *Illusions perdues* and *La Cousine Bette* he emphasises that by passion he does not just mean the passion for the acquisition of wealth or for scientific discovery which drives certain of the monomanics of *La Comédie humaine*, but particularly sexual passion, inspired by a destructive female sexuality.

The passion inspired by the actress is all the more important to the overall narrative scheme, not just because of the moral disorder which she brings about but because of the resulting disintegration of the family unit and, according to the economic code of *La Comédie humaine,* because of the dissipation of family wealth which she causes. The role of the actress/courtesan in the breakdown of the traditional family unit has been commented on by Prendergast:

---

[96] Prendergast, *Balzac, Fiction and Melodrama*, p. 180.

The actual or incipient breakdown of the integrated and hierarchical family unit is thus seen as an undermining of the essential principles of the social contract itself. And in its place – and again within the 'melodramatic' fictions – new contracts, new 'families,' bizarre and disconcerting leagues and associations begin to arise, relationships and connections which the official history would of course seek to deny (to dismiss as 'implausible', 'melodramatic'), but which it is the duty of the secret history to uncover.[97]

Balzac's treatment of the relationship between the actress and her protector contributes to his aim to write the secret history in so far as it is based in historical fact and does not feature in any of the 'official' histories of the theatre but it does more than this. The 'new contracts, new 'families,' bizarre and disconcerting leagues and associations' which are established in place of the traditional family unit become part of Balzac's vision of a society driven by money and individualism, for all of these new 'families' are based on a code of exchange. Genetic ties are replaced by financial ties and a new system is established in which the protector and the *amant de cœur* openly acknowledge and tolerate each other as members of the same 'family', for each operates according to the financial code and recognises the limits of his value to the actress.

It is significant that D'Arthez refers to the disasters caused by the passions which the female sex inspires as 'accidents infinis,' for the phrase suggests that the characters cannot be held responsible for their actions. Certainly the individual cannot stand alone against the driving forces of society and although the actress's relationships are shown to be primarily determined by money and ambition, they are also to some extent environmentally determined. Environmental determinism is not so great an issue with Balzac as it became later in the century for the Naturalists, but the corrupting influence of the theatrical environment cannot be ignored. Within the social code of the theatre certain relationships which might be unacceptable in other spheres of society are not only accepted but are positively encouraged. For all of Balzac's actresses the relationship with a protector is simply a necessary element of involvement in this environment and by choosing to move into this environment the

---

[97] Prendergast, *Balzac, Fiction and Melodrama*, p. 180.

actress automatically accepts the environment's conditions. This is true of all those who enter this environment; for example, it is not long after expressing his astonishment at Coralie's relationship with Camusot that Lucien is sufficiently corrupted also to live off Camusot's money.

Despite the criticism of the theatre world which is more or less overt from one novel to another, there is no direct authorial condemnation of the actress's lifestyle and it is difficult to discern any clear moral standpoint on this in *La Comédie humaine*. In his *Avant-Propos,* Balzac stresses the general moral stance of his fiction:

> Les actions blâmables, les fautes, les crimes, depuis les plus légers jusqu'aux plus graves y trouvent toujours leur punition humaine ou divine, éclatante ou secrète. J'ai mieux fait que l'historien, je suis plus libre.[98]

However, this cannot be borne out in any straightforward way in the destinies of his actresses and their protectors, for the conflict of vice and virtue is not simplified and separated into different characters set in opposition with each other. Balzac's development of his characters is more complex and ambiguous than in the simple antithesis of theatrical melodrama, which would allow for a strictly moralising nemesis. The actresses are no more the exclusive incarnation of vice than the society women are the incarnation of virtue. Their only real crime is to succumb to the prevailing social forces.

A moralising outcome is prohibited because the moral similarity of different groups of society is part of the total scheme of the fiction and each social group embodies aspects more usually associated with the other. Thus Coralie prostitutes herself to Camusot but is sanctified by her love for Lucien; Josépha is the clichéd portrait of the golden-hearted whore but nevertheless has no scruples about encouraging young girls into the path of vice; and the saintly Adeline Hulot not only tolerates her husband's philanderings but positively encourages him to choose inexpensive young girls rather than costly actresses. There is no strict moral judgment of the actress's lifestyle because the theatrical world is used not as a background for a struggle between vice and virtue but rather as a context for the

---

[98] *AP,* vol. I, p. 15.

struggle of the individual to succeed and overcome, a struggle which is motivated by what Balzac perceives as the relentless rise of individualism.

THEATRE AS METAPHOR IN
LA COMEDIE HUMAINE

The theatre features strongly throughout *La Comédie humaine* as a major social institution and as an industry, often providing the novels with characters, locations and intrigues firmly anchored in an accurate historical context. It is also a rich source of imagery which is fundamental to Balzac's mode of expression and closely linked to the theatrical character of Balzac's narrative technique. In discussing Balzac's use of melodrama in his novels, critics refer not only to the dramatic features of Balzac's writing but also to the tissue of images borrowed from the theatre, and through which the melodrama of the Balzacian plot with its relentless development of catastrophe, intrigue and peripeteia is often expressed.[1] Peter Brooks states in his discussion of melodrama in *Illusions perdues*:

> The model of representation in life and personal style refers us inevitably to the theatre, a principal milieu, and perhaps the dominant metaphor, of the novel. The theatre, object of Balzac's repeated ambitions and possibly the key metaphor of the nineteenth century experience of illusion and disillusionment, is also the metaphor of Balzac's methods of melodramatic presentation.[2]

Brooks goes on to explain that this second sense of metaphor consists in the persistent tension in *Illusions perdues* between the light and fascination of the theatre stage, and the obscurity and disenchantment of the backstage. This tension in turn functions as an expression of the superstructure and substructure which Balzac perceived in society at large, and which is at work not only in *Illusions perdues*, but, as will be seen later in this chapter, throughout *La Comédie humaine*. Donald Adamson also defines the theatre as a dominant metaphor in *Illusions perdues* in his discussion of chance and necessity in this novel, in which he states:

---

[1] See: Peter Brooks, *The Melodramatic Imagination*, and 'Balzac, Melodrama and Metaphor' in *The Hudson Review* (Summer, 1969), pp. 213-228; Donald Adamson 'Chance and Necessity' in *Balzac, 'Illusions perdues'*, pp. 72-74.

[2] Brooks, *The Melodramatic Imagination*, pp. 122-123.

The theatrical world in which Lucien and Coralie meet is perhaps the greatest metaphor of chance and necessity. Again, apart from a brief reference to the provincial theatre on the last page of the novel, this is a world which does not exist in or near Angoulême. It is the microcosm of Paris as the great theatre of chance, a world in which Lucien, with his fine costumes and journalistic assumption of masks, becomes one of the most colourful actors.[3]

The preceding chapters of the present work have already sought to show how the theatre facilitates the chance encounters and generates the economic necessities which Adamson speaks of here, and the issues suggested by his comment on Lucien as an actor will be treated in the course of this chapter. Indeed this chapter aims to amplify the ideas put forward by both Brooks and Adamson by showing, through a systematic analysis of imagery and terminology, how Balzac's use of theatrical metaphor applies not just to the Parisian milieu but to the whole society represented in *La Comédie humaine,* how it serves Balzac's wider narrative purposes in a variety of ways, and how ultimately, and most interestingly, it expresses Balzac's own dramaturgy.

In 1864 Victor Hugo noted the relationship between realism and metaphor when discussing dramatic style, and although his comments refer indirectly to his own work, his praise of abundant metaphor in literature indicates that in using all types of metaphor Balzac is to some extent subscribing to contemporary literary vogue.[4] Balzac's use of theatrical metaphor in particular, however, seems to have as much to do with his own distinct vision of life, and of theatre, as with the literary trend of his period. Indeed, the overall title of *La Comédie humaine* already indicates that Balzac sees the whole of human existence as a stage play, and the content and structure of the

[3] Donald Adamson, *Balzac, Illusions perdues,* pp. 72-73.

[4] Hugo, 'William Shakespeare', in *Œuvres complètes,* ed. Albin Michel (Paris: Ollendorf), vol. I, pp. 117-118: 'Etre fécond, c'est être agressif. Un poète comme Isaïe, comme Junénal, comme Shakespeare, est en vérité, exorbitant. Que diable! On doit faire un peu attention aux autres, un seul n'a pas droit à tout, la virilité toujours, l'inspiration partout, autant de métaphores que la prairie, autant d'antithèses que la chère, autant de contrastes et de profondeur que l'univers, sans cesse la génération, l'éclosion, l'hymen, l'enfantement, l'ensemble vaste, le détail exquis et robuste, la communication vivante, la fécondation, la plénitude, la production, c'est trop, cela vide le droit des autres'.

novels would seem to indicate that Balzac is perhaps less indebted to Dante for his title than he is to the notion of role-playing. Moreover, it is through the notion of life as theatre, rather than in the separate structure of the texts, that the individual novels participate in the unity of the total work.

There is some debate surrounding the exact date of Balzac's conception of his collective title.[5] However, after 1842, when this title was used for the first time in print, a surge in Balzac's use of explicit theatrical metaphor can be discerned, particularly in the third part of *Béatrix* (1844-45), where there are thirteen examples, and in *Modeste Mignon* (1844), where there are fifteen examples.[6] Although there are sixteen examples of explicit theatrical metaphors in *Les Chouans* (1828-29), this early plethora of imagery borrowed from the theatre diminishes in works written during the 1830s, even in novels such as *Le Père Goriot* (1834-35, seven examples) and *La Fille aux yeux d'or* (1834-35, one example), which rely heavily on dramatic technique, and in *Une fille d'Eve* (1838-1839, four examples), which is set largely in the theatre world. It seems therefore, that in applying the broad metaphor of *comédie* to all the human life represented in *La Comédie humaine*, at a stage when some of his major works remained to be written or completed, Balzac renewed his awareness of the expressive possibilities of theatrical imagery.

Balzac's persistent borrowing of images from the theatre reveals more, however, than a generalised notion of all of human life as a great *comédie*. Indeed, Balzac appears to strive towards a systematic employment of theatrical metaphors which divide into five key areas and make up a strict scheme of images with distinct purposes. The five categories into which Balzac's theatrical metaphors may be divided are: the character as an actor or director; social role-play as *comédie*; the theatre as a microcosm of visible society; the hidden area of the backstage as a microcosm of the social substructure; and finally, the private drama, which functions as an expression of the dramaturgy which Balzac would attempt to bring to the stage towards

---

[5] Pierre Citron, 'Du nouveau sur le titre de *la Comédie humaine*' in *RHLF* (1959), pp. 91-93, argues for 1839-1840, and F. Baldensperger, 'Une suggestion anglaise pour le titre de *la Comédie humaine*' in *RLC* (Oct-Dec 1921), makes a claim for 1835.

[6] See appendix I, for full index.

the end of his career in *La Marâtre*. Each of these categories of metaphor will be treated in turn in the course of this chapter and is supported by an index of examples drawn from *La Comédie humaine* which appears at the end of the present study. Some 600 explicit references to actual playwrights, characters and actors are listed in this index and are treated in the next section of this chapter, while a further 240 theatrical metaphors not containing comparison to any named person or character are treated in the subsequent sections.

Theatrical Metaphor in the Creation of a Typology

Balzac's vision of the drama of life, or of the human comedy, is largely intelligible to his reader because it is conveyed through characters who are recognisable types and who are capable of engaging the reader's sympathies. As is well known, Balzac, in his *Avant-Propos* to *La Comédie humaine,* had specifically declared his intention to create an extensive typology.[7] Although the nature and function of Balzac's typology have been the source of much criticism,[8] it has not been noted in more than a superficial way, that the creation of this typology is partly dependent on a system of theatrical imagery, according to which Balzac's characters are defined by reference to a catalogue of characters from the theatre.

The source and extent of Balzac's familiarity with his theatrical antecedents has been noted in the introduction to this study, where it is shown that his correspondence is replete in particular with expresssions of admiration for Racine, Corneille, and Molière. Balzac's citations of the French classical tragedians in *La Comédie humaine*, however, tend more to the admiration of their style than to the borrowing of their characters in the creation of his own typology. This is particularly so with Racine, who is for Balzac 'le désespoir des poètes',[9] since he cannot be matched, and, as seen in the introduction to the present study, is admired for his language and

---

[7] *AP*, vol. I, pp. 11-17.
[8] See: Peter Demetz, 'Balzac and the zoologists: A concept of the Type' in *The Discipline of Criticism* (Yale University Press, 1968), pp. 397-418; Guzine Dino, 'L'Aspect historique et social des types chez Balzac', in *Europe*, revue mensuelle, no. 429-430 (Jan-Feb, 1965), pp. 295-302; Willi Jung, *Theorie und Praxis des Typischen bei H. de Balzac* (Tübingen: Stauffenberg, 1983).
[9] *Corres.*, vol I, p. 35, à Laure 1819.

poetry rather than for his characterisation.[10]   There are, of course, also many references in *La Comédie humaine* to contemporary plays and to the actors and actresses who played in them.   These references tend not to be used in a metaphorical sense, however, but rather as part of what Barthes defines as 'l'effet de réel'.   Balzac's fictional characters attend plays such as *L'Auberge des adrets*, and the *Danaïdes*[11] and his actresses are often listed alongside actual actors and actresses of the day such as Talma, Mlle Mars, Mlle Georges, and Frédérick Lemaître.[12]   All these references to the current celebrities are fleeting and superficial and are used to recreate the authentic atmosphere of the period around Balzac's fictional characters.   A brief glance at the number of citations of contemporary playwrights in *La Comédie humaine* compared with those of playwrights from previous centuries illustrates their relative importance in Balzac's fiction.[13]

Earlier tradition				Contemporary theatre		
	Author	Works	Total		Author	Works	Total
Molière	67	151	218	Hugo	20	5	25
Shakespeare	26	93	119	Nodier	20	1	21
Beaumarchais	23	56	79	Scribe	10	10	20
Racine	20	32	52	Pixerécourt	2	3	5
Corneille	18	26	44	Picard	3	0	3
	Total		<u>412</u>		Total		<u>74</u>

The table above shows the five most frequently cited dramatists in each category.   Further examination of the index to this study reveals that references to contemporary works are fleeting and that few works are referred to on more than one occasion.   In almost all cases the references to contemporary works are to the name of the play and not to its characters.   Conversely, the references to dramatic

---

[10]   See above, pp. 12-13. Balzac's admiration of Racine can be seen in much of his early correspondence. See: *Corres.*, vol. I, pp. 35, 36, 52, 58, 60, 61, & 65.

[11]   See appendix II section a, for full index of contemporary plays referred to in *LCH*.

[12]   See appendix III for full index of actors and actresses referred to in *LCH*.

[13]   Full details of where these references occur in *La Comédie humaine* can be found in the index to playwrights in appendix II.

works from previous centuries are not only more abundant but repeatedly refer to the same work, and, with the exception of Racinian tragedy, these references apply more often to the characters within the plays than to the plays themselves. Clearly, the dramatists of previous centuries emerge as the more important points of reference for Balzac, and of these Molière and Shakespeare are the most important for the creation of Balzac's typology. Since metaphor depends for its effect on the reader's ability to interpret the transaction between contexts, to see the signified behind the signifier, any catalogue of characters used metaphorically in the creation of Balzac's typology must be recognisable to his reader and form part of what Barthes defines in *S/Z* as the *code culturel*. Perhaps it is for this reason that Balzac relied primarily on the plays of Shakespeare and Molière, which would be known to his readers both through performance and reading, rather than on ephemeral contemporary productions.[14] It is noteworthy that although Balzac's plots and mode of expression tend towards the melodrama, he does not borrow characters from the stage melodrama any more than from other kinds of contemporary play, to characterise his own creations.

A full index of Balzac's citations of dramatic works in *La Comédie humaine* can be found at the end of the the present work, and the points made here will be illustrated by reference to the most frequently cited dramatists only: Shakespeare and Molière.[15] The

---

[14] It has been shown in Chapter I that production runs of contemporary plays in the boulevard theatres were much shorter than those of classical plays at the larger theatres.

[15] In the overall context of this chapter the analysis here will be restricted to explicit instances of metaphor and simile and will not include any examination of perceived models of characterisation which Balzac may have borrowed from Shakespeare and Molière. Such an examination has already been conducted by P.-J. Tremewan with regard to Shakespeare, and by P. Barrière and Geneviève Delattre with regard to Molière. See: P.J. Tremewan, 'Balzac et Shakespeare', *AB* (1967), pp. 259-303. Tremewan looks in particular at *King Lear* as a model for *Le Père Goriot*, pp. 287-293. Goriot is never directly compared to Shakespeare's Lear in the course of the narrative, however. Tremewan notes that Goriot is referred to as a 'colimaçon' and a 'mollusque' and that these images are applied to Lear in Act I, scene v. These images are not considered relevant to the present analysis. See also: P. Barrière, 'Les Sources classiques de *la Comédie humaine*', in *Honoré de Balzac et la tradition littéraire classique*, pp. 74-98. Barrière examines an extensive range of possible classical sources which may have provided Balzac with the inspiration for plots and characters. He treats in particular Molière's *L'Avare* as a model for Grandet. There

success of Shakespeare with Parisian audiences in the late 1820s[16] seems to have greatly influenced Balzac in his practice of giving brief character sketches by cross-reference to the theatre. There are 93 references to Shakespeare's plays and characters in *La Comédie humaine*, far outnumbering the references to any contemporary productions, and creating the impression that Balzac was very familiar with the English playwright. Most references are taken from a small selection of major works, however, and focus on Shakespeare's most memorable characters who in Balzac's interpretation have been reduced to a single dominant character trait. These references cover the whole chronological period of *La Comédie humaine* and very few contain any judgment of the dramatist. The abundance of these allusions and the remarkable absence of comment from Balzac, seems to suggest that the references reflect literary vogue rather than Balzac's personal literary preference. The 93 citations observed in this analysis divide as follows:

Othello	30	*Hamlet*	13
Macbeth	11	*Romeo and Juliette*	15
Richard III	6	*The Tempest*	9
The Merchant of Venice	4	*Henry IV*	1
Henry V	1	*Much ado about nothing*	2
The MerryWives of Windsor	1		

It is clear that Balzac's exploitation of Shakespeare's work rests in particular on the characters of Othello, Hamlet and Macbeth.

Balzac seems to be aware of the complexity of Shakespeare's characters who, for him, are imposing, contradictory and disconcerting, but this manifests itself only in general statements about the author. This awareness is evident in *Une fille d'Eve* in the

---

is no explicit reference to Harpagon in *Eugénie Grandet*, however. Harpagon, like Lear, seems to have interested Balzac as an exception rather than as a type. In relation to Molière, see also: Geneviève Delattre, *Les Opinions littéraires de Balzac*, pp. 51-83.

[16] See: J. Bochner, 'Shakespeare en France, 1733-1830', in *RLC* (Jan.-Mar., 1965), pp. 44-65; J.L. Borgerhoff, *Le Théâtre anglais à Paris sous la Restauration* (Paris: Hachette, 1912); M. Guizot, 'Shakespeare et son temps', in *Œuvres complètes de Shakespeare* (Paris: Didier, 1821).

description of Nathan, 'qui connaissait son Shakespeare, déroula ses misères, raconta sa lutte avec les hommes et les choses, fit entrevoir ses grandeurs sans base, son génie politique inconnu, sa vie sans affection noble',[17] and also in writings outside *La Comédie humaine*.[18] When Balzac defines his own characters by comparison with individual characters of Shakespeare, however, he rarely takes into account the psychological complexity of what Genette defines in *Figures III* as the *comparant*. Rather, the references which Balzac makes to individual Shakespearian characters seem to confirm that he is aware of their principal character traits and of the main intrigue in the plays in which they appear, but that a knowledge which may appear extensive is actually based on the same few characters who are reduced to a recognisable pattern of characteristics. Balzac seizes upon one characteristic and insists upon this alone so that it becomes the dominant trait which can be recognised in all examples. This practice is consistent with Balzac's declared intention to portray humanity through the study of types and to enlarge particular aspects of character. Indeed only if he does this are these referential characters borrowed from Shakespeare useful in the creation of Balzac's typology, for only through this simplified treatment can they function as a clear signifier to the reader. Such references to Shakespeare's characters define recognisable types, link Balzac's own work to the fashionable literary trend, and often predict the character's actions and the novel's outcomes.

Othello is by far the most frequently quoted character in Balzac's figurative exploitation of Shakespeare and is used exclusively to represent dark and savage jealousy. The wildness and irrationality of Othello are not appropriate to the major characters of Balzac's fiction, however, for such a character could not survive for long in the Parisian social spheres of *La Comédie humaine*. The image of Othello can be effectively exploited only to describe single jealous actions in characters who are otherwise rational, or to describe minor

---

[17] *FE*, vol. II, p. 313.

[18] See for example *LMH*, vol. IV, p. 221, 29 February 1848, in which Balzac describes the revolution: 'Il y a eu un mélange de gaminerie, de sublimité, de force, qui a fait du jeudi un drame de Shakspeare', and *Études sur M. Beyle* where Balzac describes the duchesse de Sanseverina in *La Chartreuse de Parme* as, 'franche, naïve, sublime, résignée, remuée comme un drame de Shakespeare', *L'Œuvre de Balzac*, 16 vols. (Paris: Formes et Reflets, 1950-1953), vol. XIV, p. 1171.

characters who appear only briefly in *La Comédie humaine*. Balzac uses the image of Othello to describe the actions of Charles Mignon, the prince de Cadignan, Montriveau and de Marsay, and in each case it is the common characteristic of jealousy which prompts the comparison, although there is not the same internal conflict in Balzac's characters as there is in the Othello of Shakespeare. In each case the metaphor serves exclusively to highlight the motive of a jealous action which is highly melodramatic. For example, Montriveau's violent kidnapping of the duchesse de Langeais and his sinister threats are prompted by an unfounded jealousy in comparison to which 'Othello n'est qu'un enfant'.[19] In this way the Shakespearian metaphor becomes assimilated into Balzac's melodramatic mode of expression.

Christémio in *La Fille aux yeux d'or* is an Othello both in appearance and in temperament, but he is a minor character who appears only in this novel and is not the perpetrator of the final jealous murder:

> Jamais figure africaine n'exprima mieux la grandeur dans la vengeance, la rapidité du soupçon, la promptitude dans l'exécution d'une pensée; la force du Maure et son irréflexion d'enfant.[20]

Perhaps the most striking example of a character defined by Balzac as an Othello, in both appearance and temperament, is Montès de Montéjanos in *La Cousine Bette*. Montès is 'doué par le climat équatorial du physique et de la couleur que nous prêtons tous à l'Othello du théâtre',[21] but, unlike his model, is an 'Othello qui ne se trompe pas'.[22] When his suspicions are aroused, Montès demands visible proof of his mistress's fidelity as does Shakespeare's Othello.[23] Just as Iago in the play suggests to Othello that he should kill Desdemona, so Carabine in the novel gives Montès the same idea.[24] The final outcome of the novel, the murderous poisoning of Valérie Marneffe motivated by savage jealousy, is thus predicted in

[19] *DL*, vol. V, p. 984.
[20] *FYO*, vol. V, pp. 1075-1076.
[21] *Be.*, vol. VII, p. 210.
[22] *Be.*, VII, p. 413.
[23] Act III scene iii.
[24] *Be.*, vol. VII, p. 413-414.

the narrative from the point where Montès is introduced as a metaphorical Othello. The reader who is familiar with Shakespeare is able to recognise the type of jealousy incarnated by Montès and to expect this outcome.

Other Shakespearian characters are used by Balzac in a similar way, as brief reference points for his own, and each is reduced to a dominant feature. Comparisons with characters from *Macbeth,* for example are linked with the supernatural, with hallucinations, and with violence. Thus in the publication of *Le cousin Pons* in *Le Constitutionnel* from 18 March to 10 May 1847, Balzac added to his original manuscript the description of Mme Cibot as 'cette affreuse lady Macbeth de la rue',[25] in order to render the character more sinister and threatening. In a similar simplification, Romeo and Juliette represent ideal love. In *Modeste Mignon* Canalis, when pretending to be a sincere lover, compares himself to Romeo,[26] and Modeste to Juliette. In such comparisons the tragic aspect of Romeo and Juliette is usually neglected by Balzac in favour of his simple reduction of the play's principal characters. In the same way, Hamlet is the incarnation of the nordic type with which Balzac compares Wilfrid in *Séraphîta,* saying that he 'était beau comme Hamlet résistant à l'ombre de son père, et avec laquelle il converse en la voyant se dresser pour lui seul au milieu des vivants.'[27] Shylock is the incarnation of the Jewish moneylender. Gigonnet, identified twice with Shylock, is just as pitiless as his model in *César Birotteau.* Balzac does not take account of Shylock's love for his daughter, Jessica, for his own Jewish moneylenders are too hardened to be fathers and are only capable of the love of gold. Iago and Richard III are both seen as the incarnation of unscrupulous ambition. Cousine Bette is compared to both of them at the same time and it is difficult to see what difference Balzac perceives between them.[28] Reduced in this way the characters of Shakespeare form part of the overall system of metaphor borrowed from the theatre through which Balzac conveys his own vision of the world.

---

[25] *CP*, vol. VI, p. 667. See Donald Adamson's article on *Le Cousin Pons* in *Modern Language Review*, (April 1964).

[26] *MM,* vol. I, p. 548.

[27] *S*, vol. XI, p. 763.

[28] *Be.,* vol. VII, p. 152.

Unlike these references to Shakespeare which reflect literary vogue rather than Balzac's personal preference, the abundant references to Molière in *La Comédie humaine* are a reflection of Balzac's profound admiration for his theatrical ancestor.[29] The 151 references to Molière's works clearly indicate the dominant influence of *Le Misanthrope* and *Tartuffe* in the creation of Balzac's own typology. The range of allusions is as follows:

Le Misanthrope	46	*Tartuffe*	44
L'Ecole des femmes	19	*Les Fourberies de Scapin*	12
L'Avare	9	*Les Femmes Savantes*	9
Don Juan	8	*Le Médecin malgré lui*	6
L'Amour médecin	4	*Le Bourgeois gentilhomme*	3
Le Malade imaginaire	1		

Most of Balzac's references to *Le Misanthrope* occur in novels written between 1835 and 1847, the period of Balzac's most mature work and the period in which, as has been noted above, he seems to have most consciously and systematically exploited the theatrical metaphor suggested by the overall title of his work.

Balzac uses the character of Célimène from *Le Misanthrope* as an image of 'la femme du monde de toutes les époques'.[30] She is the *coquette* who is fleetingly alluded to as a type to characterise the vain and worldly Emilie de Fontaine,[31] Mme d'Espard,[32] Mme Firmiani[33] and Mme Evangelista.[34] Only in *Le Cabinet des antiques* (1836-38) is there a full description of how Balzac perceives Célimène:

> Parmi les organisations diverses que les physiologistes ont remarquées chez les femmes, il en est une qui a je ne sais quoi de terrible, qui comporte une vigueur d'âme, une lucidité d'aperçus, une promptitude de décision, une insouciance, ou plutôt un parti pris sur certaines choses dont s'effraierait un homme. Ces facultés sont cachées sous les dehors de la faiblesse la plus gracieuse. [...] L'une des gloires de Molière est d'avoir admirablement peint, d'un

---

[29] See above, p. 12-14.
[30] *MJM*, vol. I, p. 324.
[31] *BS*, vol. I, p. 120.
[32] *IP*, vol. V, p. 282.
[33] *Fir.*, vol. I, p. 153.
[34] *CM*, vol. III, p. 592.

seul côté seulement, ces natures de femmes dans la plus grande
figure qu'il ait taillée en plein marbre: Célimène! Célimène, qui
représente la femme aristocratique.[35]

Here the description of Célimène is used to illustrate the character of
the duchesse de Maufrigneuse, and shows that Balzac not only sees
Célimène as a coquette but also as a woman who does not allow
herself to be ruled by emotions, who is capable of facing adversity,
and who is even cruel and egotistical. This is the only example in
which the figure of Célimène is used as more than a very rapid image
of comparison. In the other twelve instances in which Balzac alludes
to her she is referred to only by her one dominant characteristic.[36]

The other characters from *Le Misanthrope* quoted frequently by
Balzac are Alceste and Philinte. In the previous century Alceste's
uncompromising virtue had been seen as a mocking satire by
comparison to the perceived reason and flexibility of Philinte. In the
nineteenth century, however, Alceste, the victim of a fatal passion,
came to be seen as a romantic hero and Philinte as a cynical
hypocrite,[37] and it is in this context that they are used by Balzac as
metaphors for the moral stances and motives of his own characters.
The first mention of Alceste occurs in *Le Père Goriot* (1834-35),
where he is defined alongside Walter Scott's Jenny Deans and her
father as 'magnifiques images de la probité'.[38] The comic element of
Molière's character has been suppressed and from now on in *La
Comédie humaine* Alceste is used to define the type who is honest,
loyal and upstanding. The contrast between Molière's Alceste and
Philinte is maintained by Balzac in his characterisation and the two
are often used in juxtaposition, with Philinte as the incarnation of
lâcheté and inconsistency. In *Une fille d'Eve* (1838-39), Nathan the
dramatist, who is also metaphorically compared to a Shakespearian
drama, is further defined through this image of contrast taken from
the dramatic tradition:

---

[35] *CA*, vol. IV, p. 1036.
[36] See appendix II b.
[37] D.B. Wyndham Lewis, *Molière, The Comic Mask* (London: Eyre, 1959), pp.
89-95.
[38] *PG*, vol. III, p. 158.

> Nul ne sait mieux jouer les sentiments, se targuer de grandeurs fausses, se parer de beautés morales, se respecter en paroles, et se poser comme un Alceste en agissant comme Philinte.[39]

In repeatedly referring to Nathan as an actor, and in describing his character by reference to Shakespeare's dramas and to Molière's characters, Balzac seems to be consciously reinforcing Nathan's position in *La Comédie humaine* as an *homme de théâtre*. Nathan fails as statesman and businessman because he steps outside his correct milieu and the sense of this is translated to the reader through the images which constantly link him to the theatre.

The contrast between Alceste and Philinte is also used in *La Muse du département* (1843), to describe the way in which Mme de la Baudraye desires to be loved:

> [L]e digne magistrat aimait à la manière d'Alceste, quand Mme de La Baudraye voulait être aimée à la manière de Philinte. Les lâchetés de l'amour s'accommodent fort peu de la loyauté du Misanthrope.[40]

It can be seen from these examples that Balzac has lost all sense of the comic in Molière's *Misanthrope* and has ignored Molière's subtle satire to reduce his characters to one characteristic. Reduced in this way, the characters of *Le Misanthrope* are also made to serve Balzac's wider purpose of exposing the process of social disillusionment. In *Splendeurs et misères des courtisanes*[41] the process of disillusionment which takes place when the individual uncovers the backstage causes lying behind the false appearance of society is described in this way: '[L]es Alcestes deviennent des Philintes, les caractères se détrempent, les talents s'abâtardissent, la foi dans les belles œuvres s'envole'.[42]

---

[39] *FE*, vol. II, p. 304.
[40] *MD*, vol. IV, p. 785.
[41] Hereafter referred to as *Splendeurs et misères*.
[42] *SetM,* vol. VI, p. 437.

The same reduction of Molière's characters can be seen in all the examples in which Balzac takes them to define his own 'actor'. In an article in *Le Constitutionnel* in 1846, Balzac writes:

> Quand Molière introduisit un Monsieur Loyal dans Tartuffe il faisait l'Huissier et non tel huissier. C'était le fait et non un homme.[43]

Molière's types are so well-known that Balzac can use them as terms of comparison for his own characters, confident in the knowledge that his reader will understand the image. The allusions are often fleeting and accompanied by little explanation. In *Le Cousin Pons* (1846-1847), Madame Cibot's machinations to infiltrate Pons's household are likened to 'les séductions à la Dorine',[44] the doctor Poulain thanks Mme Cibot with 'une moue digne de Tartuffe',[45] and has 'les yeux ardents de Tartuffe'.[46] In *La Cousine Bette* (1846), Crevel looks at Mme Hulot with 'un regard comme Tartuffe en jette à Elmire'[47] and in the final part of *Illusions perdues* (1843), Petit-Claud practises 'une de ces audaces que Tartuffe seul se serait permise'.[48]

Through these brief references Balzac consistently links his work with the established theatre, and sums up characters and actions in an instant, dispensing with the need for lengthy descriptions. The references compare both the physical and the moral aspect of the characters so that the new character presented by Balzac is described by reference to a known character who has already been morally classified. Balzac's characters are not just stereotypes, however; many are exceptional, and the theatrical references add small details to their full portrayal.[49] Through theatrical metaphor Balzac not only reinforces the sense of his characters as actors, but achieves a

---

[43] *Le Constitutionnel,* 18 Nov. 1846.

[44] *CP*, vol. VII, p. 577.

[45] *CP*, vol. VII, p. 571.

[46] *CP*, vol. VII, p. 624.

[47] *Be*, vol. VII, pp. 57.

[48] *IP*, vol. V, p. 637.

[49] The brief character portrait also, of course, demonstrates the influence not only of the theatre but of other visual art forms, for example, the contemporary trend for caricature exemplified by the works of Henry Monnier, which rely on the concentration of essential characteristics. In this sense Balzac is a caricaturist in words.

theatrical economy of form in their characterisation and links them to a known literary tradition.

The 'Comedy' of Social Role-Play

The metaphors of *comédie, scène* and *vaudeville* may broadly be treated together, since they are all used figuratively to denote the play of masks and roles within society and the deliberate development of intrigue by certain characters. Together these three terms number 35 examples in the appendix, among which the metaphor of the *comédie* is the most frequent. The metaphor of the *comédie* is usually satirical, and is used as a vehicle to denote situations of intrigue, social interaction, posturing and falsehoods deliberately perpetrated by certain characters. Through these metaphors the reader is constantly invited to penetrate beneath the mask of the comedy and discover the underlying truth. The most frequent examples are to be found in *Illusions perdues* (1836-1843),[50] not surprisingly, since this novel depends for much of its action on the social charades played out in the theatres and salons of Paris; and in *Modeste Mignon* (1844,)[51] and *Ursule Mirouèt* (1840-41),[52] in which the provincial settings are perhaps less likely scenes for the satirical exposure of social posturing and role-play.

In all of the situations which Balzac metaphorically describes as *comédies* in his novels, there is at the basis either a love interest or the play of money and ambition, which are associated with the classical tradition of comedy in the theatre, and in particular with the plays of Molière and Beaumarchais. Balzac seems to have deemed it less necessary to intervene in the narrative in order to explain and justify his metaphorical use of the *comédie* than will be seen to be the case in his use of the *drame*, and it seems likely that this is because the *comédie* was part of a more established theatrical tradition.

Balzac's metaphor of *comédie* in all cases denotes situations in which certain characters are duped by others as in Classical stage comedy. This receives its most ironic treatment in *Une fille d'Eve*

---

[50] *IP*, vol. V, pp. 557, 600, 653, & 732.
[51] *MM*, vol. I, pp. 500, 600, 612, & 648.
[52] *UM*, vol. III, pp. 799, 850, 883, & 914.

(1838-39), in which the dramatist Nathan becomes the dupe of a series of charades and social trickeries engineered by his rivals and his social superiors:

> Nathan se mit à rire de lui-même, de lui, faiseur de scènes, qui s'était laissé prendre à un jeu de scène.
> – La comédie n'est plus là, dit-il en montrant la rampe, elle est chez vous.[53]

When engaged in the role-plays of faubourg St. Germain society, Nathan, who is successful in creating convincing intrigues for the stages of the boulevard theatres, is out of his depth, for the social charade is constructed more finely and played more adeptly than any of his vaudevilles or melodramas. Nathan comes to realise this in a scene which Balzac, in a skilful mirroring of stage and public, locates in Mme d'Espard's box at the theatre. The metaphor is amplified and given wider significance by the mirroring of the intrigue played out on the theatre stage, in the intrigue played out in the boxes of the auditorium. The fact that Nathan, who deals every day in *jeux de scène* and *comédies*, cannot recognise the intrigue of which he is the victim, shows that the social *comédie*, which Balzac would have his reader believe is real, is both more contrived and, paradoxically, more convincing than any fictitious *comédie* of the stage.

The same inability of the central character to detect the social comedy played around him despite familiarity with the scenarios of the stage can be seen in *Le Cousin Pons* (1846-1847). Given his essentially naive character, this is perhaps less surprising in Pons than in Nathan, but Balzac suggests that the daily spectacle of stage intrigues had made Pons 'blasé' and perhaps this over-familiarity could also explain Nathan's apparent naivety:

> Ce bonhomme qui, depuis douze ans, voyait jouer le vaudeville, le drame et la comédie sous ses yeux, ne reconnut pas les grimaces de la comédie sociale sur lesquelles sans doute il était blasé.[54]

---

[53] *FE*, vol. II, p. 331.
[54] *CP*, vol. VII, p. 549.

Similar instances of the social comedy being juxtaposed to one on stage take place in *Illusions perdues* (1836-1843), where Lucien in the first instance witnesses the *comédies* played out in the various boxes by du Châtelet, Rastignac, de Marsay, Félix de Vandenesse and other great actors of the social stage,[55] and in the second instance becomes himself the unwitting subject of the *comédie* played out in Mme d'Espard's box.[56] In both instances there is no explicit use of the term *comédie* or *scène* in the metaphor but Balzac's satirical intentions nevertheless are clear, and as in *Une fille d'Eve*, the intrigue enacted in the boxes is more subtle, more refined and therefore more dangerous to its victims than the stage intrigue which it mirrors. Explicit use of the terms *comédie* and *scène* is only made in the third part of the novel, which is located in the provincial town of Angoulême. A possible explanation for this is that it was only after giving the title of *Comédie* and subtitles of *scènes* to the total work in 1841, by which time the first two parts of the novel had been completed,[57] that Balzac began systematically to exploit the metaphorical use of these terms. This assumption is further supported by the fact that the other two novels in which there is equally abundant metaphorical use of *scène* and *comédie*, *Modeste Mignon* (1844),[58] and *Ursule Mirouèt* (1840-41),[59] were also written after the publication of the collective title.

Another, and perhaps more convincing, reason for Balzac's explicit insistence on the metaphor of the *comédie* or *scène* only in the last part of *Illusions perdues,* might be that in the preceding Parisian episodes, appropriately located in the boxes and salons of a high society which places great emphasis on appearance, nuances of gesture and subtleties of manners, the abstract metaphor and its underlying satire can easily be understood by the reader, whereas in the provinces, where the social stage is not so easily seen to mirror the theatre world, explicit metaphor is necessary to enable the reader to discern the transaction between contexts. Lucien's repentance on

---

[55] *IP*, vol. V, p. 265.

[56] *IP*, vol. V, pp. 274-283.

[57] *Les Deux Poètes* appeared for the first time in 1837, and *Un grand homme de province à Paris* in 1839. The third part, *Les souffrances de l'inventeur*, was not written and published until 1843. See: *Histoire du texte, IP*, vol. V, pp. 1119-1126.

[58] *MM,* vol. I, pp. 500, 600, 612 & 648.

[59] *UM,* vol. III, pp. 799, 850, 883, & 914.

his return to Angoulême is a 'scène parfaitement jouée',[60] which has no more solid a foundation than his social posturings in Paris; the demise of David Séchard is a 'scène' which 'se joue assez souvent au fond du cabinet des avoués',[61] and of which he is the victim just as Lucien had been the victim of similar intrigues in Paris; Lucien's fake triumph in Angoulême is 'mis en scène [...] par un machiniste passionné',[62] in the same way that his demise is engineered by his enemies in Paris; and on the novel's final page Cérizet is said to have sought a new outlet for his capacity for intrigue and role-play 'sur la scène de province',[63] which Balzac has shown to be no less fraught with dissimulations than the more visible metaphorical stage of Paris.

The message conveyed by the explicit metaphor of the *scène* in the provincial setting of *Illusions perdues* is exactly the same as that conveyed by the implicit metaphor in the Parisian settings. Behind the deceptive façade of these sleepy provincial towns, certain characters are just as inclined to role-playing, dissimulation and intrigue as their Parisian counterparts, for human nature, as the reader is told by Vautrin in *Le Père Goriot*, is the same 'en haut, en bas, au milieu'.[64] The metaphor of the *scène* thus becomes not only the site of a satirical comment which punctuates the narrative, but part of the underlying and unifying philosophy of the narrative, which indicates the universal human propensity to corruption and the ultimate unknowability of truth.

The same can be said of *Ursule Mirouèt* (1840-41), in which the metaphorical uses of the terms *scène* and *comédie* convey the same observations of human nature. Again, the location of the action is in a provincial town and again the metaphor is made explicit to show that the propensity to role-play and intrigue is endemic throughout society and not just in Paris. In *Ursule Mirouèt*, perhaps more clearly than elsewhere, the play of money and ambition is at the root of the intrigue enacted by the extended Minoret family. Ursule is warned by Dr. Minoret of the 'comédies que les Minoret, les Crémière et les

---

[60] *IP*, vol. V, p. 557.
[61] *IP*, vol. V, p. 600.
[62] *IP*, vol. V, p. 653.
[63] *IP*, vol. V, p. 732.
[64] *PG*, vol. III p. 141.

Massin vont venir jouer'.[65] Familiar with the nature of his heirs, Dr. Minoret is well aware that after his death 'la comédie des héritiers commencera'.[66] In preparing Ursule for the deceptions and intrigue she will have to face, Balzac, through Minoret, also prepares the reader and makes him ready to accept the contortions and complexities of the intrigue which follows.

In the process of exposing through metaphor the endemic nature of social falsehood, Balzac also shows that the metaphorical *comédie* has its perpetrators and its victims. Whereas the metaphor of the *drame* in *La Comédie humaine* will be seen to indicate a tragic and often unavoidable set of circumstances in which characters become caught up, or which invade their lives without invitation, or which are dictated by their own essential nature, the metaphor of the *comédie* or *scène*, shows certain characters as perpetrators of scenarios which are enacted in full consciousness of their self-appointed roles, and other characters as unwitting or powerless victims of these intrigues and machinations. While the *drame* usually has its roots in a complex web of abstractions, the *comédie* can usually be traced to a particular individual or set of individuals with specific objectives in mind. This is certainly the case with the examples cited so far in which the *comédie* of the Minoret heirs in *Ursule Mirouèt*, of Cérizet and Lucien's enemies in *Illusions perdues*, and of Nathan's enemies in *Une fille d'Eve*, is motivated by the connected issues of money and ambition.

Similarly, it is financial interest and not love which Balzac describes as a comedy in *Le Contrat de mariage*:

> Les événements et les idées qui amenèrent le mariage de Paul avec Mlle Evangélista sont une introduction à l'œuvre, uniquement destinée à retracer la grande comédie qui précède toute vie conjugale. Jusqu'ici cette scène a été négligée par les auteurs dramatiques quoiqu'elle offre des ressources neuves à leur verve. [...] Ces comédies jouées par-devant notaire ressemblent toutes plus ou moins à celle-ci.[67]

---

[65] *UM*, vol. III, p. 850.
[66] *UM*, vol. III, p. 914.
[67] *CM*, vol. III, p. 551.

Even here, as early as 1835, Balzac is conscious of the potential of the *comédie* as a metaphorical way of referring to episodes of intrigue and scheming, and does not miss the opportunity to point out how his novel not only matches the stage comedy but surpasses it in its novelty.

In *Modeste Mignon* (1844), the motive of love rather than financial interest prompts the abundant use of theatrical metaphor, and here Balzac develops the imagery to the point of excess. There are no fewer than sixteen examples of explicit theatrical metaphor in the 255 pages of this novel, four of which relate to the *comédie* of which Modeste is the deliberate instigator, and there are a further 17 examples which compare certain characters to well-known characters from the established theatrical tradition.[68] Modeste's situation is described from the outset as the 'comédie de *La Fille mal gardée*',[69] and the 'répétition de la première scène jouée au lever du rideau de la Création';[70] the intrigue mounted by Charles and Dumay is referred to by Balzac as 'la comédie qui devait se jouer au Chalet';[71] and as the intrigue develops beyond her control Modeste decides to 'assister, en personne désintéressée, à ce qu'elle nommait le vaudeville des prétendus'.[72]

Theatrical metaphor in this novel pervades the entire narrative so that it becomes an expression of the central issues of the plot. From the outset Modeste has the impression of being able to control and direct the *comédie* which she has set in motion, and to some extent her misconception is justified. However, Modeste becomes the dupe of a further *comédie,* and throughout the first half of the novel she is a deceiver who is also deceived. The whole intrigue is expressed through theatrical metaphors which lead the reader deeper into a complex web of different levels of deception which hinge on the contrast between reality and appearance. While the intrigue deepens, Modeste and La Brière write to each other under assumed names which could be interpreted as metaphorical masks, suggestive of the masks of the *commœdia dell'arte.* In this way, not only through its

---

[68] See Appendix II. b.
[69] *MM*, vol. I, p. 500.
[70] *MM*, vol. I, p. 501.
[71] *Ibid.*, p. 600.
[72] *Ibid.*, p. 612.

explicit uses of terminology, but also through the role-play upon which the entire narrative depends, the *comédie* becomes a wider metaphor for all the false appearances portrayed by the characters, and is underpinned at every turn by literary references and comparisons to theatrical characters. In turn these references are justified by the fact that Modeste consumes huge numbers of literary works. Modeste's life comes to imitate and ultimately to surpass the theatre in the complexity and extent of its intrigues and the theatrical metaphor is fundamental to the expression of this process:

> A la période affamée de ses lectures succéda, chez Modeste, le jeu de cette étrange faculté donnée aux imaginations vives de se faire acteur dans une vie arrangée comme dans un rêve, [...] de jouer enfin en soi-même la comédie de la vie, et, au besoin celle de la mort. Modeste jouait, elle, la comédie de l'amour. Elle se supposait adorée à ses souhaits.[73]

By her own invention and by others' intervention Modeste's entire life becomes a metaphor for the 'comédie de l'amour'.

Although the metaphor of the *comédie*, here and in the examples cited previously, often announces situations which have the potential to become disastrous for the individuals concerned, the final dénouement of the intrigue usually sees some sort of order restored. Modeste marries La Brière, Ursule marries Savinien, and in *Illusions perdues* Lucien is saved from suicide and David Séchard pursues his inventions in tranquillity. It is true that there are single examples of the explicit metaphorical use of the terms *comédie, scène* or *vaudeville* in such novels as *Le Cousin Pons, Eugénie Grandet, La Fille aux yeux d'or, Le Père Goriot* and *La Cousine Bette*, which culminate in tragic endings.[74] However, on the whole, the sustained use of one category of metaphor seems virtually to preclude the use of the other and announces the nature of the final outcome of the plot from its very beginning. Consistent with this theory, in the novels in

---

[73] *MM*, vol. I, pp. 505-506.
[74] See appendix I, d.

which there is an abundant use of the term *comédie* there are very few examples of the term *drame* – none in *Le Contrat de mariage*, one in *Illusions perdues*,[75] one in *Modeste Mignon*,[76] and none in *Ursule Mirouèt*. Equally, there are few or no examples of the term *comédie* in most of the novels in which the metaphor of the *drame* dominates – none in *Les Chouans*, one in *Le Père Goriot*,[77] none in *Une ténébreuse affaire*, and none in *Pierrette*. In each novel the mode of the metaphor tends to one form or the other, to tragedy or to comedy.

In the case of the *comédie*, it has been shown that the metaphor is primarily used to effect the satirical exposure of the hypocrisies of a society in which social interaction at all levels and in all spheres is subject to dissemblance, false appearance, role-play and the propensity for intrigue. The image extends beyond a simple description of social role-play to work at a more abstract level in order to become part of Balzac's uncovering of all the falsehoods of his society and is a fundamental mode of expression for his 'histoire des mœurs'. The metaphor of the *comédie* is also, of course, a subtle satire on Balzac's own contemporary reader, for only a provisional and arbitrary privilege distinguishes the reader from the characters, since they are all part of the same human and social condition.

The World as a Stage

Whether the events of the novel are metaphorically denoted as a *comédie* or as a *drame*, a stage is required for their enactment and it is in this context that the terms of *théâtre* and *spectacle* are used by Balzac. These two groups of metaphors together number forty-nine examples and constitute approximately 20% of the total number of uses of theatrical metaphor in *La Comédie humaine* cited in the appendix. If life is a drama then the world, as Balzac reminds the reader of *Splendeurs et misères*, is the theatre stage where that drama is acted out: 'Le monde, n'est-il pas un théâtre?'[78] The image of the world as a theatre is a familiar one which suggests both stage and auditorium, action and observer. The streets of Paris are presented in

[75] *IP*, vol. V, p. 711.
[76] *MM*, vol. I, p. 480.
[77] *PG*, vol. III, p. 142.
[78] *SetM*, vol. VI, p. 828.

the opening scenes of *Ferragus* (1833) as a continual parade, and in *Une double famille* (1830), Caroline's view of the street gives her a hidden vantage point like that of actors behind the closed curtain in the theatre, from which she can witness the spectacle offered by Paris:

> Cette échappée de vue, que l'on comparerait volontiers au trou pratiqué pour les acteurs dans un rideau de théâtre, lui permettait de distinguer une multitude de voitures élégantes et une foule de monde emportées avec la rapidité des ombres chinoises.[79]

Occasionally the image of the theatre in Balzac's novels is that of a stage on which events are acted out only for the privileged viewing of the reader, and the first example of this can be found in *Les Chouans* (1828-29), where the vast Breton landscape, already noted as 'si dramatique',[80] is described as a theatre where the actions of war will be played out against a detailed backdrop: 'Une imagination exercée peut, d'après ces détails, concevoir le théâtre et les instruments de la guerre'.[81] In order to assume its full signification the image of the theatre requires the engagement of the reader's imagination.

With the reader's participation the image of the theatre in *Les Chouans* is used to denote the location and background of a dramatic action. There is only one other instance in *La Comédie humaine* in which Balzac uses the theatre to suggest a battle-ground or scene of large-scale political events and this occurs in the first part of *Béatrix* (1838), where the events of the Cent-Jours are described as a 'magique spectacle' and as a 'pièce de théâtre en trois mois'.[82] Both images suggest a vast perspective, and an action which takes place over a wide geographical area, and which reaches beyond the literal stage. In *Les Chouans* the geographical area is an empty theatre stage waiting for the actors to appear. A similar image of the background setting as a vast and empty stage can be seen much later in Balzac's work in *Une ténébreuse affaire* (1838-40), where the Gondreville

[79] *DF*, vol. II, p. 36.
[80] *Ch.*, vol. VIII, p. 913.
[81] *Ch.*, vol. VIII, pp. 919-920.
[82] *B*, vol. II, p. 692.

estate is described as a 'magnifique théâtre'[83] where the events of the novel will be played out for the reader.

In *Béatrix*, the main characters of the novel, in which the plot will largely depend on theatrical role-play, are placed from an early stage against a setting which is described as a theatre, and the sense of this comes to pervade the entire novel and to influence the characters' actions as they become aware of the sense of drama which surrounds them. The sudden revelation of Béatrix's feelings for Calyste is played out against the vista of the des Touches estate:

> En ce moment, elle était arrivée au faîte du rocher, d'où se voyait l'immense Océan d'un côté, la Bretagne de l'autre avec ses îles d'or, ses tours féodales et ses bouquets d'ajoncs. Jamais une femme ne fut sur un plus beau théâtre pour faire un si grand aveu.[84]

The metaphor of the theatre then, when used as an image of the outdoor world, denotes the geographical location of an action or intrigue which goes beyond the spatial confines of an actual theatre stage. In these instances the location is a metaphorical stage for the reader only, since the scene is not viewed by characters other than those who are directly involved.

In the social domain of Paris, however, the image of the theatre comes to denote not simply a pictorial background against which events are set for the reader to view from his privileged position, but spheres of activity in which the characters operate and from which they can be seen both by the reader and by the other characters of the novel. In this way the two distinct spheres of Cardot's social and domestic life in *La Muse du département* (1843), are described as stages on which he is active and on which he is observed by Lousteau:

> L'ennui siégeait sur tous les meubles. Les draperies pendaient tristement. La salle à manger ressemblait à celle d'Harpagon. Lousteau n'eût pas connu Malaga d'avance, à la seule inspection de ce ménage il aurait deviné que l'existence du notaire se passait sur un autre théâtre.[85]

---

[83] *TA*, vol. VIII, p. 503.
[84] *B*, vol. II, p. 819.
[85] *MD*, vol. IV, p. 740.

The image of the dull, bourgeois dining room of Molière's *L'Avare* is starkly contrasted with the image of Cardot's alternative life taking place on a different stage, and suggests, by implication of the contrast, that in this second sphere his life is full of event and intrigue. The image is doubly effective in that Cardot's social life is not only acted out in full view of society far from the strict confines of his dull home, but is acted out with a second-rate actress, Malaga, in the actual theatre environment.

In *Une fille d'Eve* (1838-39), the three spheres of Nathan's public activities are represented by the same image of the theatre stage as an area within which certain characters operate in full view of society. In order to sustain his position is society, Nathan must find the strength to be 'à la fois sur trois théâtres: le Monde, le Journal et les Coulisses'.[86] On each metaphorical stage Nathan must act out the role of dandy, journalist and dramatist accordingly, and consistently subject himself to society's critical gaze. In the Parisian setting the spectacle of the characters operating as if on a theatre stage is not offered exclusively to the reader, but is open to the whole of the society represented in *La Comédie humaine*, and that society is shown to be as harsh and as critical of any new actor as the most discerning theatre audience. Nathan's attempts to mount the political stage are as public as the staging of his vaudevilles and are thwarted because, while he is playing in centre stage and leaving himself open to public judgment, his enemies are engineering his demise from the wings.

In the same novel Marie de Vandenesse is attracted by the lights of the social stage, not just in order to witness its dazzling spectacle, but to become part of that spectacle, dreaming of the pleasure of moving 'sur un vaste théâtre, [...] devant un monde observateur'.[87] The whole of Parisian society is repeatedly portrayed by Balzac as a vast theatre in which characters move symbiotically from auditorium to stage, to see and be seen. In this respect the general image of the Parisian social realm as a theatre, like that of the external geographical setting, far exceeds the spatial constraints of the actual theatre since it also implicitly encompasses the *salons*, supper-parties, and excursions which constitute social life. However, the image frequently becomes

[86] *FE*, vol. II, p. 349.
[87] *FE*, vol. II, p. 285.

exemplified and intensified by scenes which take place in the actual theatres which are the hub of social life in the Paris of *La Comédie humaine*. Here the image works as a two-way mirror in which social life is likened to theatre and the theatre is the place of social interaction. The image of the vast social scene thus becomes contained within a confined area which is not much larger than the actual stage. This continual mirroring of stage action and social action in the Parisian theatres in *Un grand homme* (1839), and the first two parts of *Splendeurs et misères* (1839-1844), shows in particular how the metaphor of the 'théâtre du monde' consists in the fact of characters being observed by each other.

On the occasion of Esther's first visit to the Opéra in the company of Nucingen in *Splendeurs et misères*, the action on the stage is of little consequence to the members of the theatre audience, who are far more concerned by the reappearance of Esther, who becomes the sole object of their attention:

> Le lendemain, à l'Opéra, l'aventure du retour d'Esther fut la nouvelle des coulisses. Le matin, de deux heures à quatre heures tout le Paris des Champs Elysées avait reconnu la Torpille, et savait enfin quel était l'objet de la passion du baron de Nucingen. [...] A Paris, comme en province, tout se sait. La police de la rue de Jérusalem n'est pas si bien faite que celle du monde, où chacun s'espionne sans le savoir.[88]

Fully conscious of the fact that society's eyes are observing at all times, certain characters are unable ever to step out of their role and abandon the sense of being on a public stage. Esther began her career as a *petit rat* at the Opéra and although she may never have attained the position of *premier sujet*, she is no less capable of holding the centre stage.

The same message is conveyed in *Illusions perdues*, where, as has already been noted, the juxtaposition of action on stage and in the boxes perpetuates the sense of the auditorium as the real object of observation for both the reader and the fictional characters. Even from the outset in Angoulême, Lucien has the sense that the highest

---

[88] *SetM*, vol. VI, p. 623.

social sphere is 'le seul théâtre sur lequel il devait se tenir',[89] and Louise de Bargeton encourages him to feel that Paris will be 'le théâtre de vos succès!'[90] The sense of the image is that the high society of Paris is a showcase, rather than necessarily the scene of a drama, and this is borne out when Lucien makes his appearance as an observer of the 'spectacle unique'[91] offered by the audience at the Opéra, becoming absorbed in turn by the 'pompeux spectacle du ballet du cinquième acte' and the 'aspect de la salle dans laquelle son regard alla de loge en loge'.[92] Ultimately, however, Lucien's attempts to 'franchir l'espace',[93] which separates him from the stage and keeps him on the outside looking in, are thwarted and the streets of Paris become the 'théâtre de sa défaite'.[94]   Lucien's failed attempts to achieve social eminence are also expressed in the abstract metaphor of his restriction to the *coulisses* of the small theatres, for he is never able in *Illusions perdues* to make the transition from this area of obscurity, in which he associates only with actresses and journalists, to the brightly-lit stage of high society.

While the external, geographical landscape is represented as a theatre stage on which events and actions take place, and the social landscape of Paris is represented as a theatre which is above all a show-case or spectacle, a third aspect of the metaphor emerges in the internal locations of Balzac's provincial settings. Here, the claustrophobic interiors of dark and sleepy provincial houses become the closely confined stages of sinister dramas and intrigues, and the image comes closer to the actual theatre stage in which actions are confined within small spaces enclosed by scenery. Thus the 'théâtre étroit de la province', which is a recurring image in *La Comédie humaine*,[95] comes to denote the drawing rooms, kitchens and interiors where the characters come into contact. For example, in *Pierrette* the salon of Denis and Sylvie Rogron 'allait devenir le centre d'intérêts qui cherchaient un théâtre';[96] and in *Eugénie Grandet* the *salle* is

[89] *IP*, vol. V, p. 174.
[90] *Ibid.*, p. 249.
[91] *Ibid.*, p. 283.
[92] *Ibid.*, p. 284.
[93] *Ibid.*, p. 249.
[94] *Ibid.*, p. 271.
[95] *MJM*, vol. I, p. 222 & *CV*, vol. IX, p. 810.
[96] *P*, vol. IV, p. 69.

described as having the combined function of a variety of settings in which characters might typically be brought together on the stage:

> La salle est à la fois l'antichambre, le salon, le cabinet, le boudoir, la salle à manger; elle est le théâtre de la vie domestique.[97]

The provincial towns need their stage as much as Paris does, and in this way the *salle* provides both their stage and their auditorium since it is the site of the provincial dramas and the focal point of the characters' interaction, fulfilling the same function as the *planches*, *foyers* and *loges* of the Parisian theatres. The room which has been established as the theatre of domestic life at the beginning of *Eugénie Grandet* is the scene of the novel's final tragic dénouement. Here the characters gathered for their usual card games are both actors and spectators, just as in the theatres of Paris. In front of her familiar guests, Eugénie asks M. de Bonfons to remain behind after the others have left, thereby indicating that she has accepted to marry him. This simple event causes as much of a furore in the 'théâtre étroit de la province' as does Esther's appearance at the Opéra with Nucingen in *Splendeurs et misères*:

> Au moment où l'assemblée se leva en masse pour quitter le salon, il y eut un coup de théâtre qui retentit dans Saumur, de là dans l'arrondissement et dans les quatre préfectures environnantes.[98]

If the image of the theatre becomes more spatially confined in the provincial setting, its effects are no less far-reaching than those brought about in the Parisian setting.

The image of the theatre as the confined location of an action becomes further intensified in situations where it is used to describe the staging of the legal process. For example, in *Le Curé de village*, the 'drame judiciaire' brings Mme Graslin 'sur le théâtre où ses vertus brillèrent du plus vif éclat';[99] and in *Modeste Mignon* Canalis describes the courtroom as 'le plus grand théâtre du monde'.[100] The suggestions of the image require little explanation, being evocative of

---

[97] *EG*, vol. III, p. 1040.
[98] *EG*, vol. III, p. 1192.
[99] *CV*, vol. IX, p. 699.
[100] *MM*, vol. I, p. 628.

both the clash of interests and of the enclosed but nevertheless public nature of the setting, in which characters speak in turn according to a prescribed procedure.

More intensely still, the metaphor of the *théâtre* is also occasionally used to denote the play of conflict or disturbing emotion within the mind of the individual, as in the case of Eugène in *Le Père Goriot*, who is described by Vautrin as 'un théâtre où s'émeuvent les plus beaux sentiments'.[101] More often, however, the term is used, in the absence of more concrete medical or scientific terminology, to describe psychological malfunction, for example in the case of Louis Lambert who cannot be cured because 'sa tête est le théâtre de phénomènes sur lesquels la médecine n'a nul pouvoir',[102] and the daughter of M. Bernard in *L'Envers de l'histoire contemporaine*, whose 'âme a été le théâtre de tous les prodigues du somnambulisme, comme son corps est le théâtre de toutes les maladies'.[103] Here the theatrical imagery denotes psychological conflict and the interaction of heightened emotions. The description of madness through theatrical imagery also perhaps reflects the contemporary fashion for Shakespeare on the Parisian stage and for *Macbeth*, which is often quoted by Balzac in *La Comédie humaine*.[104]

It is possible to see from the examples cited that Balzac's figurative use of the terms *théâtre* and *spectacle* falls into four principal metaphorical senses none of which is confined to a specific period of his work, or to a particular type of novel. Used metaphorically the theatre may denote any place of action, and covers a wide area of reference from the open vistas of the external geographical location to the most confined area of the mind of the individual. Applied to the landscape, the image of the theatre primarily describes a backdrop or location in which events and actions take place; when applied to Paris it denotes the sense of spectacle offered by society and the desire of that society to be observed; in the provincial setting it denotes the home and fulfils the same functions as the actual Parisian theatre, being both the centre of its social activity and the site of its dramas; finally, when used to

---

[101] *PG*, vol. III, p. 186.
[102] *IP*, vol. V, pp. 419-420.
[103] *EHC*, vol. VIII, p. 339.
[104] See above, pp. 173 & 175, and appendix II b.

describe the mind and body of the individual the metaphor describes the play of excessive emotions.

The Social 'Backstage' of the Troisième Dessous and Coulisses

Just as the metaphor of the front of the theatre suggests the light of the stage and an action played out in full view, the metaphor of its wings and backstage suggests obscurity, the manipulation of machinery and the passageways which lead from light to darkness. There are relatively few examples of explicit use of theatrical terminology in these images and it is rather implicitly, depending largely on the reader's interpretation, that this group of metaphors functions in *La Comédie humaine*. In this respect the examination here, particularly in so far as it applies to the Rubempré cycle, can only expand certain points already made by Peter Brooks who has explored in some depth the broad metaphor of the theatre as a signifier of the false appearance and hidden machinations of society.[105]

Brooks's own comments on *Illusions perdues* can be used to summarise his analysis of the theatrical metaphor of the whole of the Rubempré cycle. In turn these points may also be applied to the total theatrical metaphor of *La Comédie humaine*:

> The theatre is the fascination, light, erotic lure of the scene; and also the wings, the world of backstage, which is both disenchanting and more profoundly fascinating [...]. In its double aspect, the theatre seems to offer the possiblity of both representation and machination, of play on the great stage and manipulation of the roles represented from the wings.[106]

As Brooks notes, the notions of stage and backstage, illusion and disillusionment, appearance and machination apply not only in the literal theatre where much of the action of *Illusions perdues* takes place, but to the whole of life represented by the novel, for even in the provinces events are manipulated from the backstage by the

---

[105]   Peter Brooks, 'Balzac, Melodrama and Metaphor' in *The Hudson Review*, XXII (no. 2, Summer 1969), pp. 213-228; and *The Melodramatic Imagination*, pp. 2-11, & pp. 118-130.
[106]   *Ibid.*, pp. 122-123.

Cointet brothers. The metaphor can be applied to all the novels of *La Comédie humaine* in which Balzac's concepts of plot and semi-omniscient narration are based on the notion of a social reality that is only appearance and where more sinister truths lurk behind the scenery. Balzac's 'dramatisation' of his text consists in communicating the truths lurking below the surface realities, in the wings and the backstage from where actions are manipulated.

Frequently the stage and backstage are seen to converge so that it becomes impossible for characters to distinguish between the two, to know who is 'in role' and who is not. Like the masked ball which opens *Splendeurs et misères*, Paris is a landscape of swirling travesties and false appearances behind which lie the real causes of events, but which can only be penetrated by rare characters such as Jacques Collin. It is only at the ball, disguised in a mask and cloak, that Collin can appear on the social stage, for his criminal status ordinarily confines him to the backstage whence he directs and manipulates. The masked ball, appropriately situated in the milieu of the Opéra, is theatrical both in the spectacle which it offers and in the function of exposition which it performs in the narrative. It is described as the occasion on which 'les différents cercles dont se compose la société parisienne se retrouvent, se reconnaissent et s'observent',[107] and foreshadows symbolically the interaction of different social groups that will take place in the subsequent narrative. It also suggests from the outset the play of masks and falsehoods, and interpenetration of stage and backstage which will characterise almost every encounter between the novel's characters.

Theatrical metaphor is implicit in this opening scene in which the characters at the ball seek to discover the identities, truths and intrigues which lie behind the various masks. The uncovering of hidden identity becomes the central preoccupation of the plot, as false appearances increasingly become manipulated from the hidden backstage of society by Jacques Collin. Only towards the end of the novel does Balzac concretise this image of hidden machination through an explicit theatrical metaphor which he explains to his reader. The different levels of society are likened to a theatre in which the criminal class is described as:

---

[107] *SetM*, vol. VI, p. 431.

[C]e monde souterrain qui, depuis l'origine des empires à capitale, s'agite dans les caves, dans les sentines, dans le *troisième dessous* des sociétés, pour emprunter à l'art dramatique une expression vive et saisissante. [...] Le Troisième Dessous est la dernière cave pratiquée sous les planches de l'Opéra, pour en recéler les machines, les machinistes, la rampe, les apparitions, les diables bleus que vomit l'enfer, etc.[108]

The reader is constantly invited in Balzac's theatrical metaphors to look for greater signification beyond and behind the representation. Here this is achieved by Balzac's conscious explanation of his image. The area beneath the theatre stage is not only an image of depth, and darkness denoting the lowest social level, that of the criminal class, but is also an image of the power of that class to manipulate what takes place on the front of the stage, in the visible social realm. The wider implication of the image is that the true causes of events are always to be found in the 'backstage' of society. This manipulation from the backstage is only possible because the *troisième dessous* is not an underworld which is restrained behind the façade of society, but rather is connected to that society by passageways and by the wings, and possesses the machinery to control the visible environment from behind and beneath.

In an extension of the metaphor, which is left to the reader's interpretation, Lucien's apartment and Vautrin's garret are also part of the backstage of the social theatre. Vautrin's garret is the *troisième dessous* from which he directs events and Lucien's rooms are the wings in which he waits to make his entrances into the gaze of the outside world. Through the theatrical metaphor which pervades the whole of *Splendeurs et misères,* the model of life becomes double-tiered, so that acts on the surface of society are explainable only in terms of what is going on behind and beneath, in the *bagne,* in Vautrin's garret and in Lucien's rooms. This point has already been made by Brooks who notes that, 'what is represented on the public social stage is only a figuration of what lies behind, in the domain of true power and significance'.[109]

---

[108] *Ibid.,* p. 828.
[109] Brooks, *The Melodramatic Imagination,* p. 121.

Brooks has not noted, however, that the explicit image of the *troisième dessous* occurs in two other novels of *La Comédie humaine*. In *La Cousine Bette* (1846) the image is clearly linked to the definition given in the final part of *Splendeurs et misères,* which was published for the first time in the same year. In what appears to be a conscious exploitation of the same image, Balzac describes how the sister of Jacques Collin is brought up from the underworld by the scheming of the novel's conspirators:

> Il [Victorin] reconduisit cette horrible inconnue, évoquée des antres de l'espionnage, comme du troisième dessous de l'Opéra se dresse un monstre au coup de baguette d'une fée dans un ballet-féerie.[110]

The appearance of Jacqueline Collin may seem merely accidental to those characters of the novel who are taken in by the illusion, but the image of the *troisième dessous* clearly signifies to the reader that Jacqueline belongs to the criminal underworld and that her sudden appearance has been secretly engineered. The image also occurs in *Sarrasine* (1830), where the mysterious old man 'semblait être sorti de dessous terre, poussé par quelque mécanisme de théâtre'.[111] The use of the image here differs somewhat from the later instances in *La Cousine Bette* and *Splendeurs et misères* since it contains only a sense of mystery, illusion and the paranormal, rather than the machinations of the social underworld. It seems that the fullest implications of the image only occurred to Balzac towards the end of his career, in those novels where the play of social falsehood and backstage manipulation and corruption is the central concern of the plot.

The *troisième dessous* and backstage areas of the actual theatre, as Lucien finds on his first visit to the Panorama-Dramatique, are connected to the front of the stage by the passageways and wings and this is the same in Balzac's imagery. The actual theatre represented in *La Comédie humaine* has its *loges, baignoires, parterre, coulisses* and *troisième dessous,* and directly mirrors Balzac's representation of Restoration society at large, which has its hierarchy of high-

---

[110] *Be.,* vol. VII, p. 388.

[111] *S,* vol. VI, p. 1050.

society,[112] bourgeoisie, students, artists and underworld. In both hierarchies the apparently distinct parts are connected by a labyrinthine series of dark, hidden passageways. In the opening pages of *Ferragus* Balzac tells at length of the different types of interconnecting streets which make up Paris,[113] of the 'rues de mauvaise compagnie où vous ne voudriez pas demeurer, et des rues où vous placeriez volontiers votre séjour';[114] and the beginning of *Splendeurs et misères*, tells how the maze of dark streets surrounding Esther's home connects with and winds around the fashionable boulevards:

> Ces rues étroites, sombres et boueuses, où s'exercent des industries peu soigneuses de leurs dehors, prennent à la nuit une physionomie mystérieuse et pleine de contrastes. En venant des endroits lumineux de la rue Saint-Honoré, de la rue Neuve-des-Petits-Champs et de la rue de Richelieu, où se presse une foule incessante, où reluisent les chefs-d'œuvre de l'Industrie, de la Mode et des Arts, tout homme à qui le Paris du soir est inconnu serait saisi d'une terreur triste en tombant dans le lacis de petites rues qui cercle cette lueur reflétée jusque sur le ciel. Une ombre épaisse succède à des torrents de gaz. De loin en loin, un pâle réverbère jette sa lueur incertaine et fumeuse qui n'éclaire plus certaines impasses noires.[115]

If the brightly lit social world of the fashionable boulevards is society's stage, then the dark, interconnecting passageways hidden behind can be seen as its *coulisses*. Although Peter Brooks has not noted this relationship between the streets and the *coulisses* he has said that, 'the streets and walls of Paris, under pressure of the narrator's insistence, become the elements of a Dantesque vision, leading the reader into infernal circles'.[116] In this sense the physical context of the novel's setting relates to the moral context of its theme, for all levels of society are connected by the obscure backstage of society, which is where the true causes of events are shown to lie.

---

[112] Composed of the *Ancien régime* and of the 'new' aristocracy represented by characters such as Goriot's daughters.
[113] *F*, vol. V, pp. 793-796.
[114] *Ibid.*, p. 793.
[115] *SetM*, vol. VI, p. 446.
[116] Peter Brooks, *The Melodramatic Imagination*, pp. 2-3.

Thus throughout *La Comédie humaine,* the same motivating forces can be seen at work in the *coulisses* of society, as operate in the *coulisses* of the theatre itself: the imperatives of sex, money and personal ambition, and the secret machinations of certain groups. This mirroring function of the theatrical metaphor is all the more effective because it is brought into relief by the exposure of the corrupt and materialistic forces governing the actual theatre world, which, as has been shown in the two previous chapters, has its basis in historical reality. The actual backstage of the theatre reveals not only hidden machinery, but groups such as the claque and the journalists and the protectors who engineer success. Balzac exposes the hidden forces governing the actual theatre world and at the same time uses that exposure as an image with which to describe society at large. In this way the imagery is underpinned by historical reality. As a result the reader is more readily able to accept the existence of similar, hidden groups which Balzac shows to be operative in the world at large.

Any reader of Balzac, as Peter Brooks has noted,[117] is struck by the prevalence of secret societies and occult powers. There are organizations such as the Confrérie de la Consolation, Les Grands Fanandels, the Dévorants, the Chevaliers de la Désœuvrance, and looser organizations of plotters, such as the bankers in *César Birotteau,* the Cointet brothers in *Illusions perdues,* the secret police in *Splendeurs et misères.* The sphere of activity of these groups is behind the visible stage of society, yet their actions which take place in the wings and backstage decisively govern the play of the actors in the world at large. Life is controlled, manipulated, given its true explanation and significance from behind, most often in a secret and conspiratorial realm.

In order to succeed in the society represented in *La Comédie humaine,* the individual must act on the social stage in full awareness of these powers which lie behind the scenes, and must be able to move with ease between the two spheres. Crevel in *La Cousine Bette* (1846), when discovered in Valérie's room by Marneffe 'aurait voulu descendre dans la cave par une trappe, comme cela se fait au théâtre',[118] but he is already in the *coulisses* of vice, plotting revenge

---

[117] Peter Brooks, *The Melodramatic Imagination,* pp. 119-120.
[118] *Be.,* vol. VII, p. 228.

against Hulot with Valérie, and his daily manoeuvres from his bourgeois home and business to the rue du Dauphin where he has his secret rendezvous with Valérie, are facilitated by just such a metaphorical social *trappe*. Crevel, like all the bourgeois businessmen of *La Comédie humaine* who have mistresses, has mastered the manœuvre between realms, between the front and backstage of society.

In *La Femme de trente ans* (1829-1834), the reader is told that suffering makes the individual aware of this distinction between the front and backstage of society and that once he has experienced this, 'il rentre dans le monde pour mentir au monde, pour y jouer un rôle; il connaît dès lors la coulisse où l'on se retire pour calculer, pleurer, plaisanter'.[119] The social education of the individual lies in the experience of this distinction, and his social success lies in his ability to apply that education and to move freely and at will between the two spheres. While for the reader the experience of the backstage reveals the novel's greater signification, for the characters it constitutes the loss of all their illusions about life, as Balzac explains through the duchesse de Carigliano:

> Nous autres femmes, nous devons admirer les hommes de génie, en jouir comme d'un spectacle, mais vivre avec eux! jamais. Fi donc! c'est vouloir prendre plaisir à regarder les machines de l'Opéra au lieu de rester dans une loge, à y savourer ses brillantes illusions.[120]

The experience of the social backstage results in the loss of illusions of both Eugène de Rastignac and Lucien de Rubempré. In *Le Père Goriot* (1834-35), there is no explicit use of the metaphor of the *dessous, trappe* or *coulisses* of the theatre, but Eugène's journeys from the social stage of the faubourg St Germain to the '*dessous*' of the Pension Vauquer take him through the muddy streets which can be seen as the *coulisses* and passageways of the Parisian social theatre. The light, open spaces, in which he moves in full view of society, are starkly contrasted with the dark obscurity of the Pension Vauquer and the stairways and entrances where Eugène begins to uncover the mysterious causes of events. Eugène's first social call

[119] *F30*, vol. II, p. 1106.
[120] *MCP*, vol. I, pp. 88-89.

takes him on to the centre stage of the de Restaud household where he stumbles by accident into a dark passageway. It is here, in the wings, that he sees Goriot leaving the house and makes his first discovery of what lies behind Goriot's drama. This awareness later increases as Eugène spies on Goriot and Vautrin from the dark hallways of the Pension Vauquer. Eugène's indiscretion in the de Restaud household about what he has learned from the backstage causes him to be banished back there and for his metaphorical passageway to be blocked. His success, however, lies in his ability to overcome this setback and learn to move between the two areas of stage and backstage and to assimilate the principles of distinction.

While Eugène is able to grasp the essential nature of what goes on in the backstage of society, Lucien is not. Lucien is not able sufficiently to distinguish between the two areas and allows himself repeatedly to be pushed back behind the curtain into the *coulisses*. In *Illusions perdues* this is exemplified by the scene in which he is forced by Bérénice to hide behind the curtain when Camusot arrives suddenly to visit Coralie.[121] The metaphorical importance of this scene has not so far been noted by critics, yet it is vital to the reader's understanding of Lucien's social position. Lucien will remain behind the curtain in the metaphorical backstage for as long as he lacks the wealth to compete for centre stage on equal terms, for it is wealth more than talent or beauty which gains the individual his place in the social spotlight. Only by joining himself to Jacques Collin, in the *troisième dessous* of society, can Lucien gain wealth and attain any significant social status, but again, unlike Rastignac (who moves increasingly infrequently in the social wings and whose journeys between metaphorical stage and backstage become increasingly easy until the point where he is just behind the scenery waiting to emerge at the whim of Mme de Beauséant or Delphine de Nucingen), Lucien in *Splendeurs et misères* is in the lowest depths of the social theatre, and his movements between the two spheres become so encumbered by the Parisian labyrinth that he can no longer make the journeys to and fro. Exhausted by the contrasts between stage and backstage, between a visible world which is based on appearance and an invisible world which is based on machination, Lucien can see no way out from his prison cell back into the social footlights and must

[121] *IP*, vol. V, p. 410.

kill himself. The problem for Lucien is that the 'truth' which lies behind the stage of society is even more hideous than the false appearance which conceals it.

The metaphor of stage and backstage in *Illusions perdues* is applied not only to life but to the literature which represents life. Lousteau explains this to Lucien in the course of the latter's initiation into the ways of Paris:

> La vie littéraire a ses coulisses. Les succès surpris ou mérités, voilà ce qu'applaudit le parterre; les moyens, toujours hideux, les comparses enluminés, les claqueurs et les garçons de service, voilà ce que recèlent les coulisses. Vous êtes encore au parterre. Il en est temps, abdiquez avant de mettre un pied sur la première marche du trône que se disputent tant d'ambitions, et ne vous déshonorez pas comme je le fais pour vivre.[122]

As this image makes clear, the literary *coulisses* do not simply denote the period of waiting for success, and of preparation; they denote the machinations and manipulations necessary to bring that success about. The machines, fire-men, backstage equipment and old scenery, which Lucien has seen in operation on his first visit to the Panorama-Dramatique,[123] in this way become a metaphor for the commercial aspects of the literary process itself and which literally manufacture success. The image is quoted directly by Félix Davin in his preface to the second edition of *Les Comédiens sans le savoir* in 1847 (published on this occasion as *Un provincial à Paris*), as an example of how Balzac's narrative is pervaded by his own 'combats' and 'luttes' with the 'misérables réalités de la vie', in order to establish his literary reputation. Davin's image is all the more effective because the literary *coulisses* are exposed in detail in the subsequent narrative.

The theatrical metaphor of stage and backstage is central to the full understanding of *La Comédie humaine* and of its complex system of super-structure and sub-structure, signifier and signified, false appearance and hidden cause. Through the theatrical metaphor Balzac not only represents the *comédie* of the social code, and the interplay

---

[122] *IP*, vol. V, p. 342.
[123] *Ibid.*, p. 373.

of individual destinies on the social stage, but also aims at uncovering the structures of society to reveal what lies behind and beneath. The surface of life represented in *La Comédie humaine* can only be explained through the examination of what takes place in its backstage area.

The Character as an Actor

While the events of life are described as dramas, the role-plays of society as comedies and the world as a theatre with its stage and backstage, the characters who move within this world are frequently described as actors, players, extras, directors, and authors. The index to this section lists 61 examples,[124] and there are many more which contain explicit comparison to named characters from dramatic works.[125] The world represented by *La Comédie humaine* is one in which characters are both actors and spectators simultaneously, some conscious of their roles and others less so. On the whole, only the narrator, reader and rare, semi-omniscient characters such as Vautrin and Gobseck know who is playing which role at any given moment. The roles are those of extras and puppets who are caught up in the novel's drama, actors, and particularly actresses, who play the social comedy, and more able actors who are simultaneously directors controlling the actions of others.

Along with other uses of theatrical imagery, the explicit metaphor of the character as an actor spans the whole of *La Comédie humaine*. The most frequent examples are to be found in *Les Chouans* (1828-29),[126] *Modeste Mignon* (1844),[127] and *Splendeurs et misères* (1838-1847).[128] In each case the metaphor underpins the central themes of the novel, so that in *Les Chouans* the characters are actors caught up in a historical drama, in *Modeste Mignon* they are players who assume their roles in the social comedy, and in *Splendeurs et misères* they are the masked villains of a sinister melodrama. Balzac's use of the metaphor in *Les Chouans* relates to his conception of this novel as

---

[124] See appendix I, section e.
[125] See appendix II.
[126] *Ch*, vol. VIII, pp. 925, 974, 975, 992, 1043, & 1120.
[127] *MM*, vol. I, pp. 593, 600, 612, 649-650, 673, 681, & 682.
[128] *SetM*, vol. VI, pp. 585, 735, 835, 837, & 886.

a series of dramatic events in which his characters are carried along. The references are casual and often descriptive of large groups playing out certain actions or anticipating the actions to come. The metaphor above all clarifies where the characters stand in relation to one another. From the outset the minor characters are 'les muets acteurs de cette scène, semblable à mille autres qui rendirent cette guerre la plus dramatique de toutes',[129] and the action is centred around Montauran who is the 'acteur principal [...] vu par tous, quoique absent',[130] who has willingly accepted 'un rôle dans cette tragédie'.[131] Later, the assembled opposing sides are again referred to as 'les acteurs de cette scène',[132] and in the course of the novel's tragic dénouement Marie is 'comme un acteur sublime',[133] and Montauran acts 'à la manière de grands acteurs'.[134] These images of his fictional characters as actors are consistent with Balzac's insistence that the events of Les Chouans constitute a drama in both the popular and more strictly theatrical sense of the term.[135]

Occasional metaphorical references to characters as actors caught up in the large-scale dramas of historical events can be seen throughout La Comédie humaine, up to the final part of Splendeurs et misères (1847), where Corentin is referred to as 'ce grand acteur du drame historique de notre temps'.[136] In other works, which again span much of Balzac's career, the image of the character as an actor is used to denote specific gestures which are described by comparison to the movements and habits of actors. For example,[137] in Une fille d'Eve (1838-39), Nathan begins to 'écouter comme ces acteurs qui regardent la salle au lieu d'être en scène';[138] in La Cousine Bette (1846), Crevel 'attendait pendant un moment, comme un acteur qui

---

[129] Ch., vol. VIII, p. 925.

[130] Ibid., p. 974.

[131] Ibid., p. 970.

[132] Ibid., p. 975.

[133] Ibid., p. 992.

[134] Ibid., p. 1120.

[135] The question of what Balzac means by 'drama' will be addressed in the final section of this chapter.

[136] SetM, vol. VI, p. 886.

[137] See also: DF, vol. II, p. 114; Be., vol. VII, p. 304; TA, vol. VIII, p. 648; PG, vol. III, p. 161; CM, vol. III, p. 582.

[138] FE, vol. II, 334.

marque un temps';[139] and in *Ursule Mirouèt* (1840-41), the curé 'se caressait le menton par ce geste commun aux valets de théâtre'.[140] The movements of the stage actor provide Balzac with a gestural code through which he can more graphically describe the actions of his own characters.

Throughout *La Comédie humaine*, however, it is possible to see that Balzac's use of theatrical imagery in describing his characters is more than an expression of their relative positions in the action, as 'acteurs muets',[141] and 'acteur principal',[142] for example, and of the gestures which accompany their actions, but is an integral element of the expression of his world view. In *Les Chouans* there is only one such instance, which occurs towards the end of the novel, and foretells the way in which the metaphor of the actor will be developed from now on in *La Comédie humaine*. The image here is of the abbé Gudin, who, in his address to his congregation, has 'à la manière des grands acteurs, manié tout son public comme un seul homme, en parlant aux intérêts et aux passions'.[143] In the drama of history, an individual such as Gudin has little power to control the enormity of the events which are overtaking the Breton peasants, but his particular role is subject to his own power of interpretation and enables him to influence the reactions of the peasants. This distinction between characters who are able to exercise some control over others, and characters who are merely puppets and dupes, becomes central to the interaction of Balzac's characters in later novels and is frequently expressed through images of their relative acting and directing capacities.

The social comedy in *La Comédie humaine*, as has been noted, is primarily one in which characters knowingly and deliberately adopt roles and play out intrigues in which other characters are merely puppets or dupes. Vautrin points this out in *Le Père Goriot* to Eugène:

---

[139] *Be.*, vol. VII, p. 68.
[140] *UM*, vol. III, p. 860.
[141] *Ch.*, vol. VIII, p. 925.
[142] *Ch.*, vol. VIII, p. 974.
[143] *Ch.*, vol. VIII, p. 1120.

> Mon petit, quand on ne veut pas être dupe des marionnettes, il faut entrer tout à fait dans la baraque, et ne pas se contenter de regarder par les trous de la tapisserie.[144]

The metaphorical terms used to describe the characters engaged in this *comédie* include *acteur, comédien, charlatan, valet de comédie*, and frequent reference is made to the metaphorical masks which they wear. It is remarkable how often these terms are used in the feminine form of *actrice* and *comédienne*, conveying a sense of what Balzac perhaps sees as a natural female acting capacity, or perhaps a female imperative to subscribe to the rules of the social comedy.

The characters who engage in the social comedy are at least semi-omniscient and are spectators as well as actors, for it is only in relation to the roles played by others and in awareness of the social code that they are able to judge their own performance. Valérie Marneffe in *La Cousine Bette*, always alternating between her positions as wife and mistress, acts in full awareness of her roles: 'Mme Marneffe, se sachant étudiée, se comporta comme une actrice applaudie',[145] and plays a scene of the self-sacrificing, virtuous woman with such credibility that it reduces Crevel to tears, as she quickly shifts from actress to spectator to mock both the role and Crevel's gullibility. Valérie's power lies in her semi-omniscience and her ability to distinguish between her different roles without ever losing sight of her material aims.

Some of Balzac's less well-known female characters are equally remarkable for their acting capacities, for example Honorine is a 'comédienne de bonne foi', who is capable of giving 'regards qui feraient la gloire d'une actrice',[146] and later confesses 'J'ai bien joué mon rôle de femme: j'ai trompé mon mari',[147] again like Valérie she is fully aware of the role she is playing. Similarly, the duchesse de Carigliano hides her true feelings with calm words 'dont la richesse d'intonation et l'accent inimitable eussent fait envie à la plus célèbre actrice de ce temps'.[148] Honorine and the duchesse de Carigliano act

---

[144] *PG*, vol. III, p. 119.
[145] *Be.*, vol. VII, p. 258.
[146] *H*, vol. II, pp. 570-571.
[147] *Ibid.*, p. 593.
[148] *BS*, vol. I, p. 156.

out a role which is predetermined by their sex and status, and in which the gestures, speech, and facial expressions are determined by social convention. In this sense the image of women as actresses can be applied to all of the women in *La Comédie humaine* who move in the *salons*, drawing-rooms, ball-rooms and theatres of Parisian society, for on the social stage along with Mmes d'Espard, de Langeais, de Beauséant, de Restaud and de Nucingen, they play out the roles which they have been born and married into, aware that a critical public is watching their every move. Permanent respite from the gaze of society is achieved by total withdrawal from the social stage, as in the case of the duchesse de Langeais and Mme de Beauséant, who, tired of wearing metaphorical masks, withdraw to provincial convents.[149]

The wearing of the social mask is exemplified at an early stage in Balzac's work in the figure of the estranged wife of Chabert in *Le Colonel Chabert* (1832). The demands of Mme Ferraud's roles as wife and mother and her own material interests cause her to display her acting talents:

> Il fallait être comédienne pour jeter tant d'éloquence, tant de sentiments dans un mot. [...] Pour se trouver un moment à l'aise elle monta chez elle, s'assit à son secrétaire, déposa le masque de tranquillité qu'elle conservait devant le comte Chabert, comme une actrice qui, rentrant fatiguée dans sa loge après un cinquième acte pénible, tombe demi-morte et laisse dans la salle une image d'elle-même à laquelle elle ne ressemble plus.[150]

For Mme Ferraud, as for the duchesse de Langeais and Mme de Beauséant, the wearing of the social mask is as morally and physically exhausting as the parts played in the theatres of Paris by Balzac's fictional actresses Coralie and Florine.[151] As with other uses of theatrical imagery, the metaphor gains its fullest signification

---

[149] The playing of the social comedy is a female imperative for the maintenance of reputation and virtue. See Marie-Henriette Faillie, *La Femme et le code civil dans La Comédie humaine de Honoré de Balzac* (Paris: Didier, 1968), pp. 91-164.

[150] *Col.*, vol. III, pp. 359-362.

[151] For example *FE*, vol. II, pl 320 'Pendant chaque représentation, Florine change deux ou trois fois de costume, et rentre souvent dans sa loge épuisée, demi-morte'. See also above, pp. 154-155.

when considered in relation to the historicity of Balzac's portrayal of the theatrical world in *La Comédie humaine* as a whole.

The most frequent examples of Balzac's characters metaphorically defined as players of the social comedy can be found in *Béatrix* (1838-1845), and in *Modeste Mignon* (1844), in which novels the entire plot depends on intrigue and role play. Béatrix and Modeste, however, are not just actresses playing out the roles governed by their sex and status, but are also in some sense directors of the drama in which other characters act out their given roles. The intrigue of *Modeste Mignon* centres on Modeste's self-appointed 'rôle de la jeune première',[152] and the mounting of a sub-plot in which there are to be 'deux personnages pour un rôle'.[153] Each of the characters in the subplot deploys 'le talent d'un grand acteur',[154] and Modeste's undoing is that while she believes she is playing a self-appointed role, that role is ultimately written by another hand.

Béatrix's undoing similarly results from a series of events in which she poses as an actress but which escapes her control. Béatrix's problem is that her rival, Camille Maupin, is a more accomplished, and indeed actual, dramatist who engineers the drama between herself and the other characters much as if she were literally creating a piece of theatre. Béatrix becomes aware of this in the second part of the novel where on the arrival of Conti, she declares to Camille, 'je reconnais là votre infernal talent d'auteur: la vengeance est complète, et le dénouement est parfait'.[155] The controlling position is then usurped by Conti who creates a scenario in which he plays 'l'homme soupçonneux et jaloux' and gives to Calyste 'le rôle d'un amoureux contrarié'.[156] In accepting this role Calyste becomes not only an actor but also the dupe or puppet of Conti who is both actor and director in this phase of the intrigue. When Béatrix has fled with Conti, Camille refers to her rival as 'une actrice de second ordre',[157] because she had been unable to play her role convincingly to the last. In the rivalry between Camille and Béatrix the skill of Camille as a

[152] *Ibid.*, p. 612.
[153] *MM*, vol. I, p. 600.
[154] *Ibid.*, p. 593.
[155] *B*, vol. II p. 823.
[156] *Ibid.*, p. 826.
[157] *Ibid.*, pp. 827-828.

dramatist, proves far superior in directing events to the skill of Béatrix as an actress.

In Balzac's metaphorical theatre of life the actor may only avoid becoming a puppet if he is fully aware of the role that he is playing, has learned it to perfection and is able to control the reactions of his audience. It is primarily the *lions* of the *Comédie humaine*, such as de Marsay, de Trailles, du Tillet, and du Châtelet, in their roles as dandies, financiers and politicians, who have this capacity. The individual's ability to achieve this position, Balzac explains in *Modeste Mignon*, depends on his ability to satisfy a new audience:

> Ce détail indique les dangers que court le héros d'un salon à sortir, comme Canalis, de sa sphère; il ressemble alors à l'acteur chéri d'un certain public, dont le talent se perd en quittant son cadre et abordant un théâtre superieur.[158]

In *La Comédie humaine* the transition of the young man from provincial *arriviste* to Parisian dandy, can be interpreted as that of the actor who must learn to dominate a new public. It is this ability to convince their public which marks the distinction between Eugène de Rastignac and Lucien de Rubempré as actors on the Parisian stage. While Eugène is able to control the reactions of his public by adapting to the demands of Paris, Lucien is never able adequately to do this. Eugène is never explicitly referred to as an actor, and this is indicative both of the sincerity which remains with him until his final defiant cry to society in *Le Père Goriot,* and the fact that he does not submit to the directing influence of Vautrin. In an abstract sense, however, Eugène becomes an actor as soon as he gets engaged in the social code after his first visit to the de Restaud household, immediately equipping himself with the necessary costumes and gestures to play his role, and his actions become subject to a greater director than Vautrin, to the general economic determinism which governs Parisian society. Eugène's greatest moment of awareness comes when he sees the miserable death bed of Goriot 'sous les diamants des deux sœurs',[159] and from that moment he can be seen as an actor who can make the distinction between the superficial

[158] *MM*, vol. I, pp. 649-650.
[159] *PG*, vol. III, p. 266.

appearance and the underlying truth. Eugène's final defiant declaration in the novel is a demonstration of his ability to play in the Parisian drama with sufficient awareness of what lies behind and beneath.

Lucien, on the other hand, believes himself to be an actor but is little more than a puppet, who is not aware that his actions are always being directed from beyond the immediate scene. Even Lucien's success on the narrow, provincial stage of Angoulême is engineered in the first place by Mme de Bargeton and after his return from Paris by Cérizet. Peter Brooks notes:

> Lucien experiences melodrama – the manichaestic extremes, the unbearable contrasts, the struggle of light and darkness, the accumulation of menace – without ever mastering it, without himself becoming the dramatist of experience.[160]

Lucien is always the actor who follows the directions of others and is never able to take control and direct his own actions. He is described as 'un homme à la fois prince et comédien',[161] and 'une femmelette qui aime à paraître',[162] but he is unable to distinguish his roles from his real self and continues acting in the *coulisses* of life, switching social and political allegiances, as he does in the *coulisses* of the Panorama-Dramatique. Lucien's inability to interpret and direct his own actions is a weakness which is quickly identified by Vautrin, who upon saving Lucien's life declares, 'Je suis l'auteur, tu seras le drame'. Just as he has been the dupe of du Châtelet, his enemies in the press, and the Cointet brothers, Lucien is now to be the puppet of Vautrin. Unlike Eugène who plays out his chosen role according to the general rules prescribed by society, Lucien flouts society's laws, does not adhere to the social comedy, and without a director his posturings are futile. Vautrin points out to Lucien that had he hidden his relationship with Coralie, he would have been able to marry Mme de Bargeton and achieve social respect and success:

[160] Peter Brooks, *The Melodramatic Imagination*, p. 124.
[161] *IP*, vol. V, p. 554.
[162] *Ibid.*, p. 578.

> Les grands commettent presque autant de lâchetés que les misérables; mais ils les commettent dans l'ombre et font parade de leurs vertus. [...] Vous avez eu publiquement pour maîtresse une actrice, vous avez vécu chez elle, avec elle; vous n'étiez nullement répréhensible, chacun vous trouvait l'un et l'autre parfaitement libres; mais vous rompiez en visière aux idées du monde et vous n'avez pas eu la considération que le monde accorde à ceux qui obéissent à ses lois. [...] Dès lors vous ne serez plus coupable de faire tache sur les décorations de ce grand théâtre appelé le monde.[163]

Lucien can only master the stage when he has been fully initiated into the social comedy and his every move is calculated and minutely directed by Vautrin.

Vautrin is the semi-omniscient director of all the subsequent dramas which take place in *Splendeurs et misères*. From the sphere of the underworld Vautrin functions both as actor and director. Vautrin appears on the social stage in his successive disguises, which are necessary for his transition from the *troisième dessous* to the light of the social stage. He is in no sense a puppet or even an actor fulfilling a role, rather he is one of the metaphorical actor/directors who, prompted by material interests and individual ambitions, write both their own roles and those of the characters around them. Vautrin only briefly puts himself at risk by abandoning his role:

> Aussi Jacques Collin, en garde contre lui-même, avait-il jusqu'alors admirablement bien joué son rôle d'innocent et d'étranger, soit à la Force, soit à la Conciergerie. Mais abattu par la douleur, écrasé par sa double mort, car, dans cette fatale nuit, il était mort deux fois, il redevint Jacques Collin. Le surveillant fut stupéfait de n'avoir pas à dire à ce prêtre espagnol par où l'on allait au préau. Cet acteur si parfait oublia son rôle, il descendit la vis de la tour Bonbec en habitué de la Conciergerie.[164]

Like Mme de Beauséant and the duchesse de Langeais, who in the face of suffering abandon their social roles, Vautrin's submission to

---

[163] *IP*, vol. V, p. 700.
[164] *SetM*, vol. VI, p. 835.

personal grief and to the irreversible, indomitable fact of Lucien's death, lies in the temporary abandoning of his roles.

The power to direct the drama of life in any way is given only to some in *La Comédie humaine*, to the *lions* and to the secret societies, while the rest remain at best conscious actors performing according to the social rules and at worst unwitting dupes or puppets.   Even those who seem to hold the strings are driven by a superior force, however, for the drama represented in *La Comédie humaine* is directed by the new gods of this era, by money, passion and personal ambition.   The lives and actions of all the characters of *La Comédie humaine* who are explicitly referred to as actors, or who in the context of the overall theatrical metaphor can be interpreted as actors, are governed or affected by the forces of material determinism and individual interests.

It is possible to see from these examples that the metaphor of the character as an actor serves three main narrative purposes throughout *La Comédie humaine*.   Firstly, the image of the actor is used to indicate the relative importance of the characters in the action and also to describe their gestures and expressions.   Secondly, the image describes the characters as players of the social comedy who adopt the roles prescribed by social convention, and as well as actors may also be puppets or directors.   Finally, the metaphor becomes an expression for the overall moral and ideological concerns of *La Comédie humaine*, since all characters are in some sense actors who portray false appearances and whose movements and speeches are directed not only by social conventions but by economic determinism and individual interests.

The Drama of Private and Domestic Life

In *La Comédie humaine*, while the term *comédie* is reserved for the play of masks and roles which Balzac perceives to be prevalent in both Paris and the provinces, the term *drame* usually indicates the process by which the mask and the surface appearance are penetrated to reveal the realities or further transgressions which lie beneath. The *drame* is the most prolific theatrical metaphor of *La Comédie humaine*, numbering 64 examples in the appendix to this chapter and constituting almost 27% of the total identified.[165] These examples include use of the term both in its secondary, popular sense to denote situations or sequences of events which are highly emotional, tragic, or turbulent, and in its primary, more strictly theatrical sense, as a work to be performed by actors on stage.[166] In its contemporary theatrical sense the term *drame* denotes the highly emotional and spectacular representations of the Romantic drama and may be distinguished from its original definition by Diderot in the previous century as a serious and, above all, realistic dramatic genre which was neither tragedy nor comedy.[167]

In many instances, Balzac appears to use the metaphor of the *drame* in its merely popular, secondary sense which is connected to the contemporary theatre only by association. There is, for example the 'drame de la Révolution'[168] referred to in *Les Chouans*, the 'drame commercial'[169] of *César Birotteau*, and the 'drame terrible d'une instruction criminelle' of *Splendeurs et misères*.[170] Of course, it is easy to equate Balzac's use of the *drame* as a metaphor in these instances, and particularly in *Splendeurs et misères,* with an impulse towards the contemporary melodrama which was reliant on the kind of turbulent and sensational events featured in the plots of these novels.

In certain other, more remarkable instances, Balzac's use of the metaphor of the *drame* stands in a much stricter relationship to the

---

[165] The terms of *drame* and *tragédie* have been listed together in the appendix since in Balzac's novels they are often juxtaposed and treated as synonymous. The term *tragédie,* by far the more infrequent of the two, is usually used in a popular rather than strictly dramatic sense to complement the metaphor of the drama of life which in many instances becomes a *drame tragique.* See, for example: *Ch.,* vol VIII, pp. 970, 1007, 1015, & 1186.

[166] The term *drame* had been accepted by the Académie Française for inclusion in the dictionary only in 1762, subsequent to Diderot's definition of the *drame* in his *Entretiens sur le Fils naturel* (1757) and *De la poésie dramatique* (1858). See: Jean-Pierre Sarrazac, 'Genres anciens, genre nouveau', in *Le Théâtre en France,* ed. Jacqueline de Jomaron, 2 vols. (Paris: Armand Colin, 1992), vol. I, p. 310.

[167] See: Denis Diderot, 'De la poésie dramatique' in *Œuvres complètes,* 20 vols. (Paris: Garnier, 1875). 'J'ai essayé de donner dans *Le Fils naturel* l'idée d'un drame qui fût entre la comédie et la tragédie'.

[168] *Ch.,* vol. VIII, p. 970.

[169] *CB,* vol. VI, p. 272.

[170] *SetM,* vol. VI, p. 700.

theatre. In these cases the *drame* in its contemporary stage sense functions as a contrast with Balzac's writing through which he defines how he believed the theatre should be. Critics have not remarked upon this phenomenon in *La Comédie humaine,* and indeed Balzac's own failure in the theatre is partly attributed[171] to the supposed fact that he had no clearly defined dramaturgy to offer other than the vague notion of the need to 'faire vrai'.[172] It is true that, unlike Hugo, Balzac at no stage explained his dramatic theory in any kind of separate treatise, but it is not true that this is because he had no theory. It has perhaps been the mistake of some critics of Balzac's theatre to study his dramatic works in isolation from his novels, for Balzac's dramaturgy is to be found in *La Comédie humaine* in his usage and explanations of the metaphor of the *drame,* and particularly in *Le Père Goriot* and *Eugénie Grandet.*

The opening pages of *Le Père Goriot* contain perhaps the best known example of Balzac's metaphorical use of the term *drame* with which to define his novel:

> Néanmoins, en 1819, époque à laquelle ce drame commence, il s'y trouvait une pauvre jeune fille. En quelque discrédit que soit tombé le mot drame par la manière abusive et tortionnaire dont il a été prodigué dans ces temps de douloureuse littérature, il est nécessaire de l'employer ici: non que cette histoire soit dramatique dans le sens vrai du mot; mais, l'œuvre accomplie, peut-être aura-t-on versé quelques larmes *intra muros et extra.*[173]

It is clear from Balzac's reference to 'douloureuse littérature' that he understands the 'sens vrai du mot' of the *drame* here in its literary and therefore theatrical sense rather than in a merely popular sense. For Balzac, according to these opening statements, the events of his novel do not constitute the type of highly emotional drama which could be found on the contemporary stage, but he claims that they may nevertheless produce a kind of theatrical pathos. Balzac's own sense of drama here is contrasted with the contemporary stage drama (which is seen to devalue the term *drame*), and is equated with truth

---

[171] W.S. Hastings, *The Drama of H. de Balzac,* p. 143; René Guise, Introduction to Balzac's theatre, p. XI; Milatchitch, *Le Théâtre de H. de Balzac,* p. 324.
[172] See above, pp. 14-15.
[173] *PG,* vol. III, p. 49.

which he believed to be lacking from the theatre of his day: 'Ah! sachez-le: ce drame n'est ni une fiction, ni un roman. All is true.'[174]

On first sight it seems as though Balzac might merely be making the point through metaphor that life itself is more dramatic in a popular sense than anything which is represented on the literal theatre stage. This is seen particularly in the description of the boarders, who, as part of this drama of real life, are themselves living dramas:

> Ces pensionnaires faisaient pressentir des drames accomplis ou en action; non pas de ces drames joués à la lueur des rampes, entre des toiles peintes, mais des drames vivants et muets, des drames glacés qui remuaient chaudement le cœur, des drames continus.[175]

Again, Balzac emphasises the distinction between his own definition of drama and the bright lights and spectacle of the current stage tradition. The most significant aspect of this image is that the boarders are described not as dramas which are highly visible and played out on the stage of society, but as silent and hidden dramas. It is the drama of the hidden, private and domestic realm which most interests Balzac. By insisting that the characters contain their dramas within them, Balzac strives to awaken interest and curiosity in the banality of the boarding house and in mean characters at the bottom of·the social scale.[176] Of course, Vautrin, Goriot and Rastignac are singled out for amplification, but the other boarders also remain interesting because they too have their hidden dramas which Balzac seeks to uncover.

Balzac's declared intention in these opening metaphors is of course belied by the subsequent events of the novel, which turn out to be highly emotional and melodramatic. Balzac is more successful in carrying out his declared intention in *Eugénie Grandet*, where he

---

[174] *PG,* vol. III, p. 50.

[175] *PG,* vol. III, p. 57.

[176] Ian Watt prescribes two important general conditions for the novel successfully to portray the lives of ordinary individuals: 'The society must value every individual highly enough to consider him the proper subject of its serious literature; and there must be enough variety of belief and action among ordinary people for a detailed account of them to be of interest to other ordinary people, the readers of novels.' *The Rise of the Novel* (London: Chatto & Windus, 1957), p. 60. The second of these conditions is partly fulfilled by Balzac in the creation of his fictional characters through his own idea of the dramatic.

resists the impulse towards melodrama. Here too Balzac borrows the vocabulary of the theatre to analyse and mark the stages of his creative process and to justify these to the reader, and it is in contrast to the prevailing form of the drama that he justifies to the reader the possibly disappointing ending of *Eugénie Grandet*:

> Ce dénouement trompe nécessairement la curiosité. Peut-être en est-il ainsi de tous les dénouements vrais. Les tragédies, les drames, pour parler le langage de ce temps, sont rares dans la nature. [...] Ici, nulle invention.[177]

Balzac is insistent here upon the truth of the outcome of his novel which stands in opposition to the contemporary stage drama, which he claims does not represent reality.[178] Certainly, Eugénie's ultimate resignation to the slow passage of the remainder of her provincial life is more poignant and more credible than the expedient and more melodramatic endings of other of Balzac's novels, which are brought about by sudden deaths and unexpected revelations.[179] Nevertheless, in his preface to this novel, Balzac does refer metaphorically to the events which are to unfold as a *drame*, but here he seems to be hinting not at the stage drama as understood in 'le langage de ce temps', which he refers to in the epilogue, but rather at something distinct from that:

> Si tout arrive à Paris, tout passe en province: là ni relief, ni saillie; mais là, des drames dans le silence; là, des mystères habilement dissimulés; là des dénouements dans un seul mot; là, d'énormes valeurs prêtées par le calcul et l'analyse aux actions les plus indifférentes.[180]

---

[177] *EG*, vol. III, p. 1201.

[178] See above, pp. 14-15. ᵛVictor Hugo n'est pas vrai' *LMH*, vol. II, p. 177.

[179] *La Cousine Bette*, for example, in which Balzac deems no less than seven deaths to be necessary to the resolution of the plot, or *La Fille aux yeux d'or*, in which Paquita is murdered and her lover and keeper sensationally find themselves to be brother and sister.

[180] *EG*, vol. III, p. 1025.

What Balzac appears to be formulating here, and in the opening of *Le Père Goriot,* is a notion of renewal of the *drame bourgeois* which had been defined and advocated in the previous century by Diderot. Balzac continues in his preface to *Eugénie Grandet* with metaphors borrowed from painting, speaking of 'touches de pinceau', 'tableaux' and 'clair-obscur'. This strengthens rather than detracts from the impression that through metaphor Balzac is expressing a dramaturgy after the manner of Diderot, for in his *Entretiens sur Le Fils naturel* Diderot had drawn close analogy between his vision of the *drame bourgeois* and the Flemish school of painting which depicted detailed interiors with dramatic use of light.[181] Certainly Balzac's intention to write a type of realistic, almost anti-dramatic *drame* in *Eugénie Grandet,* is carried out in the text of the novel which progresses by a series of interior scenes largely devoid of coups de théâtre.

That Balzac intends his metaphorical use of the *drame* to be understood in a specifically theatrical context, rather than as merely denoting a series of turbulent events, can be seen in a passage from *Facino Cane* (1836). Here Balzac intervenes in the narrative to tell of the plethora of dramas which he claims can be perceived beneath the surface of society:

> Vous ne sauriez imaginer combien d'aventures perdues, combien de drames oubliés dans cette ville de douleur [...] il faut descendre trop bas pour trouver ces admirables scènes ou tragiques ou comiques, chefs-d'œuvre enfantés par le hasard.[182]

Balzac's references to *scènes* and *chefs-d'œuvre* ground his metaphor in the theatre rather than in merely popular terminology. Again in *Le Cousin Pons* (1846-47), Balzac emphasises by use of complementary theatrical vocabulary that the 'drame de cette vie obscure'[183] is not merely a metaphor for a series of turbulent events:

---

[181] Diderot, *Entretiens sur 'Le Fils naturel* ': 'Je pense pour moi que si un ouvrage dramatique était bien fait et bien représenté, la scène offrirait aux spectateurs autant de tableaux réels qu'il y aurait dans l'action de moments favorables au peintre', and ' Le spectateur est au théâtre comme devant une toile où des tableaux divers se succéderaient comme par enchantement'.
[182] *FC*, vol. VI, p. 1020.
[183] *CP*, vol. VII, p. 489.

> Ici commence le drame, ou, si vous voulez, la comédie terrible de la mort d'un célibataire livré par la force des choses à la rapacité des natures cupides qui se groupent à son lit, et qui, dans ce cas, eurent pour auxiliaires la passion la plus vive, celle d'un tableaumane, l'avidité du sieur Fraisier, qui, vu dans sa caverne, va vous faire frémir, et la soif d'un Auvergnat capable de tout, même d'un crime, pour se faire un capital. Cette comédie, à laquelle cette partie du récit sert en quelque sorte d'avant-scène, a d'ailleurs pour acteurs tous les personnages qui jusqu'à présent ont occupé la scène.[184]

The juxtaposition and substitution of *comédie* and *drame* in particular call to mind Diderot's definition of the *drame* as a form which would be unhampered by restrictive, established definitions of genre. This, combined with words which might be seen to evoke theatrical pathos, such as *terrible, frémir, passion*, and more specific theatrical terms such as *avant-scène* and *acteurs*, seems to indicate that Balzac sees this private drama in relation to the actual theatre stage.

The point is noted by Félix Davin who remarks in his introduction to the *Etudes philosophiques* (1834), that it is above all the dramas of private and hidden passion which interest Balzac:

> Il est allé les chercher [ces passions et ces types] dans la famille, autour du foyer; et fouillant sous ces enveloppes en apparence si uniformes et si calmes, il en a exhumé tout à coup, des caractères tellement multiples et naturels en même temps, que tout le monde s'est demandé comment des choses aussi familières, aussi vraies, étaient restées si longtemps inconnues.[185]

Part of Balzac's gift as a novelist, and as the *historien des mœurs* is that, as the Davin text says, he is able to wrest the interesting and the dramatic from within the familiar and the real. Just as Diderot had advocated almost a century earlier, Balzac is penetrating the private sphere to show a drama enacted by the people who actually lived it, and through close alignment with the real strives to make his

---

[184] *CP*, vol. VII, p. 630.
[185] *LCH*, vol. X, p. 1208.

audience forget that it is witnessing a fiction and believe that it is party to real events.[186]

Balzac's purpose in describing hidden events and private circumstances as dramas is of course consistent with his overall process of uncovering what lies beneath social norms and apparently calm exteriors. The oxymoron of the silent drama is the means by which he makes the intangible tangible and brings in to the public arena conflicts which are not normally visible. Throughout *La Comédie humaine* Balzac uncovers the private, inner dramas which are played out both within the small theatre of the family and, more secretly still, within the heart of the individual. There is the '[...] drame se jouant dans l'âme'[187] of Colonel Chabert whose private tragedy is played out in the sombre law offices of Derville, where such scenes are described as the 'drames de la Morgue';[188] in *Mémoires de deux jeunes mariées* love is described by Louise to Renée as a tragedy or a 'drame joué au fond des cœurs';[189] in *Honorine* Octave describes his unhappy state as 'le drame de mon âme';[190] and the love intrigue of *Béatrix* is described as a 'drame diabolique' and as a 'drame tragique' which unfolds 'dans toute son étendue au fond des cœurs'.[191] Similarly, the central love interest of *La Muse du département* is described as 'une de ces longues et monotones tragédies conjugales qui demeureraient éternellement inconnues'. 'Inconnues' that is, until Balzac chooses to expose them by penetrating the private domain, metaphorically to 'stage' those hidden dramas for his public.

---

[186] The republication of Diderot's *Le Fils naturel* in 1857 included a prologue and epilogue in which Diderot claimed to have been invited by a character named Dorval to watch this family drama from a hiding place within the family home: 'J'entrai dans le salon par la fenêtre, et Dorval, qui avait écarté tout le monde, me plaça dans un coin, d'où sans être vu, je vis et j'entendis ce qu'on va lire'. Diderot strives to create the impression that he is penetrating the real, private realm, just as Balzac does in his novels.

[187] *Col.*, vol. III, p. 315.

[188] *Ibid.*, p. 369.

[189] *MJM*, vol. I, p. 292.

[190] *H*, vol. II, p. 554.

[191] *B*, vol. II, pp. 856 & 821.

In all of these examples, and there are many more,[192] love is the
metaphorical drama which is played out silently in the souls of the
characters. The notion that the drama is silent or stifled makes the
violently contrasting emotions and extreme suffering engendered by
that love all the more intense. The *drame* thus attains a
claustrophobic pressure when contained within the heart of the
individual. The tragedy of Eugénie Grandet, of Octave and of Chabert
is that this drama of love remains hidden within them forever, known
only to themselves, the narrator and the reader. Conversely the
events of the second part of *Béatrix*, which is entitled *Le Drame*,
come about because the hidden drama must be known, and the reader
is prepared for this by the mounting tension of contrasts which must
escape beyond the innermost confines of each individual. The drama
announced by the title is borne out by the explosion of real feeling
which the protagonists can no longer contain beneath a veneer of
social convention.[193]

The metaphor of the hidden drama which surfaces in the life of an
otherwise ordinary individual is perhaps best exemplified in *Pierrette*
(1839-40). A little studied work, *Pierrette* is the embodiment of the
private drama, of terrible events played out behind the closed doors
of a provincial town. It is in every sense the drama of a character
whose life would appear to be anti-dramatic. The metaphor of the
drame occurs in *Pierrette* at five intervals throughout the novella's
143 pages. In the first instance the metaphor is employed self-
consciously by Balzac to awaken the reader's interest in his subject,
which he describes as:

> Un de ces drames obscurs qui se passent en famille et qui, pour
> demeurer secrets, n'en sont pas moins terribles, si vous permettez
> toutefois d'appliquer le mot de drame à cette scène d'intérieur.[194]

As in the opening of *Le Père Goriot*, Balzac justifies his use of
dramatic metaphor to his reader and acknowledges that the events
described in the novel may not be what the reader would recognise as

---

[192]   See, for example, *Cath.*, vol. XI, p. 388: 'Le drame profondément caché'; *EG*,
vol. III, p. 1193: 'Le drame commencé depuis neuf ans'; *PMV*, vol. XII, p. 169: 'ce
drame conjugal'.

[193]   *B*, vol. II, pp. 823-824.

[194]   *P*, vol. IV, p. 34.

dramatic either in the contemporary theatrical or popular sense. Again Balzac juxtaposes dramatic metaphor with the image of the 'scène d'intérieur' borrowed from painting, as he had done in the preface to *Eugénie Grandet*, apparently unconsciously approximating his definition of the drama to that of Diderot. Through the metaphor of the private, hidden drama Balzac leads his reader to expect a similar set of tragic circumstances to that which had brought him great commercial success in *Eugénie Grandet*, and in this the reader is not to be disappointed.

As will be seen in the next chapter, the metaphor of the drama surrounding Pierrette is integrated into the narrative through theatrical presentation of the text as her life becomes 'le drame domestique que la venue de Brigaut détermina dans la maison Rogron'.[195] Pierrette's personal tragedy, like that of Eugénie Grandet, lies in the fact that the drama of her suffering and her lover's desperation, goes unheard and undiscovered until it is too late: 'Le bavardage d'un amant au désespoir éclaira ce drame domestique au médecin, sans qu'il en soupçonnât l'horreur ni l'étendue'.[196] Balzac's insistence on the term 'drame domestique' in *Pierrette* not only foretells the type of stage drama which he was later to develop in his play *La Marâtre* in 1848, but is entirely necessary for the outcomes of the plot. It is precisely because the drama is enacted behind the closed shutters of the provincial house and not in a public, Parisian setting, that its tragedy remains undetected and unavoidable, eventually culminating in what Balzac successively describes as a 'drame fatal' and a 'drame horrible'.[197]

Through this examination of the metaphor of the *drame* in Balzac's novels, it is possible to see that he had been developing since the early 1830s, and in conscious opposition to the Romantic drama, his own idea of a sort of intimate or domestic drama. Balzac eventually transferred this dramaturgy from metaphorical representation in his novels to actual stage representation in *La Marâtre*, which he called a 'tragédie bourgeoise'[198] and a 'drame comme on en peut trouver à tout moment en fouillant les mystères de

---

[195] *Ibid.*, p. 98.
[196] *P*, vol. IV, p. 141.
[197] *Ibid.*, pp. 106 & 152.
[198] *LMH*, vol. IV, p. 299.

la vie privée,'[199] and through which, according to his claims in a letter to Madame Hanska in May 1848, he hoped to revive the French stage: 'Ce que je voulais je l'ai obtenu: une rénovation, et la littérature dramatique   reconnaîtra que je vais me faire une large part.[200] Unfortunately, after the second act the play errs on the side of melodrama, but even the harshest of critics saw *La Marâtre* as a literary revolution and agreed that through it Balzac had succeeded in transferring from the novel to the stage his primary dramatic principle: 'faire vrai'.[201]

Despite the overwhelming prevalence of melodrama in many of the plots of Balzac's novels, it is possible to conclude from the examples given here that, through his use of the *drame* as a metaphor with which to describe and distinguish his novels, Balzac expresses his own dramaturgy which is that of a realistic and intimate *drame bourgeois*. It is not only the realism and intimacy of his novels, but also the specific dramaturgy which Balzac expresses in his novels and puts into practice in *La Marâtre,* which establishes him at a mid-point in the development of the modern theatre, between Diderot's theories in the previous century and the Naturalist theatre of Zola and the Théâtre Libre towards the end of the century.[202] The fact that when Balzac uses the *drame* as a metaphor, he more often than not intends the term to be understood in its theatrical sense will be underpinned in the next chapter which examines the way in which Balzac presents the text using dramatic techniques and elements of stagecraft.

---

[199] *Corres.*, vol. V, p. 315.

[200] *LMH*, vol. IV, p. 365.

[201] See: Gautier *La Presse,* 29 May, 1848; Pontmartin, *Revue des Deux Mondes,* 29 May 1848; Janin, *Les Débats,* 29 May, 1848, all of whom saw in the play's realism and originality a desirable renovation of the drama. When the play was restaged in 1859 Sarcey saw it as a 'révolution' and 'le premier essai d'une comédie nouvelle'. See: 'La Marâtre' in *L'Opinion Nationale,* 12 September, 1859.

[202] Émile Zola, *Le Naturalisme au théâtre*: 'Un fait se déroulant dans sa réalité et soulevant chez les personnages des passions et des sentiments, dont l'analyse exacte serait le seul intérêt de la pièce. Et cela dans le milieu contemporain avec le peuple qui nous entourne'. Zola's theories were finally put into practice by André Antoine at the Théâtre Libre, which opened on 30 March 1887. In his *Causerie sur la mise en scène* (1903), Antoine clearly expressed the idea of the 'quatrième mur' through which the private drama could be seen, as suggested by Diderot and Zola and practised by Balzac in his novels.

Conclusion – A Coherent System

From the examination in this chapter it is possible to see that Balzac's exploitation of the theatre as a descriptive resource is not simply the product of an indeterminate notion of the world as a theatre or of an impulse towards melodrama, but corresponds to a strict system, in which images are used to express the novels' central concerns. Within this scheme the *drame* is an image of the private, domestic realm through which Balzac formulates and expresses his dramaturgy, the *comédie* or *scène* is an image of social role-play, the *théâtre* is the image of the location of action often played out in full view of society, and the *dessous* and *coulisses* are images of the true causes of events. In accordance with this system Balzac's characters are defined as actors who are described by reference to established theatre characters, and who emerge either as puppets, *comédiens* or actor/directors, whose actions are determined by materialism and individualism.

From the analysis of this scheme it has been possible to expand the observations made by Brooks and Adamson and it is now possible to conclude that the theatrical metaphor is not only relevant to those novels situated in the labyrinth of Paris and which stand in close relationship to theatrical melodrama, such as *Illusions perdues, Splendeurs et misères* and *La Cousine Bette*, but is also fundamental to the mode of expression of other novels such as *Pierrette, Eugénie Grandet* and *Les Chouans*. Balzac's use of theatrical metaphor is both systematic and all-embracing and is an expression of the most melodramatic series of peripeteia in *Splendeurs et misères*, and of the most lingering and silent tragedy in *Eugénie Grandet*.

Furthermore, it is important to consider Balzac's use of theatrical metaphor in relation to the historicity of his treatment of the actual Parisian theatre in *La Comédie humaine*. It is only in relation to Balzac's revelations concerning the actual theatre world that his imagery attains its fullest signification, for through theatre Balzac's fictional world becomes self-contained. Balzac does not rely on assumed knowledge of the external reality to which the theatrical metaphor refers his reader, but provides that knowledge in the texts. The images of characters as actors are amplified by Balzac's exposure of life in the theatre with its physical, mental and financial demands and moral compromises. Similarly, the image of society as a theatre with its wings and backstage areas is amplified by the exposure of backstage practices in the actual theatre, by the corrupt dealings of the *feuilletons* and the *claque* and the machinations of actors, directors and dramatists, and by the economic forces which govern the theatre. The historical treatment of the theatre and the exploitation of the theatre as a source of imagery are to some extent interdependent in Balzac's vision.

It has also been shown here that Balzac's use of theatrical metaphor covers the whole thematic, locational and chronological period of *La Comédie humaine*. From the mid 1830s onwards, however, a more abundant and systematic exploitation of theatrical imagery can be seen, particularly in the allusions to established dramatic characters, and this seems to indicate Balzac's increasing preoccupation with the notions of role-play and false appearance which characterise his mature work. It would be erroneous to suggest that Balzac's use of theatrical metaphor is a direct consequence of his own attempts to write for the stage, since he did not devote himself to the theatre in any serious way until the 1840s,[203] and the theatrical metaphor is already well-developed in novels written in the mid and late 1830s. Rather the metaphor derives from the combined effect of Balzac's vision of life and of his awareness of the need to 'dramatise' the novel in order to awaken and sustain the reader's interest.

The theatre provides Balzac with an established vocabulary and typology with which to describe his novels and characters. To some extent the borrowing of theatrical vocabulary to describe the novel at the beginning of the nineteenth century was essential to Balzac since the novel had no such vocabulary of its own. While the theatrical tradition had a familiar and established terminology, the novel had no means to describe its processes. As a highly self-conscious author, Balzac borrows metaphors and vocabulary from the established literary form both in order to analyse and justify his own process of creation and in order to communicate effectively with the reader. Only through recognisable images can the reader see behind the metaphor to what is signified, and these images are to be found in what has been shown to be the dominant social institution of Balzac's period, in the theatre. It is precisely through a metaphor which has its

[203] See above, pp. 16-29.

basis in showing and seeing that Balzac reveals his process of uncovering society to the reader. The process of this exposure is expressed by Balzac in a letter to Madame Hanska by means of a theatrical metaphor which summarises his creation of *La Comédie humaine*: 'Les *mœurs* sont le *spectacle*, les *causes* sont les *coulisses et les machines*, les principes, c'est l'*auteur*.[204]

---

[204] *LMH*, vol. I, p. 270.

STAGING THE TEXT –
MISE EN SCENE IN THE *ETUDES DE MŒURS*

Il est excessivement rare de voir des prosateurs du roman posséder,
au même degré que Balzac, ce secret des effets de scène, qui semble
ne devoir appartenir qu'au théâtre.[1]

The dramatic quality of Balzac's novels has often been commented on
in relation to the construction of their plots, which so often rely for
their development and climaxes on the traditional devices of the stage
melodrama.[2] P. Bourget has noted how Balzac uses the hyperbole and
antithesis of traditional stage melodrama to force the action to a point
of crisis,[3] and, more recently, as noted in the introduction to the
present work, Peter Brooks and Christopher Prendergast have again
paid particular attention to the way in which melodrama functions as
one of Balzac's most compelling effects.[4] However, it is not only
through the melodramatic peripeteia of their plots that the novels of
La Comédie humaine become imbued with a sense of theatricality, but
also through the effect of Balzac's exploitation of theatrical metaphor
(as seen in the previous chapter), combined with his frequent use of
stagecraft in his presentation of the text. The aim of this chapter is to
examine the extent to which Balzac successfully dramatizes his text
through the use of scenery, positioning of characters, special effects,
costume, speech and gesture, and to establish the function of these
devices in Balzac's overall narrative purpose.

Although Balzac was instinctively drawn to the theatre throughout
his adult life, his main attempts at writing for the stage came towards

---

[1] Marcel Barrière, *L'Œuvre de H. de Balzac* (Paris: Calmann- Lévy, 1890), p. 255.
[2] The tradition of certain devices in the plots of stage melodrama was established
between 1800 and 1820 by Pixerécourt, the most successful exponent of the genre,
and came to include the use of unexpected and fortuitous events, masked and
mistaken identities, lost and found blood relations, physical struggle and combat, evil
villains and innocent victims. The climax of the plot in stage melodrama would
usually consist in peripeteia and its dénouement in anagnorisis. See: W.D. Howarth,
Sublime and Grotesque, a study of French Romantic Drama (London: Harrap, 1975),
pp. 61-72.
[3] P. Bourget, 'L'Art du Roman chez Balzac' in *Revue des deux mondes*, vol.
XXXI, 15 Feb. 1926, pp. 931-942.
[4] See above, pp. 9-11; Peter Brooks, *The Melodramatic Imagination*, p. 111;
Christopher Prendergast, *Balzac, Fiction and Melodrama* , pp. 15-16.

the end of his career, in the late 1830s and 1840s.[5] It is important to recognise from the outset therefore, that Balzac's use of stagecraft in his novels appears to be born out of the general influence of the drama on the novel during his lifetime, rather than from specific instances of his own experiments with the dramatic form. As the examples given later in this chapter will demonstrate, Balzac's use of theatrical technique in the novel was already well developed at the time of writing *Les Chouans* in 1828 and 1829, and is masterfully handled in *Le Père Goriot* in 1834 and 1845, where the well-known opening lines constitute a contractual engagement of the reader as a spectator of a drama:

> Les particularités de cette scène pleine d'observations et de couleurs locales ne peuvent être appréciées qu'entre les buttes de Montmartre et les hauteurs de Montrouge [...]. Ainsi ferez-vous, vous qui tenez ce livre d'une main blanche, vous qui vous enfoncez dans un mœlleux fauteuil [...]. Ah! sachez-le: ce drame n'est ni une fiction, ni un roman.[6]

From the outset of *Le Père Goriot,* having thus self-consciously defined his novel as a drama, Balzac justifies his case for doing so and implicitly invites his reader to engage in the narrative as though watching from a seat in an auditorium. Furthermore, Balzac insists to his reader that the drama which is to unfold is filled with the realistic detail and *couleur locale* which were seen as essential to the Romantic drama of the 1830s.[7]

---

[5] See above, pp. 16-29. *L'Ecole des Ménages,* 1838; *Vautrin,* 1839; *Les Ressources de Quinola,* 1841; *Paméla Giraud,* 1843; *Mercadet,* 1840-1848; *La Marâtre,* 1848.

[6] *PG,* vol. III, pp. 49-50.

[7] By the late 1820s the expressive dramaturgy of the established melodrama came to be assimilated in part into the aesthetics of the emerging Romantic drama which found its clearest expression in Hugo's *Préface de Cromwell.* Here Hugo insists on the importance of realistic setting and authentic dialogue which he terms *couleur locale*: 'On commence à comprendre de nos jours que la localité exacte est un des premiers éléments de la réalité. [...] Le lieu où telle catastrophe s'est passée en devient un témoin terrible et inséparable; et l'absence de cette sorte de personnage muet décompléterait dans le drame les plus grandes scènes de l'histoire. [...] Il faut donc que le drame soit un miroir de concentration qui, loin de les affaiblir, ramasse et condense les rayons colorants, qui fasse d'une lueur une lumière, d'une lumière une flamme. [...] Ce n'est point à la surface du drame que doit être la couleur locale, mais au fond, dans le cœur même de l'œuvre. [...] Le drame doit être radicalement

In the opening of *Ferragus* (1833), Balzac again self-consciously justifies his dramatization of the narrative by explicit reference to what he calls the *drame moderne* and highlights the importance both of extreme action and emotion, and of realistic detail:

> Mais il y a telle rue de Paris où cette rencontre [d'une femme jolie avec le premier homme de sa connaissance] peut devenir le drame le plus effroyablement terrible, un drame plein de sang et d'amour, un drame de l'Ecole moderne. Malheureusement, cette conviction, ce dramatique sera, comme le drame moderne, compris par peu de personnes, et c'est grande pitié que de raconter une histoire à un public qui n'en Epouse pas tout le mérite local.[8]

Balzac seems to be conscious of the fact that part of his own modernity as a novelist lies in his attempts to dramatize the text, and is at pains to persuade the reader of this.

As is well known among scholars of Balzac, the impulse to dramatize his narrative came to him at least partly from the influence of Walter Scott,[9] who according to Balzac's opinions expressed in his *Etudes sur M. Beyle* (1840), had achieved the kind of literary eclecticism which he believed to be necessary to the modern writer. In the same article Balzac notes the imperative for the modern novelist of borrowing techniques which had previously belonged more properly to the theatre:

imprégné de cette couleur des temps'. Victor Hugo, *Préface de Cromwell*, ed. Maurice Souriau (Paris: Société française d'imprimerie et de librairie, 1897), pp. 234-266.

[8] *F*, vol. V, p. 796.

[9] See M. Bardèche, *Balzac romancier* (Paris: Plon, 1940), p. 52: 'c'est à force de méditer sur l'art de Walter Scott, d'en rechercher les règles, que Balzac établit cette forme romancée du drame'.

See also, André Le Breton, *Balzac, l'homme et l'œuvre* (Paris: Boivin et cie., 1923) p. 89: 'En somme Walter Scott a infiniment contribué à enseigner à Balzac l'art de la composition, du dialogue, de la description et du portrait, et il lui a appris, selon un mot de Balzac lui-même, à dramatiser le roman'.

Je ne crois pas la peinture de la société moderne possible par le procédé sévère de la littérature du XVIIe et XVIIIe siècles. L'introduction de l'élément dramatique, de l'image, du tableau, de la description, du dialogue, est indispensable dans la littérature moderne.[10]

The same opinion had already been expressed indirectly by Balzac through the fictional character of Blondet in *Un grand homme* the previous year,[11] and is reiterated in a second article in 1840, in which Balzac testifies to the gradual and widespread interpenetration of genres which had taken place during his career:

La littérature a subi, depuis vingt-cinq ans, une transformation qui a changé les lois de la Poétique. La forme dramatique, la couleur et la science ont pénétré tous les genres. Les livres les plus graves sont forcés d'obéir à ce mouvement qui rend les compositions si attrayantes.[12]

Finally, in a letter to Hippolyte Castille in 1846, Balzac states clearly and definitively that, like his fictional character Blondet, he is convinced that 'le besoin de l'Epoque est le drame':[13]

J'ai entrepris l'histoire de toute la société. J'ai exprimé souvent mon plan dans cette seule phrase: 'Une génération est un drame ou cinq mille personnages saillants. Ce drame, c'est mon livre.'[14]

What will be seen in the examination of Balzac's *mise en scène* is a fusion of the mode of excess and extravagant expressionism of the melodrama and the naturalistic setting and *couleur locale* of the Romantic drama, reinforced at every stage by attempts to render the narrative visible and plastic, and to enable the reader to construct a

---

[10] 'Etudes sur M. Beyle', in *Œuvres diverses* (Le Club Français du Livre), vol. XIV, p. 1156. This article first appeared in the *Revue parisienne* on 25 September, 1840.

[11] *IP*, vol. V, p. 459.

[12] 'Lettres sur la littérature', in *Œuvres diverses* (Paris: Conard, 1836-1848), vol. III, p. 272. First published in *La Revue parisienne*, 15 July, 1840.

[13] *IP*, vol. V, p. 460.

[14] 'Lettre à Hippolyte Castille', in *Œuvres diverses*, ed. cit. vol. XIV, p. 1222. First published in *La Semaine* on 11 October, 1846.

performance from the visual data given in the text. These efforts towards a visual mode of presentation reflect not only contemporary literary trends, but in a wider sense also reflect the growing importance of all visual art forms during the first half of the nineteenth century.[15]

At the same time, Balzac's use of dramatic technique in his novels becomes part of his penetrating observation of a whole society, so that from his privileged vantage point the reader is invited to penetrate the hidden, private sphere and to perceive the underlying reality in the public sphere, in order to make a distinction between *être* and *paraître*. However, the techniques of *mise en scène* which Balzac uses to dramatize his fiction, to endow it with life, realism and *couleur locale*, and to reveal truth are, paradoxically, often the very things which cloud truth and indicate the unknowability of the real. In this way theatrical devices are used by Balzac to a dual effect – to create a visible drama which is driven forward in a dynamic manner, and to convey the more profoundly theatrical idea that the images which are represented as 'real' may themselves be illusory.

Settings and Groupings

The importance of visual entertainment in Paris during Balzac's career is perhaps best exemplified by the opening of the Diorama in 1822,[16] which in August of that year Balzac describes in a letter to his

---

[15] For example, the advances in paper manufacturing and printing, which are accurately described by Balzac in *Illusions perdues,* facilitated the wide-scale distribution of visual images and a rapid integration of image and text which resulted in a fashion for the drawings and caricatures by Daumier, Monnier, Grandville, and Gavarni. At the same time the side-shows, circus acts and fairground attractions of the boulevard du Temple offered appealing visual entertainment to a wide public. See above, pp. 34-39.

[16] The Diorama was developed by the lighting specialist Daguerre from the more primitive rolling pictorial scenes known as *panoramas.* At Daguerre's Diorama, the entertainment consisted in a pageant of pictorial scenes as the audience sat in a darkened, revolving auditorium while the visual spectacle was created by backdrop paintings against which transparent and non-transparent parts were alternated and lit from behind by a system of coloured filters. See: G.M. Bergman, *Lighting in the Theatre* (Stockholm: Almqvist & Wiksell, 1977), p. 259. The impression of the Diorama and the *panoramas* is conjoured up by Lubbock's imagery in his discussion of dramatic and pictorial narrative, in which he describes the pictorial novel as: 'a moving stream of impressions [...] or in another image it is a procession that passes before us as we sit to watch', and particularly in his examination of *Madame Bovary*

sister. His comments in this letter clearly indicate that from the very beginning of his career Balzac was aware of the realistic visual effects which could now be created in the theatre:

> J'ai vu le Diorama, Surville n'a plus de perspective à faire. Daguerre et Bouton ont étonné tout Paris; mille problèmes sont résolus depuis que, devant une toile tendue, on croit être dans une Eglise à cent pas de chaque chose. C'est la merveille du siècle, une *conquète de l'homme*, à laquelle je ne m'attendais nullement.[17]

The example of the Diorama, together with the elaborate stage sets of the contemporary melodrama, which incorporated highly convincing scenery,[18] serve to illustrate that the pictorial detail for which Balzac's descriptions of the physical setting have become renowned was already an established and vital element in the popular stage entertainment of his period.

Balzac's descriptions of location and décor have of course been commented on extensively, and they constitute one of his greatest skills as a novelist.[19] There has also been much discussion of the role of the fine arts in Balzac's novels, and many of his descriptions of setting are seen to stand in close relationship to realist painting rather than to the theatre.[20] It appears, however, that Balzac seems to have appreciated above all the dramatic, evocative quality of painting since he praised those works in which the figures:

in which he states: 'His [Flaubert's] object is to place the scene before us, so that we may take it in like a picture gradually unrolled'. Percy Lubbock, *The Craft of Fiction* (London: Jonathan Cape, 1921), p. 14, & p. 65.

[17] *Corres.*, vol. I, p. 205.

[18] Since stage melodrama had evolved partly from the boulevard theatres which had been restricted to showing *pantomimes* and simple theatrical entertainments with few speaking parts to an audience which was largely illiterate, writers and directors had relied heavily on visual techniques, and in particular on scenery. Stage sets of the period could portray background setting with sufficient realistic detail to rival the detailed descriptions of background setting found in certain novels, and the melodramatist Pixerécourt is known to have given lengthy descriptions running into several pages, of scenery and visual effects to accompany the written texts of his productions. See: M.J.A. Borgnis, *Traité complet de mécanique appliquée aux arts* (Paris: Bachelier, 1820).

[19] Danielle Dupuis, 'Spécificité et rôle du décor dans les *Scènes de la vie privée*', in *AB*, 1994, pp. 139-155.

[20] Pierre Laubriet, *L'Intelligence de l'art chez Balzac* (Paris: Didier, 1961), pp. 384-402.

semblent et parler et marcher: l'ombre devient ombre, le jour est jour, la chair est vivante, les yeux remuent, le sang coule dans les veines et les Etoffes chatoient.[21]

It is significant, and yet not widely known, that in at least one instance Balzac literally 'staged' the setting of the dramatic climax of a novel in order to explore its plastic dimensions and to convince himself of its realism. Gautier tells how he arrived at Balzac's house in the rue des Batailles to find that he had converted the square drawing room into a round room like that of Paquita in *La Fille aux yeux d'or* by dividing off the corners. According to Gautier the room was arranged exactly as in the novel with: 'pas un détail d'ajouté ou de retranché'.[22] The main purpose of the exercise, Gautier recalls, was to test whether from such a room the screams of Paquita might be heard elsewhere in the house. It seems extraordinary, if this had been his sole aim, that Balzac should have gone to the trouble of creating the smaller details of the setting. What this suggests is that Balzac's conception of setting consists not only in the two-dimensional image of the realist painter, who creates a static, merely pictorial backdrop against which events take place, but also in the three-dimensional image of the *metteur en scène*, who creates a physical environment which is as essential to the action of the novel as elaborate stage sets are to the melodrama.

A distinction has already been made in the discussion of Balzac's dramatization of the location between the 'static' setting, which serves as a merely pictorial background, and the 'active' or dynamic setting, which serves as a propulsive force in the drama. Both the static and the active settings of Balzac's novels may, however, be seen to relate to the theatre – the former to the detailed backdrops of the historical drama, and the latter to the elaborate and highly symbolic settings of the melodrama. Generally landscape descriptions, such as those found in *Les Chouans*, *Le Lys dans la Vallée*, *Le Médecin de campagne* and *Le Curé de village* belong more, although not totally, to the pictorial backdrop, whereas city and interior descriptions belong to moral atmosphere, dramatic provision of character and closing in of the scene.[23] As can be seen in the opening pages of *Le*

---

[21] *Bo.*, vol. I, p. 328.
[22] Gautier, 'Honoré de Balzac', in *Ecrivains et Artistes Romantiques* (Plon: Paris, 1933), p. 95. See above, p. 19, n. 49.
[23] See: Percy Lubbock, *The Craft of Fiction*, pp. 204-221; Erich Auerbach,

Père Goriot or *Eugénie Grandet,* the movement is from wide landscape to minute detail, from exterior to interior, from town to room. In these novels there is a gradual, but perceptible, sense of convergence so that the description increases in detail and intensity as the point of focus is approached, and décor is presented not only as atmosphere but as a foreshadowing of theme and character. Throughout *La Comédie humaine* environment and characters are seen and depicted in a state of fusion, in which décor functions as strong visual symbolism so that, for example, Grandet's character is an extension of his Spartan surroundings, Goriot's demise is reflected in the disintegration of his lodgings, and the contrasts of Esther's life are highlighted in the difference between the fashionable world which she frequents and the miserable garret in which she resides.

Interestingly, and perhaps blurring Lubbock's distinction of pictorial and dramatic narrative, descriptions which appear to be merely pictorial may also be an active force in the plot. Furthermore, this is not merely implicit in the course of the narrative, but is explicitly stated by Balzac himself in a number of novels. Balzac frequently justifies his introductory descriptions by use of a theatrical vocabulary which communicates to the reader that descriptions which may otherwise seem superfluous and incidental are in fact essential to the dynamics of the drama which is to unfold and to the psychology of the characters. In the opening pages of *Les Petits Bourgeois,* for example, Balzac tells the reader:

> Quelques indications, assez semblables à celles qui servent de sommaire aux pièces de théâtre, seront d'ailleurs d'autant moins déplacées en tête de cette esquisse, qu'elles faciliteront l'introduction des personnages.[24]

Similarly, the pictorial setting of *Les Chouans,* which constitutes one of the longest descriptions in *La Comédie humaine,* is justified by use of vocabulary borrowed from the theatre in an attempt to establish it as an active rather than static element of the narrative. The description of the landscape in the first and third parts of the novel is so definite in outline that it could easily constitute a stage backdrop,

---

Mimesis (New York: Doubleday, 1957), pp. 417-418; Maurice Bardèche, *Balzac romancier,* pp. 312-313.

[24] *Bou.,* vol. VIII, p. 23. See also: *Pay.,* vol. IX, p. 128, 'Ce précis rapide aura le mérite d'introduire quelques-uns des principaux acteurs du drame'.

but it is also more than this since it is an animated, three-dimensional theatre: 'De toutes parts, des montagnes de schiste s'élèvent en amphithéâtre', and: 'Quelques bestiaux animaient cette scène déjà si dramatique'.[25] The importance of the background is again reinforced at the beginning of the third part of the novel:

> Les derniers événements de cette histoire ayant dépendu de la disposition des lieux où ils se passèrent, il est indispensable d'en donner ici une minutieuse description, sans laquelle le dénoœment serait d'une compréhension difficile. [...] Ce lieu [...] fut précisément le théâtre où devait se dénouer le drame commencé à la Vivetière. Ainsi, quelque pittoresques que soient les autres parties de Fougères, l'attention doit être exclusivement portée sur les accidents du pays que l'on découvre en haut de la Promenade.[26]

The Breton countryside remains not only in the background but also in the foreground throughout the novel, shaping the actions of the characters, and the reader continues to be conscious of it as would a spectator at a play.

Again in *Une ténébreuse affaire* Balzac consciously justifies three pages of description by emphasising the role of the setting in the *drame*. Here too the theatrical terminology makes explicit Balzac's deliberate attempt to give a double dramatic function to the setting, in that it is both a three-dimensional location for the action, like a stage setting with plasticity and perspective, and is also part of the central tension of that action:

> Le lieu pittoresque où le régisseur avait amené Laurence devait être si fatal aux principaux personnages de ce drame et à Michu lui-même, que le devoir d'un historien est de le décrire.[27]

The sense of theatre attached to the scene is further reinforced by the image of Michu as a stage manager who has led Laurence to this scene.

Although it is outdoor scenery which is so frequently justified by dramatic terminology, its importance in the narrative is often less than that of indoor scenery. Indeed it has to be recognised that in many

---

[25] *Ch.*, vol. VIII, pp. 912 & 913.
[26] *Ch.*, vol. VIII, p. 1069.
[27] *TA*, vol. VIII, 564.

novels the outdoor scenes, which could only be adequately reproduced by the cinema, particularly those scenes which take place in moving carriages or on horse-back, are not always essential for the development of character or plot, and it is in the interiors of buildings that the 'drama' takes place. In these interior scenes Balzac's technique approaches even more closely that of the theatrical *metteur en scène*.

Only when the panoramic view of the surroundings of the Grandet house or the Pension Vauquer gives way to the contained settings of the interiors does the drama begin to unfold, and it is more often in these locations, so easily transferred to the stage,[28] that the climaxes of the plot occur. To cite but a few striking examples from *La Comédie humaine*: Birotteau learns of his bankruptcy in the back of his shop;[29] Vautrin's identity is discovered in the communal room of the Pension Vauquer;[30] the purpose of Montriveau's kidnap of the duchesse de Langeais is revealed in his drawing room;[31] and in Paquita's bedroom de Marsay discovers the shocking identity of her protector;[32] and in each instance the physical aspect of the room has been described before the dramatic anagnorisis takes place.

Even in *Les Chouans*, where Balzac is at pains to establish the significance of the wider landscape, it is in the interior scenes that the chance meetings, discoveries and revelations upon which the plot depends actually take place, since these scenes heighten the dramatic tensions by bringing the opposing sides into close physical proximity. In order to highlight this Balzac states explicitly that, '[p]our la parfaite intelligence du dénouement, il est nécessaire de rentrer dans la maison de Mlle de Verneuil avec elle'.[33] Here the climax is reached as Marie's agitation is intensified to its most acute in the confined space of her room, and the truth about the false letter sent by Corentin and Marie's unwitting treachery to her lover are revealed.

The interior setting is above all a location in which opposing parties can be positioned with symbolic significance and in which furnishings play a significant role. In *Les Chouans* this occurs in the

---

[28] The stage adaptations of *Le Père Goriot* and *Eugénie Grandet* work in this way, by picking the essential interior scenes out of the original narrative. See appendix IV.
[29] *CB*, vol. VI, p. 260.
[30] *PG*, vol. III, p. 214.
[31] *DL*, vol. V, p. 989.
[32] *FYO*, vol. V, p. 1105.
[33] *Ch.*, vol. VIII, p. 1200.

inn at Alençon where the conflicting parties are seated at opposite sides of the dinner table.[34] The inn was a popular location for the plots of contemporary melodrama, providing a convenient and confined meeting point for characters who might not otherwise come into contact,[35] and Balzac further manipulates the opportunities of this setting through the contrivance of the dinner table device. Tables are often used by Balzac as a concrete, physical means of setting characters in opposition, and in each case feature in scenes which readily lend themselves to the stage: at the dining table of the Pension Vauquer the drama of *Le Père Goriot* begins to unfold; countless intrigues are originated at the dining tables of courtisans; at Birotteau's dining table du Tillet effects the plot against him; and in *Les Petits Bourgeois* the theatrical quality of the table device is explicitly emphasised by Balzac:

> Brigitte eut la satisfaction de voir la table bordée des principaux personnages de ce drame que d'ailleurs son salon allait contenir tous, à l'exception de l'affreux Cérizet.[36]

Beyond the confines of the table, characters are set in opposition within the larger context of the room, or of adjoining rooms. In *Un grand homme*, for example, the opposition between Camusot and Lucien and the latter's social marginalisation are visually portrayed in a scene in which Lucien is at risk of being discovered in Coralie's room by her protector, Camusot. In order to avert this discovery, Bérénice lifts a curtain to enable Lucien to hide behind it. The décor thus serves both to facilitate the plot and to give symbolic representation to Lucien's standing in society,[37] for he will always be behind the curtain, hiding from one thing or another and unable to face society head on.

The physical representation of the central issues of the plot can also be found in the courtroom scene of *Une ténébreuse affaire*, which is described in a way which suggests a stage, on which the opposing

---

[34] *Ch.*, pp. 978-989.

[35] Elsewhere Balzac makes reference to one of the most successful of these, *L'Auberge des Adrets*, a three-act melodrama by Antier, Chaponnier and Lacoste, first performed at the Ambigu-Comique on 2 July 1823. See: *F*, vol. V, p. 895; & *SetM*, vol. VI, p. 919.

[36] *Bou.*, vol. VIII, p. 103.

[37] *IP*, vol. V, p. 410.

sides in the drama are symbolically located at each side of the set. Like the inn, the courtroom was also popular in contemporary melodrama, not for the opportunities for intrigue which it afforded, however, but because it clearly embodied the simple morality of the melodrama and distinguished right from wrong, good from evil, and ensured that just punishment was meted out. Similar examples of courts, tribunals, and lawyers' offices which set the different parties in clear opposition are frequent in *La Comédie humaine*,[38] but this scene is particularly striking in its attention to detail, the precision with which the furniture is located, and the strict positioning of the characters:

> Ainsi tous les personnages de ce drame, et même ceux qui n'en étaient en quelque sorte que les comparses, se trouvèrent réunis sur la scène où les destinés des deux familles se jouaient alors. [...] Au fond de quelque longue salle carrée, on voit un bureau couvert en serge verte, élevé sur une estrade, derrière lequel s'asseyent les juges dans des fauteuils vulgaires. A gauche, le siège de l'accusateur public, et, de son côté, le long de la muraille, une longue tribune, garnie de chaises pour les jurés. En face des jurés s'étend une autre tribune où se trouve un banc pour les accusés et pour les gendarmes qui les gardent.[39]

Balzac goes on to detail exactly the furniture and objects in the room, using the present tense, and omitting main verbs in order to lend his description the immediacy of a stage direction. In particular the use of 'on voit' invites the reader to visualise the scene rather than to accept passively details which might otherwise have been introduced by 'il y avait'.

Similarly the climactic scene of Vautrin's arrest in *Le Père Goriot* takes place in an interior setting in which the principal actors and the minor characters are grouped together around what can be seen as the central 'stage'.[40] The boarders who had been introduced in the novel's

---

[38] Another significant example occurs, for instance, in *Le Colonel Chabert* when Chabert and his estranged wife are placed in direct opposition to one another in Derville's office, each sitting in a different, small room which opens off the central office where Derville is situated as mediator. The physical arrangement clearly indicates the conflict and concealment on each side and Derville's role in its resolution. *Col.*, vol. III, pp. 356-358.

[39] *TA*, vol. VIII, p. 653.

[40] *PG*, vol. III, p. 214.

opening scenes are now gathered in the same communal room to witness its climax. On the arrival of the police the group's attention is directed at Vautrin 'sur qui tous les regards s'arrêtèrent irrésistiblement', and Vautrin's wig is knocked off to reveal his identity in all its horror.[41]   The scene of unmasking the villain, which was perhaps the most common *coup de théâtre* of stage melodrama, is 'staged' in the novel within the contained space of the communal room, of which one wall has been removed, as it were, to allow the reader to see inside.   The contained space of the room, with the grouping of the main characters in the centre and minor characters around the outside, is crudely theatrical, and ensures that the focus is on Vautrin since this is the climax of his particular drama within the plot.   Moreover, the setting and grouping are essential for the narrative outcome since, enclosed both by the room and by the minor characters who bar his exit, Vautrin cannot escape.

The interior settings discussed so far bring together large and often conflicting groups of individuals, but equally important, and often more intense, are more intimate groupings and settings where pacts are made, secrets are revealed and fatal relationships are established. Perhaps the most striking example of the dramatic role of intimate setting in the dynamics of the plot occurs in *Béatrix* (1838-1845). Here Félicité des Touches detains Calyste in her room, deliberately waiting until Béatrix can see her close the curtains, so as to provoke the latter's jealousy.[42] Béatrix in turn consciously uses the opulent and bohemian décor of her surroundings to contrast with the sterility of the du Guénic household in order to strengthen her hold on Calyste and thus the environment of des Touches becomes a 'lieu fatal' for him.[43]

Such intimate groupings provide the opportunity both to accelerate the plot and to reveal elements of intrigue and tension to the reader, while retaining the essential mystery between those characters who are informed and those who are ignorant. For example: in the intimate setting of the garden bench in *Modeste Mignon*, La Brière reveals to Butscha the feelings which he had wanted to hide from him, thereby enlisting his help;[44] on the 'sièges peints en vert' in the garden of the

---

[41] *Ibid.*, pp. 214-217.
[42] *B*, vol. II, p. 774.
[43] *Ibid.*, p.858. See also p. 881.
[44] *MM*, vol. I, p. 651.

Pension Vauquer Vautrin reveals the Taillefer plot to Rastignac;[45] and on a bench in the Jardin des Plantes Mlle. Michonneau and Poiret have their meeting with the police chief to discuss the plot against Vautrin.[46] Intimate settings establish who is on the inside of the drama and who is on the outside looking in. They are a sort of novelistic figuration of the proscenium arch of the theatre, thus delineating the perspectives of the different characters within the central drama. From the area of the stage in front of the proscenium arch the minor characters not only take part in but also observe the drama of the protagonists' lives.

In this sense the theatrical quality of the settings assumes a further dimension, for Balzac is not only himself an omniscient observer, inviting the reader to penetrate the intimate drama of his characters, literally to see it from without, but additionally he places other characters around them who are also looking in – Goriot wants a corner of Delphine's apartment for himself from where he can watch the pleasure which he has orchestrated; Herrera watches over Lucien, Esther and Nucingen from his adjacent room as though he were watching a drama which he had created; Gobseck witnesses the dramas of other characters with chilling emotional detachment as they pass in succession through his premises;[47] Rastignac perceives Goriot's drama by spying on him in his room at night[48] and by looking in from a hiding place as Goriot leaves the de Restaud household.[49]

These intimate scenes in which other characters look in, also serve to highlight the central theme and central characters of the drama. For example, the closing scene of *Les Chouans,* in which the expiring Montauran and Mlle. de Verneuil are brought together and surrounded by their enemies who are looking down on them, serves to illustrate, through a clear theatrical grouping of the characters, that this is not so much a political drama but rather is the lovers' drama. In particular, it is in scenes of death that Balzac consciously attempts to engage the reader's participation in the dramatic spectacle, inviting the reader by use of verbs of 'seeing' to become a spectator. This is best

[45] *PG,* vol. III, p. 135.

[46] *Ibid.,* p. 187.

[47] Gobseck has already been defined as a detached spectator by Peter Brooks. See: *The Melodramatic Imagination,* p. 115.

[48] *PG,* vol. III, p. 78.

[49] *Ibid.,* p. 102.

exemplified in the description of Coralie's room in *Illusions perdues* which symbolises the extremes of Lucien's emotional experience since it is a 'ravissante création du luxe, toute blanche et rose', which functions as part of his seduction and marks both the beginning and the end of his pleasures in Paris. In the scene of Coralie's death the reader is invited to look in on the room along with Bianchon and d'Arthez who have just arrived. By use of the words 'spectacle' and 'vue', and by emphasising the lack of dialogue, Balzac makes the scene rely entirely on its visual effect:

> Le spectacle de cette belle morte souriant à l'éternité, la vue de son amant lui achetant une tombe avec des gravelures, Barbet payant un cercueil, ces quatre chandelles autour de cette actrice dont la basquine et les bas rouges à coins verts faisaient naguère palpiter toute une salle, puis sur la porte le prêtre qui l'avait réconciliée avec Dieu retournant à l'église pour y dire une messe en faveur de celle qui avait tant aimé! ces grandeurs et ces infamies, ces douleurs écrasées sous la nécessité glacèrent le grand écrivain et le grand médecin qui s'assirent sans pouvoir proférer une parole.[50]

Balzac's descriptions of setting are an invitation both to visualise, and to penetrate and understand, for as well as reflecting the characteristics and motivations of the protagonists, Balzac's interior décor consistently acts as an external reference point, giving concrete form to abstract ideologies and to the very essence of the dramatic conflict. At the same time, however, the physical setting occasionally becomes theatrical in a more profound sense, for it is made to serve Balzac's critique of the vast charade of society and itself appears as a theatrical illusion masking an underlying reality. Nowhere is this more apparent than in the residences of Balzac's fictional actresses who inhabit sumptuous apartments and yet cannot pay for their suppers and their haberdashery.[51] Far from being a clear visual signifier of their social standing, the actresses' extravagant boudoirs and salons hide a sordid reality of debt and prostitution, and for them the drawing-room and bedroom are in every sense an extension of the theatre stage. So too César Birotteau's impending ruin is concealed from the outside world by the comfort of the new apartment and the air of prosperity in his shop; the bourgeois dining room of Cardot

---

[50] *IP*, vol. V, p. 549.
[51] *IP*, vol. IV, p. 494; *FE*, vol. II, p. 324; *HA*, vol. VII, pp. 779 & 786.

belies his life of excess and debauchery in the backstage of the theatre;[52] and in *Pierrette* the expensive décor and furnishings of the Rogron household conceal from the outside world the cruelty and deprivation to which Pierrette is subjected.

In *Pierrette* Balzac makes explicit this penetration of the surface décor to reveal the mean characters of Rogron and Sylvie, for whom luxurious furnishings have become the sole object of affection:

> Après le déjeuner, sa cousine et son cousin, heureux de l'étonnement de Pierrette et pressés d'en jouir, lui montrèrent leur beau salon pour lui apprendre à en respecter les somptuosités. [...] Rogron et Sylvie étaient arrivés à un amour immodéré pour leur mobilier et pour leur maison, qui leur avaient coûté si cher.[53]

From the point of view of the provincial society of the novel the prosperous impression given by the house and its furnishings succeeds in creating a convincing illusion of comfort and ease which is unanimously considered to be beneficial to Pierrette. The characters of the novel are not able adequately to distinguish between the *être* and the *paraître,* and only when it is too late do they discover what the reader has known from the outset – that Rogron and Sylvie have decorated their house as their own social stage, and that the appearance of this house is little more than a theatrical illusion which hides a fatal drama. In this way the society of *La Comédie humaine* becomes a victim of its own insistence on the value of appearances, for characters are duped by settings which are not valid signifiers. The physical setting is thus an integral part of Balzac's process of observing and uncovering a world in which all is theatre.

The above discussion shows that in his novels Balzac frequently exploits the setting, its furnishings, and the positioning of the characters within it, so that the physical location works in a multiple theatrical sense. At its simplest level the pictorial backdrop of certain exterior settings reflects the contemporary importance of realistic visual techniques in the theatre. More than this, however, the three-dimensional, plastic interiors, and occasionally exteriors, the intimate

[52] *MD*, vol. IV, p. 740.
[53] *P*, vol. IV, pp. 78-79.

locations, the strategic use of furnishings and the precise positioning of characters, work together to create settings which are an active force in the drama of the plot and often also a concise and concrete symbol of the novel's central conflict. The reader is constantly invited to create a mental image from the visual data given in the text, and in the process of doing this may find that this stage is itself part of the total social illusion offered up for view in *La Comédie humaine*.

Sound Effects and Lighting

In order to achieve maximum dramatic effect in the settings of his fiction, Balzac often introduces light and sound to emphasise the realism of his portrayal and to amplify certain scenes of dramatic climax in a way which reflects the use of these devices in the contemporary theatre.[54] Balzac's use of sound and light consists mainly in the juxtaposition of sound and silence, and light and obscurity, and in many instances moves the narrative forward either by highlighting the novel's central conflict, or by pointing in a symbolic way to its final dénouement.

The opposition of silence and sound in Balzac's novels is often characterised by an abrupt cessation of violent action or dialogue, so that it is the silence rather than the sound which punctuates the narrative and creates tension through a dramatic pause. Conversely, there are also instances in which sound pierces the narrative in a way

[54] Prior to the gradual introduction of gas lighting in the theatre from 1822 onwards, the sole source of light had been the *quinquet*, a type of oil lamp which produced a hazy, reddish light and which, despite its threat as a fire hazard, was used in the theatre for over forty years. The introduction of gas lighting allowed for more spectacular effects, for the more contrasted interplay of light and shade, and in particular for spotlighting. The dramatic climaxes of the melodrama which depended heavily upon sudden revelations of identity were emphasised by beams of light piercing a dimly lit background, or by the sudden movement of light from one character to another. In the emerging Romantic drama the increased sophistication of lighting facilitated a more naturalistic representation of the contrast between day and night, between indoor and outdoor scenes, and in particular between the brightly lit interiors of wealthy homes and the dimly lit hovels of poverty. Sound effects, on the other hand, had always been integral to the boulevard theatres, and in particular music and song, which had been used in place of dialogue in early forms of melodrama, and continued to be an essential element of the vaudeville throughout Balzac's lifetime. See: M.A. Allevy, *La Mise en scène en France pendant la première moitié du dix-neuvième siècle* (Paris: Droz, 1938); & G. M. Bergman, *Lighting in the Theatre*, pp. 273-279.

which resembles a theatrical, 'off-stage' sound effect in which a sudden gunshot, chime of a clock, sound of approaching footsteps, or strain of music invades the scene. In *Les Chouans*, for example, sound is consistently used in this way to emphasise the mounting tensions of the plot as the advancing military troops move concentrically around the centres of interior action and frame the scenes with sound. Sound effects are important from the opening scenes to the last and are integral to the realistic animation of the setting as well as to the sequence of the action. The peaceful Breton countryside in the opening scenes is characterised by the singing of the birds, and against this the rhythmic sound of marching footsteps is introduced, announcing the advance of the military forces and establishing an element of tension:

> Au milieu de ce silence solennel, les pas tardifs des conscrits, sous les pieds desquels le sable criait sourdement, rendaient un son régulier qui ajoutait une vague émotion à cette anxiété générale.[55]

In the obscurity and fog in which much of the subsequent action takes place, sound becomes increasingly important in the identification of the positions of the opposing forces, and at every point heightens the tension as the enemy can be heard but not seen: in the inn at Alençon Hulot hears Marche-à-Terre's special whistle, indicating that he is surrounded by 'Chouans déguisés', although he can see no-one outside; as Hulot's suspicions regarding Montauran's identity increase, the 'off-stage' sound of arms and footsteps announces the arrival of Hulot's forces and deflects attention away from the disguised Montauran;[56] later, in the wedding scene, the sound of guns and footsteps can be heard by Marie, and signals the presence of the soldiers around the house as a threatening and audible, but unseen, reminder of her pact with Corentin.[57] In a crudely theatrical way, sound is used throughout this novel to signal the position of the military forces. Thus where any action is located in an interior setting, the sound effects come from beyond the immediate scene and are made by footsteps and guns, which signal the advance of the Republicans and create a cumulative sense of entrapment and

[55] *Ch.*, vol. VIII, p. 925.
[56] *Ch.*, vol. VIII, pp. 988-991.
[57] *Ibid.*, p. 1206.

destruction since they point towards the final dénouement, in which
the lovers are surrounded and assassinated. In the scene where this
takes place, the tension between silence and sound reaches its climax,
and the tragedy which has been predicted by the advancing sounds of
the Republicans throughout the novel is finally realised in an arresting
dramatic pause:

> Le feu des Républicains n'offrit aucune interruption et fut
> continuel, impitoyable. Les victimes ne jetèrent pas un cri. Entre
> chaque décharge le silence était effrayant.[58]

Similarly, in the final part of *Illusions perdues* a dramatic pause
points towards the novel's final dénouement by highlighting Lucien's
momentary glory and predicting his subsequent fall. The young
people of Angoulême celebrate Lucien with a noisy, late-night
serenade but ten minutes later the square is empty again and 'le
silence y régnait'.[59]   The sound of the serenade invades the narrative
as it invades the the sleep of Lucien's family, but the silence which
follows it is predicative of doom, and the sense of anticipation which
it generates is rendered all the more effective by its juxtaposition to
the tumultuous noise.

Just as sound is used to heighten and predict dramatic tension, so
too it is occasionally a determining force in the drama of the plot.
This can be seen in *Pierrette* (1839-40), where Sylvie's suspicions of
her cousin are aroused by the sound of Brigaut's heavy footsteps in
the square:

> malgré sa prestesse, ses souliers ferrés, en retentissant sur le petit
> pavé de Provins, produisirent un son facile à distinguer dans la
> musique du moulin, et que put entendre la personne qui ouvrait la
> fenêtre.[60]

Sylvie's suspicions are then confirmed by the sound of Pierrette's
own footsteps as she gets out of bed in the night and crosses the room
to the window. In the course of Pierrette's hidden drama, sound leads
to suspicion, suspicion leads to maltreatment, and maltreatment leads
to death.

---

[58] *Ch.*, vol. VIII, p. 1209.
[59] *IP*, vol. V, p. 652.
[60] *P*, vol. IV, p. 32.

An equally striking example of sound shaping the plot can be found in *La Duchesse de Langeais* (1833), where the sound of *Te Deum* played by the Antoinette is juxtaposed to the silence of the Spanish convent in which she resides. The sound of this music sparks Montriveau's memory and acts as the catalyst of all the subsequent action.[61] Then on Montriveau's return to the silent convent the next day, non-verbal sound becomes the sole means of communication between him and his former mistress, as he contrives to announce his presence by making sounds in the silent cloisters: 'il y marcha bruyamment, il toussa', and the reply comes in the organ striking up the *Magnificat* and as '[l]a musique éclata dans toute sa puissance; elle échauffa l'église'.[62] This scene is brought to a close in a fusion of musical effects and metaphorical lighting effects, which emphasise the impression of theatrical *mise en scène*. The sound giving way to silence is described as though it were light giving way to darkness, and the effect is one of diminishing perspective as though the curtain were being lowered at the end of a stage scene:

> Quand les airs eurent, par degrés, cessé leurs vibrations oscillatoires, vous eussiez dit que l'église, jusque-là lumineuse rentrait dans une profonde obscurité.[63]

Balzac's use of light shows the same awareness of its dramatic potential as his use of sound. At its simplest level Balzac uses light in a descriptive sense as part of the portrayal of the scene, as if lighting a stage set in order to spotlight the principal characters or to render the mood of the scene through lighting effects. This is particularly evident in some of the death-bed scenes in which furnishings, décor and

---

[61] Music, and piano music in particular, plays an important role in certain novels. However, its function is largely narrative rather than dramatic since music and the ability to appreciate or produce it is used in Balzac's novels mainly in a descriptive sense as a signifier of social standing, good education, or artistic sensibility, rather than as a sound effect. Danielle Pistone claims that in the thirty novels she has examined for the importance of piano music, from *Annette et le criminel* (1824), to *Le Cousin Pons* (1847), there are approximately eighty pianists. In most cases the musical ability of these characters is part of creating their typology and the background setting, and does not feature as an active element of the drama. See: Danielle Pistone, 'Pianos et pianistes balzaciens', in *AB*, 1994, pp. 55-69; & L. Maurice-Anour, 'La Musique' in *Honoré de Balzac* (Paris: Flammarion, 1952).

[62] *DL*, vol. V, p. 912.

[63] *DL*, vol. V, p. 913.

characters are carefully arranged as though on a theatre stage. Goriot's death-bed, for example, is 'mal éclairé par une seule chandelle',[64] indicating his poverty and creating an obscure and miserable mood for the scene; Coralie on her death-bed is framed by 'quatre chandelles',[65] allowing her beauty to be seen and surrounding her in a peaceful light of religious reconciliation, while Lucien remains outside the frame of light and the benediction which it symbolises; Paquita's room in which her bloody corpse is sprawled has '[t]ous les flambeaux allumés',[66] serving to sustain the mood of violence and passion, and to show the scene in the full extent of its horror, as well as to facilitate the mutual recognition of the siblings.

Light is also often used to effect the transition of the reader's gaze from background to character. Thus in *Illusions perdues* 'les rayons du soleil qui se jouaient dans les pampres de la treille caressèrent les deux poètes en les enveloppant de sa lumière comme d'une auréole'.[67] The two friends are briefly but powerfully illuminated: David, strong and enduring; Lucien, effeminate and inconstant. By means of dramatic use of light the reader's attention is caught and held and before his eyes the characters take on life and significance.

In Balzac's novels light is perhaps most dramatically effective when used to create an effect of theatrical *chiaroscuro*,[68] in which dark gives way to light. In some instances this constitutes part of the naturalistic representation of the passage of time from night to day, such as could be found in productions of Romantic drama, and in others it is a more sudden moment of clarity which forms part of the melodramatic technique of revelation. In *La Duchesse de Langeais* when Montriveau finally gains an audience with Antoinette, the literal parting of a curtain in the darkness of the convent opens up a scene of light to reveal her figure, as though she were in the spotlight of a stage as the curtains part: 'Un léger bruit fit tressaillir cet homme, le rideau

---

[64] *PG*, vol. III, p. 285.

[65] *IP*, vol. V, p. 549.

[66] *FYO*, vol. V, p. 1106.

[67] *IP*, vol. V, p. 144.

[68] Although this is a term borrowed from painting, I have used it here to denote the revealing and mobile quality of light in the theatre. Balzac's use of light in his descriptions has of course often been related to the Flemish school of painting, and there are 27 references to Rembrandt in *La Comédie humaine*. See *LCH*, vol. XII, p. 1798. See also above, pp 236-237.

brun se tira; puis il vit dans la lumière une femme debout'.[69]   A
similar sudden beam of light also allows Antoinette to see the masked
men who are her kidnappers:

> Elle resta clouée par la peur, en croyant voir la lueur placée derrière
> le rideau prendre de l'intensité sous les aspirations d'un soufflet.
> Tout à coup les reflets devenus plus vifs avaient illuminé trois
> personnes masquées.[70]

Later the light shines brightly again, like a spotlight cutting through
the darkness, this time leaving Antoinette in no doubt about the
menacing presence of the masked men in the background obscurity.[71]
The light is thus used to build up the dramatic tension, so that
mysteries and plots are hatched in darkness and illuminated only for
long enough to indicate the threat which they may pose.

   This play of light and obscurity is also crucial to the action of *Les
Chouans*, since the rebels are able to hide in the darkness, their
indistinct forms being mistaken for rocks in the 'tonnerre de
brouillard', which exacerbates the difficulty facing Hulot's
Republican forces. As the obscurity begins to give way to clarity,
sound and lighting effects are combined to announce the imminence
of the battle. Corentin makes out the position of the Chouans as the
fog begins to part and the bells in the distance chime to announce
symbolically the end of the period of hiding.[72]   As the dawn
approaches, the darkness and fog, which had concealed the positions
of the opposing sides in the battle, now give way to the moonlight
which reveals. The moon beams down like a theatrical spotlight to
point at the enemy as Marie de Verneuil and Montauran now see
Corentin clearly:

> La lune, ayant dissipé le brouillard, éclairait de sa blanche lumière
> les habits, les fusils, l'impassible Corentin qui allait et venait
> comme un chacal attendant sa proie.[73]

The tension is highlighted in the positioning of the spotlight on the

---

[69] *DL*, vol. V, p. 918.
[70] *Ibid.*, p. 993.
[71] *Ibid.*, p. 997.
[72] *Ch.*, vol. VIII, pp. 1198-1199.
[73] *Ch.*, vol. VIII, p. 1208.

impatient enemy and the guns which will bring down Marie and Montauran. Balzac's use of light in this novel consistently points towards the dénouement, for each time it indicates the presence of the Republicans and their guns which will kill Montauran and Marie.

Light is also of minor significance in the play of *être* and *paraître* at the basis of Balzac's critique of society, for just as a piercing beam, or the effect of chiaroscuro may invite the reader to visualise and focus on the scene which is illuminated, so too it may invite the reader to penetrate the scene's dark recesses. This can be seen in the first part of *Le Père Goriot,* where the beams of light piercing the dark stairways of the Pension Vauquer serve to intensify the growing sense of mystery. At night the mysteries surrounding Goriot and Vautrin are perceived by Eugène, whose attention is drawn by the beams of light emitted from beneath their doors, revealing only sufficient information to allow Eugène to conclude: 'voilà bien des mystères dans une pension bourgeoise'.[74] The use of light here not only functions in the melodramatic heightening of the mystery, but also as part of the invitation to see the drama through the eyes of Eugène, spying on Goriot and Vautrin in order to penetrate their private dramas. At the same time the bright lights of the Faubourg St-Germain, the *chandelles*, the *lustres*, which allow the salons and ballrooms of the *grandes dames* of *La Comédie humaine* to be seen by the reader and by the characters in all their brilliance, may be metaphorically likened to the footlights of the theatre stage, for these lights are blinding to the characters on the social stage and far from revealing, and contrarily often conceal dark social realities of hypocrisy, infidelity and debt. It is not in the bright lights of the social stage that intrigues are mounted and crimes committed but in the darkness of its wings.

As the above discussion shows, lighting and sound effects are important elements in the dramatization of the narrative of Balzac's novels and are used in a variety of ways to animate the visual image, to create mood, and to advance the action. Balzac arranges the physical location of his novels and animates the location with sound and light to a dual theatrical effect in so far as he creates a convincing set for the action and at the same time strives towards his wider aim of penetrating society's illusions. Into this 'staged' setting Balzac then introduces his characters, who must be dressed appropriately.

[74] *PG,* vol. III, pp. 78-79.

Costume and Disguise

Balzac's use of costume in his novels shows the combined influence of the crude theatricality of the stage melodrama and the visual expressionism of the Romantic drama,[75] as well as functioning as a key element in his interpretation of society. No-one was perhaps more aware than Balzac of the importance of costume on the metaphorical stage of Parisian society, and there is certainly a sense of theatricality in Balzac's personal style, from the famously extravagant turquoise cane adopted in his period of dandyism, to the austere monk's habit donned in periods of disciplined application to his work. The value placed on appearance, which is a recurrent theme of his novels, is a maxim by which, according to Gautier, Balzac lived. Describing Balzac's house in the rue des Batailles Gautier writes:

> Il s'était arrangé là un intérieur assez luxueux, car il savait qu'à Paris on ne croit guère au talent pauvre, et que le *paraître* y amène souvent l'*être*. C'est à cette période que se rapportent ses velléités d'élégance et de dandysme, le fameux habit bleu à boutons d'or massif, la massue à pommeau de turquoises.[76]

As well as in his novels and in his personal style, Balzac's appreciation of clothing as a visual signifier is clearly expressed in his *Traité de la vie élégante* (1830), in which he divised a system of categorising his fellow citizens according to their clothing in to three types: 'l'homme qui travaille, l'homme qui pense, l'homme qui ne fait

---

[75] The devices of disguise and costume change are widely recognised as essential components of nineteenth-century stage melodrama, in which plots often depended on mistaken or concealed identities and the dramatic climax consisted in an anagnorisis which would establish family connections and true heirs, and name the villain of the piece. In the stage melodrama costume also provided clear visual signifiers of a character's role and status in the drama, which could often be reduced to crude symbolic representation so that, for example, the villain would be dressed in black and the good heroine in white. While in the emerging Romantic drama of the 1830s costume partly retained this symbolic function (See, for example Vigny's *Chatterton*), it also came to be part of the realistic representation of life, an element of what Hugo had defined in his *Préface de Cromwell* in 1827 as 'couleur locale' and constitutes part of the background setting of the drama. See: Hugo, *Préface de Cromwell*, pp. 262-267.

[76] Gautier, *Honoré de Balzac*, p. 94.

rien'.[77]

As in the *Traité de la vie élégante*, Balzac's descriptions of costume in his novels attempt to place his characters in their correct social milieu, and through his insistence on the realistic detail of their outward appearances certain characters become part of the general 'couleur locale' of the animated, visual background. The opening pages of *Les Chouans* (published in 1829, two years after Hugo's *Préface de Cromwell*), for example, contain a description of the costumes of the Breton peasants which is justified precisely by reference to the current vogue in literature for 'couleur locale':

> Ce détachement, divisé en groupes plus ou moins nombreux, offrait une collection de costumes si bizarres et une réunion d'individus appartenant à des localités ou à des professions si diverses, qu'il ne sera pas inutile de décrire leurs différences caractéristiques pour donner à cette histoire les couleurs vives auxquelles on met tant de prix aujourd'hui.[78]

The subsequent descriptions of the costumes of the opposing forces in the drama are graphic and detailed and become as much a part of the visual setting as the descriptions of the Breton landscape. Costume also gives symbolic representation here to the central political conflict, for the animal skins and rough, sack-cloth garments of the peasants stand in stark visual contrast to the gleaming buttons and leather boots of the military forces.

Similarly in *Le Père Goriot* (1834-35), the costumes of the boarders of the Pension Vauquer are linked to the physical setting, and function as part of the visual appeal of the novel. In fact, the extensive detail in the descriptions of the minor characters' costumes is completely out of proportion to the roles that they play, but they are carefully dressed by Balzac as though they were actors who could not appear on stage without costumes or only partially clothed. Throughout *La Comédie humaine* social demarcation is signified by costume and thus the social status of each member of the boarding house is denoted by his dress, which gives symbolic representation of where the characters stand in relation to society at large and to each other:

---

[77] *LCH*, ed. Pléiade, vol. XII, pp.211-257.
[78] *Ch.*, vol. VIII, p. 905.

Aussi le spectacle désolant que présentait l'intérieur de cette maison se répétait-il dans le costume de ses habitués, également délabrés. Les hommes portaient des redingotes dont la couleur était devenue problématique, des chaussures comme il s'en jette au coin des bornes dans les quartiers élégants, du linge élimé, des vêtements qui n'avaient plus que l'âme. Les femmes avaient des robes passées, reteintes, déteintes, de vieilles dentelles raccommodées, des gants glacés par l'usage des collerettes toujours rousses et des fichus éraillés.[79]

The boarders' costumes are then individually described in terms which are highly evocative and which rely for their visual impact on a coined phraseology and inventive use of language which is built up to a hyperbolic pitch. These images not only reveal minute attention to detail, but also personify, endow with life, and make plastic the pictorial descriptions. There are the 'pantoufles grimacées'[80] of Mme Vauquer and the 'étoffe lézardée' of her skirt, the 'culotte presque vide' of Poiret,[81] the 'châle à franges maigres et pleurardes'[82] of Mlle. Michonneau, and the 'tenue égrillarde'[83] of Goriot before his demise.[84] In the language used and the accumulation of the adjectives Balzac's description becomes itself part of the melodramatic mode of excess, part of the novel's theatrical expressionism.

In the first part of *Le Père Goriot,* perhaps more than anywhere else in *La Comédie humaine,* Balzac's style of presentation approaches that of the theatrical *metteur en scène,* since in logical sequence the stage is set, the characters are dressed one by one, and only then are they made to speak. With the exception of Vautrin, the boarders' characters, their status in society and the roles that they will play in the plot are defined from the outset by their costume. Furthermore, the central drama of the plot of *Le Père Goriot* is also given concrete visual representation through clothing. The contrast of Eugène's dress with the costume of Maxime de Trailles clearly highlights to him, and to the reader, the importance of clothing in the quest for social success:

[79] *PG,* vol. III, p. 57.
[80] *Ibid.,* p. 54.
[81] *Ibid.,* p. 58
[82] *Ibid.,* p. 57.
[83] *Ibid.,* p. 72.
[84] See also, for example: *IP,* vol. V, p. 470, where the 'pantalons mûrs' and 'redingotes râpées' of the claque are described.

Puis Maxime avait des bottes fines et propres, tandis que les siennes, malgré le soin qu'il avait pris en marchant, s'étaient empreintes d'une legère teinte de boue. Enfin Maxime portait une redingote qui lui serrait élégamment la taille et le faisait ressembler à une jolie femme, tandis qu'Eugène avait à deux heures et demie un habit noir. Le spirituel enfant de la Charante sentit la supériorité que la mise donnait à ce dandy.[85]

While the other boarders of the Pension Vauquer are defined from the outset by costumes which do not change in the course of the narrative, Eugène's rise in society is given visual interpretation in his increasing assimilation of the fine nuances of sartorial skill.   Conversely, Goriot's social demise from 1813 when he joins the Pension Vauquer with the 'trousseau magnifique du négociant qui ne se refuse rien en se retirant du commerce', to 1819 when the action of the novel begins,[86] is marked by the progressive states of his disintegrating attire, so that when he enters the scene he is dressed in 'une redingote de drap marron grossier, un gilet en poil de chèvre, et un pantalon gris en cuir de laine'.[87]

Vautrin's costume is not described in the opening of Le Père Goriot, for although he turns out to be a master of disguise, he is defined in this novel by his gestures, speech, and physionomy and not by his dress. Vautrin's disguise functions rather as part of the mystery of the plot, and it is in the development of Vautrin's role that Balzac's use of disguise comes closest to the contemporary stage melodrama. The ability to reinvent himself through costume is fundamental to the very conception of Vautrin and to his functions within La Comédie humaine, for only through costume and disguise is he able to escape death and live up to his name of Trompe-la mort. Each new disguise in the novels brings with it an indentity distinct from the last and represents a new life. It is significant that Vautrin is the only character whom Balzac attempted to transport in entirety from the novel to the stage, and Vautrin's suitability for stage melodrama owes as much to his propensity for convincing disguise as to the enormity of his character. In the play Vautrin (written in 1839 and produced in 1840), the leading character has no fewer than seven costume changes,[88] and

[85] PG, p. 97.
[86] Ibid., p. 63.
[87] Ibid., p. 72.
[88] See above, pp. 20-21; and Maurice Descotes, Le Drame romantique et ses

his function in the play is denoted as much by his successive disguises as by his actions and speech.

In *La Comédie humaine* it is Vautrin's disguise as the Spanish priest, Carlos Herrera, which in its mysterious and sinister aspect is the most melodramatic. Herrera is introduced towards the end of *Illusions perdues* as:

> un voyageur vêtu tout en noir, les cheveux poudrés, chaussé de souliers en veau d'Orléans à boucles d'argent, brun de visage, et couturé comme si, dans son enfance, il fût tombé dans le feu. Ce voyageur, à tournure si patemment ecclésiastique, allait lentement et fumait un cigare.[89]

On the surface, Vautrin's disguise is detailed and convincing and the reader might see a potential salvation for Lucien in the ecclesiastical dress, but there is a disturbing subtext to be discerned in the facial disfigurement, which for Vautrin is but an extension of his costume, hinting both backwards and forwards at some past trauma and at the future drama to be unfolded in *Splendeurs et misères*.

In *Splendeurs et misères* (1838-1847), Balzac's exploitation of the devices of costume and disguise is at its most extreme. Costume is not so much a realistic detail of the narrative here, as a propelling force of the plot, since disguise and impersonation are at the root of every new turn, of every deepening of the intrigue. To cite but a few examples: the action opens at the opera ball, where behind the masks and the cloaks identities can be only partially discerned;[90] Vautrin attends the opera disguised 'en militaire' and Esther is obliged to wear a veil;[91] Vautrin's wig is knocked off as it is in *Le Père Goriot*;[92] Peyrade parodies Vautrin's ecclesiastical costume by disguising himself as père Canquœlle, the opposing forces both assuming the appearance of 'good' in the guise of religion;[93] and Asie pays attention to the minutest details of her disguise as Mme de Saint-Estève in order to trick Nucingen:

grands créateurs (Paris: Presses Universitaires de France, 1955), p. 180.

[89] *IP*, vol. V, p. 689.
[90] *SetM*, vol. VI, p. 444.
[91] *Ibid.*, 470.
[92] *Ibid.*, p. 477.
[93] *Ibid.*, p. 532.

La fausse entremetteuse vint en robe de damas à fleurs, provenant
de rideaux décrochés à quelque boudoir saisi, ayant un de ces châles
de cachemire passés, usés, invendables, qui finissent leur vie au dos
de ces femmes. Elle portait une collerette en dentelles magnifiques,
mais éraillées, et un affreux chapeau; mais elle était chaussée en
souliers de peau d'Irlande, sur le bord desquels sa chair faisait
l'effet d'un bourrelet de soie noire à jour.[94]

Asie's costume is portrayed with realistic attention to detail and
functions both as an active force in the intrigue mounted to dupe
Nucingen and also as a comment on the type of woman she is to
portray. Attention to detail is necessary not only in terms of the
novel's realism but also in terms of its plot, for disguises, which in the
stage melodrama were often crude, can only be effective devices in
the novel if they are totally convincing both to the characters and to
reader.

Vautrin's disguise in *Splendeurs et misères* is in fact so effective,
and his disfigurement so complete, that in the final stages of the novel
even his fellow convicts are unable to recognise him from his
appearance, and can rely only on their natural instinct.[95] The intrigue
on which the plot depends is sustained because of the characters'
willingness to accept the codification of costume, for a time at least,
unquestioningly. Even characters who themselves deploy great skill
in disguise, and this in fact applies to nearly all the characters of the
novel, are unable immediately to decode certain outward signs in
order to recognise disguise in others.[96]

---

[94] *Ibid.*, p. 568.

[95] *Ibid.*, p. 839.

[96] Pierre Citron lists the following disguises and usurped identities in his
introduction to the Pléiade edition of *Splendeurs et misères:* 'chacun est en constante
mutation: Collin est l'abbé Herrera, Trompe-la-Mort, l'officier de paix, William
Barker, M. de Saint-Estève, un militaire; Esther, prostitué, grisette, courtisane et ange,
est la Torpille, Mme Van Bogseck, Mme de Champy. Asie est Jacqueline Collin,
mais aussi une Malaise (*sic.*), Mme Nourrisson, Mme de Saint-Estève, la marquise de
San Esteban et une baronne anonyme. [...] Corentin est aussi M. de Saint-Estève chez
Lucien, et M. de Saint-Denis chez le duc de Grandlieu; Peyrade est le père
Canquoëlle, Samuel Johnson et M. de Saint-Germain; Contenson est le baron Bryond
des Tours-Minières, un porteur de la Halle, une marchande des quatre-saisons, un
garde du commerce et un mulâtre. Bibi-Lupin se déguise en gendarme. Parmi les
criminels évoqués dans la quatrième partie, quatre, Calvi, La Pouraille, Fil-de-soie et
La Biffe, sont des experts en déguisements et en changements de noms.' *SetM*, vol.
VI, p. 420.

The effectiveness of costume as a dramatic device of the plot in *Splendeurs et misères* depends to some extent on the narrator's ability to communicate the real identities behind the disguises at the points where clarification is necessary to the reader, and these disguises are more prolific than those typically found in a stage melodrama.[97] What *Splendeurs et misères* does demonstrate is that, although Balzac perhaps pushed the device to a point of excess, he had a dramatist's conception of clothing both as a visual signifier and as a dynamic force in the plot, around which narrative complexities could be woven.

In other novels of *La Comédie humaine* disguise also functions in the dynamics of the plot in a way which is close to theatrical melodrama, but the device is not stretched to the mode of excess that is characteristic of *Splendeurs et misères*. In *Les Chouans*, for example, despite Montauran's disguise in the costume of the Ecole Polytechnique, the English origin of his companion, the false Mme du Gua, is suggested to Corentin by her 'mante d'étoffe anglaise' and the strange shape of her hat and it is this which arouses Corentin's suspicion of Montauran.[98] Just as the action of the plot is prompted by disguise, so too its final tragedy is brought about through the exploitation of the same device. In order to escape his enemies Montauran must disguise himself as a Chouan, leaving his own clothing with Marie,[99] but it is precisely this which causes her death since she dresses in his clothes to create the diversion which she hopes will facilitate his escape. Marie is shot because her identity is mistaken in her costume, and the tragic error is revealed only when it is too late: '[t]ous les soldats restèrent immobiles. Le commandant avait fait dérouler les longs cheveux noirs d'une femme'.[100] The full horror of the mistake is discovered by removal of the costume, in a setting in which, as has already been shown, the characters are

---

[97] In stage melodrama any clarification of identity could only be given more crudely by means of asides to the audience or by crude disguises which would leave the character still identifiable by the audience and require a suspension of disbelief. Too many disguises of this type within the same piece might cause the audience to lose sight of the plot altogether. According to Gautier, this was a criticism which was made of Balzac's own play *Vautrin,* in which the audience found the frequent costume changes confusing and contrived. See: *Histoire de l'art dramatique*, vol. II, p. 39.

[98] *Ch.*, vol. VIII, p. 978.

[99] *Ibid.*, p. 1208.

[100] *Ibid.*, p. 1210.

grouped as if in a stage scene.

Costume is also occasionally used to provoke sexual interest or jealousy in certain characters and thereby becomes a dynamic force in the plot. For example, in *Les Chouans* the first thing that is revealed when Montauran enters Mlle de Verneuil's room to find her in a state of enormous nervous agitation is his 'toilette du gentilhomme' with its 'air de fête et de parure qui ajoutait encore à l'éclat', and the costume is significant because it is the sight of this which causes Mlle de Verneuil to recover 'toute sa présence d'esprit'.[101] In the same way, it is costume which in *Un grand homme* causes Mme de Bargeton's and Lucien's feelings about each other to change dramatically after their arrival in Paris. On their first visit to the theatre Mme de Bargeton finds Lucien's attire 'prodigieusement ridicule' when she compares his 'redingote dont les manches étaient trop courtes, ses méchants gants de province, son gilet étriqué' to the clothing of the young people in the balcony.[102] On the occasion of their next visit to the theatre, Lucien sees his mistress as nothing but an 'os de seiche' in her tired provincial dress,[103] and his own social fate is sealed by his exaggerated costume which makes him look like a 'statue égyptienne dans sa gaine,'[104] causing him to be the object of ridicule, since for Mme de Bargeton '[d]e là, à le trouver moins spirituel, il n'y avait qu'un pas.'[105] Costume is thus treated as a visual representation of social hypocrisy and exceeds its basic theatrical function in the realistic staging of the drama to become an element of Balzac's critique of a society which operates according to often false appearances.

In *Illusions perdues* costume is multi-functional, acting as a catalyst in the action, as a codification of the social hierarchy and at the same time generating meaning for the reader. The dress of Mme de Bargeton and of Lucien clearly signifies, both to the reader and to the other characters in the novel, the ignorance of these characters of the Parisian social code, their lack of sophistication and their provincial nature. Dress also signifies to the reader and to Lucien the physical and moral transformation which he must undergo in order to achieve status in Paris. This is visually emphasised in the contrast

---

[101] *Ibid.*, p. 1201-1202.
[102] *IP*, vol. V, p. 266.
[103] *Ibid.*, p. 273.
[104] *Ibid.*, p. 279.
[105] *Ibid.*, p. 276.

between Lucien's inelegance and de Marsay's mastery of the sartorial statement with: 'une toilette appropriée à sa nature qui écrasait autour de lui tous ses rivaux'.[106] The fact that once he has a similar costume, Lucien is instantly reinstated in Mme de Bargeton's affections clearly demonstrates that it is merely the appearance of wealth and power which counts in society. Costume thus comes to generate greater meaning for the reader who can see the hypocrisy while the characters can not.

Clothing in Balzac's novels is in this sense an embodiment of the whole interplay of *être* and *paraître* which is at the root of the *Comédie* and which Gautier identifies as fundamental to Balzac's own experience of social life.[107] In *Le Père Goriot*, the necessity of the appearance of wealth for social advancement is stressed through the vehicles of Vautrin and Mme de Beauséant, and the view is echoed by Balzac in *Un grand homme,* where he emphasises that the value of appearance exists most specifically in costume:

> La question du costume est d'ailleurs énorme chez ceux qui veulent paraître avoir ce qu'ils n'ont pas, car c'est souvent le meilleur moyen de le posséder plus tard.[108]

So it is that for Eugène and Lucien the transition from poor *arriviste* to Parisian dandy is first marked not by their personal or social achievements but by their visits to the tailor.[109] This is where the matter of visual realism in Balzac's descriptions of costume becomes problematic, since in the case of the dandy, and also in some instances the *grande dame*, the image of the character is not clarified by detailed costume but is blurred by it, because the relationship between signifier and signified is no longer reliable. The theatrical use of costume to identify, typify and clarify, to give visual signposts to the plot, is subverted in the dandy's costume, since this is not a disguise to be assumed temporarily, but is a sustained and altered state of

---

[106] *Ibid.*, p. 277.

[107] See above, p. 253.

[108] *IP*, vol. V, p. 269.

[109] Peter Brooks notes that in the case of the *arriviste* costume is part of the climate of speculation: 'The tailors, hatters, bootmakers, jewelers who deck them in the necessary accessories themselves understand that they are staking a kind of risk capital which will be repaid when and if success is forthcoming'. *The Melodramatic Imagination*, p. 114.

being which no longer subscribes to a clearly differentiated code of dress and may or may not be a true reflection of wealth and status.[110] This is disguise at its most subversive and unsettling, since the details of dress are adhered to so strictly by the dandy as to defy any attempt at decodification, and his position in society remains ambiguous. Thus the fine nuance of dress, which, according to Balzac's own *Traité de la vie élégante,* should reveal a character's status, in fact comes to conceal it, and the attention to detail which had begun as part of the visual *mise en scène* of the novel and part of the convincing aspect of characterisation and disguise, becomes a metaphor for a disintegrating society which believes in appearances that are no longer a valid signifier of truth.

In its insistence on the value of these appearances, the whole of Parisian society becomes engaged in the play of disguise and impersonation which is at the root of the complexities of *Splendeurs et misères.* This novel has been treated here as the most extreme example of Balzac's use of costume as a device around which to weave the plot, but, together with *Illusions perdues,* it is also representative of the dissimulation which Balzac perceives to be endemic in society in a wider sense, since no-one can be relied upon actually to be that which is denoted by his costume. Lucien's clothing in Paris no more reveals his true self than do Coralie's stage costumes, and each prostitutes his or her talent and person respectively in order to buy the necessary costumes with which to perpetuate a false appearance. Ultimately Lucien's success in Paris proves to be as superficial as his costume and lasts only as long. On his return to Angoulême he is the pauper son of a provincial pharmacist that he was when he left, since he does not have the clothes to denote otherwise:

---

[110] In this respect Prendergast notes: ' "l'homme qui ne fait rien" is, in contemporary social conditions, an ambiguous class; it includes both the man of means and the aspirant parvenu [...]. In the case of the fashionable aristocrat form signifies a substance; his elegance is a sign of identity backed by collateral (family name, inheritance, capital). The parvenu dandy, however, masters the art of the nuance in order to appear what he is not, to give out the sign of a 'value' (a social identity) which is in fact false, a sign without a grounded signified'. *The Order of Mimesis,* p. 94.

> Ma chère Eve, dit Lucien à l'oreille de sa sœur, je me trouve absolument omme j'étais à l'Houmeau le jour où je devais aller chez Mme de Bargeton: je suis sans habit pour le dîner du préfet.[111]

The occasion of this dinner marks Lucien's final social success in Angoulême and is a triumph of his ability to pose as an actor in the costume which makes him the person he is not. Lucien adopts both the attire and the mannerisms of de Marsay, which are described in detail, even down to the gestures with a cane which draw attention to Lucien's witty remarks.[112] However, the costume is a sham and can no more make a de Marsay out of Lucien than a fine dress can make a duchess out of Coralie, and once he is without it he is but a failed poet driven to suicide.

Throughout *La Comédie humaine* costume is mistakenly accepted by society as a signifier of wealth and status, and the unreliability of any such reliance on the *paraître* is reiterated in the metaphor of the character as an actor in costume on the social stage:

> Dans le monde dissipé, dans ce tourbillon de fêtes, on admet les acteurs en scène sous leurs brillants costumes sans s'enquérir de leurs moyens.[113]

Subscribing in this way to the social rule of the *paraître*, Anastasie's concern in the final stages of *Le Père Goriot* is not for her father's declining condition, nor particularly with the ruinous state of her relationships, but with having sufficient money to pay for the 'robe larmée' and the recovery of her diamonds, for it is her brilliant costume which will establish her on the social map of Paris and obliterate the fact that she was born a Goriot. The dress is a ravishing success, but it is no more than a social disguise which hides her miserable plight, for the women of polite society are as adept in their use of costume to hide the truth as are the actresses of the boulevard theatres.[114]

Nor is this type of dissemblance through dress confined to Paris,

---

[111] *IP*, vol. V, p. 651.
[112] *IP*, vol. V, p. 675.
[113] See also appendix I, section e.
[114] See also, for example, *Le Cabinet des antiques,* in which Diane de Maufrigneuse appears at the Opera in sumptuous attire which is said to belie the debts of herself and Victurnien. *CA,* vol. IV, p. 1025.

for in *Les Chouans* Marie de Verneuil's appearance in 'tout l'éclat du
vêtement des mariées'[115] hides her inner turmoil and the knowledge of
the fate which awaits her, and in *Béatrix*, both Béatrix and Mlle des
Touches use dress as a means of ensnaring the unwitting Calyste in
their battle for his affections. Moreover, in the sleepy, provincial
setting of Provins in *Pierrette*, dress functions as a primary element in
the show of material comfort which conceals the heroine's misery.
Here the provincial characters who value appearance are no less easily
duped by fine attire than their Parisian counterparts. The pitiful
bundle which, 'ne vaut pas trois francs',[116] with which Pierrette
arrives at her cousins' house is swiftly transformed into a magnificent
trousseau to rival the wardrobes of the daughters of the town's
wealthiest families. This marks the beginning of Pierrette's misery,
for she places no value on appearance and is unable to deny her
essential nature: 'Le beau trousseau, les belles robes des dimanches et
les robes de tous les jours commencèrent le malheur de Pierrette'.[117]
Their own value system prevents the inhabitants of Provins from
suspecting that beneath the beautiful dresses and precious appearance
is a child who is ill and mistreated. In Paris the primary adverse
consequences of the false appearance of costume are financial and
emotional, but in Provins society's reliance on outward show is a
contributory cause of Pierrette's death. In this little studied work
Balzac demonstrates partly through use of costume that the interplay
between *être* and *paraître* can have more devastating effects than the
simple blurring of social identities.

From the above discussion it is possible to conclude that Balzac
uses costume in the 'staging' of his text in a variety of ways. Through
a selection of examples it has been possible to show that in some
instances costume functions as part of the realistic *mise en scène* and
'couleur locale' of the setting and is used as a visual signifier of the
role and status of the characters and occasionally of the central
concerns of the plot. In other instances costume is used as a dynamic
force in the plot in a way which comes close to stage melodrama in so
far as Balzac disguises his characters in order to weave the mysteries
of the plot around them. Beyond this, Balzac's use of costume
exceeds the boundaries of what could be contained by the

[115] *Ch.*, vol. VIII, p. 1206.
[116] *P*, vol. IV, p. 76.
[117] *Ibid.*, p. 81.

contemporary theatre and becomes a visual representation of the tissues of falsehood and hypocrisy which characterise the whole of the society of *La Comédie humaine*.

Speech and Dialogue

When the scene has been set and the characters have been dressed, they are made to speak. Balzac's use of speech in the novel, together with Hugo's, is new in so far as it embodies the literary precepts of Romanticism, and through the use of authentic dialogue, inspired partly by Walter Scott,[118] brings the novel closer to the drama.[119] Additionally, this use of dramatic dialogue in Balzac's novels demonstrates his own penetrating observation of the linguistic process. Evidence of Balzac's skill in representing diverse characteristics and emotions through dialogue can be found not only in his novels and plays themselves, but also in accounts of his own attempts to act out the parts in his plays and to imitate the differentiated speech of his characters. Gautier recalls how, at a reading of the play *Mercadet* at Les Jardies, Balzac affected a different voice to represent each of the characters, differentiating carefully between the various creditors who feature in the play and who might otherwise appear indistinguishable:

> Balzac [...], affectait une voix particulière et parfaitement reconnaissable à chaque personnage; les organes dont il dotait les différentes espèces de créanciers étaient d'un comique désopilant; il y en avait de rauques, de mielleux, de précipités, de traînards, de menaçants, de plaintifs. Cela glapissait,cela miaulait, cela grondait, cela grommelait, cela hurlait sur tous les tons possibles et impossibles.[120]

Gautier also tells how Balzac would try out the authentic dialogue effects from his novels on his friends, by imitating the German accent of Nucingen or Schmucke, or by suffixing *rama* onto nouns, like the boarders of the Pension Vauquer.[121]

---

[118] See above, p. 232.
[119] See: G. Matoré, 'Le Goût du vrai', in *Le Vocabulaire de la prose littéraire de 1833 à 1845* (Genève: Droz, 1951), pp. 121-149.
[120] Gautier, *Honoré de Balzac*, p. 113.
[121] Gautier, *Honoré de Balzac*, p. 108.

Balzac's exuberant love of words and verbal play finds expression in many animated passages in *La Comédie humaine*. For example, in *Les Chouans*, Beau-Pied and La-clef-des-cœurs, in the midst of battle, engage in a banter of semantics centred on the words 'problème' and 'emblème'; in *Le Colonel Chabert*, the rapid exhange of wit and legal jargon between the clerks in Derville's office provides a lively opening scene; in *Un début dans la vie*, Mistigris and Joseph Bridau tirelessly exhange mangled proverbs such as 'les bons comtes font les bons amis', and 'les voyages déforment la jeunesse'; in *Les Employés*, Colleville shows a passion for anagrams and predicts the destinies of his fellows according to a judicious rearrangement of their names; and of course there are the renowned *-rama*[122] and *cor-* games of *Le Père Goriot*.

Dialect and accent were the main problems that Balzac faced in his novels in rendering the speech of his characters authentic. In *Les Chouans* (1828-29), there is some attempt to reproduce the authentic dialogue of the Breton peasants and this is attempted again much later in *Les Paysans* (1838-1845). There is also a determined attempt to render authentic dialogue effects in the voices of Nucingen and Schmucke, whose German accents are laboriously reproduced in a form of written dialogue which can be understood only through the reader's active engagement in the text. The reader is required to act out the parts for himself and silently to pronounce the oddly juxtaposed syllables in order to derive the sense from the sounds, for only through enunciation can the sense of their speech be understood.

Realistic dialogue effects are also created through use of the authentic jargon of journalism, publishing, business and the legal profession, which is employed throughout *La Comédie humaine* in the speech of the characters who operate in these realms. The earliest example in *La Comédie humaine* of Balzac making his characters speak in harmony with their profession and milieu can be found in the

---

[122] This particular game is filled with historical significance, since Balzac explains how the word-play had evolved from the opening of the Diorama. See *PG*, vol. III, p. 91: 'La récente invention du Diorama, qui portait l'illusion de l'optique à un plus haut degré que dans les Panoramas, avait amené dans quelques ateliers de peinture la plaisanterie de parler en *rama*, espèce de charge qu'un jeune peintre, habitué de la pension Vauquer, y avait inoculée.' In fact the Diorama was not opened until 1822 and the action of the novel is in 1819 at this point. However, Balzac's original plans had placed the action in 1824 and he seems to have overlooked the issue of the Diorama when he resituated the action in 1819.

language of Hulot in *Les Chouans*. Hulot's language is laced with rough and expressive words and phrases, and the reader is told that he 'possédait éminemment l'art de parler le langage pittoresque du soldat', and his speeches are frequently prefaced with 'Que diable', 'Pourquoi diable', 'Où diable', and the recurring 'Tonnerre de Dieu', or 'Mille tonnerres'. Balzac informs the reader that the latter 'expression militaire [...] annonçait toujours quelque tempête', and both the reader and Hulot's soldiers come to know his moods by his language.

In his attempts to establish a close link between dialogue and milieu, it is the slang of the Parisian underworld which really seems to have captured Balzac's imagination. In the last part of *Splendeurs et misères* Balzac self-consciously justifies his use of the slang of the *bagne* to the reader:

> Il n'est pas de langue plus énergique, plus colorée que celle de ce monde souterrain qui, depuis l'origine des empires à capitale, s'agite dans les caves, dans les sentines, dans le *troisième dessous* des sociétés. [...] Chaque mot de ce langage est une image brutale, ingénieuse ou terrible [...] Tout est farouche dans cet idiome.[123]

Balzac clearly acknowledges here his recognition of the expressive qualities of this particular type of slang and he goes on at length to explain some of its terms and their evocative, onomatopoeic or metaphoric effects:

> Les syllabes qui commencent ou qui finissent les mots sont âpres et étonnent singulièrement. Une femme est une *largue*. Et quelle poésie! la paille est la *plume de Beauce*. Le mot minuit est rendu par cette périphrase: *douze plombes crossent!* Ça ne donne-t-il pas le frisson? *Rincer une cambriole* veut dire dévaliser une chambre. [...] Quelle vivacité d'images![124]

The problem with such a use of authentic slang in literature is that it requires precisely this type of authorial interpretation in order to be clearly understood by the reader, and cannot therefore be thought of as a dramatic technique in the strictest sense.[125] Although the

---

[123] *SetM*, vol. VI, pp.828-829.
[124] *SetM*, vol. VI, p. 829.
[125] The untapped and authentic resources of slang, accent and dialect were

convicts' slang is part of the 'bringing to life' of this novel it would be unintelligible to an audience in a theatre, where no detailed linguistic explanations could be given.

Notwithstanding this point, in *Splendeurs et misères* slang also fulfils a dynamic function in the plot since it enables Collin to maintain his double identity. In his disguise as the Spanish priest Carlos Herrera Collin adopts the dialogue compatible with his status and denies all knowledge of the convicts' slang in his dealings with the law, but through slang he is able to communicate privately with the convicts and protect his position: 'Ne fais pas de ragoût sur ton dâb (n'éveille pas les soupçons sur ton maître)!'.

Slang is also used in this novel to highlight in a dramatic way the contrast between the different moral states of its heroine, Esther. When the regenerated Esther is forced to return to the life of the prostitute, the moral transformation which is required of her is expressed not through an internal examination of her psychology, but through her speech which immediately changes register. As she switches roles Esther promptly switches to the slang of the courtesan and her moral crisis is rendered dramatically in her speech:

> 'J'aurais voulu que Lucien me vît ainsi, dit-elle en laissant échapper un soupir étouffé. Maintenant, reprit-elle d'une voix vibrante, *blaguons*. ...'
> En entendant ce mot Europe resta tout hébétée, comme elle eût pu l'être en entendant blasphémer un ange.
> — Eh bien, qu'as-tu donc à regarder si j'ai dans la bouche des clous de girofle au lieu de dents? Je ne suis plus maintenant qu'une infâme et immonde créature, une fille, une *voleuse*, et j'attends milord.[126]

Esther's speech lends all the more substance to Collin's insistence that she is in her very nature a prostitute and cannot escape from this fact.

---

consistent with the Romantic aesthetics of expressiveness, exoticism and the grotesque. The origins of the use of slang in literature are traced by Stephen Ullmann, who explains that interest in slang was promoted in part by publication in 1828-1829, of the memoirs of Vidocq, the ex-convict who had joined the police and had become head of the *Sûreté*. Victor Hugo's *Les derniers jours d'un condamné* (1829), was the first major literary work to use slang on a significant scale, and in the boulevard theatres it also became a popular feature of vaudeville productions. See: Stephen Ullmann, *Style in the French Novel* (Cambridge University Press, 1957), pp.74-75.

[126] *SetM*, vol. VI, p. 614.

The speech of her phase of moral regeneration is made to seem like the well-rehearsed lines of the actress, or like the 'in-character' speech of Collin in his successive disguises, since her return to slang is immediate at the point when refined language is no longer appropriate to her situation.

Frequently in *La Comédie humaine* Balzac uses dialogue in this way, adapting both the *énoncé* and the *énonciation* to reflect the innermost psychology of the speaker, so that what is said and the way in which it is said are in harmony. In the first part of *Le Père Goriot*, for example, all the characters define themselves from the outset by their speech, so that they might achieve presence and individuality by means of their voice and vocabulary, which indicate character and confirm the physical portrait. Of Vautrin we read, 'sa voix de basse-taille, en harmonie avec sa grosse gaieté, ne déplaisait point'; Mlle Michonneau, on the other hand, 'avait la voix clairette d'une cigale criant dans son buisson aux approches de l'hiver'; and the gentle Victorine has a very different kind of voice again, for when Mme Vauquer and Mme Couture curse her mean father, 'Victorine faisait entendre de douces paroles, semblables au chant du ramier blessé, dont le cri de douleur exprime encore l'amour'. Finally, Poiret is described speaking to Mlle Michonneau, who is too preoccupied to give her attention to: 'les phrases tombant une à une de la bouche de Poiret, comme les gouttes d'eau qui suintent à travers le robinet d'une fontaine mal fermée'.

Here then, as throughout *La Comédie humaine*, Balzac throws the characters into relief by means of their speech. All of the dialogue at the boarding house is sarcastic, bantering, full of significance for an understanding of the group. The comic banter of the boarders is finely woven into the fabric of the narrative so that it serves both as an apparent diversion from the main action and as a means of indicating the relationships between the characters.[127] At the same time, while there is often little correlation between what a character says and what he thinks, there is complete correlation between the sort of remark he

[127] The cross-fire of wit begins with Eugène's account of the ball which is interrupted with Vautrin's play on *roi* and *roitelet*, and echoed by Poiret. The episode serves to reveal through comic dialogue where the characters stand in relation to one another, since it undermines Eugène and establishes both Vautrin's superiority and Poiret's inferiority in his parrotting of everything the other boarders say. The game also serves to highlight the canine nature of Goriot who is the object of most of the joking and sits through it with placid impenetrability. See: *PG,* vol. III, pp.85-86.

habitually makes and his essential nature. Goriot's first speech after the action begins reveals his paternal passion; all of Rastignac's speeches in the first part reveal his ambition; Poiret's parrotting of the other boarders defines his inability to think and act independently; Mme de Langeais' superciliousness is revealed by her repeated inability to say Goriot's name even after Rastignac's corrections; Mme de Beauséant's rejection of Parisian life is predicted by her advice to Eugène which is filled with her own disillusionment. Intimate knowledge of the characters is thus revealed dramatically and in their own words, without lengthy descriptions.

The action of Balzac's novels is frequently advanced through dialogue in a way which brings the novel close to the drama, for in many cases the narrator withdraws almost completely and interrupts the dialogue only to indicate who is speaking. The sense of stage performance which this facilitates is strengthened still further through the use of asides and monologues, which form a private communication between character and reader, like that which might exist in the theatre between actor and spectator.[128] Monologues reveal sentiments, conflicts, and opinions which are otherwise hidden, and allow the reader to know the characters better by revealing inner thoughts in a dramatic way. For example, Rastignac's monologues repeatedly highlight his moral conflicts, and the monologue which comes after the proposition of the Taillefer plot by Vautrin reveals him to be torn between honour and fortune.

The speaker of the monologue does not fear being overheard, while the speaker of the aside does fear being overheard and deliberately tries not to be. This can be seen in *Les Chouans* at the inn where Mlle de Verneuil sees Montauran for the first time and remarks in an aside: 'ce jeune homme est singulièrement distingué pour un républicain'.[129] In the same scene private remarks among the characters seated at the table also function as asides which establish the suspicions of each party in the central conflict. These suspicions heighten the tension and provoke the subsequent action:

> — Et c'est avec des muscadins comme ça, dit confidentiellement Corentin à l'hâte en en épiant le visage, qu'on espère relever la

---

[128] During Balzac's lifetime both Bouffé and Lemaître were renowned for bantering quite openly with the audience and the claque.

[129] *Ch.*, vol. VIII, p. 975.

marine de la République.
— Cet homme-là, disait le jeune marin à l'oreille de l'hôtesse, est quelque espion de Fouché. Il a la police gravée sur la figure.[130]

Everywhere the dialogue in this novel reinforces other manifestations of dramatic tension. Although dialogue is frequently used by Balzac to reveal psychology and to illuminate and advance the action of his novels, it is also often used in a more profoundly theatrical sense to conceal thoughts, or to deepen the intrigue, and comes to undermine any belief in the power of language to express sure knowledge or truth. In this respect dialogue often functions in the same way as costume, as part of an assumed role. Remarks which should classify the speaker in some way are therefore not always reliable, and there is often no more relation between what a character really thinks and what he says than there is between his costume and his real identity. In the first scene of *Les Chouans* every remark on both sides is subtly phrased in order to secure information and yet not to reveal the identity of any person present. The use of dialogue to conceal thought is also evident in the conversation between Montauran and Mlle de Verneuil on the journey from Alençon to Vivetière. Of this dialogue Balzac says:

> L'entretien, frivole en apparence, par lequel ces inconnus se plurent à s'interroger mutuellement, cacha les désirs, les passions et les espérances qui les agitaient.[131]

Conversation which is apparently meaningless in this instance does not convey true feelings, but conceals a subtext which is charged with emotion. Similarly in *Pierrette*, the polite chatter of Rogron and Sylvie conceals their dislike of their cousin and, together with the outward show of furnishings and costumes, propagates a false and ultimately damaging image to the outside world. In *Le Père Goriot* an authorial comment underlines that Balzac recognised that the spoken word was often not a reliable signifier of truth: 'Quand on connaît Paris, on ne croit à rien de ce qui s'y dit',[132] but as is shown in *Pierrette* this phenomenon is not confined to Paris.

The power of speech to conceal thought, identity and fact is best

---

[130] *Ibid.*, p. 977.
[131] *Ch.*, vol. VIII, p.1002.
[132] *PG*, vol. III, p. 175.

exemplified in the character of Vautrin whose vocabulary and expressions change with each new identity as he successively adopts the nonchalant, worldly tone of Vautrin, the ecclesiastical rhetoric of Carlos Herrera and the underworld slang of Jacques Collin. At the same time, however, all of Vautrin's attempts to lecture his protégés in the ways of Parisian life testify to his own experience of life and to the character he has become, and his motivations and thoughts are everywhere expressed through the spoken word. In his speeches to Eugène in *Le Père Goriot* Vautrin reveals his personal philosophies and the qualities which define his personality,[133] and these are echoed in similar rhetorical speeches to Lucien in *Illusions perdues* and *Splendeurs et misères*. Vautrin is successfully able to manipulate speech to reveal and conceal simultaneously, for while his first speech in *Le Père Goriot* establishes him as a powerful force among the other boarders and his tirades against society are entirely in accord with his character, his mystery is deepened by conscious avoidance of talking of his own past. In his dialogues with Eugène, Vautrin may reveal some of his thoughts and the antithetical sides of his character, but at the same time his rhetoric conceals the very things by which most people identify themselves, and which are at the root of his mystery — his name and his occupation:

> Qui suis-je? Vautrin. Que fais-je? Ce qui me plaît. Passons. Voulez-vous connaître mon caractère? Je suis bon avec ceux qui me font du bien ou dont le cœur parle au mien. [...] Mais [...] je suis méchant comme le diable avec ceux qui me tracassent, ou qui ne me reviennent pas.[134]

In the stage melodrama characters would often speak directly to the audience or to the other characters in a sweeping verbal gesture which revealed their identity, but with Vautrin the naming device of the stage melodrama, the revelatory 'I am', is turned into a means of prolonging and deepening the mystery which surrounds him. Only once does Vautrin come near to making a slip when he inadvertently switches register: 'Je vous aime, foi de Tromp...(mille tonnerres!), foi

---

[133] *PG*, vol. III, pp. 136-143.
[134] *Ibid.*, p. 135

de Vautrin'.[135] This, of course, points forward to what will take place in the second part of the novel.

In *Le Père Goriot* Vautrin's presence in the boarding house is often heard even when it is not seen, and his entrances are in almost every case indicated 'off-stage' by his singing, which announces him, emphasises his prominence and creates tension. Vautrin's snippets of song are also part of his posturing, as though he is conscious of being an actor in the drama he has created for himself, and they are a specific verbal characteristic of this particular incarnation since they disappear in his subsequent personae. Vautrin's repeated nonchalant singing of 'j'ai longtemps parcouru le monde',[136] gives verbal expression to his capacity to remain free of imprisonment in each reincarnation, as well as to his worldy sophistication which sets him apart from the other boarders. In the scene where Vautrin overhears Goriot and Eugène discussing their plan to alert Taillefer to the plot against him, he sings to indicate that he has discovered them[137] and again when he has drugged them, he rounds off the scene in a way which was customary in the vaudeville, with a couplet taken from *La Somnambule:*[138] 'Donnez, mes chères amours! Pour vous je veillerai toujours'. These snippets of contemporary song which form part of the portrayal of Vautrin are both testimony to his familiarity with the theatre world and to his sharp wit, since they are carefully chosen to be ironically appropriate to his sleeping victims. Snatches of song which appear incidental to the other boarders are loaded with a private meaning of which only Vautrin and the reader are aware, and which hint at what lies behind his fine rhetoric and powerful phrases.

This type of secret communication is central to Vautrin's dialogue. After his arrest at the Pension Vauquer, Vautrin reverts to the language of the *bagne*, further confirming his real identity, since the adoption of the correct register of speech is always part of his disguise and his present disguise has now been exposed.[139] Vautrin's final words before being taken away by the police are carefully chosen to

---

[135] *Ibid.*

[136] *PG*, vol. III, p. 82.

[137] *Ibid.*, p. 199.

[138] *La Somnambule*, a vaudeville written by Scribe and Delavigne, was first performed on 6 December 1819, so Vautrin's knowledge of the theatre is firmly associated with the period in which the action is set.

[139] *PG*, vol. III, p. 219.

be understood only by himself and Eugène, however, for although his identity has now been revealed, the secrets between Vautrin and Eugène are to remain hidden.[140] The same juxtaposition of Vautrin's private language and the public language of his disguise can be seen in the dénouement of *Splendeurs et misères*: Vautrin, now known to be the real Jacques Collin:

> — Vous avez été promptement guéri?' dit Camusot.
> — Je suis pincé,' pensa Jacques Collin. Puis il répondit à haute voix: 'La joie, monsieur, est la seule panacée qui existe...'[141]

While Vautrin, now known to be the real Jacques Collin, adopts ecclesiastical rhetoric in his dialogue with Camusot, his true thoughts are expressed in dramatic asides in the colloquialisms of his private language and in his secretive whisperings to his fellow convicts. In Vautrin Balzac has succeeded in creating the paradox of a character who consistently defines himself through his speech and yet uses speech as one of the principal devices with which to propagate false impressions.

In the above discussion it can be seen that Balzac's use of dialogue serves the 'staging' of his text in multiple ways, for some attempt is made by Balzac to render the identity and psychology of his characters and set them in their proper milieu through accent, dialect, slang and jargon, and the characters frequently define themselves and their actions through their own speech, either in dialogue, monologue or theatrical 'asides', as they would in the stage drama. Ultimately Balzac also uses speech to indicate the profound theatricality of life since he demonstrates the inability of language to convey reliable truths. This is not so in the physical movements of his characters, for though they may use their environment, clothing and speech to generate a particular image of themselves, the inner self may still be revealed through gesture.

Gesture and Movement

As with the other devices with which Balzac 'stages' the text of his novels, his incorporation of the gestures and movements of his

---

[140] *PG*, vol. III, p. 221.
[141] *SetM*, vol. VI, p. 766.

metaphorical actors shows the influence of both the established stage melodrama, which relied on a repertoire of highly exaggerated and stylised movements,[142] and of the Romantic drama which favoured a more natural, although still highly expressive, style of acting.[143] Balzac's views on the expressive qualities of gesture and movement and their signification of psychology and inner thought can be found in his surprisingly neglected *Théorie de la démarche* (1833).[144] It is common knowledge that Balzac was greatly influenced by Lavater's pseudo-scientific theory of physiognomy, and in his own *Théorie de la démarche* he refers to gesture and movement as 'la physionomie du corps'.[145]   Above all, Balzac emphasises that while language is often used to conceal thought, body language frequently reveals thought involuntarily and is loaded with meaning:

[142] The importance of gesture in the boulevard theatres of the early nineteenth century was a result of the same prevailing conditions which dictated the importance of costume.   The government's restriction of speaking parts in the small theatres urged their reliance on the visual mode.   Gestures and facial expressions were consciously exaggerated to be clear even to the audience in the *paradis*, since they were not merely an embellishment of the representation but were often its primary mode of communication. The pantomimes of the late eighteenth century, from which the melodrama in part developed, relied entirely for their effect on the figurability of emotion and conflict through gesture and facial expression, and had a repertory of dramatic postures, exaggerated facial expressions such as teeth gnashing and eye rolling, and other non-naturalistic manifestations of heightened emotions.   This expressive style reached its peak in the acting of Frédérick Lemaître and Bouffé who were famed for the plasticity of their facial expressions and for the energy of their acting. See: Peter Brooks, *The Melodramatic Imagination*, p. 47; and Robert Baldick, *The Life and Times of Frédérick Lemaître* (London: Hamish Hamilton, 1959).
[143] In 1827 the successful second visit of the English Shakespeare company to the Porte-Saint-Martin theatre exercised a considerable influence upon an acting style which was already exaggeratedly expressive.   Parisian audiences were enthralled by English Actors such as Kean, Kemble and Harriet Smithson whose innovative style of performance placed great emphasis on the physical enaction of mental suffering, agonised death throes and madness.   The acting style of the English company was highly expressive but in a more naturalistic manner than in the French melodrama, and in place of the latter's repertory of standardised, stylised movements and postures was all the variety of real human expression.   The example set by the English troupe appealed to the Romantics' taste for all things authentic and expressive and their style began to be adopted in the staging of Romantic drama. See: Maurice Descotes, *Le Drame romantique et ses grands créateurs*, pp. 36-43.
[144] *LCH*, ed. Pléiade, vol. XII, pp. 259-302.
[145] *Ibid.*, p. 262, & p. 282.

N'est-il pas effrayant de penser qu'un observateur profond peut découvrir un vice, un remords, une maladie en voyant un homme en mouvement? Quel riche langage dans ces effets immédiats d'une volonté traduite avec innocence! L'inclination plus ou moins vive d'un de nos membres; la forme télégraphique dont il a contracté, malgré nous, l'habitude; l'angle ou le contour que nous lui faisons décrire, sont empreints de notre vouloir, et sont d'une effrayante signification. C'est plus que la parole, c'est la pensée en action. Un simple geste, un involontaire frémissement de lèvres peut devenir le terrible dénouement d'un drame caché longtemps entre deux cœurs.[146]

What Balzac seems to have perceived is how his narrative could be endowed with signification through the interpretation of gesture and his theory serves to underpin his fictional technique.

At its simplest level Balzac's use of gesture and movement is part of the visual portrayal of his characters' total personality. For example in *Le Curé de Tours* Birotteau's movements are a confirmation of the physical portrait, and the tone in which they are described indicates Balzac's attitude to his character: 'Le bon vicaire [...] circulait sans gravité, trottait, piétinait en paraissant rouler sur lui-même'.[147] Characters are also occasionally endowed with an idiosyncratic, recurring gesture, for example Hulot in *Les Chouans*: 'secoua [...] la tête par un geste négatif, et contracta deux gros sourcils noirs qui donnaient une expression sévère à sa physionomie'.[148] His soldiers and the reader come to know him not only by his language but 'en observant les variations de la petite grimace'.

Gesture is also frequently used by Balzac as a clear visual signifier of the central concerns of the plot, in a way which comes close to the physical expressionism of the stage melodrama. For example, in the wedding scene of *Les Chouans* simple gestures are loaded with symbolic significance for the dénouement which is to come: the couple's act of advancing towards the altar hand in hand foretells their death scene side by side; their act of kneeling[149] before the altar is a

---

[146] *Ibid.*, p. 280.
[147] *CT*, vol. IV, p. 201.
[148] *Ch.*, vol. VIII, p. 914.
[149] In *Illusions perdues,* in a similar act of kneeling, Coralie feels sanctified by her love for Lucien. The image is clearly sacrilegious since Coralie is kneeling at the bedside where Lucien is sleeping. The bed is the sacrificial altar of her passion and Lucien her religious icon. See, *IP,* vol. V, p. 410: 'Agenouillée à ce lit, heureuse de

symbolic gesture of their submission to a power greater than theirs and to the terrible fate which awaits them; Marie's stretching of her hand towards Montauran in an act of love is the hand which is leading him to his death; and Montauran's gesture of taking the hand foretells his forgiveness and his submission to the fate which Marie has brought upon them both.

Gesture between other characters in this novel also carries clear symbolic significance so that it functions not only to reveal character and advance the plot but also to underpin the novel's central themes in a plastic way. Gestures indeed speak louder than words, and are most effective when they replace dialogue entirely. This can be found in the scene between Francine and Marche-à-Terre when bidding their final farewells: 'Il saisit la main de Francine, la serra, la baisa, fit un signe de croix, et se sauva dans l'écurie, comme un chien qui vient de dérober un os.[150] Marche-à-Terre's actions to Francine symbolise the central themes of the novel: fraternity and comradeship in his handshake, romantic love in his kiss, king and country in his blessing, and his final action of stealth summarises in one movement his own position as an outlaw.

In *Le Père Goriot* symbolic gestures assume a more hyperbolic significance which underpins the melodramatic mode of the novel. For example, Eugène is given a thousand francs by Delphine as his share of the winnings from the roulette table, and in a romantic gesture of magnanimity he hands the notes over to Goriot together with his waistcoat soaked with Delphine's tears.[151] The gesture reveals Eugène's genuine feelings for Delphine, and the sympathy and generosity which are not yet eroded by Parisian life, but it also symbolises his position as a contractual conveyancer between father and daughter. The daughters' feelings, which constitute their part of the contract of exchange with their father, are always conveyed by Eugène from now on, and it is this gesture centred on the waistcoat and the thousand francs which first establishes him in this position.

The physical gesture of exchange is fundamental to the interaction of the characters of Balzac's novels. In an abstract sense exchange is at the hub of most of the texts; tacit and implicit exchanges are made in all spheres of human contact and many of these are given concrete

---

l'amour en lui-même, l'actrice se sentait sanctifiée'.

[150] *Ch.*, vol. VIII, p. 999.

[151] *PG*, vol. III, p. 176.

form in the literal handing over of bills of exchange, letters, promissory notes, jewellery and other personal effects. The abstract gesture in these instances is centred on a physical object whose importance attaches to the value placed on it by the giver and receiver or taker.[152] The use of the object to concretise the gesture of exchange thus gives it a plastic, theatrical dimension, and gives clear physical representation to an often complex ideology.

In this way Mme de Beauséant's feelings about Adjuda d'Pinto are not verbalised but are expressed in her gesture of throwing the box containing her letters to him in to the fire. Her feelings are contained in the box and are erased without trace in a single, silent gesture which is representative both of her dignity and of the demands of the Parisian social code.[153] Value is attributed to the letters only by Mme de Beauséant, and is stripped from them in her gesture. Similarly, Goriot's present from his wife is an object of some material value but is endowed with enormous sentimental value by him:

> Ceci, dit-il à Mme Vauquer en serrant un plat et une petite écuelle dont le couvercle représentait deux tourterelles qui se becquetaient, est le premier présent que m'a fait ma femme, le jour de notre anniversaire. [...] [J]'aimerais mieux gratter la terre avec mes ongles que de me séparer de cela.[154]

When Eugène sees Goriot beating this into bars and shedding a tear as he does so, already before the plot has begun to unfold Goriot's tragedy is symbolised in the action of distorting the symbol of his love.[155] The action centred on this object functions to intensify Goriot's mystery, for the reader knows the value attached by him to

---

[152] Prendergast draws attention to the fact that in the Rubempré cycle in particular many of these objects at the centre of the exchange are forgeries. The object at the centre of the gesture of exchange is often in the form of paper and the anagnorisis upon which the dramatic climax depends often consists in the discovery of the falsity of that paper's value. See: *The Order of Mimesis*, pp. 88-89. So too in *Les Chouans* the false evidence of Montauran's infidelity is handed over to Marie in the form of a letter. The final downfall of the lovers, their personal tragedy, is brought about by an exchange of information and complicity in return for a false document. The written word which should propagate truth comes, as it often does in Balzac's novels, to be the purveyor of falsehoood. Similarly the plot of *Ferragus* hinges on forged letters which are of no value.

[153] *PG*, vol. III, p. 265.

[154] *PG*, vol. III, p. 64.

[155] *Ibid.*, p. 78.

this object. At the same time, the gesture also establishes in concrete form the force of Goriot's paternal love which has now overtaken the love for his wife. The act of love as transcribed through the manipulation of the object becomes an act of distortion, just as Goriot's love for his daughters is a distortion of normal paternal affection. Marital love is thus exchanged for paternal love, as the symbol of the marriage is exchanged for cash with which to buy his daughters' affections. The latter must be purchased with the symbol of the former, which was given freely. The gesture and the object at its centre together give concrete form to the extent and complexity of Goriot's paternal feelings.

A similar value is attached by Goriot to the locket containing the hair of his daughters. In a final gesture of violation of his paternity this is taken from his corpse, an act which sums up the dehumanised characters of Sylvie and Mme Vauquer, until in a sentimental gesture it is replaced by Eugène:

> Quand le corbillard vint, Eugène fit remonter la bière, la décloua, et plaça religieusement sur la poitrine du bonhomme une image qui se rapportait à un temps où Delphine et Anastasie étaient jeunes, vierges et pures.[156]

In this gesture the paternity of which his own daughters have divested him is returned to Goriot in its purest form, as a symbol of his daughters' authentic feelings before they became a currency with which to satisfy their whims. The gesture not only restores Goriot's paternity to him but sanctifies it, renders it sublime in its final moment after the grotesque aspect of his death throes. There is no last confession or absolution for Goriot, all his love and all his guilt are contained within the locket, and the placing of it on his corpse is a final benediction more compassionate than the hurried and dehumanised prayers at the cemetery.

The gestural mode of Balzac's novels is brought close to the stage melodrama above all in some of the most climactic points of dramatic tension in *La Comédie humaine*. In these cases any subtleties of body language which might require interpretation are abandoned for violent, stage-managed actions whose meanings are clearly denoted

---

[156] *Ibid.*, p. 289.

by their figure.[157] At the point of crisis in *La Fille aux yeux d'or,* for example, the actions and gestures are precipitated one after the other in an accumulation of violence which is characteristic of melodramatic excess. In the struggle between de Marsay and Paquita which is described in just one page of text, there are no fewer than eleven described actions and very little dialogue:

1. Il sauta sur le meuble,
2. Il [...] alla prendre sa cravate et s'avança vers elle.
3. Alors elle s'élança d'un seul bond au bout de la chambre.
4. Il y eut un combat.
5. Paquita jeta dans les jambes de son amant un coussin qui le fit tomber.
6. Christémio sauta sur de Marsay, [...]
7. [...] le terrassa, lui mit le pied sur la poitrine.
8. Parleras-tu?, dit-elle en frappant du pied avec colère.
9. Pacquita se précipita sur lui.
10. Elle fit un signe à Christémio...
11. ... qui leva son pied de dessus le jeune homme.[158]

The violent action is brought to an abrupt halt and the final terrifying aspect of the drama is conveyed in the silent looks exchanged between de Marsay and Christémio, which are: 'l'annonce d'une guerre de sauvages, d'un duel où cessaient les lois ordinaires'.[159] The violence of the physical struggle is juxtaposed with the mute threat of the exchange of glances, made all the more terrible for its silence. The ending of the violence does not bring relief, and the contrasting silence adds to the melodramatic excess in its threat of worse violence to come, for movements and gestures in this scene constitute a physical, 'staged' progression to the murder which follows.

Similarly, the build-up to the climax of *Les Chouans* in which Mlle

---

[157] Peter Brooks has said that Balzac's use of gesture in the novel appears to be a 'betrayal' of theatrical gesture because Balzac is 'more concerned with the decipherment and translation of gesture than with its pure figure'. Brooks notes that description of the physical movement is often replaced by immediate interpretation of the gesture. It is true that many gestures are presented in this way, beginning with 'un geste de' or 'un geste qui', and it is not the movement but rather its meaning which is written into the text. *The Melodramatic Imagination*, pp. 75-77. The examples which I give here, show that, contrary to this, in some cases the pure figure of the gesture is often also important in the text.

[158] *FYO*, vol. V, p. 1103.

[159] *Ibid.*, pp. 1104-1105.

de Verneuil realises her fatal misjudgment of Montauran, is expressed through action. The importance of the setting and of dialogue in this episode have already been outlined, and the indications of movement are a further dimension of the theatrical quality of the scene. Just one page of text at the point of climax is punctuated with no fewer than ten indications of movement:

1. Elle poussa doucement la porte.
2. Ses lèvres [...] dessinèrent un sourire arrêté dont l'expression était plus terrible que voluptueuse.
3. Elle marcha d'un pas lent vers le jeune homme, et lui montrant du doigt la pendule [...].
4. Elle tomba sur le sopha.
5. Elle se tourna brusquement et le regarda dans les yeux.
6. Elle le poussa violemment et se leva.
7. Elle sauta vivement sur le poignard [...] et le fit briller à deux doigts de la poitrine du jeune homme surpris.
8. Bah! dit-elle en jetant cette arme.
9. Elle trépignait des pieds comme un enfant gâté.
10. Ne me touchez pas! s'écria-t-elle en se reculant par un mouvement d'horreur.[160]

Each movement is described with the brusqueness of the action itself and each successively heightens the tension of the climax, and, through the cumulative effect of the violent gestures, becomes a virtuoso expression of melodramatic excess. The gestures are not denoted by their decipherment and need no interpretation, rather it is their rapidity, disjointedness and increasing violence which reflect Mlle de Verneuil's anger and loss of reason. Even the simple gesture of pointing at the clock is loaded with meaning because it is during the time marked by Montauran's absence that the crisis has arisen, and the gesture indicates his blame. In both this scene and in de Marsay's struggle with Paquita the threat of death is the ultimate physical expression of heightened emotion and melodramatic excess.

When the trickery of the letter is discovered, Mlle de Verneuil's frenzied actions achieve their own climax in a hyperbolic expression of physical and emotional collapse, 'elle alla tomber sur le sopha, et un déluge de larmes sortit de ses yeux'. The full horror of the discovery is translated into physical expression and the cessation of

---

[160] *Ch.*, vol. VIII, pp. 1201-1202.

violent action again brings no relief. The juxtaposition of violence
and collapse rather highlights the awareness of a more terrible fate to
come.

In *Les Chouans* gesture and movement continue to be central to the
expression of the dramatic conflict as the narrative moves into its
dénouement. The lovers' awareness of the approach of death during
their final hours is signalled not through dialogue, or through an inner
examination of their feelings, but through body language and the
simple gesticulation towards the enemy:

> Et tressaillant d'horreur, elle s'élança hors du lit; le marquis étonné
> la suivit, sa femme l'amena près de la fenêtre. Après un geste
> délirant qui lui échappa, Marie releva les rideaux de la croisée, et lui
> montra du doigt sur la place une vingtaine de soldats.[161]

The gesture towards the enemy is deliberate and conscious, but the
fear which accompanies this is betrayed by an involuntary gesture.
The 'geste délirant' betrays Marie's true emotions and the fear which
she is trying to conceal but which involuntarily escapes her, for even
if her admission of her crime is stated without a verbal display of
emotion, her sense of guilt is evident in her gestures. In Marie's fear
verbal communication fails, and the final vehicle of expressivity
remains in the gesture.

This fusion of the deliberately exaggerated gesture of the stage
melodrama and the more psychologically revealing, involuntary
gesture can also be seen in the device of the unmasking of the villain
in *Le Père Goriot*. Vautrin is publicly unmasked by the action of a
policeman who 'commença par lui donner sur la tête une tape si
violemment appliquée qu'il fit sauter la perruque'.[162] The gesture is
crucial to the action, for it is this which uncovers Vautrin's disguise,
and it is only later in the formal recording of his arrest that Vautrin's
true identity is vocalised. Vautrin responds to this gesture of violence
with an equally violent physical response, confirming the revelation
which has been made:

> Il bondit sur lui-même par un mouvement empreint d'une si féroce
> énergie, il rugit si bien qu'il arracha des cris de terreur à tous les
> pensionnaires. A ce geste de lion, et s'appuyant de la clameur

---

[161] *Ch.*, vol. VIII, p. 1208.
[162] *PG*, vol. III, p. 217.

générale, les agents tirèrent leurs pistolets.[163]

Through his instinctive physical reponse Jacques Collin reveals the
terrifying criminal who lies beneath the studied nonchalance of
Vautrin and it is only at the sight of the drawn pistols does Collin
regain his composure.

In *Splendeurs et misères* involuntary action is also instrumental in
the identification of Jacques Collin by his fellow criminals, and again
becomes part of the melodramatic action of the unmasking of the
villain. Collin drags his right leg slightly because of the weight of the
shackles which he had worn as a convicted criminal,[164] and while
deformity is unnoticed by the authorities, it forms part of the secret
code of communication between the criminals:

> Chez Trompe-la-Mort, évadé depuis huit ans, ce mouvement s'était
> bien affaibli; mais, par l'effet de son absorbante méditation, il allait
> d'un pas si lent et si solennel que, quelque faible que fût ce vice de
> démarche, il devait frapper un œil exercé comme celui de La
> Pouraille.[165]

Since there is no mention of this handicap in earlier descriptions of
Collin, it appears to be a final device of the plot, contrived to confirm
the convicts' instinctive recognition of Collin despite his facial
disfigurement.

In his subtle use of involuntary gesture as a signifier of normally
hidden meanings Balzac succeeds in conveying what a good actor
conveys. Even characters who are experts in social role play and the
concealment of true feelings are not always the master of their own
movements, and their inner thoughts are betrayed by their involuntary
gestures, but at times these gestures can be interpreted only by the
narrator or by other characters who fully understand the gestural code.
In *Béatrix*, for example, through gesture and facial expression the true
emotions of Camille and Béatrix, which they have been at pains to
hide from each other, are revealed. This revelation of feelings, which
can no longer be contained beneath the veneer of social convention,

---

[163] *Ibid.*, p. 218.
[164] Pierre-Georges Castex confirms the truth of Balzac's claim that this was a
common deformity among convicts by reference to the *Mémoires* of Vidocq, vol. I, p.
266. See: *SetM*, vol. VI, p. 1466, n. 1.
[165] *SetM*, vol. VI, p. 839.

causes the irreconcilable dissolution of their friendship:

> Ce fut avec rage et sa belle figure décomposée que la marquise dit ces affreuses paroles à Camille qui essaya de cacher son bonheur par une fausse expression de tristesse; mais l'éclat de ses yeux démentait la contraction de son masque, et Béatrix se connaissait en grimaces! [...] elles se virent alors séparées par une haine profonde.[166]

Béatrix understands the gestural code in a way which enables her to interpret the implications lying beneath the false mask of her opponent's facial expression.

So too in *Le Colonel Chabert* the comtesse Ferraud's lies, which she has tried to conceal behind a mask of social convention, are revealed in her involuntary gesture when she is tricked by Derville, she 'rougit, pâlit, se cacha la figure dans les mains', and in so doing reveals her guilt, and in *Le Père Goriot* Mme de Beauséant reveals to Eugène through a sharp, impatient gesture 'la main de fer sous le gant de velours'.[167] Again it is the interpretation of the action which is important in the narrative, since the harsh side of the otherwise sympathetic Mme de Beauséant is shown in her involuntary gesture. In *Illusions perdues* gesture is used in the same way to create the reverse effect, to indicate the sympathetic side of the otherwise implacable père Séchard. David holds out his hand to his father without greeting him, the silent gesture carrying the full import of the pain caused by his father. Séchard is unmoved by his son's plight but in a silent gesture of compassion towards his grandchild shows that he is not wholly bad, 'Il alla voir et caresser l'enfant, qui lui tendit ses petites mains'.[168] Séchard is instinctively compelled to do this despite the feeling that he might have been drawn into a trap, and despite the emotionless attitude that he is determined to maintain to the last. The silence which accompanies these gestures highlights their importance, for when all other communication between characters fails, gesture is the final purveyor of meaning to the reader who looks in on the scene.

The ability of gesture to reveal inwardness to other characters is applicable only to spontaneous and involuntary gestures, however, for studied and affected gestures are also part of social role-playing.

---

[166] *B*, vol. II, pp. 823-824.
[167] *PG*, vol. III, p. 150.
[168] *IP*, vol. V, p. 615.

Characters who assume false identities, and use costume as a disguise also assimilate the nuances of gesture and the deliberate posturings appropriate to their role. This is at its most obvious in the character of Lucien whose social role play begins with the assumed aristocratic name of de Rubempré, is sustained by the dress of the young dandy, and is completed by the imitation of de Marsay's affected gestures. At Petit-Claud's wedding celebration after his return to Angoulême, Lucien waves his cane, salutes his fellow guests in a gesture of condescending affability, and postures himself 'dans une pose de grand seigneur en visite chez de petites gens'. If Lucien was only ever a walk-on actor on the social stage of Paris, he is at this point a leading player in Angoulême, and his gestures are as vital to the incarnation of his role as to any actor on the real stage. The provincial characters do not have the necessary skills to decodify Lucien's gestures and penetrate the truth which lies behind them.

    In Balzac's novels, gesture and movement thus express the inner life of the characters and impart a sense of urgency and animation to the drama. In its simplest form this use of gesture is part of the physical portrait of Balzac's characters, and in its most exaggerated form it is part of the extravagant, stylised expressionism of his mode of presentation and in this sense recalls the stage melodrama. Gesture is also used as part of Balzac's efforts to dramatize his text to give symbolic representation to the central themes of the plot, and, with the notable exception of the dandy, to express the inner psyche of the individual. In certain moments of dramatic crisis gesture remains the final vehicle of expressivity and through it Balzac invites the reader to create a mental image of the actions carried out before him.

Conclusion – Narrative and Dramatic Purpose

For Balzac the wider creative scope offered by the novel seems to have made it a more appropriate medium for his literary dramatization of life than the stage drama, particularly since it is only in the novel that he is able to intervene in the narrative, to explain the text, to educate the reader and self-consciously to examine his creative process. However, the above discussion shows that Balzac displays an adept handling of dramatic technique in his novels and consciously manipulates the plastic elements of theatrical representation. This is particularly so in certain scenes of dramatic climax which rely heavily on dialogue and action, and also, perhaps more surprisingly, in certain detailed descriptions of setting and costume. Balzac's success in dramatising both background and plot explains why so many of his novels lent themselves so readily to the stage.[169] Furthermore, the dramatic mode is fundamental to the portrayal of character for which Balzac is renowned, for his characters are depicted not by the author's descriptions of their inner psychology, but define themselves dramatically through their dialogue, actions, appearance and gestures, and so too their milieu becomes an integral part of their drama, reflecting their personalities, shaping their destinies and driving the drama forwards.

The *mise en scène* of the text is constantly reinforced by use of theatrical data, which invites the reader to create a mental stage production of the text by following Balzac's instructions as to setting, décor, lighting, costume, dialogue and gesture. Balzac's use of these devices in his novels is a reflection of a combination of influences – his own leanings towards the drama, the novels of Walter Scott, the hyperbolic expressionism of the melodrama and the visual realism of the Romantic drama, together with an innate awareness that he was writing for a public whose taste was conditioned by visual art forms, and for many of whom the theatre would have been a principal source of entertainment and social interaction.[170]

However, the visual realism with which characters and settings are portrayed, is often subverted by Balzac in so far as the image evoked often turns out to be little more than a theatrical illusion. The insistence on outward appearance, which is important both to the mode of presentation of the novels and to the society which these novels describe, is frequently shown to be misguided, and reliance on milieu, clothing, speech and even, although to a lesser extent, gesture, as signifiers of characters' status and psychology is thus undermined. The ultimate irony of Balzac's work is that he claims to present himself as an observer and historian of social reality, but since that reality is shown in many instances to resemble a theatrical illusion, truth itself remains at best ambiguous and at worst completely unknowable. Through theatrical devices Balzac is in fact playing with his reader and posturing in his novels just as he postured in his own life, convincing the reader that his attention to visual detail constitutes

---

[169] No fewer than 30 stage adaptations are known to have been made from Balzac's novels. See appendix IV.

[170] See above, chapter 1.

his accurate depiction of the *être,* while in fact it is often a manifestation of his skill in passing off the *paraître* as real. The *mise en scène* of the text is thus simultaneously part of the bringing to life of the narrative and part of the novels' more profound theatricality. It does not seem to have been an inherent inability to dramatize or to envisage the staging of his text that prevented Balzac from achieving success as a dramatist, but rather an inability to contain his vast, all-embracing notion of all of life as theatre, within an individual production of a few hours' duration. Perhaps if he had lived longer and had time to develop the experiments with the drama which he attempted only towards the end of his career, Balzac might have achieved the theatrical success which eluded him. Certainly Gautier was of this opinion and writes: 'S'il eût vécu, au bout d'une douzaine de pièces, il eût assurément trouvé sa forme et atteint le succès'.[171] In fact, just as Balzac's leanings towards the theatre and profound sense of the theatricality of life influenced his technique as a novelist, so too in a symbiotic way, the skilful *mise en scène* of his novels could only have benefited Balzac in his endeavours as a dramatist, and the next chapter will show how this is so.

---

[171] Gautier, 'Honoré de Balzac', in *Ecrivains et Artistes Romantiques,* p. 135.

CESAR BITTOTEAU, THE PROTOTYPE OF THE 'BEAU DRAME COMMERCIAL'[1]

César Birotteau is the novel from *La Comédie humaine* which perhaps stands in the most interesting relationship to Balzac's own experience of the theatre, and will serve here as a test case for some of the ideas expressed in previous parts of the thesis. With the exception of René Guise, who briefly notes some of the possible theatrical sources of *César Birotteau*,[2] and the 'tentation du théâtre' which the novel manifests, critics have so far paid little attention to the theatrical antecedents of *César Birotteau* and the apparently conscious 'dramatization' of its text. Furthermore, the relationship between *César Birotteau* and Balzac's financial play, *Mercadet*, has not previously been traced by critics. Indeed Edmond Biré, whose study of Balzac's work is divided between the novels and the plays, sees little relationship between them:

> Je ne terminerai pas ce chaptire sans faire remarquer que pas une des pièces de Balzac n'est tirée de ses romans. *Vautrin* est la seule dans laquelle il ait mis un personnage qui avait déjà figuré dans quelques-uns de ces récits. Tous les autres personnages, ainsi que le sujet même du drame et de ses développements, étaient entièrement nouveaux. [...] Aussi estimait-il plus commode et plus simple, au lieu de faire des emprunts à ses propres ouvrages, de ne mettre au contraire à la scène que des sujets et des types inédits.[3]

---

[1] *CB*, vol VI, p. 272.

[2] René Guise, Introduction to *César Birotteau* in *La Comédie humaine*, ed. Pléiade (Paris: Gallimard, 1977), vol. VI, pp. 26-27. Guise notes Beaumarchais's *Les Deux Amis ou le Négociant de Lyon* and Molière's *Tartuffe* as possible sources of *César Birotteau,* and an 'interaction difficile à évaluer' between the novel and Balzac's play *La Première Demoiselle*, but does not fully develop these points.

[3] Edmond Biré, *Honoré de Balzac* (Paris: Champion, 1897), p. 263. Chapters VIII, IX and X of Biré's study are devoted to Balzac's theatre, and chapters XI and XII, to stage adaptations of *La Comédie humaine* made by other dramatists.

Contrary to Biré's comments, however, the posthumous success of the play *Mercadet*, which continues up to the present day,[4] seems to have owed much to Balzac's earlier experience of 'dramatising' the financial theme and presenting similar characters in *César Birotteau*. The aim of this final chapter is to show through examination of *César Birotteau*, how both the contemporary and classical theatre may have influenced Balzac in the choice and treatment of his theme and characters, how certain aspects of his own attempts at writing for the stage can be discerned in the novel, and how the novel, in turn, seems to have engendered the theme for the play *Mercadet ou Le Faiseur*, which incontestably established Balzac as a successful dramatist. The development of the characters and the financial theme will be traced from their theatrical antecedents, through to *César Birotteau*, which was first conceived in 1833 and written and published in 1837, and finally through the financial drama of *Mercadet*, which was first mentioned by Balzac in 1839, and which was written during the period from 1840 to 1848.[5]

General Theatrical Antecedents of César Birotteau

Balzac was not the first or only author to make the financial theme a significant focus of interest in his work. It is generally recognised that in the Classical tradition of comedy, money held as important a place as love, and intrigues were often developed around thefts and deceptions, and large financial rewards were frequently given for virtue or genius. In 1709, Lesage had presented the character of a revenue collector who is exposed as a public robber in his play *Turcaret*, and in 1770 Beaumarchais treated the subject of bankruptcy

---

[4] See above, p. 29 and n. 101. *Mercadet ou Le Faiseur* was produced with considerable success by the Comédie-française in Paris in 1993, and jointly by the Théâtre Populaire Romand and the Théâtre Jeune Public de Strasbourg in 1992.

[5] See above, pp. 27-29 for full details of the genesis, publication and production of *Mercadet*. These details will be reiterated in the course of the present chapter in so far as they are relevant. As noted in the introduction to the present study, the date of the writing of *Mercadet* remains imprecise, and can only be situated vaguely between 1840 and 1848. It is sufficient for the purpose of the present examination, however, that both the first mention of the play and the earliest evidence that Balzac was working on it, are posterior to the publication of *César Birotteau*.

in *Les Deux Amis ou le Négociant de Lyon*.[6] It is clear from the frequent references to Beaumarchais in *La Comédie humaine* that Balzac was very familiar with his plays,[7] and René Guise is certain that the theme of *César Birotteau* shows an 'emprunt net' from *Les Deux Amis*.[8] This borrowing is difficult to prove, however, since Balzac makes no mention of this particular play in his correspondence or in his novels, and there were apparently no performances of it during his lifetime, so he cannot have seen it on stage.[9] It can only be assumed therefore, from the striking similarity of plot, that Balzac read the play and recalled it when he came to write his novel.

In both Beaumarchais' play and Balzac's novel there is a central character who is facing financial ruin, a young relative whose marriage becomes pertinent to the resolution of the disaster, and an astute employee and protégé who is instrumental in bringing about its happy outcome. In Beaumarchais' play the opening description of the central character, Aurelly, as an honest and upstanding citizen, is equally befitting to Birotteau, who is introduced in the novel as 'la probité venue sur terre'.[10] This similarity is confirmed later in the play when Melac and Dabins testify to the scrupulous character of Aurelly:

> Vous l'avez dit, il en mourra; l'homme le plus vertueux! le plus sage!.... une réputation si intacte! s'il suspend ses paiements, s'il

---

[6] Beaumarchais, 'Les Deux Amis' in *Œuvres complètes* (Paris: Crémille, 1973), pp. 103-135.

[7] I have noted 79 references to Beaumarchais and his works in *La Comédie humaine*. See appendix II part b, for details of where these occur and which plays they refer to.

[8] René Guise, Introduction to *César Birotteau*, p. 26. This claim is not substantiated by Guise, but Balzac's correspondence with Madame Hanska suggests that he was reading Beaumarchais keenly in 1837. There are no references to Beaumarchais in letters to Mme Hanska from 1832-1836, and then in 1837 there are five references. See: *LMH*, vol. I, pp. 475, 512, 533, 541, & 560.

[9] See: A. Joannidès, *La Comédie Française de 1680 à 1900, Dictionnaire général des pièces et des auteurs* (Paris: n.p.,1901); J.B. Colson, *Répertoire du Théâtre Français* (Bordeaux: Colson & Foulguier, n.d.); C.B. Wicks, *The Parisian Stage 1800-1900: Alphabetical Indexes of Plays and Authors* (Alabama: University of Alabama Press, 1950-1979).

[10] *CB*, vol. VI, p. 39.

faut que son honneur... Il en mourra, l'infortuné: voilà ce qu'il y a de bien certain.[11]

Aurelly has been granted *lettres de noblesse*, which are to be celebrated by his supporters and friends. This is repeated in Balzac's novel with Birotteau's appointment to the *Légion d'honneur*, which is celebrated by a ball and unanimously congratulated by Birotteau's family and friends. In two parallel scenes of intense dramatic irony a further similarity between the two characters is demonstrated. In Beaumarchais's play, Aurelly launches a tirade against the infamy of bankrupts and calls for more stringent laws to ensure that business is conducted in an honest manner, while at the same time Melac is trying to warn him of the imminence of his own financial ruin.[12] This episode is mirrored almost exactly in Balzac's novel in a scene where Birotteau also rails against the disgraceful nature of all bankrupts, and proclaims the inadequacy of the present laws to Ragon and Pillerault just before his creditors begin to call.[13]

Beaumarchais does not treat the financial aspect of his comedy in any detailed way, however, and it remains a side issue to the matter of the daughter's marriage. Indeed, no dramatist prior to the nineteenth century shows the processes of financial speculation through which their characters enlarge their fortunes, or the mechanisms of their transactions with creditors and investors. Not until the nineteenth century does the financial theme come to be treated by dramatists in a more realistic way, as the central and dominant point of dramatic interest. The importance of the financial theme in the literature of the nineteenth century is noted by Gautier in *La Presse* on 24 January, 1848:

C'est une chose singulière et digne de remarque, que l'introduction de l'argent dans la littérature comme but, comme moyen et comme idéal; on n'en trouve aucune trace sérieuse avant notre époque. Dans les pistolets dérobées aux tuteurs et aux pères par les mauvais sujets de la comédie ancienne, c'est l'originalité de l'expédient et non la valeur de la somme que l'on considérait.

---

[11] Act I, scene ix.
[12] Act I, scene xi.
[13] *CB*, vol. VI, p. 184.

In 1801, at the Théâtre Louvois, Picard introduced a detailed portrayal of financial transactions to the Parisian theatre audience with his play *Duhautcours, ou le contrat d'union*.[14] In this play Picard exposes the practices of dishonest financiers through the character of the morally upstanding Durville, who is impoverished through the malpractice of his financial associates, just as César Birotteau would be in Balzac's novel some thirty-six years later. Picard's Duhautcours is an undeveloped representation of the type of unscrupulous banker that Balzac would later portray in detail in the characters of du Tillet and Nucingen. The dramatic contrast of luxury and penury in *Duhautcours* is concretised in the sumptuous dinner given by the banker while his creditors wait outside. The same contrast is highlighted in Balzac's novel by the sumptuous ball which immediately precedes Birotteau's bankruptcy.

There is no mention of *Duhautcours* in Balzac's correspondence or novels, and there are only three general references to Picard in *La Comédie humaine*, so it remains difficult to prove whether Balzac knew the play. Certainly there was no production of the play after 1801, so Balzac cannot have seen it performed.[15] However, after its first publication in 1801 the play was also included in the first complete edition of Picard's work which appeared in 1821,[16] at which time Balzac was living in Villeparisis and making frequent trips into Paris,[17] and it is possible that he may have read it. At best the similarity of theme in Balzac's novel suggests only a possible, vague recollection of Picard's play rather than a deliberate borrowing of models.

It is possible that some inspiration for *César Birotteau* came from the work of Balzac's contemporary, Eugène Scribe.[18] Balzac's

[14] Picard [1769-1828], *Duhautcours ou le contrat d'union* (Paris: Charon, 1801), and Picard, 'Duhautcours ou le contrat d'union' in *La France dramatique au dix-neuvième siècle* (Paris: Barba, Delloye & Bezou, 1841), vol. V.

[15] See: C.B. Wicks, *The Parisian Stage 1800-1900: Alphabetical Indexes of Plays and Authors*, and J.B. Colson, *Repertoire du Théâtre Français*. Also verified by scanning of *Le Miroir des théâtres* for period 1821-1828.

[16] Picard, *Œuvres complètes*, 10 vols. (Paris: Barba, 1821).

[17] Roger Pierrot, 'Chronologie de Balzac', in *Œuvres complètes*, ed. Pléiade (Paris: Gallimard, 1976), vol. I, p. LXXXV.

[18] A certain 'huile de Macassar' features in Scribe's play *Le Coiffeur et le perruquier* written in 1824. However, I have not noted this as a possible source of the 'huile de Macassar' produced by Birotteau's competitors and often mentioned in

admiration of Scribe is openly acknowledged in his preface to *La Peau de chagrin,* where he is described as, 'celui de nos Favart qui traduit avec le plus de finesse, de grâce et d'esprit les nuances insaisissables de nos petites mœurs bourgeoises'.[19] Certain aspects of *César Birotteau* seem to derive directly from Scribe's play *Les Adieux au comptoir,* which was first performed at the Gymnase in 1824.[20] Again, Balzac makes no mention of this play in his work or correspondence, but as he was in Paris during this year it is possible that he saw the play performed or read its reviews.[21]

The opening scene of Scribe's play shows the wife of the fabric merchant Dubreuil entreating him to retire from business and enjoy a comfortable life. Similarly, *César Birotteau* opens with a scene in which Constance is trying to dissuade her husband from uncertain business ventures and extravagant expenditure. The first act of Scribe's play involves preparations for a magnificent, celebratory ball, the second is taken up with the ball itself, the third involves scenes with various creditors and suppliers clamouring for payment, the actual bankruptcy occurs in the fourth act, and the fifth sees the resolution and the restoration of moral order. Scribe's play and Balzac's novel differ in detail and in characterisation but the principal elements of the ball, the bankruptcy and the reinstatement are common to both, and the sequence of events follows the same pattern, with the greater part of the text being devoted to the build-up to the catastrophe and a smaller section concerned with the dénouement.

The examples given so far show how the financial theme gradually developed in the French theatre from the beginning of the previous century up to the period of Balzac's work, and how Balzac mayhave been influenced by this development in the writing of

Balzac's novel. It seems more probable that Balzac's source can be found in his own activities as a printer. In 1827 Balzac printed a catalogue for the pharmacists Dissey and Pivier, in which appear: item 135, 'Huile comogène pour la pousse des cheveux' and items 136 and 137, 'Huile de Macasar' either 'en bouteilles paquetées avec livres' or 'avec étuis à coulisses, à filets d'or'. This catalogue is conserved at the Bibliothèque Nationale, Imprimés, 8° Wz 3909.

[19] *PCh.,* vol. X, p. 48.

[20] Eugène Scribe, 'Les Adieux au comptoir' in *Théâtre de Scribe* (Paris: Lévy Frères, 1856-1859).

[21] Roger Pierrot, 'Chronologie de Balzac', p. LXXXVI.

César Birotteau. While there is no evidence to prove that Balzac consciously took inspiration from the works cited here, mentions of these authors by Balzac and similarities between their works and his make it probable that they exercised influence on him.

Balzac's Plays and Theatrical Models in César Birotteau

The theme of bankruptcy appears to have been in Balzac's mind from as early as 1830. Milatchitch notes that the idea for a play entitled *La Faillite* was listed in Balzac's notebook of that year, along with the names of other plays which were never written.[22] Despite these early intentions, however, the first time that Balzac realised his idea of treating the subject of bankruptcy in his work was in the novel *César Birotteau,* which was first promised to the publisher Gosselin in November 1833, but not written until 1837.[23] In the intervening period Balzac made various attempts to write a successful play, and in order to do so consciously took models and inspiration from the work of other dramatists. Faced with an inability to translate his own interpretations of these models into theatrical success, Balzac appears to have integrated certain aspects of them into *César Birotteau.*

In 1835 Balzac began to think of writing a sequel to Molière's *Tartuffe,* which he would call *Orgon,*[24] and by 1837 he seems to have become almost obsessed by Molière's play.[25] In this year Balzac began work on a play which he first called *La Première Demoiselle,* and which the following year he would rename as *L'Ecole des*

---

[22] Milatchitch, *Le Théâtre inédit de H. de Balzac,* p. 15. See also appendix VI for full list of Balzac's unfinished dramatic projects.

[23] René Guise, 'Histoire du texte', in *LCH,* vol. VI, pp. 1119-1132.

[24] Milatchitch, *Le Théâtre inédit de H. de Balzac,* pp. 162-166. Milatchitch notes here that although Balzac apparently did not begin work on this play until 1847, he must have first conceived of it in 1835, since the actors which Balzac had appointed to the various roles in his notebook would have been simultaneously available only at this time.

[25] At this point *Tartuffe* had been played by the Comédie-Française every year since Balzac's birth. See: A. Joannidès, *La Comédie Française de 1680 à 1900,* no page numbers given; see tables of annual productions from 1799 to 1837. The 44 references to this single play in *La Comédie humaine* attest to the extent of Balzac's familiarity with its subject and characters. See Appendix II part b.

ménages.[26] *La Première Demoiselle,* Balzac explained in February 1837 to Mme Hanska, would be the drama of 'Tartuffe en jupons':

> Je fais en ce moment avec fureur, une pièce de théâtre, car là est mon salut. Il faut vivre du théâtre et de ma prose concurremment. Elle s'appelle *la Première demoiselle.* Je l'ai choisie pour mon début parce qu'elle est entièrement bourgeoise. Figurez-vous une maison de la rue St-Denis comme *la Maison du Chat-qui-pelote,* où je mettrai un intérêt dramatique et tragique d'une extrême violence. [...] Personne n'a encore songé à faire un Tartuffe femelle, et sa maîtresse sera Tartuffe en jupons.[27]

Balzac goes on to explain the plot of the play with enthusiasm, adding briefly that he must also set to work on *César Birotteau* without further delay.   Balzac worked on *L'Ecole des ménages* throughout 1837 and at the same time wrote *César Birotteau.*

In Balzac's play, as in Molière's original version of *Tartuffe,* the home is disrupted by a stranger who has been charitably welcomed into the family circle; each father leads his family to ruin as a result of his misplaced affection for this stranger, and those who suffer join forces to rectify the situation.   However, Adrienne is not entirely a 'Tartuffe en jupons', for her character is portrayed by Balzac with sympathy; she is a fine and sensitive young woman who is wrongly accused out of jealousy, and who cannot be held responsible for the disaster which she unwittingly causes.

As Balzac worked simultaneously on *César Birotteau* and *La Première Demoiselle* in 1837, he seems to have deviated from his initial intentions, and the characteristics of Molière's Tartuffe seem to have been transferred rather to du Tillet in the novel than to Adrienne in Balzac's play. Du Tillet enters the Birotteau household, the reader is told, 'dans les intentions de Tartuffe'.[28] In his attempts to seduce Constance Birotteau, and in engineering the ruination of the family for his own gain while convincing the head of the family of his good intentions, du Tillet entirely fulfils the expectations awakened in the reader by this early comparison to a familiar scoundrel.   Birotteau on the other hand, although metaphorically

---

[26] See above, pp. 18-19 for fuller details of the history of Balzac's play.

[27] *LMH,* vol. I, p. 485.

[28] *CB,* vol. VI, p. 74.

referred to as Orgon,[29] is more than a reincarnation of Molière's character. Birotteau is guilty of the egotism and naiveté typically associated with the comic protagonists of Molière but he is also a tragic character who is: 'la victime de la civilisation parisienne'. The model offered in Orgon is thus transformed by Balzac into a character who is both the caricature of a bourgeois type and an individual capable of engaging the reader's sympathies.

The model of the typical bourgeois character was to be found by Balzac not only in the works of Molière, but also in the character of Joseph Prudhomme, who had been created by Henry Monnier.[30] Balzac had experimented with the idea of writing a play with Prudhomme as its central character since the latter's first appearance in 1830 in Monnier's *Scènes populaires*, where Prudhomme appeared

---

[29] *Ibid.*

[30] Monnier (Henry-Bonaventure) [1799-1877] was primarily known as a caricaturist, but was also a writer and actor. He found fame through his series of caricatures, the *Scènes populaires* (1830), and *La Physiologie du bourgeois* (1841), and through his plays *La Famille improvisée* (1831), in which he played the role of Joseph Prudhomme when the play was performed at the Vaudeville, and *Grandeur et décadence de Joseph Prudhomme* (1852). See: Champfleury, *Henry Monnier sa vie, son œuvre* (Paris: Dentu, 1879), pp. 130-144 and 320-321. For Balzac's relationship with Monnier see: André Le Breton, *Balzac l'homme et l'œuvre*, pp. 104-108; Milatchitch, *Le Théâtre Inédit de H. de Balzac*, p. 17. Monnier had been chosen by Balzac to play the role of Gérard in *L'Ecole des ménages* before the play was rejected by the Théâtre de la Renaissance in February 1839. See: Balzac, *Corres.*, vol. IV, p. 839 and A. Meininger 'Balzac et Henry Monnier', in *AB* (1966).

as a caricature. The following year Prudhomme was also incarnated on stage at the Vaudeville in Monnier's play *La Famille improvisée*. Balzac makes reference to this play in *Un homme d'affaires* (1845), and it seems certain that he was familiar with it.[31]

In January 1834, when Balzac was making his initial plans for *César Birotteau*, he also noted an idea for a play entitled *Prudhomme bigame*.[32] At the beginning of September 1837, while the need to complete *César Birotteau* was becoming increasingly urgent, Balzac wrote to Mme Hanska that he was about to begin work on a five-act comedy entitled *Joseph Prudhomme*, and the following month, as he was finally completing *César Birotteau*, he explained his intention to borrow the character, exactly as Monnier had created him, for another projected play, *Le Mariage de Mademoiselle Prudhomme:*

> Vous connaissez M. Prudhomme, le type trouvé par Monnier, je le prends hardiment, car pour surprendre un succès, il ne faut pas avoir une création à faire accepter, il faut [...] l'acheter tout fait.[33]

In the same letter Balzac goes on to describe how he recognised the opportunity to exploit Prudhomme as an established type:

> Prudhomme, comme type de notre bourgeoisie actuelle, comme image des Ganneron, des Aubé, des gardes nationaux, de cette classe moyenne sur laquelle s'appuie il padrone, est un personnage bien plus comique que Turcaret, plus drôle que Figaro, il est tout le temps actuel.[34]

Balzac had declared his intentions to create a typology of characters in his *Avant-Propos* to *La Comédie humaine*, and here he seems to suggest that immediate theatrical success might be achieved by the borrowing of an established and recognisable type. There would be no need to characterise Prudhomme through the drama and Balzac could simply emphasise his known comic traits. Balzac did not carry out any of his plans to bring Prudhomme to the stage, but as Monnier's character occupied his thoughts during the writing of

---

[31] *HA*, vol. VII, p. 787.
[32] Milatchitch, *Le Théâtre Inédit de H. de Balzac*, pp. 18-19.
[33] *LMH*, vol. I, p. 541.
[34] *Ibid.*

César Birotteau, the character of Birotteau seems to have been infiltrated by certain of Prudhomme's comic mannerisms and pompous characteristics.

Dramatization of the Narrative in César Birotteau

During the course of 1837, with his thoughts thus occupied by his own play *L'Ecole des ménages,* and by the characters of Molière's Tartuffe and Monnier's Prudhomme, Balzac wrote his novel *César Birotteau.* It is not surprising therefore, that having been produced in a state of mind pervaded by themes and characters from the theatre, the novel is highly dramatized, both in the treatment of its theme and in the style of its narrative. It is often difficult in Balzac's novels to separate the antitheses and conflicts which constitute the drama of the plot, from specific aspects of theatrical technique used in the narrative, for the latter is often the mode of expression of the former. Nevertheless, some attempt will be made here to examine first the general dramatization of the theme in *César Birotteau* and then to examine how this is expressed through specific dramatic devices.

The full title of this novel immediately introduces the antithesis which is to be central to the drama of the plot: *Histoire de la grandeur et de la décadence de César Birotteau, marchand parfumer, adjoint au maire du deuxième arrondissement de Paris, chevalier de la Légion d'honneur, etc.* The *grandeur* and *décadence* announced by the title instantly suggest to the reader a plot which will contain the extreme contrast and reversal of fortune typically associated with the popular stage melodrama of the 1820s and 1830s.[35] Attached to this announcement of antithesis is an insistence upon Birotteau's elevated social status, which from the outset suggests the comic aspect of his pompous self-congratulation. Moreover, it is by opposition to this elevated social promotion, which is introduced in

---

[35] The stage melodrama, as has been noted in the previous chapter (see above, p. 247 n. 2), traditionally relied upon hyperbolic expression, violent contrasts, reversals of fortune and a strict moral ordering of the universe. A simple moral system and structure of plot prevailed. The exposition would define the characters as good or evil; in the intrigue good would be opposed and temporarily overcome by evil; in the dénouement the moral order would be restored and virtue and altruism would be rewarded.

the title and developed in the early stages of the novel, that the polarised extreme of Birotteau's social reversal is to be judged. Through the course of the novel the melodramatic antitheses of luxury and indigence, good and evil are central to the plot. Birotteau is promoted to the highest level of social success in his appointment to the *Légion d'honneur* and reduced to the lowest level of disgrace, in which state he is faced with the prospect of borrowing funds from his former employees. The characters of the novel are also consistent with the dramaturgy of the Melodrama. They are grouped in strictly opposing camps of good and evil, with Birotteau, Constance, Césarine, Popinot, and the extended Birotteau family placed as upstanding, moral citizens on one side of the conflict, and du Tillet, Claparon, Roguin and the conspirators firmly placed on the opposing side of evil. Within each of the two groups is a character who is closely linked to Birotteau's business activities and who rallies the other members of the group: in one group du Tillet, and in the other Popinot, 'cet admirable et sublime contrepied de du Tillet'. The characters are morally polarised in one camp or the other.[36] No character stands between the two camps or redeems himself from a previous wrongdoing by a subsequent act of altruism. Unlike his fellow bourgeois businessmen in *La Comédie humaine*, such as Camusot, Crevel and Matifat, Birotteau loves his wife too much and has too great a sense of morality ever to take a mistress.[37] A clear moral order prevails throughout the novel and establishes it in close

---

[36] Birotteau commits only one act which might be perceived as immoral in a twentieth-century context. He deliberately exaggerates the properties of his hair treatment oil in his publicity material. This act can be discounted, however, in the light of prevailing nineteenth-century attitudes to publicity material. In the new spirit of enterprise and industry which characterises this period of commercial activity, the notion of misrepresentation had not yet become a serious issue or become the subject of legal control. The advancement of printing and paper-manufacturing technology described by Balzac in *Illusions perdues* had facilitated a sudden and enormous growth in printed publicity, and legislative processes were slow to assimilate this commercial development. In all commercial matters it was rather the legal principle of 'buyer beware' which prevailed. See: René Bouvier, *Balzac, homme d'affaires* (Paris: Champion, 1930).

[37] *CB*, vol. VI, p. 39: 'Aurait-il une maîtresse? Il est trop bête, reprit-elle, et d'ailleurs, il m'aime trop pour cela. N'a-t-il pas dit à Mme Roguin qu'il ne m'avait jamais fait d'infidélité, même en pensée. C'est la probité venue sur terre, cet homme-là. Si quelqu'un mérite le paradis, n'est-ce pas lui?'

relationship to the the stage melodrama, which was similarly reliant upon a moral ordering of the universe.

Balzac's moralising intentions in *César Birotteau* are explained in his address to Zulma Carraud in his dedication of *La Maison Nucingen* in November 1837:

> Vous et quelques âmes, belles comme la vôtre, comprendront ma pensée en lisant *La Maison Nucingen* accolée à *César Birotteau.* Dans ce contraste, n'y a-t-il pas tout un enseignement social?[38]

The point is reiterated by Balzac in his preface to *Pierrette* in 1840, where he again refers to the morality represented in the contrast of good and evil in *César Birotteau:*

> Si, lisant cette histoire vivante des mœurs modernes, vous n'aimez pas mieux, toi boutiquier, mourir avec César Birotteau ou vivre comme Pillerault, que d'être du Tillet ou Roguin [...], le but de l'auteur serait manqué.[39]

The morality of the ending of Balzac's novel deviates somewhat from the punitive endings associated with the stage melodrama, however. In Balzac's novel it is true that virtue and probity are rewarded, for Birotteau is socially reinstated in a scene of emotional excess, Popinot's loyalty is acclaimed, and the previously forbidden marriage between Popinot and Birotteau's daughter is allowed to go ahead. The perpetrators of the financial crime, however, escape without punishment.[40] Notwithstanding the question of whether it is strictly moral to have the wicked escape justice in this way, the plot largely adheres to the melodramatic aesthetic announced in its title.

Balzac also seems to have consciously aimed at a dramatization of his plot when making his outline plans for the novel. The initial list of chapters which he made in Frapesle in April of 1834 was replaced

---

[38] *MN,* vol. VI, p. 329.
[39] *P,* vol. IV, pp. 25-26.
[40] The extent of this injustice is only apparent to the reader of the whole *Comédie humaine,* for du Tillet goes on to become one of the richest bankers in Paris and in 1831 marries the daughter of the comte de Grandville (*FE,* vol. II, p. 274); by 1845 he is also an influential politician (*CSS,* vol. VII, pp.1159, 1160, &1210).

in September of the same year with a more clearly and concisely defined list:[41]

April 1834	September 1834
Une altercation de ménage	Altercation
Comment prospéra la Reine des fleurs	Union
Spéculations	Spéculation
Apogée de Birotteau	Elévation
Malheur	Perdition
César en faillite	Persécution
Décadence et persécution	Résignation
Popinot et Cie	Réhabilitation
	Emotion

The second list of chapters already indicates a more dramatic conception of the novel with a clear accumulation of tension to the point of dramatic crisis situated exactly in the middle. In the second list, the juxtaposition of *Elévation* and *Perdition* at the point of reversal suggests a more acute contrast than the *Apogée de Birotteau* and the comparatively weak *Malheur* in the first list. Furthermore, the nouns of the second list suggest the representation of a series of actions and events, rather than the descriptions of situations suggested by the phrases of the first list. In particular, the addition of the term *Emotion* in the second list demonstrates a movement in Balzac's conception of his novel towards an intense and dramatic ending of emotional excess, rather than the simple continuation of life and business in a new generation, which is suggested in the first list by *Popinot et Cie*.

In the course of the narrative this movement towards a dramatic conception of his plot is translated by Balzac into theatrical metaphors, which are fundamental to his contrivance of a dramatic mode of expression. The characters of the novel are introduced as the 'principaux personnages de cette scène',[42] and the viewing of the new apartments by the Birotteau family is referred to as 'la répétition générale',[43] for the episode is indeed like a dress rehearsal for the

---

[41] *Lov.* A 92, f° I - 30. See also: *LCH, Histoire du texte*, vol VI, pp. 1123-1125.
[42] *CB*, vol. VI, p. 54.
[43] *Ibid.*, p. 168.

magnificent ball which is to follow. Theatrical metaphor is above all used to express the machinations of du Tillet and the troupe of players enlisted by this Tartuffe to assist him in his duping of Birotteau. The metaphors used emphasise both the drama of Birotteau's perilous situation, in which his fate may be reversed at any time, and the play of false appearance of which he becomes the victim. The meticulously stage-managed plot to engineer the bankruptcy and disgrace of Birotteau is presented explicitly by Balzac as a drama in which du Tillet is the director, Roguin and Claperon are leading actors, and a host of money-lenders, property speculators, tradesmen and bankers, including Nucingen, play minor roles. Under this direction Roguin, who is du Tillet's principal agent, assumes his role with ease, for he is adept in the manifestation of false appearance: 'Dès qu'un homme se résout à jouer le rôle que du Tillet avait donné à Roguin, il acquiert les talents du plus grand comédien'.[44] He goes on to play his part with a convincing and natural manner which cannot be matched by Claparon, who is a 'ham' actor by comparison, ill-versed in the social comedy of Parisian life:

> Claparon avait l'air d'un comédien de province qui sait tous les rôles, qui fait la parade, sur la joue duquel le rouge ne tient plus [...]. Aussi fallut-il à Claperon de longues études mimiques avant de parvenir à se composer un maintien en harmonie avec son importance postiche. Du Tillet avait assisté à la toilette de Claparon, comme un directeur de spectacle inquiet du début de son principal acteur.[45]

The metaphor is continued less explicitly as Roguin also becomes concerned about the 'entrée en scène' of Claparon. The concerns of du Tillet and Roguin are justified, for at Birotteau's dinner party Claparon exaggerates his acting to such an extent that he causes Pillerault to become suspicious and to ask questions, which, being accomplished neither as a banker nor as an actor, Claparon is ill-equipped to answer. This comic scene serves as a prelude to the main

---

[44] *Ibid.*, p. 92.
[45] *Ibid.*, p. 147.

dramatic action of the novel, which concerns the bankruptcy itself, and which is also expressed through theatrical metaphor:

> Ce beau drame commercial a trois actes distincts: l'acte de l'agent, l'acte des syndics, l'acte du concordat. Comme toutes les pièces de théâtre, il offre un double spectacle: il a sa mise en scène pour le public et ses moyens cachés, il y a la représentation vue du parterre et la représentation vue des coulisses. Dans les coulisses sont le failli et son agréé, l'avoué des commerçants, les syndics et l'argent, enfin le juge-commissaire.[46]

The theatrical metaphor indicates to the reader that the financial reversal is a public spectacle and a private tragedy, of which the public sees only the effects but not the hidden causes and complex processes. The metaphor of the *coulisses* invites the reader to see behind the image of the bankrupt in order to penetrate the legal and commerical machinery of which Birotteau becomes a mere puppet. On the social stage Birotteau must face his creditors and subject himself to the judgement of society, and at the same time, behind him, the legal process operates all his movements. The theatrical metaphor of the *coulisses* here, as in other novels, is both part of the novel's dramatic mode of expression and part of the uncovering of the hidden forces governing society, which Balzac has taken it upon himself to expose.

Together with the reversals and antitheses of his theme and the theatrical metaphors through which these are expressed, Balzac also employs the techniques of a theatrical *mise en scène* to dramatize his text. Perhaps the most striking of these is the use of dialogue, which predominates in this novel more than in any other of *La Comédie humaine*. As noted in the previous chapter, Balzac often consciously aimed at dramatising his narrative through dialogue after the manner of Scott, which had been assimilated into French Romantic aesthetics.[47] In this way *César Birotteau* opens *in medias res* in Constance's bedroom.[48] The narratorial voice is immediately withdrawn and the exposition is expressed through the character of Constance Birotteau, who, in a lengthy monologue, defines

---

[46] *Ibid.*, p. 272.
[47] See above, pp. 249-250 & 286-296.
[48] H.J. Hunt notes this in *Balzac's Comédie humaine,* p. 192.

Birotteau's character and the situation of the family and business. The monologue is dramatically contrived, for there is no reason for Constance to make these observations aloud to herself other than to inform the reader. Like the secondary character who appears on stage to set the scene before the appearance of the principal character, Constance tells that Birotteau has been 'adjoint au maire' for two years, that his business is a great success and that he is a paragon of probity.[49]

As the scene continues the narrative voice intervenes, but only to describe the characters' movements with the brevity of a stage direction and to introduce Birotteau, before withdrawing once more to allow the dialogue to continue. Birotteau completes this theatrically contrived exposition with an explanation of the political background,[50] and an explanation of why he has been promoted to the *Légion d'honneur*.[51] At this point in the dialogue Constance warns her husband that his *grandeurs* will be his downfall. From the outset the dialogue points forward to the point of dramatic crisis. The subsequent dialogue becomes more naturalistic as Birotteau informs his wife, and at the same time the reader, of his financial speculations and the development of the new hair oil. In all of this dialogue, which occupies some 600 lines of text, the narrative voice is reduced to a bare minimum.

This opening dialogue is far removed from the opening of other novels such as *Le Père Goriot* (1834-35), which opens with some thirty pages of background description before embarking upon the events of the plot, or *La Fille aux yeux d'or* (1834-35), in which Balzac devotes the initial twenty pages out of a total of only seventy three to a description of Paris and the Parisians, much of which is only loosely connected with the subsequent narrative. In *César Birotteau*, not only does Balzac dramatize the opening scene by putting the entire exposition into the mouths of his characters, but in the course of the novel he repeatedly withdraws the narrative voice for sustained periods.

The opening dialogue is succeeded by thirty five pages of descriptive narrative, in which Balzac explains the Birotteau family,

[49] *CB*, vol. VI, pp. 38-40.
[50] *CB*, vol. VI, p. 41.
[51] *CB*, vol. VI, p. 42.

their business and Birotteau's social promotion. Much of this description is superfluous to the plot, however, since the characters have already defined themselves and their situation, and serves merely to place them even more precisely in their social and historical context. There are no other extended descriptive passages until the final stages of the novel where Balzac intervenes in his narrative to give a detailed explanation of the legal processes of bankruptcy.[52] Apart from these two passages of descriptive narrative there are only a further thirty-three pages, distributed throughout the novel, which contain no dialogue at all. The remainder of the novel's 312 pages consist largely in dialogue, forty-five pages of which are entirely uninterrupted and many more of which are punctuated only by references (functioning almost as stage directions) to tone of voice, facial expression and the entrance or exit of certain characters.

Birotteau is a master of the theatrical gesture and line. His mannerisms, mutterings, asides and gesticulations invite the reader to realize in his own mind the scenes in which he appears:

> Sa figure offrait une sorte d'assurance comique, de fatuité mêlée de bonhomie [...] Habituellement, en parlant, il se croisait les mains derrière le dos. Quand il croyait avoir dit quelque chose de galant ou de saillant, il se levait imperceptiblement sur la pointe des pieds, à deux reprises, et retombait sur ses talons lourdement, comme pour appuyer sur sa phrase.[53]

Birotteau's reputation is not so much the result of his action in defending the royalist cause, as the result of the way in which he has publicised, promoted, and delivered the detail of this action to other people. Birotteau is both the actor and director of a small scenario which he repeatedly offers to his public. Rocking back and forth on his toes, he pauses for effect and ruminates on his success, revealing his pride in an event which marks an otherwise unremarkable existence:

> [P]eut-être me suis-je rendu digne de cette insigne et royale faveur en siégant au tribunal consulaire et en combattant pour la cause

---

[52] *CB*, vol VI, pp. 270-279.
[53] *CB*, vol. VI, p. 78.

royale au treize vendémiaire à Saint-Roch, où je fus blessé par Napoléon.[54]

Birotteau's carefully orchestrated and comic manner of delivering his self-congratulatory speech is conveyed by Balzac through careful attention to punctuation which invites the reader to visualise and hear Birotteau in his own mind. The reader's response to Birotteau is to visualise him, precisely because of the way he is repeatedly characterised by his own demeanour, bearing and gestures. As Birotteau's fortunes change so his customary, spontaneous gesture of rocking back and forth disappears. The man who at the beginning of the novel had proudly and pompously rocked and ruminated, by the end of the novel cannot look up from the ground to meet the gaze of others: 'Il allait tête baissée par les rues, dérobant à tous les regards son visage abattu, décomposé, stupide'. Birotteau's fall is dramatically figured in a pitiful transformation of gesture, which gives the contrast of his two states symbolic visual representation.

At the point of the novel's climax, which marks this contrast between Birotteau's two states, Balzac makes use of the dramatic devices of *coup de théâtre* and peripeteia. The first of these occurs as Birotteau is in the process of erroneously denouncing his loyal employée Popinot as a traitor. The Birotteau family start in amazement at this unprecedented outburst, and at that timely moment Popinot enters:

> Anselme [...] retourna chez lui [...] en sorte qu'au moment où Césarine, sa mère et leur oncle Pillerault regardaient le parfumeur, surpris du ton sépulcral avec lequel il avait prononcé ce mot: 'Ingrat!' en réponse à la question de sa fille, la porte du salon s'ouvrit et Popinot parut.[55]

This unexpected, contrived and conveniently timed entrance has the effect of a *coup de théâtre,* both for the reader and for the other characters who are simultaneously actors and spectators in the scene. The scene also features dramatic irony, since the reader knows that

[54] *CB*, vol. VI, p. 142.
[55] *CB*, vol. VI, p. 251.

Birotteau has passed an erroneous judgement and is to be surprised by Popinot's magnanimous gesture.

Popinot hands over the bank notes which represent his savings and with which he hopes to alleviate Birotteau's financial predicament. Just as the reader expects Birotteau to recognise his error and accept Popinot's aid, and the dramatic tension to subside, Pillerault intervenes and in a spectacular gesture snatches the bank notes and tears them up to unanimous exclamations of 'Mon oncle!' from the stunned onlookers. This second coup marks the point of peripeteia in the plot, for it is at this point with his only means of assistance torn into shreds, that the demise of the protagonist commences. In this way the climax of the novel is rendered theatrical not only because it is the episode of tension which stands between the contrasting situations of Birotteau's *grandeur* and *décadence*, but also because it is presented in dialogue and by means of specific theatrical devices.

The scene of climax takes place within an enclosed space in a single room, with the major characters placed in the centre, the secondary characters placed both as spectators and participants around the outside of the room, and conveniently located doors to facilitate the speedy entrance and exit of characters as necessary. This attention to the positioning of the characters, as though on a theatre stage, can be seen throughout the novel and particularly in the scenes which are essential to the action. All of these scenes take place in the confined space of an interior setting from which one wall has been removed, as it were, to allow the reader to 'see' inside. The opening scene reveals Constance in her bedroom, where she delivers the exposition until she joins Birotteau in 'la pièce voisine' and the exposition is continued in their dialogue. The apotheosis of Birotteau occurs in the splendid interior of his shop, La Reine des Roses, where he is surrounded by his admiring employees. The intrigue is acted out at a dinner party where the conspirators are seated on one side of the table and Birotteau and Pillerault on the opposite side. The climax takes place in Birotteau's apartment, and here too the members of the extended family are grouped around Birotteau to witness his final resignation to his bankruptcy:

– Ma résignation est sans bornes, dit César avec calme. Le déshonneur est venu, je ne dois songer qu'à la réparation. [...] J'ai rêvé pendant vingt-deux ans, je me réveille aujourd'hui mon gourdin à la main.[...] César aperçut sa femme, Anselme et Célestin. Les papiers que tenait le premier commis étaient bien significatifs. César contempla tranquillement ce groupe où tous les regards étaient tristes mais amis.

– Un moment! dit-il en détachant sa croix qu'il tendit à l'abbé Loraux, vous me la rendrez quand je pourrai la porter sans honte.[56]

In this scene, observed by those who had congratulated him on his success, Birotteau faces his final humiliation. The physical gesture of the removal of the cross, and the verbal gesture which accompanies it, are rendered all the more poignant precisely because the award had been so lavishly celebrated and had been the source of such inflated self-esteem. The central theme of the novel is thus given a concrete and visual presence in the symbol of the cross. This visual sign, the gesture of removing it, the rhetorical tone of Birotteau's speech, and the positioning of the onlookers around Birotteau are devices employed to present the lowest point of Birotteau's social and financial decline in a way which invites the reader to visualise the scene.

The same dramatic devices are used in the final scene of the novel's dénouement, where the themes of the plot again receive concrete representation in objects and gestures, and the action is advanced by means of a dramatic device. Birotteau's probity is recognised by the King who makes the final contribution by which Birotteau is able to clear his debts and become socially reintegrated. Admittedly, the sum offered by the King is relatively small compared to the vast sums raised by the efforts of Birotteau, Popinot and the Birotteau family, but the recognition has a huge impact on Birotteau and publicly confirms his regeneration. The abstract idea of Birotteau's rehabilitation is thus symbolically represented in the king's gesture, which also functions in a similar way to the *deus ex machina* of Classical theatre, since it brings about the final clearing

[56] *CB*, vol. VI, p. 260.

of the debt and contributes to Birotteau's excessive emotion which eventually causes his heart-attack.

With his probity thus restored and royally approved, Birotteau returns to his former apartments to find them exactly as he had left them, and his wife and daughter dressed in the same gowns they had worn for his celebratory ball. His regeneration is now given concrete visual form; there has been a complete return to his former glory and this can be seen in the apartment and the costumes, and the same guests gathered around him to celebrate his rehabilitation and the marriage of Césarine and Popinot. With his family and friends gathered around him and with the priest at his side and his head on his wife's breast Birotteau dies. The grouping of the characters is highly symbolic here, for Birotteau, the god-fearing man who has led an honest and just life and conducted himself as a loyal and devoted husband, dies positioned between his wife and the abbé, who visually represent these two aspects of his impeccable character and surrounded by his admiring friends who represent the general social approval of his conduct. The scene is visual, symbolic and sentimentalised, and in these aspects closely resembles the death scenes represented on stage in the Romantic dramas of the period.[57] The final words of the novel, pronounced by abbé Loraux, are a verbal gesture which closes the scene with the same image of Birotteau as Constance's description of him at the beginning of the novel: 'Voilà la mort du juste'.

Throughout the novel it is possible to discern Balzac's prevailing preoccupation with the theatre during 1837. The novel's exposition, intrigue, climax and dénouement are all expressed through dialogue, gesture and theatrical devices, in scenes where the central theme is given visual representation in the grouping of the characters, and in the symbolic value attached to objects. The reader is continually encouraged to realize a mental performance of the novel because the data he is given belong to the drama rather than to a descriptive narrative. In *César Birotteau* Balzac has succeeded in rendering the subject of bankruptcy dynamic and dramatic, and the same skills

---

[57] The representation of death on stage, which was previously forbidden by the Classical dramatic aesthetics, was a particular preoccupation of the Romantic dramatists. See: Howarth, *Sublime and Grotesque, a Study of French Romantic Drama.*

employed in this process would serve him well when he came to work on his financial play, *Mercadet,* in 1840.

César Birotteau *and* Mercadet – *A Common Theme*

The theme of the play *Mercadet* is first described by Balzac in a letter to Madame Hanska on 10 May, 1840, in which he writes:

> *Mercadet* est le combat d'un homme contre ses créanciers, les ruses dont il se sert pour leur échapper. C'est exclusivement une comédie, et j'espère cette fois avoir un succès et satisfaire les exigences littéraires.[58]

Although Balzac has not explicitly stated anywhere in his works, prefaces or correspondence that *Mercadet* in any way evolved from *César Birotteau,* the principal themes and characters of the play and the novel have unmistakable similarities. As in the novel, the play shows the central character living in luxurious surroundings, but in a state of financial crisis, which is partly brought about by misjudged speculations and a substantial 'theft' perpetrated by his business associate. In both the novel and the play there is also the matter of a daughter to be married and a dowry to be provided. Similarly, the characters of the play mirror almost exactly those of the novel:

Mercadet	*César Birotteau*
Mercadet, businessman	Birotteau, businessman
Mme Mercadet, wife	Mme Birotteau, wife
Julie, daughter	Césarine, daughter
Minard, suitor of Julie	Popinot, suitor of Césarine
La Brive, false associate/suitor	du Tillet, false associate/would-be seducer
Godeau, voyageur commercial	Gaudissart, voyageur commercial
Various creditors, servants, etc.	Various creditors, family, employees.

---

[58] *LMH,* vol. I, p. 675.

It should be acknowledged from the outset that Mercadet, as Balzac notes in his own description of the play to Madame Hanska, is something of a financial rogue who is cunning and unscrupulous, and at first sight very different from the morally upstanding Birotteau. Mercadet is a broker, alert, resourceful and occupied mainly with attempts to outdo his creditors. In this respect he perhaps owes more to the character of du Tillet in the novel than to that of Birotteau, for he seeks fortune at any price and has the fever of a gambler who undertakes his speculations with ardour and bravado, claiming that without liquid funds, 'on paie d'audace'.[59] Mercadet's ruses to outwit his creditors are excused only by the fact that, without exception, the creditors are shown to be more unscrupulous and parasitic than Mercadet himself, each successively seizing the opportunity to add unreasonable sums of interest to his debt and employing devious means to extort money from Mercadet.

Notwithstanding the apparent difference in the essential natures of Birotteau and Mercadet, the two bourgeois businessmen share many of the same characteristics. Indeed, Birotteau is also tempted by all possible means to augment his fortune, believes that all is fair in business, devises exaggerated publicity materials, and becomes involved in property investments which are little more than a large-scale gamble. Both are excited by the prospect of financial gain as much for the benefit of the family and for the augmentation of their daughters' dowries as for their personal comfort, for Meracdet, like his precursor Birotteau, is a devoted father and loyal husband. These redeeming qualities of Mercadet are recognised by Gautier in his review of the play in *La Presse* on 1 September 1851, where he writes:

> Mercadet est ce qu'on appelle un faiseur, espèce inconnue autrefois et produite par notre civilisation. [...] On pourrait écrire sur la tombe de Monsieur Mercadet: 'Bon père, bon époux, bon garde national', il va comme tout le monde jusqu'à la limite du code civil, pensant que ce qui n'est pas défendu est permis; il a des qualités, il est serviable, il a du cœur; il aime sa femme et sa fille.

[59] Act I, scene 13.

Gautier does not mention Birotteau, but the similarity is clear to the reader who is familiar with the novel. Like Birotteau, Mercadet also shows genuine sympathy towards his creditors and is a man of pride. When confronted by Père Violette, a pleading and supposedly destitute creditor, Mercadet takes pity on the old man and parts with the family's last few francs, becoming the victim of the *comédie* which the creditor has acted out before him. Faced with the offer of financial help from his future son-in-law Mercadet's principles cause him to refuse, just as Birotteau refuses the offer of Popinot.

Mercadet is also given to Birotteau's pomposity and sense of occasion; he loves an expensive dinner and makes as much of a show of this as Birotteau does of his ball, speaking in the feigned language of a connoisseur about the silver and the family arms of his guest, De La Brive. He is also inclined to torrents of mock-heroic eloquence like Birotteau: 'l'union fait la force! la maxime des écus de la République',[60] and is similarly a man of pompous gestures: 'Permettez-moi de vous serrer la main à l'anglaise',[61] and rejoices in his good fortune with the same studied phrases and absurd rhetoric as Birotteau ruminating on his success:

> Salut, reine des rois, archiduchesse des emprunts, princesse des actions et mère du crédit!... Salut fortune tant recherchée ici, et qui, pour la millième fois, arrive des Indes![62]

Mercadet, unlike Birotteau, is a professional speculator, but is no less inept in his financial dealings. Both are characterised by their bourgeois mediocrity, excited by business deals in which the true professional might recognise flaws. Both characters would be well advised to follow the advice of their wives, which results from instinctive caution rather than superior knowledge of the financial market. Mercadet belongs no more to the world of high finance which is operated by skilled speculators such as du Tillet and Nucingen in *La Comédie humaine,* than does Birotteau, for he delights at the prospect of investing in mines and marshes at a time

---

[60] Act I, scene 10.
[61] Act 3, scene 8.
[62] Act V, scene 6.

when these no longer represent a worthwhile opportunity, and the well-informed are investing in railways and industries.[63]

At Mercadet's side throughout the financial crisis stands a devoted wife who, like Madame Birotteau, sees her husband as an image of probity, and echoes Constance's apotheosis of Birotteau: 'J'ai voulu vous voir rester probe, loyal, courageux, enfin tout ce que vous avez été jusqu'à présent'.[64] Madame Mercadet, like Madame Birotteau, is perspicacious in advising her husband against risky financial speculations, for if she does not know the financial marketplace, she certainly knows her husband's limitations. Just as Birotteau's success is reflected in his wife's elegant ball-gown, so Mme Mercadet is required to dress 'd'une élégance',[65] which will indicate wealth to the outside world, and both wives are equally relieved to return to a life of unostentatious, comfortable security when the crisis has been resolved.

The daughter in the play, like the daughter in the novel, is only lightly sketched and is significant only in so far as her marriage and dowry are pertinent to the plot. In both the play and the novel the marriage of the daughter to her earnest and modest suitor is prevented by the absence of a dowry. In the play the lack of a dowry is an obstacle because Minard considers himself incapable of supporting Julie without her dowry, and in the novel it is because Birotteau is too proud to permit Césarine to marry Popinot without a dowry and considers a handsome sum to be necessary to his daughter's happiness. In both cases the suitor is prompted out of devotion to his prospective wife and father-in-law to offer up his own fortune as a means of partially alleviating the financial plight. In both cases the aid is refused for reasons of both pride and practicality, for the sums

---

[63] In 1815 Nucingen makes money out of mines, *MN*, vol. IV, p. 338, *CB*, VI, p. 93, and in 1818 du Tillet makes a fortune in the speculation in land of which Birotteau is the victim. By the 1840s, however, both Nucingen and du Tillet are investing in railways, *CSS*, VII, 1180. The action of *Mercadet* is set in approximately 1839-1840. Mercadet's dealings thus seem rather retarded by comparison to those of Nucingen and du Tillet.

[64] Act IV, scene 17.

[65] Act I, scene 13: 'Une femme est une enseigne pour un spéculateur. Quand à l'Opéra vous vous montrez avec une nouvelle parure, le public se dit: les Asphaltes vont bien, ou la Providence des Familles est en hausse, car Madame Mercadet est d'une élégance!'

offered are insufficient to pay off the debts and the interest, and would plunge the loyal Popinot and Minard into penury without preventing the impending bankruptcy.

In the play Mercadet sees the prospect of salvation in the character of La Brive who poses as a wealthy suitor to Julie. In fact, however, La Brive is as penniless as Mercadet himself and is a social actor. In his convincing portrayal of false appearance La Brive closely resembles du Tillet in the novel. Like du Tillet, he is a stranger who enters the home under false pretences and entices the central character into a false financial arrangement, the particulars of which are acted out over a sumptuous dinner. La Brive is as adept and convincing in trapping his prey as du Tillet is, and hopes to seize Mercadet's fortune by marrying his daughter. Here the play diverges somewhat from the novel, for unlike Birotteau, Mercadet no longer has a fortune to be stolen and is acting a role similar to that of his opponent, claiming riches and investments which are entirely false. One hopes to gain a wealthy father-in-law, the other a wealthy son-in-law, but in fact both are without financial resources. The discovery of the false posturing of each character by the other is central to the comedy of the plot. While the character and ruses of La Brive may owe much to du Tillet, his fate in the plot is rather different from that of his precursor. Rather than being cast out by Mercadet when the truth is discovered, La Brive is employed by Mercadet to help him to act out a further scenario intended to head off the creditors for long enough for the desperate pair to pull off a financial coup together.

The character of Mercadet's legitimate business partner and commercial traveller, Godeau, also seems to derive partly from du Tillet. Since Godeau's departure for India with Mercadet's investment, nothing has been heard of him and it is assumed that Mercadet, like Birotteau, has been the victim of an elaborate commercial theft. Ultimately, however, Godeau proves himself more akin to the character Gaudissart in the novel, who in his role as a commercial traveller assists in the restoration of Birotteau's fortune by his successful promotion and sale of Birotteau's cosmetic products, finally returning to hand over the results of his efforts to

Birotteau. In the play the long-awaited Godeau[66] similarly returns at the eleventh hour to restore to Mercadet his lost fortune. With his fortune restored Mercadet, like Birotteau, pays his creditors, renounces speculations for ever, and permits his daughter's marriage to go ahead.[67] The most pertinent difference between the play and the novel being that in the stage comedy the central character is permitted to survive and enjoy his good fortune.

The structure of the play also diverges somewhat from that of the novel, but only in so far as this is necessary for representation of the action on stage. In order to speed up the action the play opens at the point of financial crisis and, despite the misleading luxury of Mercadet's apartments, the audience soon learns that he is in a state of ruin. In the novel, however, Balzac can afford to take his time in building up to the crisis which appears at its midpoint. It is perhaps for this reason that the same subject which had been treated largely as a melodrama in the novel is treated as a comedy in the play, for it is the repeated and sustained elevation of Birotteau to a great social height which renders his fall all the more melodramatic. Balzac's intentions in the novel, as has been noted, were moralistic whereas in the play they are more satirical, although here too a moral standpoint is evident.

In both the play and the novel the central character is almost constantly before the audience, and only in the scenes which reveal the hidden machinations of La Brive and du Tillet respectively is the central character not present. Both Mercadet and Birotteau, as fathers and heads of families, are the focus of the plot and the embodiment of

[66] In his introduction to Balzac's *Théâtre*, René Guise raises the interesting question 'Beckett a-t-il lu Mercadet?' See *Œuvres complètes*, ed. cit. p.XXI. I have not taken up this point here. It is ironic, however, that the 'Godot' of theatrical success for which Balzac waited in vain throughout his life should come about posthumously in a play which is resolved by the fortuitous arrival of a character named Godeau.

[67] It is tempting to claim that, through a subtle use of English, Balzac might deliberately be highlighting his use of the *Deus ex machina* of Classical theatre in the name of his character. The resolution of the play is brought about entirely by Godeau's intervention. It seems more likely, however, that the name suggested to Balzac a character concerned with money, since it calls to mind certain characters of *La Comédie humaine* who share this characteristic, such as Godain, the miser without gold, see: *Pay.*, vol. IX, p. 227; Goddard, the *commis* at the *Ministère des Finances*, see: *E*, vol. VII, p. 964; and Goddet, the banker from Issoudun, see: *R*, IV, 430.

its moral principle. In both the play and the novel, the welfare of the family rests on the prudent conduct of its head, who is made to learn the error of his imprudent speculations. In speculating with the family's wealth each father also speculates with its stability and happiness, and the renunciation of future speculations by each father is an indication that the moral lesson has been assimilated. As each plot is brought to its conclusion by means of a *deus ex machina* the moral order is restored, the father is reinstated as the rightful head of the family, renounces his erroneous speculations and now bestows wealth on the young lovers who are assured a prosperous marriage. Thus, from beginning to end, the similarities between the two works are undeniable.

Conclusion – Theatrical Success

The posthumous production of *Mercadet* in 1851[68] brought Balzac the theatrical success which he had strived for throughout his life. None of his other attempts with the drama comes so close to the *Comédie humaine* in its characterisation or treatment of theme.[69] The subject of finance, which Balzac had already successfully 'dramatized' in *César Birotteau,* was clearly one which he understood better than the subjects chosen for his other plays, which owe little to *La Comédie humaine.* It seems that the enduring success of *Mercadet* is at least partly owed to Balzac's experience of treating similar characters and themes in *César Birotteau.* In the writing of *César Birotteau,* itself inspired by theatrical works and expressed by means of theatrical techniques, Balzac seems unwittingly to have found a formula which prepared him for the successful treatment of the same theme in *Mercadet.* Had Balzac become conscious of this formula, and had he lived long enough to exploit it, he might have succeeded in bringing more of the themes treated in *La Comédie humaine* to the stage.

Other dramatists have certainly exploited Balzac's novels[70] with considerable success, and none more so than *César Birotteau.*[71] One

---

[68] See above, p. 29.

[69] The play *Vautrin,* as has been noted in the Introduction to the thesis, took this familiar character and placed him in a setting which was incongruous with his previous areas of activity in *La Comédie humaine.*

[70] See Appendix IV for list of stage adaptations of Balzac's novels.

is left to wonder why Balzac did not make more use of the rich subjects of his novels in his own efforts to write for the theatre instead of attempting to diverge almost entirely from *La Comédie humaine*. *Mercadet* is, after all, the enduring proof that Balzac had the potential to be a successful dramatist as well as a successful novelist, and for Gautier, who was perhaps best equipped to judge the merit of the play in its contemporary context, *Mercadet* left Balzac's dramatic skill in no doubt:

> Chaque soir la salle est comble, et le public écoute avec une attention soutenue ce dialogue plein d'idées, d'aperçus, d'observations, de mots bouffons et profonds empruntés de cette joyeuseté terrible particulière à Balzac, et chacun s'en retourne en pensant qu'une seule tombe couvre en même temps un grand romancier et un grand auteur comique.[72]

---

[71] There have been three adaptations of *César Birotteau* for the stage. The first of these was a three act *Drame-Vaudeville* by Cormon and Legrange which was first performed at the Théâtre du Panthéon on 4 April 1838. See: *Théâtre de Cormon*, (Paris: Barba, Bezou & Quay, 1838). This piece retains most of the main characters of the novel and treats the principal elements of its plot in a simplified form. The main alteration occurs in the final scene: Birotteau does not die and the final scene shows Constance pinning the cross of the *Légion d'honneur* onto his lapel in a gesture which symbolises his rehabilitation. The second adaptation was made by Emile Fabre. This *drame social* was first performed on 7 October 1910 at the Théâtre Antoine. See: 'César Birotteau', in *L'Illustration théâtrale* no. 162 (Paris, 1910). Fabre extracted most of the play's dialogue directly from the novel. Gaston Sorbets writes in his introduction to this publication of the play: 'En des décors et sous des costumes réalisant les visions qui nous étaient suggérées par le texte de Balzac, les artistes du Théâtre Antoine ont animé et fait palpiter cette tragédie.' The third adaptation was made by Henry Monnier whose character Prudhomme had originally inspired Balzac back in 1837. Monnier's *Grandeur et décadence de Joseph Prudhomme* was first performed at the Odéon on 23 November, 1852, and Monnier himself played the title role. The plot is largely a parody of Balzac's novel. See: Monnier, *Grandeur et décadence de Joseph Prudhomme* (Paris: Lévy Frères, 1852).
[72] Gautier, 'Mercadet' in *La Presse,* 1 September, 1851.

CONCLUSION

In this study theatre in *La Comédie humaine* has been examined both for its influence on Balzac's techniques and modes of presentation in his novels, and as a theme in itself. Where appropriate, the examination has been related to Balzac's own opinions and experience of the theatre as recalled in the introduction to the present work. In the first three chapters the focus was on the historicity of Balzac's portrayal of the theatrical world, his representation of the theatre being placed in relation to primary historical sources. The geographical and social aspects of the theatres themselves led on to a demonstration of how Balzac uses the theatre environment not only as a realistic and historically grounded milieu, but also as a means of facilitating the chance encounters and strange coincidences upon which the events of his plots often depend. The examination then focused on Balzac's representation of activities within the theatre, and demonstrated how the portrayal of these serves Balzac's purpose as the writer of the *histoire secrète,* in which he exposes a society governed by the imperatives of money, ambition and sexual impulse.

The following two chapters demonstrated how the theatre provided Balzac with a rich seam of metaphor and bank of expressive devices through which he communicates his critique of society, expresses his own dramaturgy, and develops a stratagem by means of which he stimulates in the reader an attitude of penetration and observation. The examination was conducted in the context of prevailing literary influences and technical possibilities in the theatre, and showed how, in his exploitation of theatrical metaphors and stagecraft in his novels, Balzac engages the reader through a system of encodable and decodable signs in a text which can be viewed in the 'virtual dimension' like a piece of theatre. The final chapter examined the symbiotic influence of the drama and the novel in Balzac's work, tracing a common thread through a novel and a play. This chapter showed how the techniques which Balzac borrowed from the theatre and put to practice in his novel eventually resulted in posthumous theatrical success.

Collectively and cumulatively these chapters illustrate the importance of theatre in Balzac's novels, both in terms of their content and their style, and demonstrate that the theatrical quality of Balzac's writing is not simply a manifestation of his impulse towards melodrama. Theatre in its broadest sense – as influence, technique, milieu and metaphor – pervades *La Comédie humaine,* and the discussion of this all-embracing theatricality leads to the conclusion that it is partly through the notion of theatre that the individual novels attain a sense of cohesion within the collective work. Indeed the overall form of *La Comédie humaine,* which was first imposed in publication only in 1842,[1] when only fifteen works or parts of works remained to be written or completed,[2] is superimposed and stands only in metaphorical relationship to the stage *comédie.* The title of the complete work and its division into *études* and *scènes* has little relationship to the actual structure of the novels and their divisions, for although the title is suggestive of the theatre there is no actual resemblance to a strict dramatic structure in the way the novels are grouped together. Georg Lukács points out that, although the economy of form necessary to drama may exist within individual novels of *La Comédie humaine,* it does not exist in the work as a whole.[3] According to Lukács, the sense of 'totality' in *La Comédie humaine* derives from its material rather than from its form. This is

---

[1] See above, p. 171 & n. 5.

[2] *Modeste Mignon* (1844); *Béatrix* (1838-1845); *La Muse du Département* (1843); Part III of *Illusions perdues, Les Souffrances de l'Inventeur* (1839-1843); *Splendeurs et misères des courtisanes* (1838-1847); *La Cousine Bette* (1846); *Le Cousin Pons* (1846-1847); *Un homme d'affaires* (1844); *Gaudissart II* (1844); *Les Comédiens sans le savoir* (1844-1846); *Les Petits Bourgeois* (1843-1844); *L'Envers de l'histoire contemporaine* (1842-1847); *Le Député d'Arcis* (1839-1847); *Les Paysans* (1838-1845); *Petites Misères de la vie conjugale* (1830-1845).

[3] Georg Lukács, *The Theory of the Novel,* translated from the German by Anna Bostock (London: Merlin Press, 1971), pp. 108-109: 'However, this triumph of form occurs only in each individual novel, not in *The Human Comedy* as a whole. True, the prerequisite for it is there: the magnificent unity of the work's all-embracing material. [...] But ultimately this totality is not born purely out of the form: what makes the whole truly a whole is, in the end, only the effective experience of a common basis of life and the recognition that this experience corresponds to the essence of life as lived at that moment. [...] None of the parts seen from the viewpoint of the whole, possesses an organic necessity of existence; if it were not there at all, the whole would not suffer; conversely, any number of new parts might be added and no evidence of inner completeness would prove them superfluous'.

true of course, and from the points made in the present work, it is possible to conclude that the sense of cohesion which Lukács identifies in the 'all-embracing material' of the novels, owes much to Balzac's exploitation of the theatre, if not as form, then certainly as theme, metaphor and mode of presentation. In *La Comédie humaine*, just as in the society which it represents, all is theatre and 'tout s'enchaîne'.

Within this cohesive scheme, the nature of the actual theatre history represented in Balzac's novels thus underpins the way in which theatre is used in multiple senses as a metaphor for the world at large. The historical and social forces which govern the outside world are intensified in the microcosm of the theatre, which functions on lines of corruption according to economic and sexual imperatives, and the secret history of the theatre is a metaphor for the underside of social history in its widest sense. At the same time the theatrical metaphors and presentation modes of the novels serve to endow the banal and ordinary bourgeois world beyond the theatre with social and historical importance. Partly through insistence on dramatic vocabulary and by integrating techniques of stagecraft into his text, Balzac succeeds in making the private sphere visible, alive and interesting. Each manifestation of theatre in the novels underpins the others and all are to some extent dependent on the others for their fullest effect. The notion of totality and completeness achieved through the interdependency of the various manifestations of theatre in Balzac's novels can be expressed most simply in the form of a diagram:

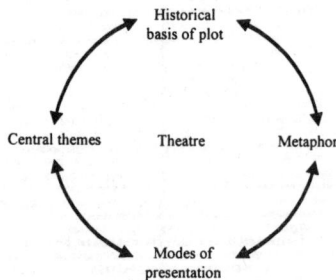

At the centre of the Balzacian world seen from this point of view is theatre. The various manifestations of theatre in the novels radiate out from a central point and are joined in a circle which has been deliberately chosen here for its value as a symbol of completeness. If we enter the circle at the point of central themes (which I am treating here as the interplay of surface and depth, chance and necessity, true and false, which are at the root of Balzac's secret history and which are the principal themes of the total work), we can find the most intense representation of these in the treatment of actual theatre history in the novels. This history then underpins and clarifies Balzac's use of theatrical metaphor, which attains its fullest signification in our understanding of the Balzacian worldview by relation to the corruption, falseness, and role-playing of the theatre. The combination of theatre as theme and metaphor urges towards the 'dramatic' presentation of the text, so that Balzac's social critique may be 'staged' and offered up for view and the invisible social substructure may be made visible. This of course, in turn, brings us back to our starting point with the central themes of surface and depth, true and false, which it is Balzac's declared intention to uncover.

To end simply with the idea that in *La Comédie humaine* all is theatre is perhaps too convenient a conclusion, however, in respect of a writer so full of contradictions and ambiguities as Balzac. In fact the notion of theatre as a unifying thread in the total work raises more questions than it resolves, for the theatre, which is at the centre of this complete and self-contained world, is itself an illusion, a mirage without substance, corrupt, unstable, and perpetrating falsehoods. Once this illusion is exploded it leaves a void, for the circle which has been used as a symbol of unity, is also the symbol of emptiness, a hole, a vacuum. If not only actresses but vast sections of the population shown in *La Comédie humaine* are always acting; if the historically validated representation of the theatre as corrupt, hypocritical, and concealing a sordid and false substructure, functions as a metaphor for the world at large, where does this leave us with the notion of Balzac's realism? Surely as levels of falsehood are peeled away in order to reveal further transgressions, hypocrisies and mysteries, any impression of realism must be in some sense devalued? If what lies beneath the false surface of the theatre and of society is also false and if all of life is theatre then the 'real' remains unknowable. Thus Balzac's treatment of the theatre in his novels becomes self-subverting, and reveals that his self-appointed task is simply not achievable – the *histoire secrète* is as false as the *histoire officielle*.

Although this has not been a biographical study, it is important also to remember that in his own life Balzac was perhaps as great a charlatan as any of his fictional characters, professing knowledge of all things, switching roles according to circumstances, engaging in the very capitalistic enterprises which he criticised, writing under pseudonyms, posturing as artist and businessman, monk and lover, moralist and observer, poet and journalist, and Balzac we must remember is not only the observer but also very much the product of the society which he set out to uncover. As Graham Robb's recent biography of Balzac confirms, it is impossible to ascribe any fixed notion of reality or truth to Balzac's own, individual life, let alone to the vast, swirling, turbulent life represented in his novels.[4] The artist is himself the purveyor of appearances (as Balzac so clearly demonstrates in *Illusions perdues*), at his best able to convince his audience of whatever he wishes. It would certainly be a great stroke of irony on Balzac's part if, even after informing us of this, he were able to make us believe in the 'truth' of his secret history. So is the *Comédie* in fact one long theatrical illusion of which we are the dupes? Balzac's use of the *comédie* as a metaphor within his novels suggests that it might be, since almost without exception the *comédie* signifies a role-play scenario in which characters engage with varying degrees of awareness. Is the corpus a reliable social history or a brilliantly stage-managed piece of theatre? Is Balzac the father of Realism or a literary charlatan who draws us into his dream-world with such attention to physical detail that nebulous phenomena are endowed with a seemingly concrete appearance? Certainly it is possible to claim that this is so with his representation of the theatre, for although the portrayal has been shown to be historically valid, it remains partial and selective. The text, even when the total corpus is taken into consideration, refuses to yield total knowledge, for the reader is allowed to penetrate the theatre environment only on limited terms and at certain points which are convenient to Balzac. While characters within the theatre enjoy a panoramic view, our own view is constantly frustrated and obscured – we are able to penetrate

[4] Graham Robb, *Balzac* (London: Picador, 1994).

certain boxes but not others, only selected areas of the *parterre* and backstage. Reality in the theatre world of *La Comédie humaine*, as in the world at large, is ultimately unknowable.

If the notion of theatre in *La Comédie humaine* in any way undermines its position as the intertext of the realist literature of the nineteenth century then this is compensated by the way in which it reaches forward to the theatre of the modern day. Balzac's use of melodrama in particular might be seen to root him in his period, but, as Prendergast points out, melodrama in *La Comédie humaine* bears only a tenuous connection with the reassuring and ordering melodrama of the stage tradition.[5] Prendergast shows how Balzac subverts the stage melodrama principally by undermining the family unity by which it was traditionally underpinned and in which its plots were usually resolved. It is true that Balzac reworks the melodrama in this way according to his more serious purposes, and that in doing so he predicts the modern age in which the traditional family unit is no longer the basis of society. However, the points made in the present work have shown that theatre in Balzac's novels amounts to more than melodrama, and at its most profound the pervasive theatricality of *La Comédie humaine* links Balzac even more firmly with the modern age. Through the notion that 'all is theatre', and by undermining belief in the power of language, clothing and external signs to reveal 'truth', by revealing a world in which apparent order is precariously balanced over the gaping chaos of a crumbling social substructure, Balzac conveys the unknowability of the real and foreshadows the modern anxieties of the theatre of Pirandello, and Ionesco and the Absurdists.

When the fullest implications of theatre in *La Comédie humaine* are taken in to account it is impossible to dismiss Balzac as a crude melodramatist who is rooted in the nineteenth century, for his exploitation of theatre in his novels reaches back to the theatre of Molière, Shakespeare and Diderot, encompasses the influences of the Melodrama and Romantic drama, expresses his theory of the *drame bourgeois,* and reworks these in the service of a modern artistic purpose which is to suggest the theatricality of life itself and the unknowability of the real. In this respect *La Comédie humaine* remains a rich and worthy subject of study in the twentieth century,

[5] Prendergast, *Balzac: Fiction and Melodrama*, pp. 175-179.

the possibilities of which remain, as asserted by Michel Butor, far from exhausted:

> L'œuvre de Balzac est incomparablement plus révolutionnaire qu'il n'apparaît à une lecture superficielle et fragmentaire; parmi les nouveautés qu'elle apporte, certaines ont été exploitées systématiquement au cours du XIXe siècle, d'autres n'ont trouvé d'échos que dans les œuvres les plus originales du XIXe, et cette fécondité est bien loin d'être encore épuisée.[6]

[6] Michel Butor, 'Balzac et la réalité', in *Répertoire I* (Paris: Minuit,1960), p. 81. Butor goes on to explain that these 'nouveautés' include Balzac's promotion of experimentation with the novel form (through the agent of Daniel d'Arthez in *Illusions perdues*), and the scheme of recurring characters which creates a multiplication of temporal planes within the total work.

APPENDIX I

INDEX OF THEATRICAL METAPHORS
IN *LA COMEDIE HUMAINE*

This index, which does not claim to be exhaustive, gives examples of metaphorical references to the theatre and its related professions, which do not contain explicit comparisons to named playwrights, characters or actors. The references, which are grouped according to the scheme employed in chapter 4, give the title of the novel according to the list of abbreviations given on pages 5-8 of the present work, followed by the volume and page number of the Pléiade edition of *La Comédie humaine*.

I.a.   *Comédie, scène, vaudeville*

This category of metaphor relates in particular to situations of social role-play, posturing, concealment of truth and social intrigue.

B, II, 827	*IP*, V, 557
B, II, 856	*IP*, V, 600
Be., VII, 381	*IP*, V, 653
BS, I, 124	*IP*, V, 732
CA, IV, 1020	*MM*, I, 500
CA, IV, 1025	*MM*, I, 600
CM, III, 551	*MM*, I, 612
CM, III, 561	*MM*, I, 648
CM, III, 582	*PG*, III, 142
CP, VII, 549	*R*, IV, 403
CP, VII, 630	*SetM*, VI, 545
EG, III, 1092	*SetM*, VI, 567
EG, III, 1148	*UM*, III, 799
F, V, 898	*UM*, III, 850
FYO, V, 1071	*UM*, III, 883
Gau., VII, 849	*UM*, III, 914
Gb., II, 976	

I.b.   *Drame, tragédie, drame bourgeois*

The metaphor of the *drame* is almost always synonymous with the notion of *tragédie*. Most of these metaphors contain the sense of reversals of fortune and catastrophic events in lives which are otherwise ordinary and unremarkable, and in many instances serve to define Balzac's vision of the *drame bourgeois*.

Ad., IX, 1014	*Mes.*, II, 395
B, II, 605	*MD*, IV, 649
B, II, 626	*MD*, IV, 657
B, II, 748	*MJM*, I, 267
B, II, 821	*MJM*, I, 292
B, II, 856	*MM*, I, 480
Cath., XI, 388	*P*, IV, 34
CB, VI, 272	*P*, IV, 98
Ch., VIII, 908	*P*, IV, 141
Ch., VIII, 970	*P*, IV, 152
Ch., VIII, 1007	*Pay.*, IX, 65
Ch., VIII, 1015	*Pay.*, IX, 134
Ch., VIII, 1025	*Pay.*, IX, 253
Col., III, 315	*PCh.*, X, 97
Col., III, 369	*PG*, III, 49 x2
CP, VII, 489	*PG*, III, 113
CP, VII, 535	*PMV*, XII, 169
CP, VII, 630	*RA*, IX, 683
CT, IV, 200	*SetM*, VI, 674
CV, IX, 690	*SetM*, VI, 700
CV, IX, 699	*SetM*, VI, 789
DA, VIII, 755	*SetM*, VI, 854
DA, VIII, 771	*SPC*, VI, 979
DF, II, 114	*SPC*, VI, 991
DL, V, 934	*SPC*, VI, 997
DV, I, 746	*TA*, VIII, 607
EG, III, 1193	*TA*, VIII, 643
F, V, 796	*TA*, VIII, 653
F, V, 812	
F, V, 866	

I.c.   *Théâtre, spectacle, mise en scène, coulisses*

In these examples the image of the theatre is used to denote a location for action, a spectacle to be seen, or an event waiting to happen.

Ad., X, 1000	*Ma.*, IX, 1082
B, II, 692	*MCP*, I, 89
B, II, 819	*MD*, IV, 731
BS, I, 156	*MD*, IV, 740
CA, IV, 1011	*MJM*, I, 222
Ch., VIII, 919	*MM*, I, 502
CM, III, 544	*MM*, I, 623-624
CP, VII, 559	*MM*, I, 628
CV, IX, 699	*MM*, I, 649-650
CV, IX, 810	*P*, IV, 69
E, VII, 895	*P*, IV, 625
E, VII, 944	*P*, IV, 700
E, VII, 946	*PC*, XII, 800
EG, III, 1040	*PG*, III, 179
EHC, VIII, 339	*PG*, III, 186
FE, II, 285	*PMV*, XII, 171
FE, II, 310	*SetM*, VI, 828
FE, II, 349	*TA*, VIII, 503-504
F30, II, 1106	*TA*, VIII, 648
H, II, 593	
IP, V, 174	
IP, V, 249	
IP, V, 270	
IP, V, 279	
IP, V, 419	
IP, V, 655	

I.d.   *Troisième dessous, machines, trappe*

These images occur frequently in *Illusions perdues,* where much of the action takes place in the backstage of the Panorama-Dramatique (see chapter 4, pp. 212-221), but may also be found in a small number of other novels.

Be., VII, 228	*PMV,* II, 172
Be., VII, 388	*S.* VI, 1050
DF, II, 36	*SetM,* VI, 828
MCP, I, 89	

I.e.   *Acteur, comédien, auteur, directeur*

The image of the actor or actress in most instances relates to the metaphor of social role play. The author or director is often used as an image to convey the control which certain characters have over the lives of others.

B, II, 826	*Mes.,* II, 395
B, II, 902	*MM,* I, 593
B, II, 932-933	*MM,* I, 600
Be., VII, 68	*MM,* I, 612
Be., VII, 258	*MM,* I, 649-650
Be., VII, 304	*MM,* I, 673
BS, I, 124	*MM,* I, 681
BS, I, 156	*MM,* I, 682
CA, IV, 1010	*Pay.,* IX, 128
CA, IV, 1020	*PG,* III, 161
Ch., VIII, 925	*PMV,* XII, 171
Ch., VIII, 974	*S,* VI, 1063
Ch., VIII, 975	*SetM,* VI, 585
Ch., VIII, 992	*SetM,* VI, 735
Ch., VIII, 1043	*SetM,* VI, 835
Ch., VIII, 1120	*SetM,* VI, 837
Col., III, 359	*SetM,* VI, 886
Col., III, 362	*SPC,* VI, 949
CP, VII, 552	*SPC,* VI, 972

CM, III, 582
DA, VIII, 731
DA, VIII, 755
E, VII, 919
E, VII, 960
EG, III, 1092
EG, III, 1052
EM, IX, 910
FE, II, 334
F30, II, 1084
F30, II, 1106
Gau., VII, 848
Gb., II, 976
H, II, 570
H, II, 593
IP, V, 554
IP, V, 578
IP, V, 732

SPC, VI, 989
SPC, VI, 1004
TA, VIII, 552
TA, VIII, 564
TA, VIII, 653
UM, III, 883

I.f.   *Dénouement, exposition, acte*

The vocabulary of the formal structures of the play is often used in a figurative sense to mark the different episodes of action and description in the novels.

B, II, 818
Be., VII, 186
Bou., VIII, 23
BS, I, 124
Ch., VIII, 1065
Ch., VIII, 1069
Ch., VIII, 1186
Ch., VIII, 1200
CV, IV, 200
EG, III, 1192
EG, III, 1193
EG, III, 1201

Gau., VII,
IP, V, 711
MJM, I, 292
Pay., IX, 128
PCh., X, 97
PG, III, 126
PG, III, 154
PMV, XII, 169
SetM, VI, 798
UM, III, 883

APPENDIX II

INDEX OF REFERENCES TO DRAMATISTS AND THEIR WORKS IN *LA COMEDIE HUMAINE*

The name of the dramatist is followed by details of the references to his name. These are followed by details of references to specific works and to characters within the works. Although all general references to the name of the author have been included, references to any individual works outside the dramatic field have not been listed.

II.a.   Contemporary Dramatists

ANTIER (Benjamin) [1787-1870], dramatist.
　　L'Auberge des Adrets: F, V, 895; *SetM*, VI, 919; *DA*, VIII, 740.
　　Robert Macaire, Robert Macaire: *FM*, II, 234; *R*, VI, 328; *MN*, VI, 358; *SetM*, VI, 920; *DA*, VIII, 797; *PMV*, XII, 47.

BRAZIER (Nicolas) [1783-1838], dramatist and lyricist.
　　Les Cuisinières: CB, VI, 137.
　　La Famille improvisée: HA, VII, 787.

CARMOUCHE (Pierre-François-Adolphe) [1797-1868], dramatist.
　　La Neige ou l'Eginard de campagne: PVS, XII, 269.

COURCY (Frédéric de) [1795-1862], dramatist who collaborated with Scribe at the Gymnase during the Restoration period: *IP*, V, 435, 436.

DELAVIGNE (Germain) [1790-1868], vaudevilliste.
　　L'Héritière: MM, I, 618.
　　Robert le Diable: IP, V, 706; *Be.*, VII, 95; *Gam.*, X, 499-510.

DELAVIGNE (Jean-François-Casimir) [1793-1843], brother of the above, poet and dramatist: *IP*, V, 152, 299, 337, 352, 368, 369, 648.

Marino Faliero: *MI*, XII, 731.

DUCANGE (Victor-Henri-Joseph Brahain, dit) [1783-1833], writer and dramatist: *IP*, V, 300-302, 351, 362, 469.
  Calas: IP, V, 469.
  Trente ans ou la Vie d'un joueur: *R*, IV, 472.

DUMAS (Alexandre Dumas Davy de La Pailleterie, dit Alexandre) [1802-1870], writer and dramatist.
  Richard d'Arlington: *SetM*, VI, 619, 620, 628.

DUMERSAN (Théophile Marion du Mersan, dit) [1780-1849], dramatist.
  Les Anglaises pour rire: *AS*, I, 916.
  Les Cuisinières: CB, VI, 137.
  Les Saltimbanques: E, VII, 947; *CSS*, VII, 1162, 1163, 1208.
  Bilboquet: *E*, VII, 947.
  Le Soldat laboureur: *R*, IV, 313.

DUPATY (Victor-Guy, baron) [1775-1851], poet and dramatist: *ES*, XII, 542.

DUPETIT-MERE (Frédéric) [1785-1827], dramatist: *IP*, V, 469.
  La Famille d'Anglade: *DV*, I, 865.
  Le Fils banni: R, IV, 340.
  La Vallée du torrent: F30, II, 1151.

HUGO (Victor-Marie, vicomte) [1802-1885], writer: *IP*, V, 123; *MM*, I, 496, 505, 510, 517; *AS*, I, 920; *MD*, IV, 673, 707; *IP*, V, 152, 164, 238, 337, 368, 369, 400, 454, 648; *Pre.E*, VII, 888; *CSS*, VII, 1203, 1205.
  Lucrèce Borgia: Be., VII, 235; *CSS*, VII, 1181.
  Marion Delorme: Ma., X, 1067.
  Ruy Blas: MJM, I, 246 (n. 2); *MM*, I, 573 (n. 1).

MARTAINVILLE (Alphonse-Louis-Dieudonne) [1776-1830], dramatist and founder of the *Drapeau blanc: IP*, V, 515, 516, 519,

520, 524, 528, 529, 531, 538, 542. These references to Martainville are in the context of his journalistic rather than dramatic activities.

MATURIN (Charles Robert) [1782-1824], dramatist and novelist: *MM*, I 508; *F30*, II, 1096; *CA*, IV, 976; *IP*, V, 373; *SetM*, VI, 813; *Pré.PCh.*, X, 47; *MR*, X, 387.
  Bertram ou le Château de Saint-Aldobrand: *IP*, V, 373; *Pre.PCh.*, X, 47.

MERVILLE (Pierre-François Camus, dit) [1781-1853], actor and dramatist: *IP*, V, 310.

NODIER (Jean-Charles-Emmanuel) [1780-1844], writer: *MM*, I, 508, 513; *AS*, I, 920; *H*, II, 546; *AEF*, III, 704, 705; *MD*, IV, 673, 682; *IP*, V, 373, 648; *SetM*, VI, 829; *Pr.B*, VII, 810; *PVS*, XII, 249, 261, 262, 296; *Ech.*, XII, 488; *DxA*, XII, 679; *AIH*, XII, 775, 785.
  Bertram ou le Pirate: *IP*, V, 373 (n. 1).

PICARD (Louis-Benoit) [1769-1828], comic actor and dramatist: *P*, IV, 123; *IP*, V, 302, 426.
  La Maison en loterie: *MM*, I, 667; *P*, IV, 123; *IP*, V, 426.
  Rigaudin(Trigaudin): *MM*, I, 667; *P*, IV, 123; *IP*, V, 426; *Pr.B*, VII, 811.

PIXERECOURT (René-Charles Guilbert de) [1773-1844], dramatist: *MD*, IV, 707; *E*, VII, 951 (n. 1).
  Le Mont sauvage: *PG*, III, 203.
  Les Ruines de Babylone: *DV*, I, 857, 868.

SCRIBE (Augustin-Eugène) [1791-1861], dramatist: *MD*, IV, 673, 759; *IP*, V, 366, 435; *SetM*, VI, 603; *PGr.*, VI, 1094; *E*, VII, 951; *Pre.PCh.*, X, 48 (n. 2); *Phy.*, XI, 1158 (n. 3); *Ep.T.* XII, 433.
  Le Charlatanisme: *IP*, V, 113.
  La Dame blanche: *CA*, IV, 1015; *Ad.*, X, 979; *Gam.*, X, 513.
  Gustave III or *le Bal masqué*: *FM*, II, 233; *MN*, VI, 330
  L'Héritière: *MM*, I, 618.
  La Muette de Portici: *Pré. PCh.*, X, 55.
  L'Ours et le Pacha: *SetM*, VI, 603 (n. 1).

Robert le Diable: IP, V, 706; *Be.,* VII, 95;*Gam.,* X, 499-510.
Valentine: MD, IV, 688.

VAREZ (François) [circa. 1780-1857], dramatist and producer at the Ambigu-Comique and the Gaîté.
Calas: IP, V, 469.

VIGNY (Alfred-Victor, comte de) [1797-1863], writer: *MM,* I, 517; *DL,* V, 1012.
Chatterton: FE, II, 'le suicide régnait alors à Paris' 354.

II. b. Dramatists belonging to previous centuries

BEAUMARCHAIS (Pierre-Augustin Caron de) [1732-1799], writer: *FE,* II, 343; *B,* II, 731; *VF,* IV, 842; *CA,* IV, 987, 996; *Pré.IP,* V, 116; *IP,* V, 171, 208, 378, 522; *SetM,* VI, 522, 605; *Be.,* VII, 245; *CP,* VII, 631; *Pré.E,* VII, 885, 886; *MC,* IX, 490; *Cath.,* XI, 168, *PVS,* XII, 291; *MI,*XII,721.
Le Barbier de Séville: H, II, 555; *IG,* IV, 577; *VF,* IV, 875 (n. 1); *Pré.E,* VII, 892.
Almaviva: *IP,* V, 397; *Bou.,* VIII, 'Lindor' 33; *Gam.,* X, 461; *Phy.,* XI, 1034.
Bartholo: *F,* V, 849; *Ma.,* X, 1042, 1043; *Phy.,* XI, 1038.
Bazile: *UM,* III, 907.
Figaro: *MJM,* I, 293, 391; *DV,* I, 787; *H,* II, 555; *In.,* III, 425; *CA,* IV, 1036; *Pré. IP,* V, 116; *IP,* V 208; *FYO,* V, 1071; *SetM,* VI, 522; *Be.,* VII, 245; *Phy.,* XI, 1034; *Cath.,* IX, 445.
Rosine: *Gam.,* X, 461.
Le Mariage de Figaro: MD, IV, 680; *CA,* IV, 1003; *SetM,* VI, 592; *Pré.E,* VII, 892; *EHC,* VIII, 261; *DA,* VIII, 766; *PCh.,* X, 123; *Phy.,* XI, 930.
Chérubin: *B,* II, 706, 731; *PG,* III, 157; *VF,* IV, 842; *FYO,* V, 1057; *CP,* VII, 647, 683; *E,* VII, 945; *Phy.,* XI, 930.
Figaro: *E,* VII, 928; *Phy.,* XI, 947.
Marceline: *VF,* IV, 842.
Suzanne: *CB,* VI, 227; *Phy.,* XI, 1040.
La Mère coupable. Begearss: *Cath.,* XI, 168.

CORNEILLE (Pierre) [1606-1684], dramatist: *Pré.CH*, I, 7; *MJM*, I, 250; *MM*, I, 549 (n. 1); *UM*, III, 863 (n. 1); *VF*, IV, 926; *IP*, V, 177, 457; *CB*, VI, 166, 174; *Pré.E*, VII, 886, 889; *Pré.PCh.*, X, 55; *Gam.*, X, 496; *Ma.*, X, 1067; *LL*, XI, 649; *Phy.*, XI, 942; *Pré.*, XII, 812, 813.
  Le Cid: *MJM*, I, 233; *Fré.*, XII, 817.
  Chimène: *MJM*, I, 233.
  Rodrigue: *MJM*, I, 233; *CB*, VI, 138; *Fré.*, XII, 817.
  Cinna: *B*, II, p32 (n. 1); *PG*, III, 130 (n. 1); *Be.*, VII, 183 (n. 3); *CP*, VIII, 653 (n. 1); *CSS*, VII, 1181 (n. 2).
  Auguste: *Bou.*, VIII, 56.
  Cinna: *IP*, V, 457.
  Octave: *IP*, V, 457.
  Héraclius: *MM*, I, 673 (n. 1).
  Horace: *Be.*, VII, 122 (n. 2)
  Médée, Médée: *MJM*, I, 316; *FE*, II, 352; *DL*, V, 935; *MC*, IX, 390; *CV*, IX, 696.
  Nicomède, Nicomède: *SetM*, VI, 920.

LOPE DE VEGA (Lope-Félix de Vega Carpio, dit) [1562-1635] Spanish poet and dramatist: *B*, II, 688; *MD*, IV, 759; *DL*, V, 947; *Pré.E*, VII, 888; *Fré.*, XII, 812.
  Le Chien du jardinier (*El Perro del Hortelano*): *DL*, V, 947; *DA*, VIII, 746 (n. 1).

MOLIERE (Jean-Baptiste Poquelin, dit) [1622-1673], player and comic dramatist: *Pré.CH*, I, 7; *MJM*, I, 324; *MM*, I, 508, 517, 525, 527, 545, 551, 642, 645, 652; *DV*, I, 803, 815; *AS*, I, 931; *Pré.FE*, II, 269; *FE*, II, 300, 314, 317; *B*, II, 912; *PG*, III, 158; *Ath.*, III, 393; *P*, IV, 147; *MD*, IV, 745; *VF*, IV, 859; *Pré.CA*, IV, 963; *CA*, IV, 1034; *Pré.IP*, V, 116; *IP*, V, 123, 207, 208, 295, 314, 316, 317, 397, 457, 459; *CB*, VI, 69, 166, 190; *SetM*, VI, 691, 733; *VF*, VI, 839; *Gau.*, VII, 848; *Pré.E.*, VII, 880; *Bou.*, VIII, 52, 90; *Pay.*, IX, 131; *CV*, IX, 644; *Lys.*, IX, 1108 *ELV*, XI, 486; *LL*, XI, 649; *Phy.*, XI, 985, 987, 1093; *PVS*, XII, 277, 278; *VV*, XII, 357; *HP*, XII, 577; *AIH*, XII, 779; *Fré.*, XII, 812, 813.
  L'Amour médecin, Josse: *UM*, III, 846; *P*, IV, 60; *MN*, VI, 373; *Phy.*, XI, 1119.
  L'Avare: *PMV*, XII, 85 (n. 3).

Harpagon: *R*, IV, 426; *MD*, IV, 740; *CB*, VI, 243; *SPC*, VI, 954; *CP*, VII, 575; *Pay.*, IX, 242; *CV*, IX, 644; *Cath.*, XI, 341.

Le Bourgeois gentilhomme: IP, V, 426.

Jourdain: *PVS*, XIII, 261.

Le Mamamouchi: *IP*, V, 426.

Le Dépit amoureux, Gros-René: *Be.*, VII, 319 (n. 1)

Don Juan: CA, IV, 1034.

Dimanche: *Gb.*, II, 976; *IP*, V, 662; *EHC*, VIII, 350; *ELV*, XI, 486.

Don Juan: *AEF*, III, 712; *IP*, V, 662; *ELV*, XI, 486.

L'Ecole des femmes: DV, I, 803 (n. 1); *B*, II, 912 (n. 4); *MD*, IV, 680; *Phy.*, XI, 970; *PMV*, XII, 119 (n. 1).

Agnès: *AS*, I, 931, 931; *FE*, II, 283; *MD*, IV, 677; *VF*, IV, 859; *CA*, IV, 1015; *PMV*, XII, 119.

Alain: *Be.*, VII, 319 (n. 1).

Arnolphe: *DV*, I, 803; *FE*, II, 283; *B*, II, 912; *MD*, IV, 677.

L'Etourdi: MM, I, 548 (n. 3); *CM*, III, 640 (n. 1); *Phy.*, XI, 974 (n. 2).

L'Etourdi: *E*, VII, 1049.

Mascarille: *E*, VII, 1049; *Phy.*, XI, 1108.

Les Femmes savantes: MM, I, 645 (n. 1); *IP*, V, 434 (n. 2); *Pré.E.*, VII, 886 (n. 2).

Bélise: *MM*, I, 542.

Chrysale: *MM*, I, 546, 548; *CB*, VI, 174.

Henriette: *MM*, I, 542.

Les Fourberies de Scapin: MM, I, 545 (n. 1).

Argante: *MM*, I, 548.

Géronte: *MM*, I, 545; *MD*, IV, 745; *Fré.*, XII, 816.

Léandre: *MD*, IV, 745.

Scapin: *R*, IV, 379, 447; *CB*, VI, 276; *CP*, VII, 577; *Ch.*, VIII, 1191;   *Fré.*, XII, 816.

Georges Dandin, Georges Dandin: *Phy.*, XI, 915.

Le Malade imaginaire, Argan: *H*, II, 529.

Le Médecin malgré lui: F30, II, 263 (n. 1); *E*, VII, 968 (n. 1); *PCh.*, X, 263 (n. 1).

Géronte: *CA*, IV, 1024.

Sganarelle: *F30*, II, 124; *CA*, IV, 1024.

Le Misanthrope: MJM, I, 324; *MM*, I, 545; *MN,* VI, 362.

Alceste: *MM*, I, 527, 'le sublime raisonneur' 545; *Fir.*, II, 153; *FE*, II, 304; *PG*, III, 158; *CM*, III, 575; *MD*, IV, 785; *IP*, V, 208; *Pré.CB*, VI, 35; *SetM*, VI, 437, 624; *CP*, VII, 568, 624; *Lys*, IX, 1088; *PMV*, XII, 103.

Arsinoé: *CM*, III, 592; *PCh.*, X, 157.

Célimène: *BS*, I, 120; *MJM*, I, 324; *Fir.*, II, 153; *FE*, II, 283; *B*, II, 931; *CM*, III, 592; *CA*, IV, 1036, 1093; *IP*, V, 282; *Be.*, VII, 257; *E*, VII, 928; *DA*, VIII, 769; *PMV*, XII, 135.

Eliante: *FE*, II, 300; *CP*, VII, 492.

Oronte: *MM*, I, 548.

Philinte: *FE*, II, 304; *MD*, IV, 785; *Pré.IP*, V, 116; *IP*, V, 457; *Pré.CB*, VI, 35; *SetM*, VI, 437; *Pay.*, IX, 135; *Lys*, IX, 1088; *PMV*, XII, 103.

Monsieur de Pourceaugnac, Pourceaugnac: *Pay.*, IX, 270.

Les Précieuses ridicules: CB, VI, 72 (n. 2); *Ech.*, XII, 489.

Mascarille: *BS*, I, 116; *CA*, IV, 1024; *Phy.*, XI, 1018; *ES*, XII, 544.

Tartuffe: FE, II, 305 (n. 2); *MD*, IV, 680, 697; *IP*, V, 205 (n. 1); *SPC*, VI, 979; *Bou.*, VIII, 66; *Pay.*, IX, 131.

Dorine: *SetM*, VI, 742; *CP*, VII, 577; *CSS*, VII, 1174; *HP*, XII, 572, 580.

Elmire: *SetM*, VI, 505; *Be.*, VII, 57.

Laurent: *E*, VII, 1074.

Loyal: *Th.*, XII, 591.

Marianne: *DxA*, XII, 678.

Orgon: *MM*, I, 603; *B*, II, 926; *MD*, IV, 697; *CB*, VI, 74; *Pay.*, IX, 131

Tartuffe: *FM*, II, 213; *FE*, II, 305 (n. 2); *Ath.*, III, 393; *P*, IV, 83, 130; *Pré.IP*, V, 116; *IP*, V, 404, 637; *CB*, VI, 74; *MN*, VI, 334 (n. 1); *SetM*, VI, 505, 592, 765 (n. 1); *Be.*, VII, 57; *CP*, VII, 571, 624, 710; *Bou.*, VIII, 21, 66, 67, 90; *Pay.*, IX, 131; *PMV*, XII, 156; *MI*, XII, 731.

Valère: *DxA*, XII, 678.

RACINE (Jean) [1639-1699], poète dramatique: *MJM*, I, 285; *MM*, I, 517; *FE*, II, 321; *IP*, V, 171, 177; *CB*, VI, 69, 95, 104, 166, 174; *Be.*, VII, 325; *Pré.E*, VII, 888; *EHC*, VIII, 252; *PCh.*, X, 218; *Gam.*, X,

496; *LL*, XI, 649; *PVS*, XII, 293; *VV*, XII, 355-357; *AIH*, XII, 779; *Fré.*, XII, 812, 813.

> *Andromaque*: *MJM*, I, 360 (n. 1); *MD*, IV, 680.
> Pyrrhus: *FD*, XII, 502.
> *Athalie*: *AS*, I, 916; *Be.*, VII, 325 (n. 3).
> *Bajazet*: *MD*, IV, 674 (n. 1); *Be.*, VII, 435 (n. 1).
> *Bérénice*: *MJM*, I, 285; *CB*, VI, 95; *Be.*, VII, 179 (n. 1).
> *Britannicus*: *DV*, I, 850; *Pr.B*, VII, 811; *Lys*, IX, 978.
> Agrippine: *R*, IV, 403.
> Néron: *DV*, I, 850; *Col.*, III, 319; *Lys*, IX, 811; *Th.*, XII, 593.
> *Mithridate:MD*, IV, 680.
> *Phedre:* *MD*, IV, 680; *IP*, V, 706; *Be.*, VII, 131 (n. 1), 179 (n. 1), 262, 358 (n. 4); *AR*, XI, 119 (n. 2).

SHAKESPEARE (William) [1564-1616], dramatist, player and poet: *MJM*, I, 229; *MM*, I, 603, 612; *Ven.*, I, 1089; *FM*, II, 223; *FE*, II, 313; *B*, II, 688, 912; *AEF*, III, 681; *Pré.P*, IV, 27; *IP*, V, 459; *SetM*, VI, 515; *PP*, VII, 53; *Be.*, VII, 105, 119, 245, 403; *CP*, VII, 586, 591; *Lys*, IX, 1142; *PCh.*, X, 112; *Cath.*, XI, 168; *Phy.*, XI, 1009; *PMV*, XII, 88; *PVS*, XII, 278; *MI*, XII, 720.

> *Beaucoup de bruit pour rien*: *MM*, I, 612.
> Béatrix: *MM*, I, 612.
> *Hamlet:* *Be.*, VII, 105; *CP*, VII, 591; *Phy.*, XI, 1009.
> Claudius: *CB*, VI, 248; *Lys*,IX, 1142; *Sér.*, XI, 763.
> Hamlet: *MM*, I, 546, 576; *CB*, VI, 248; *Lys*, IX, 1142; *Sér.*, XI, 763.
> *Henry IV*, Falstaff: *Cath.*, xI, 168.
> *Henry V*, Henry V: *R*, IV, 366.
> *Les Joyeuses Commères de Windsor*, Falstaff: *Cath.*, XI, 168.
> *Macbeth*: *Be.*, VII, 403; *PCh.*, X, 123, 181.
> Banquo: *DA*, VIII, 807; *PCh.*, X, 181.
> Lady Macbeth: *CP*, VII, 628.
> Macbeth: *IP*, V, 422; *Lys*, IX, 1086.
> Sorcières (les trois): *IP*, V, 422; *PCh.*, X, 123.
> *Le Marchand de Venise*, Shylock: *FE*, II, 369; *IP*, V, 354; *CB*, VI, 107; *E*, VII, 1094.
> *Othello*: *AEF*, III, 681; *SetM*, VI, 484; *Phy.*, XI, 119.

Desdemona: *MJM,* I, 229; *AEF,* III, 683; *CA,* IV, 1041; *PMV,* XII, 88.

Iago: *H,* II, 585; *B,* II, 912; *Be.,* VII, 152.

Othello: *MJM,* I, 229; *MM,* I, 679; *H,* II, 544, 585; *B,* II, 912; *F30,* II, 1182; *AEF,* III, 679, 681-683; *CA,* IV, 1041; *DL,* V, 984; *FYO,* V, 1075; *SetM,* VI, 484; *SPC,* VI, 994; *Be.,* VII, 210, 223, 397, 413; *Phy.,* XI, 1050, 119; *PMV,* XII, 88, 181.

Richard III, Margaret: *R,* IV, 515.

Richard: *R,* IV, 515; *VF,* IV, 892, 930; *Be.,* VII, 152; *ZM,* VIII, 843; *RA,* X, 785.

Roméo et Juliette, Capulet (les): *Do.,* X, 610.

Juliette: *MM,* I, 548; *Ven.,* I, 1089; *Mes.,* II, 399; *SetM,* VI, 688, 787; *DA,* VIIII, 791; *Lys,* IX, 1142.

Montaigu (les): *Do.,* X, 610.

Roméo: *MM,* I, 548; *Ven.,* I, 1089; *SetM,* VI, 688, 787; *DA,* VIII, 791; *Lys,* IX, 1142.

La Tempête: Be., VII, 119.

Ariel: *Be.,* VII, 119.

Caliban: *UM,* III, 770; *Be.,* VII, 119; *PCh.,* X, 68.

Prospero: *Be.,* VII, 119.

VOLTAIRE (François-Marie Arouet, dit) [1694-1778], writer: *MM,* I, 517, 641, 647, 662; *DV,* I, 767, 780, 836; *PM,* II, 115; *Fir.,* II, 149; *Pré.FE,* II, 269; *B,* II, 720; *Gb.,* II, 986, 990; *PG,* III, 51; *AEF,* III, 697; *UM,* III, 784, 786, 822; *Pré.P,* IV, 27; *CT,* IV, 216; *MD,* IV, 759; *CA,* IV, 996; *IP,* V, 171, 222, 305, 330, 443, 460, 648, 653, 707; *F,* V, 817; *DL,* V, 950; *CB,* VI, 69, 150, 164, 166, 174, 220; *SetM,* VI, 523, 605; *Be.,* VII, 106, 115, 246, 348, 434; *Pre.E,* VII, 883, 885, 886, 887, 894; *CSS,* VII, 1204, 1205; *Gam.,* X, 491; *Cath.,* XI, 167, 338, 449; *LL,* XI, 640, 649.

Alzire: Pre.Ch., VIII, 899.

Mahomet: Gam., X, 491.

Mahomet: *VF,* IV, 876.

Olympie: CB, VI, 220.

Tancrède: DA, VII, 795.

Zaïre, Zaire: *Be.,* VII, 158.

Chatillon: *PCh.,* X, 209.

Nérestan: *VF,* IV, 922; *MC,* IX, 516.

APPENDIX III

INDEX OF REAL ACTORS, ACTRESSES AND DIRECTORS
REFERRED TO IN *LA COMEDIE HUMAINE*

BAPTISTE (Nicolas-Baptiste Anselme, dit) [1761-1835], actor with the Comédie-Française from 1793 to 1828: *IP*, V, 299.

BAPTISTE cadet (Paul-Eustache Anselme, dit) [1765-1839], brother of the above, actor with the Comédie-Française from 1792 to 1822: *IP*, V, 299; *Pay.*, IX, 77.

BARON père (André Boyron, dit) [circa. 1600-1655], actor: *R*, I, 360.

BARON (Michel Boyron, dit) [1653-1729], son of the above, actor with Molière's troupe: *MM*, I, 642; *FE*, II, 321; *Fre.*, XII, 781.

BOUFFE (Hugues-Marie-Desiré) [1800-1888], comic actor who began his career at the Panorama-Dramatique in 1822: *MD*, IV, 674; *IP*, V, 391, 396, 397; *HA*, VII, 794.

BRUNET (Jean-Joseph Mira, dit) [1766-1853], comic actor: *AS*, I, 916.

CLAIRON (Claire-Joseph Leris, dite Hippolyte Leris de la Tude, puis Mlle) [1723-1803], actress with the Comédie-Française from 1743 to 1765: *FE*, II, 321.

CONTAT (Louise-Françoise) [1760-1813], actress witht he Comédie-Française from 1777 to 1803: *FE*, II, 321.

CORSSE (Jean-Baptiste Labenette, dit) [1759-1815], actor and director at the Ambigu-Comique from 1800: *Th.*, XII, 594.

CORSSE (Henriette-Bastienne Ponsignon, dite Mme), wife of the above who played at the Montansier theatre and at the Ambigu-Comique: *Th.*, XII, 594.

DEJAZET (Pauline-Virginie) [1789-1875], actress: *CSS*, VII, 1212 (n. 1); *Be.*, VII, 160.

DORVAL (Marie-Thomase-Amélie) [1798-1849], actress: *Postface* H_{13}, V, IIII.

DUPONT (Charlotte-Louise-Valentine Rougeault de La Fosse, dite Mlle) [1791-1864], actress with the Comédie-Française from 1812 to 1840: *SetM*, VI, 581.

DUPUIS (Antoinette-Nicole, dite Adèle) [1789-1847], actress known as the Mlle Mars of the boulevard: *IP*, V, 469.

ELSSLER (Franziska, dite Fanny) [1810-1884], Austrian dancer who made her début in Paris in 1834: *FM*, II, 'Essler' 222; *MD*, IV, 700 (n. 2); *SetM*, VI, 494; *CSS*, VII, 1160; *PMV*, XII, 99 (n. 2).

FAY (Jeanne-Louise-Léontine Baron, dite Léontine) [1810-1876], actress who established her career at the Gymnase before joining the Comédie-Française in 1835 where she remained until 1840: *IP*, V, 536.

FLEURIET, dite LOLOTTE (Elisabeth-Florestine) [1804-1823], actress at the Gymnase: *CM*, III, 644; *IP*, V, 536.

FLEURY (Abraham-Joseph Laute de Fleury, dit) [1750-1822], actor with the Comédie-Française from 1774-1818: *VF*, IV, 815 (n. 2); *IP*, V, 299.

FLORVILLE (Mlle) [dates unknown], actress employed at the Panorama-Dramatique as *sixième-amoureuse*: *IP*, V, 373, 374, 375.

GEORGE (Marguerite-Joséphine Weimer, dite Mlle) [1787-1867], actress with the Comédie-Française from 1802-1808 and from 1813-1818: *H,* II, 530 (n. 3); *R,* IV, 403; *MD,* IV, 674; *Be.,* VII, 74.

GREVIN (Antoine Tauge, dit) [1785-1828], actor at the Gaîté from 1818: *Th.,* XII, 593 (var. b.).

LAFON (Pierre Rapenouille, dit) [1773-1846], actor with the Comédie-Française from 1800 to 1830: *CB,* VI, 138; *Bou.,* VIII, 92 (n. 2).

LAGUERRE (Marie-Josephine ou Marie-Sophie) [1755-1783], lead soprano at the Opéra before the Revolution: *Pr.B,* VII, 810; *Pay.* IX, 57, 59, 60, 64, 129-131, 149, 150, 201, 256, 258, 260, 261, 264, 279 (n. 1).

LE KAIN (Henri-Louis Cain, dit) [1729-1778], actor with the Comédie-Française from 1750 until his death: Balzac refers to him as 'Lekain': *MCP,* I, 67; *FE,* II, 321.

LEMAITRE (Antoine-Louis-Prosper Lemaître, dit Frédérick) [1800-1876], actor and dramatist: *R,* IV, 472 (n. 1), 524; *MD,* IV, 674; *SetM,* VI, 534, 619; *CSS,* VII, 1162, 1697; *Bou.,* VIII, 128.

MALAGA fille (Françoise-Catherine Bénéfand, dite) [1786-unknown], daughter of a tight-rope walker, dancer and the mistress of Laurent-Jan, who is perhaps evoked in: *Phy.,* XI, 1028; *PMV,* XII, 177.

MARS (Anne-Françoise-Hippolyte Boutet, dite Mlle) [1779-1841], daughter of two actors, Jacques-Marie Boutet, known as Monvel and Jeanne-Marguerite Salvetat, known as Madame Mars. Mlle Mars was part of the troupe of the Comédie-Française from 1795 until her death: *MM,* I, 626; *FE,* II, 321, 346; *MD,* IV, 674; *CA,* IV, 1038; *IP,* V, 382, 393; *CB,* VI, 69, 138, 227; *MN,* VI, 350; *Bou.,* VIII, 128; *DA,* VIII, 760; *Phy.,* XI, 1165.

MICHOT (Antoine Michaut, dit) [1765-1826], actor with the Comédie-Française from 1791 to 1821: *IP*, V, 299; *Pay.*, IX, 77.

MILLOT (Marie-Louise-Félcité, dite Mlle), actress at the Gaîté from 1819 to 1826 and then, after a brief spell at the Porte-Saint-Martin, at the Cirque Olympique from 1827 to 1834: *IP*, V, 469.

MINETTE (Jeanne-Marie-Françoise Ménestrier, dite Mlle), later became Mme Margueritte [1789-1853], actress at the Vaudeville from 1813 to 1827 and them at the Gymnase: *IP*, V, 348.

MOLE (François-René) [1734-1802], actor with the Comédie-Française from 1760 until his death. Best known for his interpretation of the role of Almaviva in Beaumarchais' *Le Barbier de Seville*: *VF*, IV, 812, 815, 816; *Be.*, VII, 106.

MONVEL (Jaques-Marie Boutet, dit) [1745-1812], dramatist and actor at the Comédie-Française from 1770 to 1806 and father of Mlle Mars: *FE*, II, 321; *Bou.*, VIII, 56.

ODRY (Jacques-Charles) [1770-1853], actor at the Porte-Saint-Martin from 1804 to 1817 then at the Variétés unit 1841: *Pre.P*, IV, 22; *E*, VII, 1008; *CSS*, VII, 1162, 1163, 1196, 1208; *PVS*, XII, 269 (n. 2); *Ech.*, XII, 482 (n. 4).

PERCILLIEE (Marie-Anne) [1795-1852], actress at the Odéon from 1820 to 1822: *E*, VII, 1028.

PERLET (Adrien) [1795-1850], actor who divided his career between London and the Gymnase in Paris: *MR*, X, 362 (n. 3), 367.

RACHEL (Elisabeth-Félix, dite) [1821-1858], actress with the Comédie-Française from 1838 until her death: *IP*, V, 493 (n. 2), 706 (n. 1).

RAUCOURT (Françoise Clairien, dite Mlle) [1753-1815], actress with the Comédie-Française from 1772 until her death: *F*, V, 896, 897; *MC*, IX, 390.

TAGLIONI (Filippo) [1777-1871], Italian dancer and choreographer: *B*, II, 711; *SetM*, VI, 442 (n. 5); *PVS*, XII, 270; *FM*, II, 220 (n. 2).

TAGLIONI (Maria) [1804-18884], daughter of the above, dancer who first performed at the Opéra in Paris in 1827 and was principal dancer from 1829 to 1847: *DF*, II, 79; *AEF*, III, 702; *MD*, IV, 674; *FYO*, V, 1044; *Pre.B*, VII, 826; *CSS*, VII, 1160; *PVS*, XII, 262, 290, 323.

TALMA (François-Joseph) [1763-1826], tragedian with the Comédie-Française from 1787 until his death: *DV*, I, as Nero, 850; *DF*, II, 80; *FE*, II, 314, 321; *B*, II, 695; *Col.*, III, as Nero, 319; *MD*, IV, as Leicester, 789; *IP*, V, 299, 368, as Manilus, 453; *FYO*, V, as Othello, 1075; *CB*, VI, 69; *SetM*, VI, as Manilus, 479, as Nicomède, 920; *E*, VII, 1077; *Bou.*, VIII, 52, 128; *Lys.*, IX, as Nero, 978; *RA*, X, 823; *Phy.*, XI, 1083; *ES*, XII, 543; *Th.*, XII, 587, 591, as Nero 593.

VERNET (Charles-Edme) [1789-1848], actor for forty years at the Variétés: *PVS*, XII, 269.

APPENDIX IV

STAGE ADAPTATIONS OF BALZAC'S NOVELS

There have been many stage adaptations of Balzac's novels made by other dramatists. A brief summary of these appears here and further details can be found in the following works: Edmond Biré, 'La Comédie humaine au théâtre', in Honoré de Balzac, ch. XI and ch. XII, pp. 265-316; Ray Bowen, The Dramatic Construction of Balzac's Novels, pp. 124-126; and Mary Bryden, 'Staging Balzac', in French Studies Bulletin (Autumn 1994), pp. 7-11.

Le Bal de Sceaux

In September 1859, the Odéon staged Noblesse oblige, comédie en cinq actes, by Ange Le Roy de Deranious which was based on Le Bal de Sceaux. The Play was given a happy ending and was a great success.

César Birotteau

In April 1838, at the Théâtre du Panthéon, the well-known playwright Eugène Cormon presented César Birotteau, drame-vaudeville en trois actes. Cormon gave the play a happy ending, which was quite out of keeping with Balzac's conception of the story.

In October 1910, at the Théâtre Antoine, Emile Fabre presented a second version of César Birotteau, as a pièce en cinq actes. Much of the original dialogue of the novel was used, and the ending was the same as that in the novel. See: L'Illusration théatrale (1910), part 2, no. 9.

Les Chouans

In June 1837, at the Ambigu-Comique, Anthony Bérand presented Le Gars, drame en cinq actes et en six tableaux. The dénouement differed considerably from that of the novel and the play was a success.

In April 1894, the Ambigu-Comique staged a second version entitled *Les Chouans*, by Berton and Blavet, which proved to be an enormous success. The most popular scenes, including the tragic dénouement, were taken from the novel almost without alteration.

Le Colonel Chabert

In July 1832, Arago and Lurine presented *Chabert, drame-vaudeville en deux actes*, at the Vaudeville. Except for the dénouement, the plot closely followed that of the novel and much of the novel's dialogue was used. It proved a great success.

In 1852, Paul de Faulquement presented *Colonel Chabert*, with the subtitle, *La Femme à deux maris*, at the Beaumarchais theatre.

In 1888, Guyot presented *Le Colonel Chabert, comédie en deux actes,* at the Molière theatre in Brussels. The play's happy ending diverged considerably from the tragic ending of the novel.

La Cousine Bette

In January 1849, the Gymnase staged a *drame vaudeville* by Clairville entitled *Madame Marneffe*. The character of Bette was omitted from the play and Madame Marneffe was considerably altered. The play was reasonably successful and earned a considerable sum for Balzac.

Le Cousin Pons

In April 1873, the Théâtre de Cluny presented *Le Cousin Pons, drame en cinq actes*. The author introduced a love theme to the play and altered the conclusion so that Schmucke might inherit the art collection.

Eugénie Grandet

In January 1835, Bayard and Paulin presented *La Fille de l'avare* at the Gymnase. Although greatly changed from the original, the play enjoyed a great success and more than 300 performances were given.

L'Histoire des Treize

In October 1834, Ancelot and Comberousse presented a version of *La Duchesse de Langeais* at the Vaudeville under the title *l'Ami Grandet, comédie de trois actes mêlée de chants*. Again one of Balzac's most 'dramatic' works was spoiled by a banal ending.

In April 1839, Scribe and Duport presented *Les Treize* at the Opéra-Comique. The music was by Halévy.

In December 1867, Dugué and Peaucellier also presented a version of *Les Treize* at the Gaîté. The novel was skilfully adapted and the play proved a great success.

Honorine

In December 1846, the Gymnase staged Scribe's *La Protégée sans le savoir* which was taken from Balzac's Honorine and which was a great success.

Le Lys dans la vallée

In June 1853, the Comédie-Française, after having refused Balzac's own play *Mercadet* in 1849, accepted *Le Lys dans la vallée, drame en cinq actes et en prose*, by Barrière and de Beauplan. The authors included all the characters of the novel but failed to reproduce its poetry and changed the ending.

La Peau de chagrin

In February 1846, at the Cirque-Olympique, Villain de Saint-Hilaire put on *Le Cheval du diable, drame fantastique en cinq actes et sept tableaux,* with a prologue and epilogue. The play followed the novel almost step by step, reproducing the principal scenes in the life of Raphaèl de Valentin. The final tableau reveals, however, that the hero is still alive and has merely suffered a disturbing dream. This conclusion spoiled the play according to the critics who had greatly admired Balzac's handling of the theme. Nevertheless the play was cordially received by the public.

An English stage adaptation of this novel was made by Helen Parkinson in 1994 and was staged at the Bridewell Theatre in London. The philosophical and religious discussions of the novel were omitted, and emphasis was placed on the scenes with visual potential, such as the meeting with the mysterious antiques dealer, the supper party, and the trip to the theatre with Fœdora.

Le Père Goriot

In April 1835, Théaulon, de Comberousse and Jaime presented a version of *Le Père Goriot* in three acts at the Variétés. The play was very different from the novel.

A second version was presented on the same date at the Vaudeville by Ancelot and Paulin. Although this version also differed somewhat from the novel, it bore more resemblance to Balzac's original than the version staged at the Variétés.

In October 1891, Adolphe Tabarand presented a third version of *Le Père Goriot* at the Théâtre Libre. This version followed the original more closely: act I, the Vauquer boarding house; act II, the attic rooms of Goriot and Rastignac; act III, the little apartment rented by Delphine de Nucingen for Rastignac; acts IV and V, again the attic room of Goriot.

An English adaptation of *Le Père Goriot* was made by Geoffrey Beevers and staged at the Orange Tree Theatre in Richmond in Spring 1994. With imaginative use of space Beevers recreated the Maison Vauquer and the high society settings of Balzac's novel. Beevers realised the auditory potential of the original by exploiting the 'rama' game, the characteristic phrases of the boarders, and Vautrin's snatches of song to full effect.

Physiologie du mariage

In February 1839, at the Palais Royal, Ancelot and Duport staged *Dieu vous bénisse* taken from 'Méditation XXI' of the *Physiologie du mariage*.

In April 1833, Alfred de Vigny presented his *Quitte pour la peur* at the Opéra. This may have been taken from 'Méditation XXVII'.

In May 1837, at the Panthéon-Dramatique, Charles-Hubert Nô presented *La Victoire du mari* which was taken from 'MéditationXIII'.

Maître Cornélius

In September 1839, Scribe staged *Le Shérif*, which was based on *Maître Cornélius*. The music was by Halévy.

La Rabouilleuse

In 1904, Emile Fabre presented a version of *La Rabouilleuse*.

La Recherche de l'Absolu

In November 1837, the Gymnase staged *A plus Mg = O plus X, ou le Rêve d'un savant* by Bazard and de Biéville. The play barely resembled Balzac's novel and was a complete failure. Balzac commented in a letter to Madame Hanska: 'Quelques personnes m'avaient dit, en passant, que les journaux et Janin surtout, m'avaient beaucoup loué à propos d'une petite pièce prise dans *La Recherche de l'Absolu*, et tombée'. See: *LMH*, vol. II, p. 577.

Splendeurs et misères des courtisanes

In September 1882, the Théâtre des Nations staged a rendering of this long novel by Albert Miral which he called *Lydie*. The play was a complete failure.

In December 1908, the Théâtre Sarah Bernhardt presented *La Résurrection de Vautrin, pièce en un acte*, by Henriot Maigrot.

APPENDIX V

LIST OF BALZAC'S PROJECTED AND UNFINISHED PLAYS

This list has been compiled according to Balzac's correspondence and to the second volume of Milatchitch's survey of Balzac's theatre, *Le Théâtre inédit de H. de Balzac* (Paris: Hachette, 1940). Prior to 1834 the projects are difficult to date, but after this Balzac's letters to Madame Hanska are a rich source of information.

Initial Projects from 1819 to 1830

Les Deux Philosophes	1819	*Le Républicain*	1830
Sylla	1822	*La Faillite*	n.d.
Le Damné	1822	*Le Prince*	n.d.
Le Mendiant	1822	*L'Artiste*	1830
Les Courtisans	n.d.	*L'Héritier présomptif*	n.d.
La Conspiration	n.d.	*La Morte*	n.d.
L'Homme et la vie	n.d.	*L'Enfant naturel*	n.d.
L'Ecole des hommes	n.d.	*L'Homme incapable*	n.d.

Further Projects from 1830 to 1848

Les Prudhomme	1830-1848	*Les Parents pauvres*	1848
Le Roi des mendiants	1830-1849	*Monte-Cristo*	1848
L'Education du prince	1830-1848	*La Fausse Maîtresse*	1848
La Grande Mademoiselle	1834-1835	*La Femme abandonnée*	1848
Marie Touchet	1834-1837	*La Folle Epreuve*	1848
Les Roués Bourgeois	1838	*Le Vagabond*	1848
L'Aubain	1838	*La Comédie de l'amour*	1848
L'Héros ignoré	1843-1844	*La Succession Pons*	1848
Le Roi des Traînards	1844-1848	*Le Ministre*	1848
Pierre et Catherine	1847-1848	*L'Armée roulante*	1848
Le Père prodigue	1848	*Anunziatat*	1848
Le Père Goriot	1848		

Unfinished plays

Le Corsaire	1819
Catilina	1830
Le Lazaroni	1822
Richard Cœurd'Eponge	1830
Alceste	1823
La Vieillesse de Don Juan	1832
Pièce sans titre	1830 (circa.)
Philippe-le-Réservé	1834
Tableau d'une vie privée	1830 (circa.)
La Gina	1838-1848
Les Trois Manières	1830 (circa.)
Orgon	1847
La Mandragore	1830 (circa.)
Les Petits Bourgeois	1848
Sujet anglais	1830 (circa.)

LIST OF WORKS CONSULTED

I.   *Primary Sources*

I.a.   *Writings by Balzac*

La Comédie humaine, édition publiée sous la direction de Pierre-Georges Castex, Bibliothèque de la Pléiade, 12 vols. (Paris: Gallimard, 1976-1981).

Correspondance, Textes réunis, classés et annotés par Roger Pierrot, 5 vols. (Paris: Garnier, 1960-1969).

Lettres à Madame Hanska, Textes réunis, classés et annotés par Roger Pierrot, 4 vols. (Paris: Bibliophiles de l'Originale & Editions du Delta, 1967-1971).

L'Œuvre de Balzac, publiée sous la direction de Albert Béguin et Jean A. Ducourneau, 16 vols. (Paris: Formes et reflets & Le Club Français du Livre, 1950-1953).

Œuvres complètes, ed. Maurice Bardèche, 28 vols. (Paris: Société des Études Balzaciennes & Club de l'Honnête homme, 1955-1963).

Œuvres complètes illustrées, ed. J. Ducourneau, 30 vols. (Paris: Les Bibliophiles de l'originale, 1965-1976).

Œuvres diverses, édition publiée sous la direction de Pierre-Georges Castex, Bibliothèque de la Pléiade (Paris: Gallimard, 1990), vol. I.

Théâtre, in *Œuvres complètes de H. de Balzac*, 24 vols. (Paris: Michel Lévy,   1869-1876) vol. XVIII.

Monographie de la Presse parisienne dans la grande ville (Paris: Pauvert, 1965).

Pensées, sujets, fragmens, édition originale avec une préface et des notes de Jacques Crépet (Paris: Blaizot, 1910).

I.b.   *Other Primary Sources (excluding periodicals)*

Alhoy, M., *Grande Biographie dramatique, ou Silhouette des acteurs, actrices, chanteurs, cantatrices, danseurs, danseuses, etc. de Paris et des départements* (Paris: chez les marchands de nouveautés, 1824).

Anon., *L'Art de la claque* (Paris: Pillet, 1817). Bibliothèque de l'Opéra.

Astruc, J., *Le Droit privé du théâtre, ou Rapports des directeurs avec les auteurs, les artistes et le public* (Macon: Protat frères, 1897).

Bachaumont, *Mémoires secrets*, 36 vols. (London: Adamson, 1763-1789), vol. VII.

Beaumarchais, 'Les Deux Amis', in *Œuvres complètes* (Paris: Crémille, 1973).

Bouffé, *Mes souvenirs, 1800-1880* (Paris: Dentu, 1880).

Borgnis, M.J.A., *Traité complet de mécanique appliquée aux arts* (Paris: Bachelier, 1820).

Brazier, N., *Chroniques des petits théâtres de Paris depuis leur origine*, 2 vols. (Paris: Allardin, 1837).

Buguet, *Foyers et Coulisses, histoire anecdotique de tous les théâtres de Paris,* 15 vols. (Paris: Tresse, 1875).

Colombier, M., *Mémoires, Fin d'Empire* (Paris: Flammarion, 1898).

Cormon, E., *Théâtre de Cormon* (Paris: Barba, Bezou & Quay, 1838).

De Boigne, C., *Petits mémoires de l'Opéra* (Paris: Librairie Nouvelle, 1857).

Descombes, C.M. (known as Charles-Maurice), *Histoire anecdotique du théâtre, de la littérature et de diverses impressions contemporaines*, 2 vols. (Paris: Plon, 1856).

Diderot, D., *Œuvres complètes*, 20 vols. (Paris: Garnier, 1975).

Diderot, D., *Œuvres esthétiques*, ed. Paul Verière (Paris: Garnier, 1959).

Duflot, J., *Les Secrets des coulisses des théâtres de Paris* (Paris: Michel Lévy, 1865).

Dumas, A., *Mes mémoires*, 5 vols. (Paris: Gallimard, 1954-68), vol. IV.

Gautier, T., 'Honoré de Balzac' in *Ecrivains et Artistes Romantiques*, préface by Camille Mauclair, in series *Les Maîtres de l'histoire* (Paris: Plon, 1933).
—, *Histoire de l'art dramatique en France depuis vingt-cinq ans*, 6 vols. (Paris: Hetzel, 1858).
—, *Souvenirs de théâtre, d'art et de critique* (Paris: Charpentier, 1882).

Gavarni, *Œuvres choisies, avec des notices par MM. Théophile Gautier et Laurent-Jan* (Paris: Hetzel, 1846).

Guizot, M., 'Shakespeare et son temps', in *Œuvres complètes de Shakespeare* (Paris: Didier, 1821).

Harel, F., *Dictionnaire théâtral* (Paris: Barba, 1824).

Heilly, G., d', *Le Scandale au théâtre* (Paris: Jules Taride, 1861).

Hugo, V., *Préface de Cromwell* [1827], ed. Maurice Souriau (Paris: Société d'imprimerie, 1897).
—, 'William Shakespeare', in *Œuvres complètes*, ed. Albin Michel (Paris: Ollendorf), vol. I.

Janin, J., *Critique dramatique* (Paris: Librairie des Bibliophiles, 1877).
—, *Histoire de la littérature dramatique*, 6 vols. (Paris: Michel Lévy, 1855–1858).

Kaufmann, J.A., *L'Architectonographie des théâtres, 2e série, théâtres construits depuis 1820* (Paris: L. Mathias, 1840).

Lacan, A. and C. Paulmier, *Traité de la législation et de la jurisprudence des théâtres*, 2 vols. (Paris: Durand, 1853).

Lemaître, F., *Souvenirs publiés par son fils* (Paris: Ollendorf, 1880).

Lemonnier, A., *Les Abus du théâtre* (Paris: Tresse & Stock, 1895).

Lepeintre, J., *Pot-pourri à propos de la première et dernière représentation de Vautrin* (Paris: Vassal, 1840).

Molière, *Œuvres complètes* (Paris: Garnier, 1863-1864).

Monnier, H., *La Famille improvisée* (Paris: Barba, 1831).
—, *Grandeur et décadence de M. Joseph Prudhomme* (Paris: Lévy, 1852).
—, *La Physiologie du bourgeois* (Paris: Hetzel, 1846).
—, *Scènes populaires* (Paris: Urbain Canel, 1830).

Montigny, *Le Provincial à Paris*, 3 vols. (Paris: Ladvocat, 1825).

Moynet, M.J., *L'Envers du théâtre: machines et décorations*,(Paris: Hachette, 1875).

Muret, T., *L'Histoire par le théâtre, 1789-1851* (Paris: Amyot, 1865).

Picard, L.B., *Duhautcours ou le Contrat d'union* (Paris: Charon, 1801).
—, *Œuvres complètes*, 10 vols. (Paris: Barba, 1821).

Parent-Duchâtelet, *De la Prostitution dans la ville de Paris, Troisième édition completée par des documents nouveaux et des notes,* (Paris: J.B. Baillière et fils, 1857).

Porel P. et Monval, G., *L'Odéon, histoire administrative, anecdotique et littéraire du second théâtre français (1818-1853)* (Paris: Alphonse Lemerre, 1882).

Royer, A., *Histoire de l'Opéra* (Paris: Bachelin, 1875).
—, *Histoire universelle du théâtre*, 6 vols. (Paris: Ollendorf, 1878).

Samson, J.I., *Mémoires de la Comédie Française* (Paris: Ollendorff, 1882).
—, *De l'Association de secours mutuels entre les artistes* (Paris: Brière, 1855).

Scribe, E., 'Les Adieux au comptoir', in *Théâtre de Scribe* (Paris: Lévy Frères, 1856-1859).

Ségaud, E., *Question d'honneur littéraire et artistique: A bas la claque!* (Paris: Imprimerie Centrale de Napoléon, 1849) (Opéra, C 3072/4).

Véron, *Mémoires d'un bourgeois de Paris*, 6 vols., (Paris: Gabriel de Gonet, 1853-55).

Shakespeare, *The Complete Works*, ed. Wells and Taylor (Oxford: at the University Press, 1988).

I.c.   *Articles and periodicals used as primary sources*

Fabre, E., 'César Birotteau, pièce en trois actes', *L'Illustration Théâtrale,* vol. 162 (1910).
—, 'La Rabouilleuse, pièce en trois actes', *La Petite Illustration théâtrale,* vol. 403 (1936).

Gautier, T., 'Mercadet', in *La Presse* (1 Sept. 1851).

Goulard, C., 'Le Claqueur', in *Lettres sur les spectacles de Paris* (Paris: Duneuil, 1829) (Opéra, C 3072/3).

Picard, 'Duhautcours ou le contrat d'union', *La France dramatique au dix-neuvième siècle* (Paris: Barba, Delloye & Bezou, 1841), vol. VI.

Scribe, E., 'Le Coiffeur et le perruquier', *La France dramatique au dix-neuvième siècle* (Paris: Barba, Delloye & Bezou, 1841), vol. V.

I.d.   *Press publications used for historical surveys and theatre reviews*

La Caricature (1831 & March 1840).

Le Chronique de Paris (1836).

Le Corsaire (August 1851).

Les Débats (March 1840, March 1842, October 1843, August 1851).

La Démocratie Pacifique (October 1843).

Le Diable boiteux (1823).

Le Drapeau blanc (Sept. – Nov. 1821).

L'Echo du théâtre (March 1840).

358

Le Miroir des spectacles (Sept. – Nov. 1821, 1822 and 1823).

Le Moniteur Universel (October 1843, September 1859, October 1868).

La Nation (October 1843).

La Presse (March 1839 & October 1843).

La Quotidienne (March 1842).

Revue et Gazette des théâtres (August 1851).

Revue parisienne (September 1840).

Le Temps (March 1840).

II. *Secondary Sources*

II.a. *Secondary materials relating to Balzac and his work (excl. periodicals)*

Adamson, D., *Balzac: 'Illusions perdues'* (London: Grant & Cutler, 1981).

Arrigon, L.J., *Les Années romantiques de Balzac* (Paris: Perrin, 1927).

Barbéris, P. *Balzac, une mythologie réaliste* (Paris: Larousse, 1971).
—, *Le Monde de Balzac* (Paris: Artaud, 1973).

Bardèche, M., *Une lecture de Balzac* (Paris: Les Sept Couleurs, 1964).

Barrière, M., *L'Œuvre de H. de Balzac* (Paris: Calmann-Lévy, 1890).
—, *Honoré de Balzac et la tradition littéraire classique* (Paris: Hachette, 1928).

Béguin, A., *Balzac visionnaire* (Paris: Skira, 1946).

Bellos, D., *Balzac: 'La Cousine Bette'* (London: Grant & Cutler, 1980).

Biré, E., *Honoré de Balzac* (Paris: Champion, 1897).

Bouvier, R., *Balzac, homme d'affaires* (Paris: Champion, 1930).
—, *Les Comptes dramatiques de Balzac* (Paris: Sorlot, 1938).

Bowen, R.P., *The Dramatic Construction of Balzac's Novels* (Eugene: University of Oregon Monographs, 1940).

Brunetière, F. *Honoré de Balzac* (Paris: Calmann-Lévy, 1906).

Cazenove, M., *Le Drame de Balzac* (Paris: Delmas, 1950).

Champion, E., *Les Pièces de théâtre tirées de Balzac* (Paris: Champion, 1937).

Chollet, R., Introduction to *Illusions perdues*, Bibliothèque de la Pléiade (Paris: Gallimard, 1977), *LCH,* vol. V, pp. 3-108.
—, Introduction to Balzac's theatre, in *Les Œuvres de Balzac,* 30 vols. (Lausanne: Ed. Rencontre, 1958-1962), vol. XXVII.
—, *Balzac journaliste: Le Tournant de 1830* (Paris: Klincksieck, 1983).

Delattre, G., *Les Opinions littéraires de Balzac* (Paris: Presses Universitaires de France, 1961).

Descaves, P., *Balzac dramatiste* (Paris: La Table Ronde, 1960).

Faillie, M.H., *La Femme et le code civil dans La Comédie humaine de H. de Balzac* (Paris: Didier, 1968).

Frappier-Mazur, L., *L'Expression métaphorique dans la Comédie humaine* (Paris: Klincksieck, 1976).

360

Garnand, H.J., *The Influence of Walter Scott on the Works of Balzac*, (New York: Colombia University Press, 1926).

Gozlan, L., *Balzac chez lui* (Paris: Michel Lévy, 1862).
—, *Balzac en pantoufles* (Paris: Michel Lévy & J. Hetzel, 1856).

Guise, R., Introduction to Balzac's theatre, in *Îuvres complètes illustrées*, sous la direction de Jean Ducourneau, 30 vols. (Paris: Bibliophiles de l'Originale, 1965-1976), vol. XXI.

Hastings, W.S., *The Drama of Honoré de Balzac* (Wisconsin: George Banta, 1917).

Hemmings, F.W.J., *Balzac: An interpretation of 'La Comédie humaine'* (New York: Random House, 1967).

Hanotaux G., et G. Vicaire, *La Jeunesse de Balzac* (Paris: Ferroud, 1921).

Hunt, H.J., *Balzac's Comédie humaine* (London: Athlone Press, 1959).

Jung, W., *Theorie und Praxis des Typischen bei H. de Balzac* (Tübingen: Stauffenberg, 1983).

Lahlou, A., 'Balzac dramaturge dans les *Scènes de la vie privée*' (unpublished doctoral thesis, University of Paris-Sorbonne, 1981).

Laubriet, P., *L'Intelligence de l'art chez Balzac* (Paris: Didier, 1961).

Le Breton, A., *Balzac, l'homme et l'Îuvre* (Paris: Bovin et cie, 1923).

Lemer, J., *Balzac: sa vie, son Œuvre* , 2nd edn. (Paris: Hachette, 1965).

Lock, P.W. 'Balzac's Method of Presenting Character' (unpublished doctoral thesis, University of California, Berkeley, 1963).

Marceau, F., *Les Personnages de 'La Comédie humaine'* (Paris: Gallimard, 1977).

Maurice-Anour, L., *Honoré de Balzac* (Paris: Flammarion, 1952).

Maurois, A., *Prométhée, ou la vie de Balzac* (Paris: Hachette, 1965).

Milatchitch, D., *Le Théâtre de H. de Balzac* (Paris: Hachette, 1930).
—, *Le Théâtre inédit de H. de Balzac* (Paris: Hachette, 1930).

Prendergast, C., *Balzac, Fiction and Melodrama* (New York: Holmes & Meier, 1978).
—, 'Balzac, Narrative Contracts', in *The Order of Mimesis* (Cambridge University Press, 1988), pp. 83-118.

Pugh, A., *Balzac's Recurring Characters* (London: Duckworth, 1975).

Robb, G., *Balzac, a biography* (London: Picador, 1994).

Seillère, E., *Balzac et la morale romantique* (Paris: Alcan, 1922).

Stevenson, N., *Paris dans 'La Comédie humaine' de Balzac* (Paris: Courville, 1938).

Surville, L., *Balzac sa vie et ses Œuvres d'après sa correspondance* (Paris: Calmann-Lévy, 1878).

Van der Gun, W.H., *La Courtisane romantique et son rôle dans 'la Comédie humaine' de Balzac* (Assen, Holland: Van Goram, 1963).

Werdet, E., *Portrait intime de Balzac: sa vie, son humeur et son caractère* (Paris: Dentu, 1859).

Wurmser, *La Comédie inhumaine* (Paris: Gallimard, 1964).

II.b.   *Secondary Material Relating to Theatre History and Literary Criticism*

Albert, M., *Les Théâtres des boulevards, 1789-1848* (Paris: Société française d'imprimerie, 1902).

Allevy, M.A., *La Mise en scène en France pendant la première moitié du dix-neuvième siècle* (Paris: Droz, 1938).

Auerbach, E., *Mimesis* (New York: Doubleday, 1957).

Baldick, R., *The Life and Times of Frédérick Lemaître* (London: Hamish Hamilton, 1959).

Beaulieu, H., *Les Théâtres du boulevard du crime (1752-1862)* (Paris: Daragon, 1905).

Bénichou, P., *The Anti-Bourgeois* (New Jersey: Prentice-Hall, 1964).

Bentley, E., *The Life of the Drama* (London: Methuen, 1964).

Bergman, G.M., *Lighting in the Theatre* (Stockholm: Almqvist & Wiksell, 1977).

Berthier, P., *Le Théâtre au XIXe siècle* (Paris: Presses Universitaires de France, 1986).

Borgerhoff, J.L., *Le Théâtre anglais à Paris sous la Restauration* (Paris: Hachette, 1912).

Braun, S.D., *The Courtesan in the French Theatre from Hugo to Becque* (Paris: Société des Belles Lettres, 1947).

Brooks, P., *The Melodramatic Imagination* (New York: Colombia University Press, 1976).

Butor, M., *Répertoire I* (Paris: Minuit, 1960).

363

Carlson, M., *The French Stage in the Nineteenth Century* (Metuchen: Scarecrow Press, 1972).

Champfleury, *Henry Monnier, sa vie, son œuvre* (Paris: Dentu, 1879).

Collins, F.H., *Talma, A Biography of an Actor* (London: Faber, 1964).

Collins, I., *Government and Newspaper Press in France 1814-1881* (Oxford: at the University Press, 1959).

Colson, J.B., *Répertoire du Théâtre Français* (Bordeaux: Colson & Foulguier, n.d.).

Descotes, M., *Le Public de théâtre et son histoire* (Paris: Presses Universitaires de France, 1964).
—, *Le Drame romantique et ses grand créateurs* (Paris: Presses Universitaires de France, 1955).

Dumur, G., *Histoire des spectacles* (Paris: Gallimard, 1963).

Genette, G., *Figures III* (Paris: Seuil, 1972).

Guex, J., *Le Théâtre et la société française de 1815 à 1848* (Geneva: Slatkine, 1973).

Hemmings, F.W.J., *The Theatre Industry in Nineteenth-Century France* (Cambridge University Press, 1993).

Howarth, *Sublime and Grotesque, a Study of French Romantic Drama* (London: Harrap, 1975).

Jakobson, *Essais de linguistique générale* (Paris: Seuil, 1963).

Jakoby, R., *Das Feuilleton des Journal des Débats von 1814 bis 1830* (Tübingen: Narr, 1988).

Joannidès, A., *La Comédie-Française de 1680 à 1900, Dictionnaire général des pièces et des auteurs* (Paris: n.pub. 1901).

Jomaron, J. de (ed.), *Le Théâtre en France*, 2 vols. (Paris: Armand Colin, 1988-89).

Jouvet, L., *Témoignages sur le théâtre* (Paris: Flammarion, 1952).

Lecomte, H., *Histoire des théâtres de Paris: Le Panorama-Dramatique* (Paris: Daragon, 1907).
—, *Un comédien du XIXe siècle, Frédérick Lemaître*, 2 vols. (Paris: Hetzel, 1888).

Lintilhac, *Histoire générale du théâtre en France* (Paris: Flammarion, 1910).

Lubbock, P., *The Craft of Fiction* (London: Jonathan Cape, 1921).

Lukács, G., *The Theory of the Novel*, translated from the German by Anna Bostock (London: Merlin Press, 1971).

Matoré, G., *Le Vocabulaire de la prose littéraire de 1833 à 1845* (Genève: Droz, 1951).

Melcher, E., *The Life and Times of Henry Monnier* (London: Oxford University Press, 1950).

Montague, E., *Theatre in Mind, A Study of the Theatrical Elements in Victor Hugo's Novels* (unpublished doctoral thesis, University of London, Kings College, 1993).

Ricœur, P., *La Métaphore vive* (Paris: Seuil, 1975).

Steiner, G., *The Death of Tragedy* (New York: Hill & Wang, 1961).

Ullmann, S., *Style in the French Novel* (Cambridge: at the University Press, 1957).

Watt, I., *The Rise of the Novel* (London: Chatto & Windus, 1957).

Wicks, C.B., *The Parisian Stage 1800-1900: Alphabetical Indexes of Plays and Authors* (Alabama: University of Alabama Press, 1950-1979).

II.c.   *Articles and Periodicals used as Secondary Materials*

Baldensperger, F., 'Une suggestion anglaise pour le titre de *La Comédie humaine*', in *Revue de littérature comparée* (Oct-Dec 1921), pp. 638-639.

Bochner, J., 'Shakespeare en France, 1733-1830', *Revue de littérature comparée* (Jan-Mar 1965), pp. 44-65.

Bourget, P., 'L'Art du roman chez Balzac', *Revue des deux mondes*, XXXI (15 February, 1926), pp. 931-942.

Braun S.D., 'The Courtesan in the French Theatre, 1831-1880', *The French Review* (Dec. 1946), pp. 201-228.

Brooks, P., 'Balzac, Melodrama and Metaphor', *Hudson Review*, XXII (Summer, 1969), pp. 213-228.

Citron, P., 'Aux Sources d'*Une fille d'Eve*', *Année balzacienne* (1965), pp. 149-160.
—, 'Du nouveau sur le titre de *la Comédie humaine*', *RHLF* (1959), pp. 105-109.
—, 'Les Affreux du miroir', *Europe* (Jan-Feb   1965), pp. 94-104.

Descharmes R., 'César Birotteau de Cormon', *Le Mercure de France* (Sept. 16, 1911).

Descotes, M., 'Les Comédiens dans *la Comédie humaine*', *Revue d'histoire du théâtre*, vol. IV (1956), pp. 287-298.

Dupuis, D., 'Spécificité et rôle du décor dans les *Scènes de la vie privée*', *Année balzacienne*(1994), pp. 139-155.

Felkay, N., 'Un banquier des auteurs dramatiques: Porcher-Braulard', *Année balzacienne* (1972), pp. 201-222.

Gourmont, R., 'Les Maîtres de Balzac', *Promenades littéraires 2e série* (1906), pp. 109-120.

Guise, R., 'Un grand homme du roman à la scène, ou les illusions reparaissantes de Balzac', published in four parts in *Année balzacienne* (1966), pp. 171-216; (1967), pp. 177-214; (1968), pp. 337-368; (1969), pp. 247-280.

Hemmings, F.W.J., 'Co-authorship in French plays', *French Studies,* vol. 41 (1987), pp. 37-51.

Hunt, H.J., 'Balzac's Pressmen', *French Studies,* vol. XI, (1957), pp. 230-245.

Krakovitch, O., 'Balzac dramaturge et la censure', *Année balzacienne* (1994), pp. 273-309.

Laubriet, P., 'L'Elaboration des personnages dans *César Birotteau*', *Année balzacienne* (1964), pp. 251-271.

Meininger, A., 'Balzac et Henry Monnier', *Année balzacienne* (1966), pp. 240-262.
—, 'Théâtre et petits faits vrais', *Année balzacienne* (1968), pp. 369-382.

Pistone, D., 'Pianos et pianistes balzaciens. De l'Art des sons à l'art des mots', *Année balzacienne* (1994), pp. 55-69.

Tremewan, P.J., 'Balzac et Shakespeare', in *Année balzacienne* (1967), pp. 259-303.

III. *Bibliographies and Aids to Research*

Anon., *Nouvelle Biographie générale depuis les temps les plus reculés jusqu'à nos jours*, 46 vols. (Paris: Firmin Didot Frères, 1850-1860).

Hatin, E., *Bibliographie de la presse périodique française* (Paris: Anthropos, 1865).

Larousse, P., *Grand dictionnaire universel du XIXe siècle* (Paris: Larousse, 1864-1886).
—, *Grand Larousse Encyclopédique*, 10 vols. (Paris: Larousse, 1960-1964).

Lovenjoul, Vicomte Spœlberch de, *Histoire des Œuvres de H. de Balzac,* troisième édition (Paris: Calmann-Lévy, 1888).

Lyonnet, H., *Dictionnaire des comédiens français*, 2 vols. (Paris: Jorel, 1908-1912).

Michaud, L., *Biographie universelle ancienne et moderne* (Paris: n.p., 1843).

Royce, W.H., *A Balzac Bibliography*, 2 vols. (Chicago: University of Chicago Press, 1929-1930).

INDEX OF REFERENCES TO WORKS FROM
LA COMEDIE HUMAINE

INDEX OF REFERENCES TO CHARACTERS FROM
LA COMEDIE HUMAINE

INDEX OF REFERENCES TO PROPER NAMES